CAREERS AND OCCUPATIONS

LOOKING TO THE FUTURE

ISSN 1532-1169

CAREERS AND OCCUPATIONS

LOOKING TO THE FUTURE

Donna Lawrence

INFORMATION PLUS® REFERENCE SERIES
Formerly published by Information Plus, Wylie, Texas

GALE®

THOMSON

GALE

Detroit • New York • San Diego • San Francisco • Cleveland • New Haven, Conn. • Waterville, Maine • London • Munich

THOMSON

GALE

Careers and Occupations: Looking to the Future

Donna Lawrence

Project Editor
Ellice Engdahl

Editorial
Paula Cutcher-Jackson, Kathleen Edgar, Christy Justice, Debra Kirby, Prindle LaBarge, Elizabeth Manar, Kathleen Meek, Charles B. Montney, Heather Price

Permissions
Margaret A. Chamberlain

Product Design
Michael Logusz

Composition and Electronic Prepress
Evi Seoud

Manufacturing
Keith Helmling

For permission to use material from this prod-uct, submit your request via Web at http://www.gale-edit.com/permissions, or you may download our Permissions Request form and submit your request by fax or mail to:

Permissions Department
The Gale Group, Inc.
27500 Drake Rd.
Farmington Hills, MI 48331-3535
Permissions Hotline:
248-699-8006 or 800-877-4253; ext. 8006
Fax: 248-699-8074 or 800-762-4058

Cover photograph reproduced by permission of PhotoDisc.

Since this page cannot legibly accommodate all copyright notices, the acknowledgments consti-tute an extension of the copyright notice.

While every effort has been made to ensure the reliability of the information presented in this publication, The Gale Group, Inc. does not guarantee the accuracy of the data contained herein. The Gale Group, Inc. accepts no pay-ment for listing; and inclusion in the publica-tion of any organization, agency, institution, publication, service, or individual does not imply endorsement of the editors or publisher. Errors brought to the attention of the publish-er and verified to the satisfaction of the pub-lisher will be corrected in future editions.

LIBRARY OF CONGRESS CATALOGING-IN-PUBLICATION DATA

ISBN 0-7876-5103-6 (set)
ISBN 0-7876-6061-2
ISSN 1532-1169

TABLE OF CONTENTS

CHAPTER 1
Today's Labor Force. 1

The American labor force continues to grow rapidly, and includes people of all races, ethnicities, ages, genders, and backgrounds. This chapter looks at employment by industry, occupation, and tenure, and also covers issues such as seeking work, labor unions, work stoppages, occupational injuries, and workplace violence.

CHAPTER 2
The Changing American Workforce 39

The American workforce has transitioned in many ways. It has gone from producing goods to providing services. Many people are working longer workweeks or are adopting nonstandard work arrangements. They are working at home, as well as utilizing flexible schedules and shift work. Americans are also exposed to displacement and other threats to job security.

CHAPTER 3
Unemployment. 63

American unemployment rates are examined here by a variety of characteristics, such as age, race and ethnicity, gender, and educational level. Certain occupations and industries are also more susceptible to unemployment than others. The duration of and reasons for unemployment among workers differ across all segments of society.

CHAPTER 4
The Education of American Workers 77

Americans, and American workers, are better educated than ever before. Adults with higher levels of education are more likely to participate in the labor force than those with less education. Generally, the higher the level of one's educational attainment, the higher one's salary level.

CHAPTER 5
The Workforce of Tomorrow 107

The workforce of the future will contain older workers, more women,

and more minorities. Employment growth rates by industry, occupation, and educational requirements are examined here.

CHAPTER 6
Earnings and Benefits 129

Average earnings by occupation and demographic characteristics are examined in-depth in this chapter. In addition to wages, most workers receive benefits like paid holidays and vacations, among others. Employer-sponsored health insurance and savings plans are provided by many businesses.

CHAPTER 7
Getting a Job 151

There are many places a person can go for career information. There are also many methods for finding a job, such as using classified ads, employment agencies, and the Internet. Submitting a resume and interviewing are the last steps in landing a job.

CHAPTER 8
Workers' Rights 155

Federal, state, and local governments create laws, rules, and regulations to protect the rights of workers. Major work-related laws cover wages and hours, family and medical leave, unemployment, on-the-job safety, workers' compensation, discrimination and harassment, unions, and various types of testing.

CHAPTER 9
Business Opportunities 161

Every year, people start thousands of businesses. Other firms fail, discontinue, are sold, or continue operating. This chapter examines business start-ups and failures, as well as characteristics of business owners.

PREFACE

Careers and Occupations: Looking to the Future is one of the latest volumes in the Information Plus Reference Series. Previously published by the Information Plus company of Wylie, Texas, the Information Plus Reference Series (and its companion set, the Information Plus Compact Series) became a Gale Group product when Gale and Information Plus merged in early 2000. Those of you familiar with the series as published by Information Plus will notice a few changes from the 2000 edition. Gale has adopted a new layout and style that we hope you will find easy to use. Other improvements include greatly expanded indexes in each book, and more descriptive tables of contents.

While some changes have been made to the design, the purpose of the Information Plus Reference Series remains the same. Each volume of the series presents the latest facts on a topic of pressing concern in modern American life. These topics include today's most controversial and most studied social issues: abortion, capital punishment, care for the elderly, crime, health care, the environment, immigration, minorities, social welfare, women, youth, and many more. Although written especially for the high school and undergraduate student, this series is an excellent resource for anyone in need of factual information on current affairs.

By presenting the facts, it is Gale's intention to provide its readers with everything they need to reach an informed opinion on current issues. To that end, there is a particular emphasis in this series on the presentation of scientific studies, surveys, and statistics. These data are generally presented in the form of tables, charts, and other graphics placed within the text of each book. Every graphic is directly referred to and carefully explained in the text. The source of each graphic is presented within the graphic itself. The data used in these graphics are drawn from the most reputable and reliable sources, in particular from the various branches of the U.S. government and from major independent polling organizations.

Every effort has been made to secure the most recent information available. The reader should bear in mind that many major studies take years to conduct, and that additional years often pass before the data from these studies are made available to the public. Therefore, in many cases the most recent information available in 2002 dated from 1999 or 2000. Older statistics are sometimes presented as well, if they are of particular interest and no more recent information exists.

Although statistics are a major focus of the Information Plus Reference Series, they are by no means its only content. Each book also presents the widely held positions and important ideas that shape how the book's subject is discussed in the United States. These positions are explained in detail and, where possible, in the words of their proponents. Some of the other material to be found in these books includes: historical background; descriptions of major events related to the subject; relevant laws and court cases; and examples of how these issues play out in American life. Some books also feature primary documents, or have pro and con debate sections giving the words and opinions of prominent Americans on both sides of a controversial topic. All material is presented in an even-handed and unbiased manner; the reader will never be encouraged to accept one view of an issue over another.

HOW TO USE THIS BOOK

Work is a huge part of American life, yet the working world is changing, and at a seemingly ever more rapid pace. Technology is changing the way businesses operate, service industries are replacing traditional manufacturing jobs, businesses are moving from downtown skyscrapers to suburban office parks, and more and more Americans are working from home or as temps rather than seeking more traditional or long-term careers. This book examines all of these trends and more, providing the latest information on what Americans do for a living, how much they earn, how they find work, and what factors influence these key issues.

Careers and Occupations: Looking to the Future consists of nine chapters and three appendices. Each chapter is devoted to a particular aspect of the American workforce. For a summary of the information covered in each chapter, please see the synopses provided in the Table of Contents at the front of the book. Chapters generally begin with an overview of the basic facts and background information on the chapter's topic, then proceed to examine sub-topics of particular interest. For example, Chapter 6: Earnings and Benefits begins with an overview of the average earnings of American workers, including a breakdown of earnings by category (i.e., gender, industry, and particular careers). The average starting salaries for college graduates are also discussed. The chapter then moves on to an overview of employee benefits in the United States. The typical benefits available at employers of different sizes and types are examined. Health care benefits and retirement savings plans are given special attention. Readers can find their way through a chapter by looking for the section and sub-section headings, which are clearly set off from the text. Or, they can refer to the book's extensive index if they already know what they are looking for.

Statistical Information

The tables and figures featured throughout *Careers and Occupations: Looking to the Future* will be of particular use to the reader in learning about this issue. These tables and figures represent an extensive collection of the most recent and important statistics on the American workforce, as well as related issues—for example, graphics in the book cover employment status by age and gender; the number of layoffs in the past several years; employment rates for people of varying educational attainment; industries with increasing and decreasing salary prospects; and the number of businesses started annually. Gale believes that making this information available to the reader is the most important way in which we fulfill the goal of this book: to help readers understand the issues and controversies surrounding the American workforce and reach their own conclusions about them.

Each table or figure has a unique identifier appearing above it, for ease of identification and reference. Titles for the tables and figures explain their purpose. At the end of each table or figure, the original source of the data is provided.

In order to help readers understand these often complicated statistics, all tables and figures are explained in the text. References in the text direct the reader to the relevant statistics. Furthermore, the contents of all tables and figures are fully indexed. Please see the opening section of the index at the back of this volume for a description of how to find tables and figures within it.

Appendices

In addition to the main body text and images, *Careers and Occupations: Looking to the Future* has three appendices. The first is the Important Names and Addresses directory. Here the reader will find contact information for a number of government and private organizations that can provide further information on aspects of careers and occupations. The second appendix is the Resources section, which can also assist the reader in conducting his or her own research. In this section, the author and editors of *Careers and Occupations: Looking to the Future* describe some of the sources that were most useful during the compilation of this book. The final appendix is the book's index. It has been greatly expanded from previous editions, and should make it even easier to find specific topics in this book.

ADVISORY BOARD CONTRIBUTIONS

The staff of Information Plus would like to extend their heartfelt appreciation to the Information Plus Advisory Board. This dedicated group of media professionals provides feedback on the series on an ongoing basis. Their comments allow the editorial staff who work on the project to continually make the series better and more user-friendly. Our top priorities are to produce the highest-quality and most useful books possible, and the Advisory Board's contributions to this process are invaluable.

The members of the Information Plus Advisory Board are:

- Kathleen R. Bonn, Librarian, Newbury Park High School, Newbury Park, California
- Madelyn Garner, Librarian, San Jacinto College—North Campus, Houston, Texas
- Anne Oxenrider, Media Specialist, Dundee High School, Dundee, Michigan
- Charles R. Rodgers, Director of Libraries, Pasco-Hernando Community College, Dade City, Florida
- James N. Zitzelsberger, Library Media Department Chairman, Oshkosh West High School, Oshkosh, Wisconsin

COMMENTS AND SUGGESTIONS

The editors of the Information Plus Reference Series welcome your feedback on *Careers and Occupations: Looking to the Future*. Please direct all correspondence to:

Editors
Information Plus Reference Series
27500 Drake Rd.
Farmington Hills, MI 48331-3535

ACKNOWLEDGMENTS

The editors wish to thank the copyright holders of material included in this volume and the permissions managers of many book and magazine publishing companies for assisting us in securing reproduction rights. We are also grateful to the staffs of the Detroit Public Library, the Library of Congress, the University of Detroit Mercy Library, Wayne State University Purdy/Kresge Library Complex, and the University of Michigan Libraries for making their resources available to us.

Following is a list of the copyright holders who have granted us permission to reproduce material in Information Plus: Careers and Occupations. *Every effort has been made to trace copyright, but if omissions have been made, please let us know.*

For more detailed source citations, please see the sources listed under each individual table and figure.

Centers for Disease Control and Prevention, National Center for Health Statistics, Hyattsville, MD: Figure 6.5, Table 6.12, Table 6.13

***Contemporary Times*, v. 17, 1998. National Association of Temporary and Staffing Services. Reproduced by permission:** Table 2.14

The Dun and Bradstreet Corp., Murray Hill, NJ: Neil DiBernardo, *Business Failure Record*, 1998: Figure 9.3 (from "Number of Failures," reproduced by permission), Table 9.3 (from "Failure Trends since 1927," reproduced by permission)

The Dun and Bradstreet Corp., Murray Hill, NJ: Neil DiBernardo, *Business Starts Record*, 1998: Figure 9.1 (from "1994-1997 Yearly Business Starts," reproduced by permission), Figure 9.2 (from "1997 Business Starts Distribution by Employment Size" [chart], reproduced by permission), Table 9.2 (from "Business Starts Distribution by Employment Size" [table], reproduced by permission)

The Dun and Bradstreet Corp., Economics Analysis Department, Murray Hill, NJ: Table 9.1 (May 31, 2000, reproduced by permission), Table 9.12 and Table 9.13 (May 25, 2000, reproduced by permission)

The Gallup Organization, Princeton, NJ, 2000. Reproduced by permission. http://www.gallup.com/poll/indicators/indwork.asp: Figure 2.6

U.S. Census Bureau, Washington, DC: Figure 2.4, Figure 2.5, Figure 6.1, Table 6.3, Figure 9.4, Table 9.4, Table 9.5, Table 9.6, Table 9.7, Table 9.8, Table 9.9, Table 9.10, Table 9.11

U.S. Chamber of Commerce, Washington, DC: Figure 6.2, Figure 6.3, Figure 6.4, Table 6.10, Table 6.11

U.S. Department of Education, Office of Educational Research and Improvement, National Center for Education Statistics, Washington, DC: Figure 4.1, Figure 4.2, Figure 4.3, Figure 4.4, Figure 4.5, Figure 4.6, Figure 4.7, Table 4.1, Table 4.2, Table 4.3, Table 4.4, Table 4.5, Table 4.6, Table 4.7, Table 4.8, Table 4.9, Table 4.10, Table 4.11, Table 4.12, Table 4.13, Table 4.14, Table 4.15, Table 4.16

U.S. Department of Labor, Bureau of Labor Statistics, Washington, DC: Figure 1.1, Figure 1.2, Figure 1.3, Table 1.1, Table 1.2, Table 1.3, Table 1.4, Table 1.5, Table 1.6, Table 1.7, Table 1.8, Table 1.9, Table 1.10, Table 1.11, Table 1.12, Table 1.13, Table 1.14, Table 1.15, Table 1.16, Table 1.17, Table 1.18, Table 1.19, Table 1.20, Table 1.21, Table 1.22, Table 1.23, Table 1.24, Table 1.25, Table 1.26, Table 1.27, Table 1.28, Table 1.29, Table 1.30, Table 1.31, Table 1.32, Table 1.33, Figure 2.1, Figure 2.2, Figure 2.3, Table 2.1, Table 2.2, Table 2.3, Table 2.4, Table 2.5, Table 2.6, Table 2.7, Table 2.8, Table 2.9, Table 2.10, Table 2.11, Table 2.12, Table 2.13, Table 2.15, Table 2.16, Table 2.17, Table 2.18, Table 2.19, Table 2.20, Table 2.21, Table 2.22, Figure 3.1, Table 3.1, Table 3.2, Table 3.3, Table 3.4, Table 3.5, Table 3.6, Table 3.7, Table 3.8, Table 3.9, Table 3.10, Table 3.11, Table 3.12, Table 3.13, Table 3.14, Table 4.17, Figure 5.1, Figure 5.2, Figure 5.3, Figure 5.4, Figure 5.5, Figure 5.6, Figure 5.7, Figure 5.8, Figure 5.9, Figure 5.10, Figure 5.11, Figure 5.12, Figure 5.13, Figure 5.14, Figure 5.15, Figure 5.16, Figure 5.17, Figure 5.18, Figure 5.19, Figure 5.20, Figure 5.21, Figure 5.22, Figure 5.23, Figure 5.24, Table 5.3, Table 5.4, Table 5.5, Table 5.6, Table 5.7, Table 6.1, Table 6.2, Table 6.4, Table 6.5, Table 6.6, Table 6.7, Table 6.8, Table 6.9, Table 7.1, Table 7.2, Table 7.3, Table 8.1, Table 8.2

U.S. Department of Labor, Bureau of Labor Statistics, Office of Occupational Statistics and Employment Projections, Washington, DC: Table 5.1

U.S. General Accounting Office, Washington, DC: Table 5.2

CHAPTER 1
TODAY'S LABOR FORCE

The American labor force grew rapidly from 1970 to 2001. The number of workers in the American civilian noninstitutionalized labor force, or workers not in the army, school, jail, or mental health facilities, almost doubled from 82.8 million men and women working in 1970 to 141.8 million men and women working in 2001. This labor force includes those who are working part- or full-time or are unemployed, but actively looking for jobs. During this period, the proportion of the population in the labor force rose from 60.4 percent to 66.9 percent. (See Table 1.1.) This growth may be attributed to the introduction of the post-World War II baby-boom children and an increase in the number of women in the workforce.

GENDER, AGE, RACE, AND ETHNIC ORIGIN

In 2001, 76.4 percent of the male population and 60.9 percent of the female population 20 years and older participated in the labor force. A slightly higher percentage of whites were in the labor force (67.2 percent) than blacks (65.4 percent). Black women (65.4 percent) were somewhat more likely to be in the labor force than white women (60.2 percent), while a somewhat higher percentage of white men (76.8 percent) were in the labor force as compared to black men (72.1 percent). More than two-thirds (68.1 percent) of those of Hispanic origin participated in the labor force—83.1 percent of the men and 58.5 percent of the women. (See Table 1.2.)

Americans were most likely to be working between the ages of 25 and 54. In 2001, 91.3 percent of men and 76.4 percent of women 25 to 54 years old were in the workforce. The percentage dropped to 68.1 percent for men and 53 percent for women among those 55 to 64 years of age. (See Table 1.3.) The proportion of men in the labor force in this age group generally had declined, while the percentage of women increased. In addition, a growing percentage of jobs held by this age group were part-time instead of full-time. The low unemployment rate (3.1 percent in 2001) indicated

among this older group (shown in Table 1.3) reflects the fact that many of the older workers had retired and were no longer in the labor force. More than two of five adults who were not in the labor force were more than 65 years old.

Older workers leave the workforce for many reasons, ranging from disability to a genuine desire to retire. For many older people, however, leaving the workforce is not a voluntary act. Companies trying to cut expenses sometimes find it in their financial interest to force older, more highly paid workers into retirement and replace them with younger, lower-paid workers. The increasing desire of many companies to streamline their staffs, frequently by eliminating many middle-management positions, has had detrimental effects on this age group. They are frequently offered early retirement with some fringe benefits, but may be laid off with no benefits if they refuse early retirement. Older people are also more expensive to insure.

Student Workers

In 1998 more than one in four (nearly 27 percent) American high schoolers, ages 15 to 17, worked primarily part-time while going to school. This was down from 30 percent in the late 1970s. (See Figure 1.1.) During the summer months in 1998, about 35 percent of youths worked. In college, even more students worked (61.9 percent according to 1995 census figures). Approximately 32 percent worked full-time, and 30 percent worked part-time. In both high school and college, equal percentages of male and female students worked. The Centers for Disease Control and Prevention's web site (http://www.cdc.gov/niosh/99-141-2.html) provides an article, *The Facts About Young Worker Safety and Health*, which states that 80 percent of high school students will hold at least one job before graduation.

The *Third International Math and Science Study,* conducted in 1995, found that 61 percent of high school seniors worked an average of 3.1 hours daily. Only about

TABLE 1.1

Employment status of the civilian noninstitutional population 16 years and over by sex, 1970–2001

(Numbers in thousands)

Year	Civilian noninsti-tutional population	Civilian labor force Total	Percent of population	Employed Total	Percent of population	Agri-culture	Nonagri-cultural industries	Unemployed Number	Percent of labor force	Not in labor force
						Men				
1970	64,304	51,228	79.7	48,990	76.2	2,862	46,128	2,238	4.4	13,076
1971	65,942	52,180	79.1	49,390	74.9	2,795	46,595	2,789	5.3	13,762
1972[1]	67,835	53,555	78.9	50,896	75.0	2,849	48,047	2,659	5.0	14,280
1973[1]	69,292	54,624	78.8	52,349	75.5	2,847	49,502	2,275	4.2	14,667
1974	70,808	55,739	78.7	53,024	74.9	2,919	50,105	2,714	4.9	15,069
1975	72,291	56,299	77.9	51,857	71.7	2,824	49,032	4,442	7.9	15,993
1976	73,759	57,174	77.5	53,138	72.0	2,744	50,394	4,036	7.1	16,585
1977	75,193	58,396	77.7	54,728	72.8	2,671	52,057	3,667	6.3	16,797
1978[1]	76,576	59,620	77.9	56,479	73.8	2,718	53,761	3,142	5.3	16,956
1979	78,020	60,726	77.8	57,607	73.8	2,686	54,921	3,120	5.1	17,293
1980	79,398	61,453	77.4	57,186	72.0	2,709	54,477	4,267	6.9	17,945
1981	80,511	61,974	77.0	57,397	71.3	2,700	54,697	4,577	7.4	18,537
1982	81,523	62,450	76.6	56,271	69.0	2,736	53,534	6,179	9.9	19,073
1983	82,531	63,047	76.4	56,787	68.8	2,704	54,083	6,260	9.9	19,484
1984	83,605	63,835	76.4	59,091	70.7	2,668	56,423	4,744	7.4	19,771
1985	84,469	64,411	76.3	59,891	70.9	2,535	57,356	4,521	7.0	20,058
1986[1]	85,798	65,422	76.3	60,892	71.0	2,511	58,381	4,530	6.9	20,376
1987	86,899	66,207	76.2	62,107	71.5	2,543	59,564	4,101	6.2	20,692
1988	87,857	66,927	76.2	63,273	72.0	2,493	60,780	3,655	5.5	20,930
1989	88,762	67,840	76.4	64,315	72.5	2,513	61,802	3,525	5.2	20,923
1990[1]	90,377	69,011	76.4	65,104	72.0	2,546	62,559	3,906	5.7	21,367
1991	91,278	69,168	75.8	64,223	70.4	2,589	61,634	4,946	7.2	22,110
1992	92,270	69,964	75.8	64,440	69.8	2,575	61,866	5,523	7.9	22,306
1993	93,332	70,404	75.4	65,349	70.0	2,478	62,871	5,055	7.2	22,927
1994[1]	94,355	70,817	75.1	66,450	70.4	2,554	63,896	4,367	6.2	23,538
1995	95,178	71,360	75.0	67,377	70.8	2,559	64,818	3,983	5.6	23,818
1996	96,206	72,087	74.9	68,207	70.9	2,573	65,634	3,880	5.4	24,119
1997[1]	97,715	73,261	75.0	69,685	71.3	2,552	67,133	3,577	4.9	24,454
1998[1]	98,758	73,959	74.9	70,693	71.6	2,553	68,140	3,266	4.4	24,799
1999[1]	99,722	74,512	74.7	71,446	71.6	2,432	69,014	3,066	4.1	25,210
2000[1]	100,731	75,247	74.7	72,293	71.8	2,434	69,859	2,954	3.9	25,484
2001	101,858	75,743	74.4	72,080	70.8	2,275	69,805	3,663	4.8	26,114

28 percent of seniors in other countries worked, and they averaged 1.2 hours daily.

Many adults are concerned that high school students are working too many hours. They feel that the main "job" of young people is getting educated—not earning money. Laurence Steinberg, a psychologist at Temple University, in a 10-year survey (1985–1995) of 20,000 high school students in California and Wisconsin, found that almost one-third of students who had jobs were often too tired to do their homework. Students who worked more than 20 hours per week earned lower grades and cut more classes than students who did not work or worked fewer hours.

Some experts have concluded that student jobs, such as cashiers, sales clerks, and fast food service workers, often aren't challenging enough, yet are stressful and time consuming. They thought the students would benefit more from student activities and reading. Others claim that jobs challenge students and teach them greater responsibility.

Past surveys suggest that students worked for various reasons, including spending money, purchasing some-thing expensive, saving for future schooling, supporting their families, and supporting themselves.

EDUCATION

The more years of education, the more likely the person will be part of the labor force and the less likely to be unemployed. In 2001 college graduates had the highest labor force participation (79 percent) and the lowest unemployment rate (2.3 percent). However, those with less than a high school diploma had a labor force participation rate of 43.6 percent and an unemployment rate of 7.3 percent. Better-educated workers of any gender or racial group were also more likely to be in the labor force and employed. (See Table 1.4.)

FAMILIES

In 2001, 82.9 percent of the nation's nearly 72 million families had at least one employed person. Black families continued to be less likely to include an employed member (80 percent) than were either white or Hispanic families (83.1 percent and 86.9 percent, respectively). (See

TABLE 1.1

Employment status of the civilian noninstitutional population 16 years and over by sex, 1970–2001 [CONTINUED]

(Numbers in thousands)

Year	Civilian noninsti-tutional population	Civilian labor force						Unemployed		Not in labor force
				Employed						
		Total	Percent of population	Total	Percent of population	Agri-culture	Nonagri-cultural industries	Number	Percent of labor force	
					Women					
1970	72,782	31,543	43.3	29,688	40.8	601	29,087	1,855	5.9	41,239
1971	74,274	32,202	43.4	29,976	40.4	599	29,377	2,227	6.9	42,072
1972[1]	76,290	33,479	43.9	31,257	41.0	635	30,622	2,222	6.6	42,811
1973[1]	77,804	34,804	44.7	32,715	42.0	622	32,093	2,089	6.0	43,000
1974	79,312	36,211	45.7	33,769	42.6	596	33,173	2,441	6.7	43,101
1975	80,860	37,475	46.3	33,989	42.0	584	33,404	3,486	9.3	43,386
1976	82,390	38,983	47.3	35,615	43.2	588	35,027	3,369	8.6	43,406
1977	83,840	40,613	48.4	37,289	44.5	612	36,677	3,324	8.2	43,227
1978[1]	85,334	42,631	50.0	39,569	46.4	669	38,900	3,061	7.2	42,703
1979	86,843	44,235	50.9	41,217	47.5	661	40,556	3,018	6.8	42,608
1980	88,348	45,487	51.5	42,117	47.7	656	41,461	3,370	7.4	42,861
1981	89,618	46,696	52.1	43,000	48.0	667	42,333	3,696	7.9	42,922
1982	90,748	47,755	52.6	43,256	47.7	665	42,591	4,499	9.4	42,993
1983	91,684	48,503	52.9	44,047	48.0	680	43,367	4,457	9.2	43,181
1984	92,778	49,709	53.6	45,915	49.5	653	45,262	3,794	7.6	43,068
1985	93,736	51,050	54.5	47,259	50.4	644	46,615	3,791	7.4	42,686
1986[1]	94,789	52,413	55.3	48,706	51.4	652	48,054	3,707	7.1	42,376
1987	95,853	53,658	56.0	50,334	52.5	666	49,668	3,324	6.2	42,195
1988	96,756	54,742	56.6	51,696	53.4	676	51,020	3,046	5.6	42,014
1989	97,630	56,030	57.4	53,027	54.3	687	52,341	3,003	5.4	41,601
1990[1]	98,787	56,829	57.5	53,689	54.3	678	53,011	3,140	5.5	41,957
1991	99,646	57,178	57.4	53,496	53.7	680	52,815	3,683	6.4	42,468
1992	100,535	58,141	57.8	54,052	53.8	672	53,380	4,090	7.0	42,394
1993	101,506	58,795	57.9	54,910	54.1	637	54,273	3,885	6.6	42,711
1994[1]	102,460	60,239	58.8	56,610	55.3	855	55,755	3,629	6.0	42,221
1995	103,406	60,944	58.9	57,523	55.6	881	56,642	3,421	5.6	42,462
1996	104,385	61,857	59.3	58,501	56.0	871	57,630	3,356	5.4	42,528
1997[1]	105,418	63,036	59.8	59,873	56.8	847	59,026	3,162	5.0	42,382
1998[1]	106,462	63,714	59.8	60,771	57.1	825	59,945	2,944	4.6	42,748
1999[1]	108,031	64,855	60.0	62,042	57.4	849	61,193	2,814	4.3	43,175
2000[1]	108,968	65,616	60.2	62,915	57.7	871	62,044	2,701	4.1	43,352
2001	110,007	66,071	60.1	62,992	57.3	869	62,124	3,079	4.7	43,935

[1] Not strictly comparable with data for prior years.

SOURCE: "2. Employment status of the civilian noninstitutional population 16 years and over by sex, 1970 to date," in *Employment and Earnings,* vol. 49, no. 1, January 2002

Table 1.5.) It should be noted that these data include families that may have members who are beyond the generally accepted working age.

About 4.8 million families (6.6 percent of all families) had at least one person who was unemployed in 2001. More than 72 percent of all families that included an unemployed person also contained at least one employed family member. White families were considerably less likely to have an unemployed person (5.8 percent) than were black (11.4 percent) or Hispanic (9.9 percent) families. (See Table 1.5.)

In 2001, in 28.8 million families, both the husband and wife worked. These employed couples comprised a little over half of all married couples (52.7 million) in that year. There were about 10.6 million "traditional" couples in which only the husband was employed outside the house. In another nearly 3.2 million families, only the wife worked. (See Table 1.6.)

Married-couple families (83.9 percent) and families maintained by men (86 percent) were more likely to include an employed person than families maintained by women (77.7 percent). (See Table 1.6.) There were far fewer families with an unemployed member that were maintained by men (433,000) than women (about 1.3 million). (See Table 1.7.)

About eight of ten married-couple families (82.8 percent) with an unemployed member also contained at least one employed family member. In contrast, roughly half of the families with unemployment maintained by men (59.6 percent) or women (51.4 percent) also included an employed person. (See Table 1.7.)

In 2001 both parents were employed in 63.2 percent of married-couple families with children under 18 years old. In just 29.5 percent of two-parent families, the father, but not the mother, was employed. The proportion (37.7 percent) in which the father, but not the mother, was

TABLE 1.2

Employment status of the civilian noninstitutional population by sex, age, race, and Hispanic origin, 2000–01

(Numbers in thousands)

Employment status, sex, and age	Total 2000	Total 2001	White 2000	White 2001	Black 2000	Black 2001	Hispanic origin 2000	Hispanic origin 2001
TOTAL								
Civilian noninstitutional population	209,699	211,864	174,428	175,888	25,218	25,559	22,393	23,122
Civilian labor force	140,863	141,815	117,574	118,144	16,603	16,719	15,368	15,751
Percent of population	67.2	66.9	67.4	67.2	65.8	65.4	68.6	68.1
Employed	135,208	135,073	113,475	113,220	15,334	15,270	14,492	14,714
Agriculture	3,305	3,144	3,099	2,968	138	114	745	639
Nonagricultural industries	131,903	131,929	110,376	110,252	15,196	15,156	13,747	14,075
Unemployed	5,655	6,742	4,099	4,923	1,269	1,450	876	1,037
Unemployment rate	4.0	4.8	3.5	4.2	7.6	8.7	5.7	6.6
Not in labor force	68,836	70,050	56,854	57,744	8,615	8,840	7,025	7,371
Men, 16 years and over								
Civilian noninstitutional population	100,731	101,858	84,647	85,421	11,320	11,468	11,064	11,400
Civilian labor force	75,247	75,743	63,861	64,141	7,816	7,858	8,919	9,098
Percent of population	74.7	74.4	75.4	75.1	69.0	68.5	80.6	79.8
Employed	72,293	72,080	61,696	61,411	7,180	7,127	8,478	8,556
Agriculture	2,434	2,275	2,266	2,130	116	101	639	547
Nonagricultural industries	69,859	69,805	59,429	59,281	7,064	7,026	7,839	8,009
Unemployed	2,954	3,663	2,165	2,730	636	731	441	542
Unemployment rate	3.9	4.8	3.4	4.3	8.1	9.3	4.9	6.0
Not in labor force	25,484	26,114	20,786	21,280	3,504	3,610	2,145	2,302
Men, 20 years and over								
Civilian noninstitutional population	92,580	93,659	78,151	78,888	10,107	10,250	9,859	10,170
Civilian labor force	70,930	71,590	60,182	60,609	7,343	7,395	8,306	8,453
Percent of population	76.6	76.4	77.0	76.8	72.6	72.1	84.2	83.1
Employed	68,580	68,587	58,469	58,367	6,832	6,805	7,961	8,022
Agriculture	2,252	2,102	2,092	1,961	111	99	601	515
Nonagricultural industries	66,328	66,485	56,377	56,406	6,720	6,707	7,360	7,508
Unemployed	2,350	3,003	1,713	2,242	511	590	345	431
Unemployment rate	3.3	4.2	2.8	3.7	7.0	8.0	4.2	5.1
Not in labor force	21,650	22,069	17,969	18,279	2,765	2,855	1,554	1,717
Women, 16 years and over								
Civilian noninstitutional population	108,968	110,007	89,781	90,467	13,898	14,091	11,329	11,722
Civilian labor force	65,616	66,071	53,714	54,003	8,787	8,861	6,449	6,653
Percent of population	60.2	60.1	59.8	59.7	63.2	62.9	56.9	56.8
Employed	62,915	62,992	51,780	51,810	8,154	8,143	6,014	6,159
Agriculture	871	869	833	839	21	12	106	92
Nonagricultural industries	62,044	62,124	50,947	50,971	8,133	8,130	5,908	6,066
Unemployed	2,701	3,079	1,934	2,193	633	719	435	495
Unemployment rate	4.1	4.7	3.6	4.1	7.2	8.1	6.7	7.4
Not in labor force	43,352	43,935	36,068	36,464	5,111	5,230	4,880	5,069
Women, 20 years and over								
Civilian noninstitutional population	101,078	102,060	83,570	84,214	12,643	12,830	10,193	10,559
Civilian labor force	61,565	62,148	50,318	50,700	8,293	8,390	5,979	6,176
Percent of population	60.9	60.9	60.2	60.2	65.6	65.4	58.7	58.5
Employed	59,352	59,596	48,736	48,884	7,774	7,801	5,629	5,769
Agriculture	818	817	784	790	20	11	100	87
Nonagricultural industries	58,535	58,779	47,953	48,094	7,754	7,790	5,529	5,682
Unemployed	2,212	2,551	1,581	1,815	519	589	350	407
Unemployment rate	3.6	4.1	3.1	3.6	6.3	7.0	5.9	6.6
Not in labor force	39,513	39,912	33,253	33,514	4,350	4,440	4,214	4,383
Both sexes, 16 to 19 years								
Civilian noninstitutional population	16,042	16,146	12,707	12,786	2,468	2,479	2,341	2,393
Civilian labor force	8,369	8,077	7,075	6,835	967	934	1,083	1,122
Percent of population	52.2	50.0	55.7	53.5	39.2	37.7	46.3	46.9
Employed	7,276	6,889	6,270	5,969	729	663	902	923
Agriculture	235	225	224	217	7	4	44	38
Nonagricultural industries	7,041	6,664	6,046	5,752	722	660	858	886
Unemployed	1,093	1,187	805	866	239	271	181	199
Unemployment rate	13.1	14.7	11.4	12.7	24.7	29.0	16.7	17.7
Not in labor force	7,673	8,069	5,632	5,951	1,500	1,545	1,258	1,271

NOTE: Detail for the above race and Hispanic-origin groups will not sum to totals because data for the "other races" group are not presented and Hispanics are included in both the white and black population groups.

SOURCE: "5. Employment status of the civilian noninstitutional population by sex, age, race, and Hispanic origin," in *Employment and Earnings,* vol. 49, no. 1, January 2002

TABLE 1.3

Employment status of the civilian noninstitutional population by age and sex, 2001

(Numbers in thousands)

		2001								
		Civilian labor force								
				Employed				Unemployed		
Age and sex	Civilian noninstitutional population	Total	Percent of population	Total	Percent of population	Agriculture	Nonagricultural industries	Number	Percent of labor force	Not in labor force
TOTAL										
16 years and over	211,864	141,815	66.9	135,073	63.8	3,144	131,929	6,742	4.8	70,050
16 to 19 years	16,146	8,077	50.0	6,889	42.7	225	6,664	1,187	14.7	8,069
16 to 17 years	8,044	3,105	38.6	2,573	32.0	93	2,480	532	17.1	4,939
18 to 19 years	8,101	4,972	61.4	4,316	53.3	132	4,184	655	13.2	3,130
20 to 24 years	18,879	14,565	77.1	13,361	70.8	302	13,060	1,203	8.3	4,315
25 to 54 years	119,787	100,291	83.7	96,515	80.6	1,899	94,616	3,777	3.8	19,495
25 to 34 years	37,055	31,144	84.0	29,697	80.1	565	29,132	1,447	4.6	5,911
25 to 29 years	17,535	14,674	83.7	13,943	79.5	255	13,688	731	5.0	2,861
30 to 34 years	19,520	16,470	84.4	15,754	80.7	310	15,444	716	4.3	3,050
35 to 44 years	44,390	37,585	84.7	36,226	81.6	754	35,472	1,359	3.6	6,806
35 to 39 years	21,609	18,228	84.4	17,535	81.1	365	17,171	692	3.8	3,382
40 to 44 years	22,781	19,357	85.0	18,691	82.0	390	18,301	666	3.4	3,424
45 to 54 years	38,341	31,563	82.3	30,592	79.8	580	30,012	972	3.1	6,778
45 to 49 years	20,461	17,240	84.3	16,688	81.6	320	16,368	552	3.2	3,221
50 to 54 years	17,881	14,324	80.1	13,903	77.8	259	13,644	420	2.9	3,557
55 to 64 years	24,203	14,579	60.2	14,133	58.4	421	13,712	446	3.1	9,625
55 to 59 years	13,481	9,317	69.1	9,035	67.0	234	8,802	282	3.0	4,164
60 to 64 years	10,723	5,262	49.1	5,098	47.5	188	4,910	164	3.1	5,461
65 years and over	32,849	4,303	13.1	4,174	12.7	297	3,878	129	3.0	28,546
65 to 69 years	9,297	2,300	24.7	2,228	24.0	128	2,100	73	3.2	6,996
70 to 74 years	8,460	1,190	14.1	1,157	13.7	88	1,068	34	2.8	7,270
75 years and over	15,092	812	5.4	790	5.2	80	710	22	2.8	14,280
Men										
16 years and over	101,858	75,743	74.4	72,080	70.8	2,275	69,805	3,663	4.8	26,114
16 to 19 years	8,199	4,153	50.7	3,493	42.6	173	3,320	660	15.9	4,046
16 to 17 years	4,125	1,581	38.3	1,283	31.1	73	1,210	298	18.8	2,544
18 to 19 years	4,074	2,572	63.1	2,210	54.3	100	2,110	362	14.1	1,501
20 to 24 years	9,366	7,629	81.5	6,949	74.2	228	6,722	680	8.9	1,736
25 to 54 years	58,728	53,613	91.3	51,630	87.9	1,361	50,269	1,983	3.7	5,115
25 to 34 years	18,147	16,817	92.7	16,086	88.6	415	15,671	731	4.3	1,330
25 to 29 years	8,579	7,861	91.6	7,476	87.1	185	7,291	385	4.9	718
30 to 34 years	9,568	8,956	93.6	8,610	90.0	230	8,380	346	3.9	612
35 to 44 years	21,864	20,222	92.5	19,500	89.2	532	18,969	722	3.6	1,641
35 to 39 years	10,613	9,859	92.9	9,498	89.5	264	9,233	362	3.7	754
40 to 44 years	11,250	10,363	92.1	10,003	88.9	267	9,735	360	3.5	887
45 to 54 years	18,718	16,574	88.5	16,043	85.7	413	15,630	531	3.2	2,144
45 to 49 years	10,010	9,039	90.3	8,751	87.4	229	8,522	287	3.2	971
50 to 54 years	8,708	7,535	86.5	7,292	83.7	184	7,108	243	3.2	1,173
55 to 64 years	11,544	7,866	68.1	7,601	65.8	297	7,304	265	3.4	3,678
55 to 59 years	6,471	5,000	77.3	4,839	74.8	160	4,678	162	3.2	1,471
60 to 64 years	5,073	2,866	56.5	2,763	54.5	137	2,626	103	3.6	2,207
65 years and over	14,022	2,482	17.7	2,407	17.2	216	2,190	76	3.0	11,540
65 to 69 years	4,298	1,301	30.3	1,258	29.3	96	1,162	43	3.3	2,997
70 to 74 years	3,766	682	18.1	662	17.6	60	603	19	2.8	3,084
75 years and over	5,958	500	8.4	486	8.2	61	425	14	2.7	5,458

employed was much higher among families with preschool children (under six years of age) than it was in families whose youngest child was 6 to 17 years old (22.9 percent). (See Table 1.8.)

In 2001 more than nine of ten fathers (94.6 percent) and seven of ten mothers (72.1 percent) were labor-force participants. Among the mothers, the participation rate (78.7 percent) for those who were unmarried (single, widowed, divorced, or separated) was slightly higher than the rate for married mothers (69.6 percent). (See Table 1.9.)

In 2001 the unemployment rate of married mothers was 3.4 percent, compared to an 8 percent rate for unmarried mothers. The unemployment rate for mothers with preschool children (6 percent) continued to be higher than the rate for mothers whose youngest child was of school age (3.9 percent). (See Table 1.9.)

In 2000 more than half (54.6 percent) of all mothers of children under one year old were in the labor force. This proportion rose among mothers with children two years of age (64.5 percent). These proportions remained nearly the same in 2001, with 54.9 percent of all mothers

TABLE 1.3

Employment status of the civilian noninstitutional population by age and sex, 2001 [CONTINUED]

(Numbers in thousands)

Age and sex	Civilian noninsti-tutional population	2001 Civilian labor force Total	Percent of population	Employed Total	Percent of population	Agri-culture	Nonagri-cultural industries	Unemployed Number	Percent of labor force	Not in labor force
Women										
16 years and over	110,007	66,071	60.1	62,992	57.3	869	62,124	3,079	4.7	43,935
16 to 19 years	7,947	3,924	49.4	3,396	42.7	52	3,344	527	13.4	4,023
16 to 17 years	3,919	1,524	38.9	1,290	32.9	20	1,270	234	15.3	2,395
18 to 19 years	4,027	2,399	59.6	2,106	52.3	31	2,074	294	12.2	1,628
20 to 24 years	9,514	6,936	72.9	6,412	67.4	74	6,338	523	7.5	2,578
25 to 54 years	61,059	46,678	76.4	44,885	73.5	538	44,347	1,793	3.8	14,380
25 to 34 years	18,908	14,326	75.8	13,611	72.0	150	13,461	716	5.0	4,582
25 to 29 years	8,956	6,813	76.1	6,467	72.2	70	6,397	346	5.1	2,144
30 to 34 years	9,952	7,514	75.5	7,144	71.8	80	7,064	370	4.9	2,438
35 to 44 years	22,527	17,362	77.1	16,726	74.2	222	16,503	637	3.7	5,164
35 to 39 years	10,996	8,368	76.1	8,037	73.1	100	7,937	331	4.0	2,627
40 to 44 years	11,531	8,994	78.0	8,688	75.3	122	8,566	306	3.4	2,537
45 to 54 years	19,624	14,990	76.4	14,549	74.1	166	14,382	441	2.9	4,634
45 to 49 years	10,451	8,201	78.5	7,937	75.9	91	7,846	264	3.2	2,250
50 to 54 years	9,173	6,788	74.0	6,612	72.1	75	6,537	177	2.6	2,385
55 to 64 years	12,660	6,713	53.0	6,532	51.6	124	6,407	181	2.7	5,947
55 to 59 years	7,010	4,317	61.6	4,197	59.9	73	4,123	120	2.8	2,693
60 to 64 years	5,650	2,396	42.4	2,335	41.3	51	2,284	61	2.5	3,254
65 years and over	18,828	1,821	9.7	1,768	9.4	80	1,687	53	2.9	17,007
65 to 69 years	4,999	1,000	20.0	970	19.4	32	937	30	3.0	3,999
70 to 74 years	4,694	509	10.8	494	10.5	29	466	14	2.8	4,186
75 years and over	9,135	313	3.4	304	3.3	19	284	9	2.8	8,822

SOURCE: Adapted from "3. Employment status of the civilian noninstitutional population by age, sex, and race," in *Employment and Earnings,* vol. 49, no. 1, January 2002

FIGURE 1.1

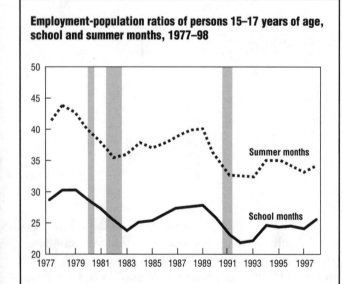

Employment-population ratios of persons 15–17 years of age, school and summer months, 1977–98

NOTE: Shaded areas are recessionary periods, as designated by the National Bureau of Economic Research.

SOURCE: "Chart 4.1. Employment-population ratios of persons 15 to 17 years of age, school and summer months, 1977–98," in *Report on the Youth Labor Force, Chapter 4,* U.S. Department of Labor, Bureau of Labor Statistics, Washington, DC, revised 2000

with children under one year in the labor force and 65.8 of mothers in the labor force with children two years of age. (See Table 1.10.)

Unmarried mothers during 2000 with children under one year of age were somewhat more likely to be in the labor force (58.8 percent) than were married mothers with children the same age (53.3 percent). In 2001, 58.3 percent of unmarried mothers with children under one year were in the workforce, while 77 percent of unmarried mothers with children that were two years old were in the workforce. (See Table 1.10.)

THE WORKING POOR

In 1999, 32.3 million persons (11.8 percent of the population) lived at or below the official poverty level. This was a reduction of 2.2 million from 1998. Although the nation's poor were primarily children and adults who were not in the labor force, about 6.8 million persons in the labor force were classified as "working poor." The working poor are individuals who spend at least 27 weeks in the labor force but whose income still falls below the official poverty threshold. In 1999 the poverty threshold for one person was $7,990, and the poverty rate for those who worked for at least 27 weeks was 4.9 percent. (See Table 1.11.)

TABLE 1.4

Employment status of the civilian noninstitutional population 25 years and over by educational attainment, sex, race, and Hispanic origin, 2000–01

(Numbers in thousands)

Educational attainment	Total 2000	Total 2001	Men 2000	Men 2001	Women 2000	Women 2001	White 2000	White 2001	Black 2000	Black 2001	Hispanic origin 2000	Hispanic origin 2001
TOTAL												
Civilian noninstitutional population	175,247	176,839	83,426	84,294	91,821	92,546	147,000	148,021	20,060	20,333	17,277	17,850
Civilian labor force	118,148	119,173	63,372	63,961	54,777	55,212	98,737	99,367	13,704	13,863	12,129	12,446
Percent of population	67.4	67.4	76.0	75.9	59.7	59.7	67.2	67.1	68.3	68.2	70.2	69.7
Employed	114,612	114,822	61,571	61,638	53,041	53,184	96,127	96,137	12,964	12,996	11,596	11,787
Employment-population ratio	65.4	64.9	73.8	73.1	57.8	57.5	65.4	64.9	64.6	63.9	67.1	66.0
Unemployed	3,537	4,351	1,800	2,323	1,736	2,028	2,610	3,230	740	867	533	659
Unemployment rate	3.0	3.7	2.8	3.6	3.2	3.7	2.6	3.3	5.4	6.3	4.4	5.3
Less than a high school diploma												
Civilian noninstitutional population	27,942	27,790	13,219	13,195	14,722	14,595	22,357	22,250	4,271	4,241	7,419	7,736
Civilian labor force	12,054	12,112	7,287	7,333	4,767	4,778	9,783	9,834	1,669	1,696	4,471	4,593
Percent of population	43.1	43.6	55.1	55.6	32.4	32.7	43.8	44.2	39.1	40.0	60.3	59.4
Employed	11,283	11,229	6,889	6,858	4,394	4,372	9,232	9,194	1,490	1,494	4,190	4,249
Employment-population ratio	40.4	40.4	52.1	52.0	29.8	30.0	41.3	41.3	34.9	35.2	56.5	54.9
Unemployed	771	883	398	476	373	407	550	640	179	202	282	344
Unemployment rate	6.4	7.3	5.5	6.5	7.8	8.5	5.6	6.5	10.7	11.9	6.3	7.5
High school graduates, no college												
Civilian noninstitutional population	57,559	57,367	26,337	26,542	31,222	30,825	48,510	48,277	7,046	7,094	4,794	4,911
Civilian labor force	37,170	36,949	19,762	19,758	17,409	17,191	30,927	30,706	4,929	4,908	3,549	3,631
Percent of population	64.6	64.4	75.0	74.4	55.8	55.8	63.8	63.6	69.9	69.2	74.0	73.9
Employed	35,886	35,412	19,086	18,912	16,799	16,500	30,015	29,602	4,609	4,542	3,410	3,471
Employment-population ratio	62.3	61.7	72.5	71.3	53.8	53.5	61.9	61.3	65.4	64.0	71.1	70.7
Unemployed	1,285	1,537	675	846	609	691	913	1,104	320	366	139	160
Unemployment rate	3.5	4.2	3.4	4.3	3.5	4.0	3.0	3.6	6.5	7.5	3.9	4.4
Less than a bachelor's degree[1]												
Civilian noninstitutional population	44,364	45,081	20,412	20,554	23,951	24,528	37,260	37,739	5,414	5,587	3,109	3,198
Civilian labor force	32,844	33,284	16,515	16,614	16,329	16,671	27,271	27,546	4,295	4,403	2,489	2,575
Percent of population	74.0	73.8	80.9	80.8	68.2	68.0	73.2	73.0	79.3	78.8	80.1	80.5
Employed	31,965	32,186	16,093	16,062	15,871	16,124	26,610	26,728	4,124	4,181	2,412	2,478
Employment-population ratio	72.1	71.4	78.8	78.1	66.3	65.7	71.4	70.8	76.2	74.8	77.6	77.5
Unemployed	879	1,098	422	552	458	546	661	818	171	222	78	97
Unemployment rate	2.7	3.3	2.6	3.3	2.8	3.3	2.4	3.0	4.0	5.0	3.1	3.8
Some college, no degree												
Civilian noninstitutional population	30,481	30,529	14,412	14,300	16,069	16,229	25,453	25,441	3,923	3,968	2,219	2,281
Civilian labor force	22,001	21,953	11,439	11,280	10,562	10,672	18,086	18,010	3,076	3,093	1,763	1,830
Percent of population	72.2	71.9	79.4	78.9	65.7	65.8	71.1	70.8	78.4	78.0	79.4	80.2
Employed	21,374	21,182	11,133	10,892	10,240	10,289	17,615	17,432	2,949	2,936	1,706	1,761
Employment-population ratio	70.1	69.4	77.3	76.2	63.7	63.4	69.2	68.5	75.2	74.0	76.9	77.2
Unemployed	628	771	306	388	322	383	471	578	128	157	57	69
Unemployment rate	2.9	3.5	2.7	3.4	3.0	3.6	2.6	3.2	4.2	5.1	3.2	3.8
Associate degree												
Civilian noninstitutional population	13,883	14,553	6,000	6,254	7,883	8,299	11,807	12,298	1,491	1,619	890	917
Civilian labor force	10,843	11,332	5,075	5,333	5,767	5,998	9,186	9,537	1,219	1,310	727	745
Percent of population	78.1	77.9	84.6	85.3	73.2	72.3	77.8	77.5	81.8	80.9	81.6	81.2
Employed	10,591	11,004	4,960	5,170	5,631	5,835	8,995	9,297	1,176	1,245	706	717
Employment-population ratio	76.3	75.6	82.7	82.7	71.4	70.3	76.2	75.6	78.9	76.9	79.3	78.2
Unemployed	252	327	116	164	136	163	190	240	43	65	21	27
Unemployment rate	2.3	2.9	2.3	3.1	2.4	2.7	2.1	2.5	3.5	4.9	2.8	3.7
College graduates												
Civilian noninstitutional population	45,382	46,601	23,457	24,002	21,925	22,599	38,873	39,754	3,328	3,411	1,955	2,005
Civilian labor force	36,080	36,828	19,808	20,256	16,272	16,573	30,756	31,281	2,810	2,856	1,620	1,647
Percent of population	79.5	79.0	84.4	84.4	74.2	73.3	79.1	78.7	84.4	83.7	82.9	82.1
Employed	35,478	35,995	19,503	19,806	15,975	16,189	30,270	30,614	2,741	2,779	1,585	1,588
Employment-population ratio	78.2	77.2	83.1	82.5	72.9	71.6	77.9	77.0	82.3	81.5	81.1	79.2
Unemployed	602	833	305	450	296	384	486	668	70	77	35	59
Unemployment rate	1.7	2.3	1.5	2.2	1.8	2.3	1.6	2.1	2.5	2.7	2.2	3.6

[1] Includes the categories, some college, no degree, and associate degree.

Note: Detail for the above race and Hispanic-origin groups will not sum to totals because data for the "other races" group are not presented and Hispanics are included in both the white and black population groups.

SOURCE: "7. Employment status of the civilian noninstitutional population 25 years and over by educational attainment, sex, race, and Hispanic origin," in *Employment and Earnings*, vol. 49, no. 1, January 2002

TABLE 1.5

Employment and unemployment in families by race and Hispanic origin, 2000–01 annual averages

(Numbers in thousands)

Characteristic	2000	2001
TOTAL		
Total families	71,680	71,980
With employed member(s)	59,626	59,699
As percent of total families	83.2	82.9
Some usually work full time[1]	55,683	55,599
With no employed member	12,054	12,281
As percent of total families	16.8	17.1
With unemployed member(s)	4,110	4,775
As percent of total families	5.7	6.6
Some member(s) employed	2,973	3,441
As percent of families with unemployed member(s)	72.3	72.1
Some usually work full time[1]	2,675	3,076
As percent of families with unemployed member(s)	65.1	64.4
White		
Total families	59,918	59,943
With employed member(s)	49,877	49,804
As percent of total families	83.2	83.1
Some usually work full time[1]	46,639	46,429
With no employed member	10,042	10,140
As percent of total families	16.8	16.9
With unemployed member(s)	3,010	3,506
As percent of total families	5.0	5.8
Some member(s) employed	2,276	2,629
As percent of families with unemployed member(s)	75.6	75.0
Some usually work full time[1]	2,052	2,351
As percent of families with unemployed member(s)	68.2	67.1
Black		
Total families	8,600	8,737
With employed member(s)	6,964	6,988
As percent of total families	81.0	80.0
Some usually work full time[1]	6,401	6,425
With no employed member	1,636	1,749
As percent of total families	19.0	20.0
With unemployed member(s)	881	1,000
As percent of total families	10.2	11.4
Some member(s) employed	535	601
As percent of families with unemployed member(s)	60.8	60.1
Some usually work full time[1]	476	538
As percent of families with unemployed member(s)	54.1	53.8
Hispanic origin		
Total families	7,581	7,766
With employed member(s)	6,633	6,746
As percent of total families	87.5	86.9
Some usually work full time[1]	6,255	6,355
With no employed member	947	1,020
As percent of total families	12.5	13.1
With unemployed member(s)	679	771
As percent of total families	9.0	9.9
Some member(s) employed	493	567
As percent of families with unemployed member(s)	72.7	73.5
Some usually work full time[1]	446	514
As percent of families with unemployed member(s)	65.8	66.7

[1]Usually work 35 hours or more a week at all jobs.

Note: Detail for the above race and Hispanic-origin groups will not sum to totals because data for the "other races" group are not presented and Hispanics are included in both the white and black population groups. Detail may not sum to totals due to rounding.

SOURCE: "Table 1. Employment and unemployment in families by race and Hispanic origin, 2000-01 annual averages," in *Employment Characteristics of Families in 2001*, U.S. Department of Labor, Bureau of Labor Statistics, Washington, DC, March 29, 2002

More than half of the workers below the poverty level (56 percent) usually worked full-time—even though full-time work substantially lowers a person's probability of being poor. Among persons in the labor force for 27 weeks or more, the poverty rate for those usually employed full-time was 3.9 percent compared with 10.5 percent for part-time workers. (See Table 1.11.) Only 6 percent of the workers below the poverty level actively looked for a job for more than six months in 1999, but ended up not working at all.

Gender, Race, and Age

Of all the persons in the labor force for at least 27 weeks in 1999, more women (about 3.6 million) than men (nearly 3.2 million) were poor. Due to the fact that fewer women than men made up the labor force, there was an even greater discrepancy between the percentages of working women living in poverty than working men. The rate of working women who were considered poor was 5.9 percent as compared to 4.4 percent of working men. (See Table 1.12.)

While nearly three-fourths of the working poor were white workers, black and Hispanic workers continued to experience poverty rates that were more than twice the rates of whites. The percentages of white working women (4.6 percent) in the labor force for more than half of the year and living in poverty were almost equal to the men (4.1 percent) in the same category. By contrast, black working women had a poverty rate of 13.6 percent, more than twice the rate of black working men (6.2 percent). (See Table 1.12.)

Younger workers were most vulnerable to being poor, particularly minority teenagers. (See Table 1.12.) High poverty rates among younger workers largely reflect the lower earnings and higher rates of unemployment associated with having relatively little education and work experience.

Education

Among all the people in the labor force for at least half of 1999, those with less than a high school diploma had a higher poverty rate (14.3 percent) than high school graduates (6 percent). Workers with an associate degree (2.9 percent) or college graduates (1.3 percent) reported the lowest poverty rates. Poverty rates generally were higher for black workers than for white workers at all education levels. (See Table 1.13.)

The poverty rate for black women workers with less than a high school diploma was 32.3 percent, compared to 14.9 percent for black men. Among high school graduates, the poverty rate for black women (17 percent) was more than twice that of black men (6.5 percent). Among black college graduates, however, poverty rates decreased, though black women still had a poverty rate of almost twice (2.3 percent) that of black men (1.3 percent). Poverty rates of white men and women were fairly similar at all education levels. (See Table 1.13.)

Occupations

During 1999 approximately three-fourths of the working poor were operators, fabricators, and laborers, or were employed in one of the following occupational groups: service, technical, sales, and administrative support. Not surprisingly, people working in managerial and professional specialty occupations have the lowest probability of being poor. In all occupational groups, women were more likely than men to be poor, and blacks were more likely to be below the poverty level than whites. (See Table 1.14.)

About 10.8 percent of those employed in service occupations were living in poverty. Female service work-

TABLE 1.6

Families by presence and relationship of employed members and family type, 2000–01 annual averages

(Numbers in thousands)

Characteristic	Number		Percent distribution	
	2000	2001	2000	2001
Married-Couple Families				
Total	54,704	54,665	100.0	100.0
Member(s) employed, total	45,967	45,868	84.0	83.9
Husband only	10,500	10,598	19.2	19.4
Wife only	2,946	3,183	5.4	5.8
Husband and wife	29,128	28,801	53.2	52.7
Other employment combinations	3,394	3,287	6.2	6.0
No member(s) employed	8,737	8,796	16.0	16.1
Families Maintained by Women[1]				
Total	12,775	12,880	100.0	100.0
Members(s) employed, total	10,026	10,014	78.5	77.7
Householder only	5,581	5,623	43.7	43.7
Householder and other member(s)	2,806	2,741	22.0	21.3
Other member(s), not householder	1,639	1,650	12.8	12.8
No member(s) employed	2,749	2,865	21.5	22.2
Families Maintained by Men[1]				
Total	4,200	4,435	100.0	100.0
Members(s) employed, total	3,632	3,816	86.5	86.0
Householder only	1,761	1,854	41.9	41.8
Householder and other member(s)	1,358	1,400	32.3	31.6
Other member(s), not householder	514	563	12.2	12.7
No member(s) employed	567	619	13.5	14.0

[1]No spouse present.
Note: Detail may not sum to totals due to rounding.

SOURCE: "Table 2. Families by presence and relationship of employed members and family type, 2000-01 annual averages," in *Employment Characteristics of Families in 2001*, U.S. Department of Labor, Bureau of Labor Statistics, Washington, DC, March 29, 2002

ers (12.9 percent) had a higher poverty rate than their male counterparts (7.8 percent). Household service workers (housekeepers, child-care workers, and cooks), almost all of whom were women, had a poverty rate of 23.6 percent. Protective service providers, such as firefighters, police officers, and guards, about 83 percent of whom were men, reported a poverty rate of only 3.2 percent. The overall poverty rate for black service providers (16.9 percent) was considerably higher than that for whites (9.3 percent). (See Table 1.14.)

The poverty rates for women and men employed in administrative support occupations were 3.3 percent and 2.5 percent respectively. Poverty rates for working women (1.5 percent) and men (2.1 percent) in technical occupations were similar. However, the poverty rate for women employed in sales occupations (8.9 percent) was more than two times that of their male counterparts (3.1 percent). (See Table 1.14.) In fact, the earnings difference between men and women in sales is larger than it is in any other major occupational group. Generally, women are more likely to work in lower-paying retail sales positions, while men are more likely to work in higher-paying wholesale sales positions.

TABLE 1.7

Unemployment in families by presence and relationship of employed members and family type, 2000–01 annual averages

(Numbers in thousands)

	Number		Percent distribution	
Characteristic	2000	2001	2000	2001
Married-Couple Families				
With unemployed member(s), total	2,584	3,028	100.0	100.0
No member employed	411	520	15.9	17.2
Some member(s) employed	2,174	2,507	84.1	82.8
Husband unemployed	836	1,137	32.3	37.5
Wife employed	531	722	20.5	23.8
Wife unemployed	789	899	30.5	29.7
Husband employed	694	792	26.8	26.2
Other family member unemployed	959	992	37.1	32.8
Families Maintained by Women[1]				
With unemployed member(s), total	1,194	1,315	100.0	100.0
No member employed	587	638	49.1	48.5
Some member(s) employed	607	676	50.9	51.4
Householder unemployed	522	590	43.7	44.9
Other member(s) employed	102	127	8.5	9.7
Other member(s) unemployed	672	725	56.3	55.1
Families Maintained by Men[1]				
With unemployed member(s), total	331	433	100.0	100.0
No member employed	139	175	42.0	40.4
Some member(s) employed	192	258	58.0	59.6
Householder unemployed	173	229	52.2	52.9
Other member(s) employed	67	93	20.4	21.5
Other member(s) unemployed	158	204	47.8	47.1

[1]No spouse present.

Note: Detail may not sum to totals due to rounding.

SOURCE: "Table 3. Unemployment in families by presence and relationship of employed members and family type, 2000-01 annual averages," in *Employment Characteristics of Families in 2001*, U.S. Department of Labor, Bureau of Labor Statistics, Washington, DC, March 29, 2002

Family Structure

In 1999 nearly 3.8 million families lived below the poverty level despite having at least one member in the labor market for 27 weeks or more. Of these, nearly half were families maintained by women (1.65 million). The poverty rate for families (the ratio of poor families with workers to all families with workers) was 6.2 percent. Not surprisingly, the poverty rate for families with just one member in the labor force (12.8 percent) was over seven times more than that of families with two or more members in the workforce (1.7 percent). Families maintained by women with only one member in the labor force (with a poverty rate of 23.5 percent) were nearly two times more likely to be poor than similar families maintained by men (11.5 percent). Married-couple families with two or more members in the labor force had the lowest poverty rate (1.4 percent). (See Table 1.15.)

EMPLOYMENT BY INDUSTRY

In 2002, four times as many people worked in the service-producing industry (107.2 million) than in the

TABLE 1.8

Employment status of parents in families with own children by age of youngest child and family type, 2000–01 annual averages

(Numbers in thousands)

	Number		Percent distribution	
Characteristic	2000	2001	2000	2001
With own children under 18 years				
Total	34,340	34,365	100.0	100.0
Parent(s) employed	31,601	31,412	92.0	91.4
No parent employed	2,739	2,953	8.0	8.6
Married-couple families	24,915	24,810	100.0	100.0
Parent(s) employed	24,282	24,092	97.5	97.1
Mother employed	17,012	16,782	68.3	67.6
Both parents employed	15,996	15,676	64.2	63.2
Mother employed, not father	1,016	1,105	4.1	4.5
Father employed, not mother	7,270	7,311	29.2	29.5
Neither parent employed	633	718	2.5	2.9
Families maintained by women[1]	7,613	7,665	100.0	100.0
Mother employed	5,751	5,710	75.5	74.5
Mother not employed	1,862	1,955	24.5	25.5
Families maintained by men[1]	1,812	1,890	100.0	100.0
Father employed	1,568	1,610	86.5	85.2
Father not employed	244	280	13.5	14.8
With own children 6 to 17 years, none younger				
Total	19,382	19,608	100.0	100.0
Parent(s) employed	17,892	18,026	92.3	91.9
No parent employed	1,490	1,580	7.7	8.1
Married-couple families	13,628	13,743	100.0	100.0
Parent(s) employed	13,248	13,339	97.2	97.1
Mother employed	10,247	10,196	75.2	74.2
Both parents employed	9,575	9,488	70.3	69.0
Mother employed, not father	672	707	4.9	5.1
Father employed, not mother	3,001	3,144	22.0	22.9
Neither parent employed	380	403	2.8	2.9
Families maintained by women[1]	4,668	4,750	100.0	100.0
Mother employed	3,715	3,743	79.6	78.8
Mother not employed	954	1,006	20.4	21.2
Families maintained by men[1]	1,086	1,114	100.0	100.0
Father employed	929	944	85.6	84.7
Father not employed	157	171	14.4	15.4
With own children under 6 years				
Total	14,958	14,758	100.0	100.0
Parent(s) employed	13,708	13,386	91.6	90.7
No parent employed	1,249	1,373	8.4	9.3
Married-couple families	11,287	11,067	100.0	100.0
Parent(s) employed	11,034	10,753	97.8	97.2
Mother employed	6,765	6,586	59.9	59.5
Both parents employed	6,421	6,188	56.9	55.9
Mother employed, not father	344	398	3.0	3.6
Father employed, not mother	4,269	4,167	37.8	37.7
Neither parent employed	254	314	2.2	2.8
Families maintained by women[1]	2,945	2,916	100.0	100.0
Mother employed	2,036	1,967	69.1	67.5
Mother not employed	909	949	30.9	32.5
Families maintained by men[1]	726	775	100.0	100.0
Father employed	639	666	88.0	85.9
Father not employed	87	110	12.0	14.2

[1]No spouse present.

Note: Own children include sons, daughters, stepchildren, and adopted children. Not included are nieces, nephews, grandchildren, and other related and unrelated children. Detail may not sum to totals due to rounding.

SOURCE: "Table 4. Families with own children: Employment status of parents by age of youngest child and family type, 2000-01 annual averages," in *Employment Characteristics of Families in 2001*, U.S. Department of Labor, Bureau of Labor Statistics, Washington, DC, March 29, 2002

TABLE 1.9

Employment status of the population by sex, marital status, and presence and age of own children under 18, 2000–01 annual averages

(Numbers in thousands)

Characteristic	2000			2001		
	Total	Men	Women	Total	Men	Women
WITH OWN CHILDREN UNDER 18 YEARS						
Civilian noninstitutional population	63,267	27,673	35,595	63,185	27,641	35,543
Civilian labor force	51,944	26,202	25,742	51,775	26,142	25,633
Participation rate	82.1	94.7	72.3	81.9	94.6	72.1
Employed	50,259	25,622	24,637	49,773	25,358	24,415
Employment-population ratio	79.4	92.6	69.2	78.8	91.7	68.7
Full-time workers[1]	43,365	24,922	18,443	42,815	24,586	18,229
Part-time workers[2]	6,894	699	6,195	6,958	773	6,186
Unemployed	1,685	581	1,104	2,002	784	1,218
Unemployment rate	3.2	2.2	4.3	3.9	3.0	4.8
Married, spouse present						
Civilian noninstitutional population	51,415	25,540	25,874	51,175	25,390	25,785
Civilian labor force	42,361	24,290	18,072	42,083	24,129	17,954
Participation rate	82.4	95.1	69.8	82.2	95.0	69.6
Employed	41,357	23,816	17,541	40,828	23,481	17,347
Employment-population ratio	80.4	93.2	67.8	79.8	92.5	67.3
Full-time workers[1]	35,793	23,212	12,581	35,232	22,813	12,419
Part-time workers[2]	5,564	604	4,960	5,597	668	4,928
Unemployed	1,004	474	531	1,255	648	607
Unemployment rate	2.4	2.0	2.9	3.0	2.7	3.4
Other marital status[3]						
Civilian noninstitutional population	11,853	2,132	9,720	12,010	2,252	9,758
Civilian labor force	9,583	1,913	7,670	9,693	2,013	7,679
Participation rate	80.8	89.7	78.9	80.7	89.4	78.7
Employed	8,902	1,806	7,096	8,945	1,877	7,068
Employment-population ratio	75.1	84.7	73.0	74.5	83.3	72.4
Full-time workers[1]	7,572	1,710	5,862	7,584	1,773	5,811
Part-time workers[2]	1,330	96	1,234	1,361	105	1,257
Unemployed	681	107	574	747	136	611
Unemployment rate	7.1	5.6	7.5	7.7	6.8	8.0
WITH OWN CHILDREN 6 TO 17 YEARS, NONE YOUNGER						
Civilian noninstitutional population	34,737	15,165	19,572	35,191	15,341	19,850
Civilian labor force	29,576	14,178	15,398	29,908	14,358	15,550
Participation rate	85.1	93.5	78.7	85.0	93.6	78.3
Employed	28,744	13,877	14,868	28,912	13,970	14,942
Employment-population ratio	82.7	91.5	76.0	82.2	91.1	75.3
Full-time workers[1]	25,042	13,513	11,529	25,148	13,568	11,580
Part-time workers[2]	3,703	364	3,339	3,764	402	3,362
Unemployed	832	302	530	995	387	608
Unemployment rate	2.8	2.1	3.4	3.3	2.7	3.9
WITH OWN CHILDREN UNDER 6 YEARS						
Civilian noninstitutional population	28,530	12,508	16,022	27,993	12,301	15,693
Civilian labor force	22,368	12,024	10,344	21,867	11,784	10,083
Participation rate	78.4	96.1	64.6	78.1	95.8	64.3
Employed	21,515	11,745	9,770	20,861	11,388	9,473
Employment-population ratio	75.4	93.9	61.0	74.5	92.6	60.4
Full-time workers[1]	18,323	11,410	6,914	17,667	11,017	6,649
Part-time workers[2]	3,191	335	2,856	3,194	370	2,824
Unemployed	853	279	574	1,006	396	610
Unemployment rate	3.8	2.3	5.6	4.6	3.4	6.0
WITH NO OWN CHILDREN UNDER 18 YEARS						
Civilian noninstitutional population	145,199	71,825	73,374	147,196	72,733	74,464
Civilian labor force	88,014	48,140	39,874	88,948	48,510	40,438
Participation rate	60.6	67.0	54.3	60.4	66.7	54.3
Employed	84,058	45,781	38,278	84,227	45,650	38,577
Employment-population ratio	57.9	63.7	52.2	57.2	62.8	51.8
Full-time workers[1]	68,046	39,136	28,910	67,977	38,898	29,079
Part-time workers[2]	16,012	6,645	9,367	16,250	6,752	9,498
Unemployed	3,956	2,359	1,596	4,721	2,860	1,861
Unemployment rate	4.5	4.9	4.0	5.3	5.9	4.6

[1]Usually work 35 hours or more a week at all jobs.
[2]Usually work less than 35 hours a week at all jobs.
[3]Includes never-married, divorced, separated, and widowed persons.

Note: Own children include sons, daughters, stepchildren, and adopted children. Not included are nieces, nephews, grandchildren, and other related and unrelated children. Detail may not sum to totals due to rounding.

SOURCE: "Table 5. Employment status of the population by sex, marital status, and presence and age of own children under 18, 2000-01 annual averages," in *Employment Characteristics of Families in 2001*, U.S. Department of Labor, Bureau of Labor Statistics, Washington, DC, March 29, 2002

TABLE 1.10

Employment status of mothers with own children under 3 years old by single year of age of youngest child and marital status, 2000–01 annual averages

(Numbers in thousands)

Characteristic	Civilian noninsti- tutional population	Total	Percent of popula- tion	Total	Percent of popula- tion	Full-time workers[1]	Part-time workers[2]	Number	Percent of labor force
		Civilian labor force		**Employed**				**Unemployed**	
2000									
TOTAL MOTHERS									
With own children under 3 years old	9,356	5,653	60.4	5,311	56.8	3,614	1,697	342	6.0
2 years	2,803	1,807	64.5	1,712	61.1	1,193	519	95	5.3
1 year	3,300	2,069	62.7	1,939	58.8	1,310	629	130	6.3
Under 1 year	3,253	1,777	54.6	1,660	51.0	1,112	548	117	6.6
Married, spouse present									
With own children under 3 years old	7,056	4,090	58.0	3,940	55.8	2,613	1,327	150	3.7
2 years	2,096	1,276	60.9	1,233	58.9	823	411	42	3.3
1 year	2,499	1,503	60.1	1,448	57.9	953	495	55	3.6
Under 1 year	2,461	1,312	53.3	1,259	51.1	837	421	53	4.1
Other marital status[3]									
With own children under 3 years old	2,300	1,563	67.9	1,371	59.6	1,002	370	191	12.2
2 years	707	531	75.1	478	67.6	370	108	53	9.9
1 year	801	566	70.7	491	61.3	357	134	75	13.2
Under 1 year	792	465	58.8	402	50.7	275	127	64	13.7
2001									
TOTAL MOTHERS									
With own children under 3 years old	9,177	5,526	60.2	5,142	56.0	3,527	1,616	383	6.9
2 years	2,787	1,834	65.8	1,719	61.7	1,194	525	115	6.3
1 year	3,344	2,020	60.4	1,881	56.2	1,285	597	139	6.9
Under 1 year	3,046	1,672	54.9	1,542	50.6	1,048	494	129	7.7
Married, spouse present									
With own children under 3 years old	6,921	3,979	57.5	3,808	55.0	2,546	1,263	171	4.3
2 years	2,069	1,280	61.9	1,229	59.4	818	411	51	4.0
1 year	2,533	1,450	57.2	1,389	54.8	920	469	62	4.3
Under 1 year	2,319	1,249	53.9	1,190	51.3	808	383	58	4.6
Other marital status[3]									
With own children under 3 years old	2,256	1,546	68.5	1,335	59.2	982	354	213	13.8
2 years	718	553	77.0	490	68.2	378	114	65	11.8
1 year	812	570	70.2	493	60.7	365	129	77	13.5
Under 1 year	726	423	58.3	352	48.5	239	111	71	16.8

[1] Usually work 35 hours or more a week at all jobs.
[2] Usually work less than 35 hours a week at all jobs.
[3] Includes never-married, divorced, separated, and widowed persons.
Note: Own children include sons, daughters, stepchildren, and adopted children. Not included are nephews, grandchildren, and other related and unrelated children. Detail may not sum to totals due to rounding.

SOURCE: "Table 6. Employment status of mothers with own children under 3 years old by single year of age of youngest child, and marital status, 2000-01 annual averages," in *Employment Characteristics of Families in 2001*, U.S. Department of Labor, Bureau of Labor Statistics, Washington, DC, March 29, 2002

goods-producing industry (24.1 million). Almost 17 million of those in the goods-producing industry worked in manufacturing. More than half (nearly 60 percent) of those produced durable goods, while about 40 percent produced nondurable goods.

In the service-producing industry sector, more than one-third (38.4 percent) of the people were employed in services, such as health, legal, and educational, and another 21.9 percent in the retail trade. (See Table 1.16.) It is important to understand the difference between a service industry and a service occupation. A service industry provides a service to the economy but employs more than service work-ers. For example, a restaurant is a service industry. It may employ workers involved in service, such as waiters, but also employs secretaries, managers, and accountants, whose occupations are not considered service occupations.

EMPLOYMENT BY OCCUPATION

In 1997 white-collar employment accounted for 59 percent of the total U.S. workforce; blue-collar for 25 percent; service jobs for 14 percent; and farming, fishing, and forestry for 3 percent. Professional, administrative, and managerial workers each accounted for approximately one-quarter of the white-collar work force. (See Figure 1.2.)

In 2001 nearly equal proportions of workers were employed in managerial or professional jobs (31 percent) and in technical, sales, or administration fields (28.9 percent). Other leading occupational categories were operators, fabricators, and laborers (13.1 percent); service occupations (13.6 percent); and precision production, craft, and repair (11 percent). (See Table 1.17.)

Women were far more likely than men to work in administrative support, including clerical, and in service occupations. Men dominated such categories as precision production, craft, and repair; fabrication and labor; and farming, forestry, and fishing. (See Table 1.17.)

Blacks were less likely than whites to work in managerial and professional specialties, sales, and precision production positions. Blacks were more likely than whites to work as operators, fabricators, and laborers and in service occupations. Black women were more likely to be in managerial and professional specialties, sales positions, administrative support positions, and service jobs than black men. (See Table 1.17.)

Almost one-quarter (24 percent) of Hispanic-origin workers were in the technical, sales, and administrative support field, with more than half of those people working in administrative support, including clerical. Operators, fabricators, and laborers accounted for another 21 percent, while one-fifth (20 percent) labored in service occupations. (See Table 1.18.) (Hispanic refers to an ethnic group, not a racial category. Hispanics can be of any race.)

Less than 15 percent of Hispanic-origin employees were in the managerial and professional specialty occupations, compared to 22 percent of blacks and 32 percent of whites. Although only 4.8 percent of Hispanics worked in farming, forestry, and fishing, they were more likely to do so than whites (2.7 percent) and blacks (1.1 percent). (See Table 1.18.)

EMPLOYEE TENURE

Data on tenure (how long a person has worked for his/her current employer) are often used to gauge employment security. Some observers regard increases in tenure as a sign of improving security and decreases in tenure as a sign of deteriorating security. There are shortcomings associated with this assumption due to other economic conditions. For example, during recessions or other periods of declining job security, the proportion of median tenure and long tenure workers could rise because less-senior workers are more likely to lose their jobs than are workers with longer tenure.

During periods of economic growth, the proportion of median tenure and long tenure workers could fall, because more job opportunities are available for new job entrants,

TABLE 1.11

Poverty status and work experience of people in the labor force by weeks in the labor force, 1999

(Numbers in thousands)

Poverty status and work experience	Total in the labor force	27 weeks or more in the labor force	
		Total	50 to 52 weeks
Total			
Total in labor force	149,042	133,651	119,376
Did not work during the year	1,503	547	476
Worked during the year	147,539	133,104	118,901
Usual full-time workers	118,368	111,992	103,620
Usual part-time workers	29,171	21,111	15,281
Involuntary part-time workers	3,717	2,956	2,333
Voluntary part-time workers	25,454	18,155	12,947
At or above poverty level			
Total in labor force	139,376	126,855	113,989
Did not work during the year	940	311	273
Worked during the year	138,436	126,544	113,716
Usual full-time workers	112,692	107,644	100,073
Usual part-time workers	25,744	18,900	13,643
Involuntary part-time workers	2,854	2,333	1,830
Voluntary part-time workers	22,890	16,568	11,813
Below poverty level			
Total in labor force	9,666	6,796	5,387
Did not work during the year	563	236	202
Worked during the year	9,103	6,559	5,185
Usual full-time workers	5,676	4,348	3,547
Usual part-time workers	3,427	2,211	1,638
Involuntary part-time workers	863	624	504
Voluntary part-time workers	2,564	1,587	1,134
Poverty rate[1]			
Total in labor force	6.5	5.1	4.5
Did not work during the year	37.5	43.2	42.5
Worked during the year	6.2	4.9	4.4
Usual full-time workers	4.8	3.9	3.4
Usual part-time workers	11.7	10.5	10.7
Involuntary part-time workers	23.2	21.1	21.6
Voluntary part-time workers	10.1	8.7	8.8

[1] Number below the poverty level as a percent of the total in the labor force.

Note: Data refer to persons 16 years and older. Data for 1999 are not strictly comparable with data for 1998 and earlier years because of the introduction of revised population controls used in the survey.

SOURCE: "Table 1. Persons in the labor force: Poverty status and work experience by weeks in the labor force, 1999," in *A Profile of the Working Poor, 1999,* U.S. Department of Labor, Bureau of Labor Statistics, Washington, DC, February 2001

and experienced workers have more opportunities to change employers and take better jobs. However, tenure also could rise under improving economic conditions, as fewer layoffs occur and good job matches develop between workers and employers.

In February 1998 and 2000 median male tenure (the point at which half the workers had more tenure and half had less) was 3.8 years, slightly less than the figures obtained in January of 1983, 1987, 1991, and February 1996. (See Table 1.19.) Since 1983 nearly every age group of men experienced a decline in median tenure, except among men ages 65 and older. For men in the 55- to 64-year category, median years of tenure increased between 1996 and 1998 from 10.5 to 11.2 years—the first

TABLE 1.12

Poverty status among persons in the labor force for 27 weeks or more, by age, sex, race, and Hispanic origin, 1999

(Numbers in thousands)

Age and sex	Total	White	Black	Hispanic origin	Below poverty level Total	White	Black	Hispanic origin	Poverty rate[1] Total	White	Black	Hispanic origin
Total, 16 years and older	133,651	111,714	15,698	13,971	6,796	4,830	1,596	1,496	5.1	4.3	10.2	10.7
16 to 19 years	5,207	4,405	596	622	527	365	127	93	10.1	8.3	21.4	15.0
20 to 24 years	12,412	10,240	1,675	1,866	1,312	894	367	253	10.6	8.7	21.9	13.6
25 to 34 years	30,695	24,839	4,096	4,178	1,835	1,290	433	486	6.0	5.2	10.6	11.6
35 to 44 years	36,945	30,612	4,564	3,917	1,726	1,246	387	417	4.7	4.1	8.5	10.7
45 to 54 years	29,965	25,468	3,158	2,255	851	631	165	167	2.8	2.5	5.2	7.4
55 to 64 years	14,066	12,240	1,271	938	419	313	89	64	3.0	2.6	7.0	6.8
65 years and older	4,361	3,909	338	195	127	91	27	15	2.9	2.3	8.0	7.7
Men, 16 years and older	71,790	61,163	7,260	8,267	3,165	2,526	447	898	4.4	4.1	6.2	10.9
16 to 19 years	2,700	2,312	264	383	234	183	29	60	8.7	7.9	10.9	15.6
20 to 24 years	6,488	5,487	741	1,152	575	438	115	156	8.9	8.0	15.5	13.5
25 to 34 years	16,728	13,865	1,899	2,558	852	707	93	315	5.1	5.1	4.9	12.3
35 to 44 years	19,949	16,877	2,153	2,254	833	674	119	243	4.2	4.0	5.5	10.8
45 to 54 years	15,764	13,594	1,455	1,253	402	311	52	91	2.5	2.3	3.5	7.3
55 to 64 years	7,595	6,704	582	546	200	159	30	28	2.6	2.4	5.2	5.1
65 years and older	2,566	2,325	166	122	69	53	10	6	2.7	2.3	5.8	4.9
Women, 16 years and older	61,861	50,551	8,438	5,704	3,631	2,303	1,149	598	5.9	4.6	13.6	10.5
16 to 19 years	2,507	2,093	332	239	293	181	99	34	11.7	8.7	29.7	14.1
20 to 24 years	5,924	4,753	934	714	737	456	252	98	12.4	9.6	27.0	13.7
25 to 34 years	13,967	10,975	2,197	1,620	983	582	340	172	7.0	5.3	15.5	10.6
35 to 44 years	16,996	13,735	2,411	1,663	893	571	269	174	5.3	4.2	11.1	10.5
45 to 54 years	14,201	11,874	1,703	1,002	450	320	114	76	3.2	2.7	6.7	7.6
55 to 64 years	6,472	5,537	689	393	219	154	58	36	3.4	2.8	8.5	9.2
65 years and older	1,795	1,584	172	73	57	38	17	9	3.2	2.4	10.1	(2)

[1] Number below the poverty level as a percent of the total in the labor force for 27 weeks or more.
[2] Data not shown where base is less than 75,000.

Note: Detail for race and Hispanic-origin groups will not sum to totals because data for the "other races" group are not presented and Hispanics are included in both the white and black population groups. Data for 1999 are not strictly comparable with data for 1998 and earlier years because of the introduction of revised population controls used in the survey.

SOURCE: "Table 2. Persons in the labor force for 27 weeks or more: Poverty status by age, sex, race, and Hispanic origin, 1999," in *A Profile of the Working Poor, 1999,* U.S. Department of Labor, Bureau of Labor Statistics, Washington, DC, February 2001

time the data showed an increase for this age group since 1983. It dropped again to 10.2 years in 2000.

During this period the age of the workforce generally shifted upward to older workers, who generally have longer tenure with their current employers. For example, median tenure for 25- to 34-year-old men was 2.7 years in February 2000, compared with 5.4 years for 35- to 44-year-olds and 10.2 years for 55- to 64-year-olds. (See Table 1.19.) This shift in the age distribution would, by itself, have raised median tenure. This age shift, however, was counterbalanced by the decline in median tenure for men in most age groups, leaving the overall median tenure for men essentially unchanged.

Among women, overall median tenure rose somewhat between 1987 and 1996, with nearly all of the gain taking place from 1991 to 1996, declining slightly in 1998 and 2000. (See Table 1.19.) The growth between 1991 and 1996 was partly due to increases in median tenure among 35- to 44-year-olds and 45- to 54-year-olds. These increases, even though small, were just the opposite of what was happening among men.

In addition to trends in median tenure, the Bureau of Labor Statistics (BLS) examined trends in the proportion of workers with relatively long tenure of ten years or

more. During the 1983 to 2000 period, the proportion of men who had worked for their current employer ten years or longer fell from 37.7 percent to 34 percent, while the proportion of women with such long tenure rose from 24.9 percent to 30 percent.

Table 1.20 provides more detailed information on the length of time workers had been with their current employers in February 2000. About one-quarter (26.8 percent) of wage and salary workers had worked for their current employer 12 months or less. These included workers who had recently entered the workforce, as well as workers who had changed employers in the previous year. More than three-quarters of 16- to 19-year-olds had such short tenure, as did over half of the workers age 20 to 24. By comparison, among 55- to 64-year-olds, 11.2 percent had 12 months or less of tenure, while 27.5 percent had worked for their current employer 20 years or more.

Among women and men in nearly every age group, workers who did not have a high school diploma had lower median tenure than those with more education. There appears to be little relationship between tenure and educational attainment for workers who have a high school diploma or higher level of education.

TABLE 1.13

Poverty status among persons in the labor force for 27 weeks or more, by educational attainment, race, and sex, 1999

(Numbers in thousands)

Educational attainment and race	Total	Men	Women	Below poverty level			Poverty rate[1]		
				Total	Men	Women	Total	Men	Women
Total, 16 years and older	133,651	71,790	61,861	6,796	3,165	3,631	5.1	4.4	5.9
Less than a high school diploma	15,991	9,728	6,263	2,287	1,257	1,030	14.3	12.9	16.4
Less than 1 year of high school	4,589	2,999	1,591	701	446	255	15.3	14.9	16.1
1-3 years of high school	9,914	5,861	4,054	1,412	720	692	14.2	12.3	17.1
4 years of high school, no diploma	1,487	868	619	174	91	83	11.7	10.5	13.3
High school graduates, no college	42,601	22,904	19,697	2,535	1,042	1,493	6.0	4.6	7.6
Some college, no degree	27,294	13,840	13,454	1,192	486	706	4.4	3.5	5.2
Associate degree	11,146	5,334	5,812	319	122	196	2.9	2.3	3.4
College graduates	36,619	19,984	16,635	463	257	206	1.3	1.3	1.2
White, 16 years and older	111,714	61,163	50,551	4,830	2,526	2,303	4.3	4.1	4.6
Less than a high school diploma	13,046	8,160	4,887	1,650	1,019	632	12.6	12.5	12.9
Less than 1 year of high school	3,967	2,660	1,307	592	410	182	14.9	15.4	13.9
1-3 years of high school	7,954	4,822	3,132	944	545	399	11.9	11.3	12.8
4 years of high school, no diploma	1,126	678	448	114	64	50	10.1	9.4	11.3
High school graduates, no college	35,536	19,448	16,088	1,758	816	942	4.9	4.2	5.9
Some college, no degree	22,412	11,605	10,807	844	377	467	3.8	3.2	4.3
Associate degree	9,507	4,646	4,861	213	93	119	2.2	2.0	2.5
College graduates	31,213	17,304	13,908	365	222	143	1.2	1.3	1.0
Black, 16 years and older	15,698	7,260	8,438	1,596	447	1,149	10.2	6.2	13.6
Less than a high school diploma	2,206	1,126	1,080	517	168	349	23.4	14.9	32.3
Less than 1 year of high school	365	213	151	74	17	57	20.2	7.8	37.7
1-3 years of high school	1,585	785	800	399	134	264	25.2	17.1	33.0
4 years of high school, no diploma	257	128	128	44	17	27	17.3	13.5	21.1
High school graduates, no college	5,632	2,733	2,899	668	177	491	11.9	6.5	17.0
Some college, no degree	3,790	1,644	2,146	276	71	205	7.3	4.3	9.6
Associate degree	1,172	457	715	81	14	67	6.9	3.1	9.4
College graduates	2,898	1,299	1,598	54	17	37	1.9	1.3	2.3

[1] Number below the poverty level as a percent of the total in the labor force for 27 weeks or more.

Note: Data for 1999 are not strictly comparable with data for 1998 and earlier years because of the introduction of revised population controls used in the survey.

SOURCE: "Table 3. Persons in the labor force for 27 weeks or more: Poverty status by educational attainment, race, and sex, 1999," in *A Profile of the Working Poor, 1999,* U.S. Department of Labor, Bureau of Labor Statistics, Washington, DC, February 2001

Industry

In February 2000 workers in mining had the highest median tenure (6.5 years) of any major private-sector industry. The median for mining rose from 3.4 years in January 1983 to a peak of 6.5 years in 2000. (See Table 1.21.) The number of workers in mining in the late 1990s and 2000 was only half of its peak of the early 1980s. Little hiring has occurred in the industry since the early to mid-1990s, and many lower-tenured workers have lost their jobs, resulting in a large increase in median tenure.

In February 2000 median tenure in manufacturing was 5 years. Some industries within manufacturing have experienced sizable movements in median tenure. For example, workers in motor vehicles and equipment had far less tenure with their employers in 2000 (5.8 years) than in 1983 (13 years). In aircraft and parts manufacturing, the median rose from 6.4 years in 1983 to 9.7 years in 2000. (See Table 1.21.)

The median length of time that workers in finance, insurance, and real estate had been with their current employer rose from 3.2 years in 1983 to 3.5 years in 1998. The services industry also experienced an increase in median tenure, from 2.5 years in 1983 to 2.9 years in 2000. (See Table 1.21.) Within services, private households, social services, hospitals, other health services, and business services all showed substantial increases from 1983 to 2000.

In transportation and public utilities, median tenure was 4.4 years in February 2000, a significant decline from 5.8 years in 1983. Wholesale and retail-trade workers showed little change in their median tenure, with retail trade continuing to have the lowest median (2 years) among the major private-sector industry groups. The median length of time government employees had worked for their current employer rose from 5.8 years in 1983 to 7.2 years in 2000. (See Table 1.21.)

NUMBER OF JOBS HELD

From 1978 to 1998, Americans held an average of 9.2 different jobs between the ages of 18 and 34. Men held 9.6 of these jobs and women 8.8. Those men and women who eventually obtained college degrees usually worked at more places between the ages of 18 and 24 than those who graduated from high school but did not attend college. (See Table 1.22.) The relatively larger number of jobs among those

TABLE 1.14

Poverty status among persons in the labor force for 27 weeks or more who worked during the year, by occupation or longest job held, race, and sex, 1999

(Numbers in thousands)

Occupation and race	Total	Men	Women	Below poverty level			Poverty rate[1]		
				Total	Men	Women	Total	Men	Women
Total, 16 years and older[2]	133,104	71,451	61,652	6,559	3,017	3,543	4.9	4.2	5.7
Managerial and professional specialty	39,908	20,235	19,674	611	289	322	1.5	1.4	1.6
Executive, administrative, and managerial	19,857	10,917	8,940	339	182	157	1.7	1.7	1.8
Professional specialty	20,051	9,318	10,734	272	107	165	1.4	1.1	1.5
Technical, sales, and administrative support	38,875	13,879	24,996	1,610	387	1,222	4.1	2.8	4.9
Technicians and related support	4,495	2,076	2,419	79	43	36	1.8	2.1	1.5
Sales occupations	15,969	8,069	7,900	955	249	705	6.0	3.1	8.9
Administrative support, including clerical	18,411	3,735	14,676	576	95	482	3.1	2.5	3.3
Service occupations	17,928	7,335	10,593	1,937	570	1,367	10.8	7.8	12.9
Private household	848	46	803	199	9	190	23.4	(3)	23.6
Protective service	2,381	1,964	417	76	47	29	3.2	2.4	6.9
Service, except private household and protective	14,699	5,325	9,374	1,662	514	1,148	11.3	9.6	12.3
Precision production, craft, and repair	14,543	13,155	1,388	621	537	85	4.3	4.1	6.1
Operators, fabricators, and laborers	18,418	14,090	4,328	1,263	830	432	6.9	5.9	10.0
Machine operators, assemblers, and inspectors	7,524	4,811	2,714	483	235	248	6.4	4.9	9.1
Transportation and material moving occupations	5,638	5,059	579	278	228	50	4.9	4.5	8.6
Handlers, equipment cleaners, helpers, and laborers	5,256	4,221	1,036	502	367	135	9.5	8.7	13.0
Farming, forestry, and fishing	3,294	2,642	652	518	404	114	15.7	15.3	17.4
White, 16 years and older[2]	111,384	60,949	50,435	4,705	2,438	2,267	4.2	4.0	4.5
Managerial and professional specialty	34,291	17,754	16,537	494	257	236	1.4	1.4	1.4
Executive, administrative, and managerial	17,311	9,805	7,505	283	164	118	1.6	1.7	1.6
Professional specialty	16,980	7,948	9,032	211	93	118	1.2	1.2	1.3
Technical, sales, and administrative support	32,774	11,922	20,852	1,061	318	743	3.2	2.7	3.6
Technicians and related support	3,738	1,743	1,995	63	43	20	1.7	2.5	1.0
Sales occupations	13,892	7,241	6,651	618	206	412	4.4	2.8	6.2
Administrative support, including clerical	15,144	2,939	12,206	380	68	311	2.5	2.3	2.6
Service occupations	13,613	5,636	7,977	1,266	403	863	9.3	7.1	10.8
Private household	634	29	605	133	3	130	21.0	(3)	21.5
Protective service	1,805	1,544	261	34	20	14	1.9	1.3	5.5
Service, except private household and protective	11,173	4,062	7,112	1,098	380	719	9.8	9.4	10.1
Precision production, craft, and repair	12,845	11,689	1,157	522	460	62	4.1	3.9	5.4
Operators, fabricators, and laborers	14,654	11,381	3,274	888	634	254	6.1	5.6	7.8
Machine operators, assemblers, and inspectors	5,971	3,919	2,052	325	174	151	5.4	4.4	7.4
Transportation and material moving occupations	4,551	4,108	443	209	180	29	4.6	4.4	6.5
Handlers, equipment cleaners, helpers, and laborers	4,132	3,353	779	354	280	74	8.6	8.3	9.5
Farming, forestry, and fishing	3,098	2,475	623	473	365	108	15.3	14.8	17.3
Black, 16 years and older[2]	15,528	7,165	8,363	1,502	402	1,100	9.7	5.6	13.1
Managerial and professional specialty	3,352	1,270	2,082	76	17	59	2.3	1.4	2.8
Executive, administrative, and managerial	1,547	620	927	35	7	28	2.3	1.1	3.1
Professional specialty	1,805	650	1,155	40	10	30	2.2	1.6	2.6
Technical, sales, and administrative support	4,401	1,219	3,182	457	39	419	10.4	3.2	13.2
Technicians and related support	495	181	314	12	0	12	2.3	0.0	3.7
Sales occupations	1,374	484	889	282	19	263	20.5	4.0	29.5
Administrative support, including clerical	2,532	553	1,979	164	20	145	6.5	3.5	7.3
Service occupations	3,415	1,280	2,135	577	126	451	16.9	9.8	21.1
Private household	156	8	147	58	6	52	37.2	(3)	35.2
Protective service	508	360	148	38	24	14	7.4	6.5	9.5
Service, except private household and protective	2,751	912	1,839	481	96	385	17.5	10.6	20.9
Precision production, craft, and repair	1,273	1,116	157	65	46	19	5.1	4.1	11.9
Operators, fabricators, and laborers	2,930	2,144	785	292	144	147	10.0	6.7	18.8
Machine operators, assemblers, and inspectors	1,113	648	465	126	48	79	11.3	7.3	16.9
Transportation and material moving occupations	925	802	122	54	33	21	5.9	4.1	17.3
Handlers, equipment cleaners, helpers, and laborers	892	694	198	111	64	48	12.5	9.2	24.0
Farming, forestry, and fishing	132	117	15	35	30	5	26.9	25.6	(3)

[1] Number below the poverty level as a percent of the total in the labor force who worked during the year.
[2] Includes a small number of persons whose last job was in the Armed Forces.
[3] Data not shown where base is less than 75,000.

Note: Data for 1999 are not strictly comparable with data for 1998 and earlier years because of the introduction of revised population controls used in the survey.

SOURCE: "Table 4. Persons in the labor force for 27 weeks or more who worked during the year: Poverty status by occupation or longest job held, race, and sex, 1999," in *A Profile of the Working Poor, 1999,* U.S. Department of Labor, Bureau of Labor Statistics, Washington, DC, February 2001

TABLE 1.15

Poverty status, presence of related children, and work experience of family members in the labor force for 27 weeks or more among primary families, 1999

(Numbers in thousands)

Characteristic	Total families	At or above poverty level	Below poverty level	Poverty rate[1]
Total primary families	60,454	56,699	3,755	6.2
With related children under 18	34,542	31,337	3,205	9.3
Without children	25,912	25,362	550	2.1
With one member in the labor force	24,649	21,506	3,143	12.8
With two or more members in the labor force	35,805	35,193	612	1.7
With two members	29,970	29,421	550	1.8
With three or more members	5,835	5,772	62	1.1
Married-couple families				
With related children under 18	25,658	24,314	1,343	5.2
Without children	21,158	20,845	313	1.5
With one member in the labor force	15,285	14,083	1,202	7.9
Husband	11,413	10,476	937	8.2
Wife	3,175	2,967	207	6.5
Relative	698	639	58	8.4
With two or more members in the labor force	31,530	31,076	454	1.4
With two members	26,518	26,112	406	1.5
With three or more members	5,012	4,964	48	1.0
Families maintained by women				
With related children under 18	6,920	5,269	1,651	23.9
Without children	3,154	2,973	181	5.7
With one member in the labor force	7,189	5,498	1,691	23.5
Householder	5,870	4,380	1,490	25.4
Relative	1,319	1,118	201	15.2
With two or more members in the labor force	2,885	2,744	141	4.9
Families maintained by men				
With related children under 18	1,965	1,754	211	10.7
Without children	1,600	1,543	56	3.5
With one member in the labor force	2,175	1,925	250	11.5
Householder	1,795	1,602	193	10.8
Relative	380	323	57	14.9
With two or more members in the labor force	1,390	1,372	18	1.3

[1] Number below the poverty level as a percent of the total in the labor force for 27 weeks or more.

Note: Data relate to primary families with at least one member in the labor force for 27 weeks or more. Data for 1999 are not strictly comparable with data for 1998 and earlier years because of the introduction of revised population controls used in the survey.

SOURCE: "Table 6. Primary families: Poverty status, presence of related children, and work experience of family members in the labor force for 27 weeks or more, 1999," in *A Profile of the Working Poor, 1999,* U.S. Department of Labor, Bureau of Labor Statistics, Washington, DC, February 2001

who attended college may be due to the fact that college students are likely to hold summer jobs as well as part-time positions while attending school. At older ages, the number of jobs did not vary much by education, suggesting that people tended to settle into more stable jobs at older ages.

From age 18 to 34, whites held more jobs than either blacks or Hispanics. The differences were more pronounced at younger ages. Between the ages of 18 and 24, whites held 5.8 jobs as compared to 4.7 for blacks and 5 for Hispanics. These racial differences nearly disappeared at older ages with the number of jobs held by blacks, whites, and Hispanics almost identical between ages 30 and 34. (See Table 1.22.)

SEEKING WORK WHILE EMPLOYED

Until the late 1990s, very little was known about job searches among those who were already employed. In 1995, about 6 million people or 5.6 percent of wage and salary workers actively looked for a new job. This was reduced to 4.5 percent in 1999. (See Table 1.23.)

Age Made a Difference

Among adult workers, the job search rate (the proportion of wage and salary workers actively seeking new positions) decreased with age from February 1995 to 1999. (See Table 1.23.) As workers age, many find suitable job matches and become less likely to seek other employment opportunities. Also, older workers may become more reluctant to change jobs as they could jeopardize earnings and lose benefits (premiums such as pensions and paid vacations gained through service with the company).

However, young adults often hold a series of short-term or part-time jobs during their school years. Upon graduation they are apt to try various jobs in order to find

TABLE 1.16

Employees on nonfarm payrolls by industry, 2001–02

(In thousands)

Industry	Not seasonally adjusted				Seasonally adjusted					
	Apr. 2001	Feb. 2002	Mar. 2002ᴾ	Apr. 2002ᴾ	Apr. 2001	Dec. 2001	Jan. 2002	Feb. 2002	Mar. 2002ᴾ	Apr. 2002ᴾ
Total	132,377	129,787	130,353	131,138	132,489	131,321	131,212	131,208	131,187	131,230
Total private	111,213	108,372	108,818	109,610	111,742	110,260	110,142	110,123	110,068	110,109
Goods-producing	25,195	23,667	23,712	23,863	25,421	24,453	24,273	24,242	24,159	24,068
Mining	554	544	544	555	560	564	563	558	554	561
Metal mining	36.7	30.0	30.1	30.6	37	33	31	30	31	31
Coal mining	75.5	81.0	80.6	80.7	75	82	82	81	80	81
Oil and gas extraction	330.1	329.1	326.0	331.4	335	336	339	335	331	336
Nonmetallic minerals, except fuels	111.6	104.0	107.2	111.9	113	113	111	112	112	113
Construction	6,709	6,333	6,404	6,558	6,852	6,850	6,787	6,815	6,774	6,695
General building contractors	1,511.8	1,473.1	1,481.2	1,497.3	1,548	1,559	1,552	1,552	1,548	1,536
Heavy construction, except building	899.4	803.9	824.2	878.4	915	944	928	938	905	899
Special trade contractors	4,298.1	4,056.4	4,098.6	4,182.1	4,389	4,347	4,307	4,325	4,321	4,260
Manufacturing	17,932	16,790	16,764	16,750	18,009	17,039	16,923	16,869	16,831	16,812
Production workers	12,116	11,224	11,215	11,217	12,166	11,405	11,328	11,294	11,267	11,256
Durable goods	10,844	9,990	9,965	9,969	10,870	10,158	10,048	10,018	9,988	9,987
Production workers	7,296	6,629	6,620	6,630	7,308	6,744	6,675	6,657	6,638	6,634
Lumber and wood products	789.0	767.2	767.0	773.5	800	780	781	784	783	784
Furniture and fixtures	544.1	496.7	496.7	501.4	543	499	497	499	497	500
Stone, clay, and glass products	574.4	537.6	544.4	551.2	577	559	554	551	553	552
Primary metal industries	664.3	599.3	597.6	595.6	667	613	600	596	599	597
Blast furnaces and basic steel products	212.7	188.8	188.5	187.8	(1)	(1)	(1)	(1)	(1)	(1)
Fabricated metal products	1,497.5	1,414.1	1,410.6	1,416.5	1,503	1,428	1,416	1,417	1,415	1,420
Industrial machinery and equipment	2,071.0	1,861.8	1,857.1	1,853.3	2,072	1,892	1,870	1,857	1,850	1,853
Computer and office equipment	363.2	326.9	325.3	322.4	367	335	327	326	326	325
Electronic and other electrical equipment	1,678.3	1,441.4	1,428.6	1,422.6	1,684	1,474	1,456	1,434	1,424	1,424
Electronic components and accessories	684.0	564.7	557.2	553.7	686	583	571	561	555	554
Transportation equipment	1,771.1	1,665.5	1,660.4	1,651.5	1,768	1,696	1,661	1,671	1,661	1,651
Motor vehicles and equipment	950.9	893.8	896.2	891.3	950	901	878	897	899	891
Aircraft and parts	463.6	431.2	423.0	417.7	464	452	440	432	423	419
Instruments and related products	864.5	832.6	828.3	823.5	866	839	835	833	830	826
Miscellaneous manufacturing	389.4	373.5	374.5	379.4	390	378	378	376	376	380
Nondurable goods	7,088	6,800	6,799	6,781	7,139	6,881	6,875	6,851	6,843	6,825
Production workers	4,820	4,595	4,595	4,587	4,858	4,661	4,653	4,637	4,629	4,622
Food and kindred products	1,651.7	1,654.6	1,653.9	1,654.6	1,687	1,682	1,684	1,685	1,685	1,687
Tobacco products	31.2	33.3	32.6	32.3	32	32	33	33	33	33
Textile mill products	487.1	435.7	435.5	434.1	489	442	440	439	437	435
Apparel and other textile products	581.4	522.2	524.7	523.3	581	531	534	527	525	523
Paper and allied products	636.8	619.9	619.8	615.9	641	624	624	622	622	619
Printing and publishing	1,507.0	1,420.1	1,414.0	1,407.9	1,512	1,444	1,434	1,423	1,416	1,412
Chemicals and allied products	1,034.2	1,018.0	1,015.0	1,008.1	1,036	1,021	1,020	1,019	1,017	1,010
Petroleum and coal products	127.1	123.7	127.1	129.8	128	127	128	128	130	130
Rubber and misc. plastics products	965.7	914.4	917.1	917.4	967	920	919	916	919	918
Leather and leather products	65.7	58.4	59.0	58.0	66	58	59	59	59	58
Service-producing	107,182	106,120	106,641	107,275	107,068	106,868	106,939	106,966	107,028	107,162
Transportation and public utilities	7,087	6,826	6,834	6,858	7,119	6,915	6,898	6,895	6,881	6,886
Transportation	4,552	4,319	4,330	4,364	4,576	4,387	4,381	4,381	4,369	4,387
Railroad transportation	229.7	223.3	225.2	226.8	230	227	228	226	227	227
Local and interurban passenger transit	492.2	494.6	497.2	500.8	477	485	482	484	484	489
Trucking and warehousing	1,841.4	1,788.3	1,795.6	1,807.2	1,864	1,832	1,830	1,827	1,826	1,830
Water transportation	199.6	194.4	195.1	204.3	202	206	204	205	203	206
Transportation by air	1,299.9	1,176.6	1,175.1	1,181.8	1,313	1,189	1,192	1,195	1,187	1,192
Pipelines, except natural gas	13.6	13.8	13.9	13.9	14	14	14	14	14	14
Transportation services	475.1	428.2	427.7	429.0	476	434	431	430	428	429
Communications and public utilities	2,535	2,507	2,504	2,494	2,543	2,528	2,517	2,514	2,512	2,499
Communications	1,692.5	1,665.9	1,664.3	1,654.6	1,696	1,683	1,670	1,669	1,668	1,655
Electric, gas, and sanitary services	842.5	841.4	839.7	839.4	847	845	847	845	844	844
Wholesale trade	7,034	6,870	6,879	6,894	7,053	6,938	6,933	6,917	6,911	6,910
Durable goods	4,177	4,051	4,048	4,053	4,187	4,086	4,076	4,067	4,061	4,060
Nondurable goods	2,857	2,819	2,831	2,841	2,866	2,852	2,857	2,850	2,850	2,850
Retail trade	23,289	22,927	23,006	23,244	23,530	23,365	23,408	23,466	23,452	23,475
Building materials and garden supplies	1,018.5	971.1	1,005.3	1,053.6	999	1,013	1,022	1,028	1,035	1,039
General merchandise stores	2,708.1	2,687.9	2,688.7	2,694.5	2,804	2,755	2,710	2,793	2,793	2,792
Department stores	2,374.1	2,347.4	2,351.0	2,356.0	2,459	2,410	2,369	2,435	2,442	2,443
Food stores	3,524.2	3,469.8	3,449.5	3,452.7	3,562	3,525	3,519	3,502	3,494	3,484

TABLE 1.16

Employees on nonfarm payrolls by industry, 2001–02 [CONTINUED]

(In thousands)

Industry	Not seasonally adjusted				Seasonally adjusted					
	Apr. 2001	Feb. 2002	Mar. 2002ᵖ	Apr. 2002ᵖ	Apr. 2001	Dec. 2001	Jan. 2002	Feb. 2002	Mar. 2002ᵖ	Apr. 2002ᵖ
Automotive dealers and service stations	2,417.3	2,400.3	2,405.4	2,425.1	2,421	2,428	2,436	2,430	2,427	2,433
New and used car dealers	1,121.1	1,139.8	1,142.8	1,145.5	1,122	1,141	1,145	1,147	1,147	1,147
Apparel and accessory stores	1,194.6	1,177.3	1,184.6	1,183.2	1,226	1,192	1,221	1,218	1,222	1,214
Furniture and home furnishings stores	1,129.3	1,133.3	1,133.4	1,134.5	1,140	1,143	1,138	1,142	1,143	1,146
Eating and drinking places	8,201.1	7,966.4	8,057.9	8,220.2	8,213	8,209	8,213	8,206	8,192	8,223
Miscellaneous retail establishments	3,095.8	3,120.4	3,081.4	3,080.5	3,165	3,100	3,149	3,147	3,146	3,144
Finance, insurance, and real estate	7,599	7,572	7,581	7,610	7,626	7,632	7,638	7,626	7,616	7,634
Finance	3,751	3,759	3,760	3,759	3,761	3,774	3,778	3,769	3,764	3,767
Depository institutions	2,027.1	2,037.4	2,037.5	2,041.6	2,032	2,044	2,046	2,043	2,042	2,046
Commercial banks	1,417.4	1,421.8	1,420.6	1,422.8	1,421	1,427	1,429	1,427	1,425	1,427
Savings institutions	254.0	260.8	261.9	263.8	255	260	262	261	263	264
Nondepository institutions	689.9	729.6	730.2	728.1	691	728	731	731	729	729
Mortgage bankers and brokers	308.1	346.7	346.5	344.6	308	342	346	349	347	345
Security and commodity brokers	774.0	735.1	735.5	735.5	780	744	742	738	738	739
Holding and other investment offices	259.9	257.2	256.7	254.1	258	258	259	257	255	253
Insurance	2,351	2,342	2,341	2,347	2,356	2,352	2,351	2,347	2,342	2,351
Insurance carriers	1,592.1	1,586.2	1,585.1	1,589.9	1,596	1,594	1,594	1,589	1,585	1,593
Insurance agents, brokers, and service	759.3	755.9	756.2	757.3	760	758	757	758	757	758
Real estate	1,497	1,471	1,480	1,504	1,509	1,506	1,509	1,510	1,510	1,516
Services[2]	41,009	40,510	40,806	41,141	40,993	40,957	40,992	40,977	41,049	41,136
Agricultural services	839.8	719.4	759.1	848.8	824	846	843	844	846	835
Hotels and other lodging places	1,895.4	1,761.2	1,789.7	1,813.4	1,944	1,845	1,854	1,858	1,860	1,856
Personal services	1,335.6	1,361.6	1,359.9	1,362.8	1,267	1,294	1,295	1,285	1,293	1,296
Business services	9,604.9	9,114.8	9,205.0	9,282.4	9,729	9,346	9,317	9,286	9,339	9,408
Services to buildings	1,007.0	966.6	970.4	981.3	1,009	992	982	976	977	981
Personnel supply services	3,504.6	3,084.8	3,183.4	3,258.7	3,600	3,252	3,237	3,237	3,306	3,358
Help supply services	3,112.7	2,748.9	2,840.4	2,907.2	3,202	2,894	2,881	2,891	2,951	3,017
Computer and data processing services	2,200.1	2,187.7	2,184.1	2,173.5	2,199	2,189	2,186	2,184	2,177	2,170
Auto repair, services, and parking	1,301.0	1,302.9	1,301.8	1,302.7	1,300	1,304	1,308	1,307	1,302	1,301
Miscellaneous repair services	363.7	356.5	354.4	354.7	364	359	358	361	357	355
Motion pictures	598.2	576.2	576.8	581.7	601	580	589	579	576	584
Amusement and recreation services	1,737.5	1,544.5	1,591.3	1,690.9	1,764	1,777	1,772	1,756	1,746	1,722
Health services	10,264.1	10,504.4	10,545.0	10,554.6	10,280	10,483	10,504	10,528	10,558	10,573
Offices and clinics of medical doctors	1,964.2	2,010.7	2,018.5	2,020.2	1,967	2,002	2,007	2,016	2,023	2,023
Nursing and personal care facilities	1,811.3	1,842.9	1,850.5	1,854.2	1,816	1,842	1,848	1,847	1,852	1,858
Hospitals	4,056.3	4,170.1	4,180.3	4,182.4	4,062	4,158	4,167	4,174	4,183	4,191
Home health care services	646.2	657.5	661.6	662.9	646	659	663	662	662	663
Legal services	1,014.7	1,023.9	1,024.1	1,024.8	1,021	1,031	1,030	1,030	1,029	1,033
Educational services	2,533.7	2,617.1	2,627.6	2,628.0	2,388	2,457	2,472	2,486	2,478	2,485
Social services	3,044.2	3,123.5	3,139.8	3,148.2	3,023	3,105	3,122	3,120	3,124	3,128
Child day care services	764.2	768.7	774.9	780.4	743	757	756	754	755	758
Residential care	833.2	856.7	860.8	860.1	835	853	860	860	863	863
Museums and botanical and zoological gardens	107.9	101.0	103.8	108.0	109	110	110	110	110	110
Membership organizations	2,477.6	2,485.0	2,494.9	2,499.5	2,489	2,506	2,504	2,505	2,506	2,512
Engineering and management services	3,518.3	3,546.7	3,561.9	3,570.0	3,517	3,541	3,542	3,550	3,553	3,567
Engineering and architectural services	1,045.0	1,049.7	1,054.5	1,058.9	1,053	1,063	1,064	1,061	1,066	1,068
Management and public relations	1,120.6	1,123.0	1,124.5	1,130.3	1,124	1,125	1,132	1,131	1,128	1,133
Services, nec	50.8	49.8	49.2	49.3	(1)	(1)	(1)	(1)	(1)	(1)
Government	21,164	21,415	21,535	21,528	20,747	21,061	21,070	21,085	21,119	21,121
Federal	2,611	2,596	2,597	2,599	2,615	2,615	2,607	2,608	2,605	2,605
Federal, except Postal Service	1,756.5	1,767.3	1,771.9	1,776.4	1,756	1,775	1,775	1,777	1,777	1,778
State	4,984	5,030	5,068	5,070	4,847	4,928	4,934	4,928	4,931	4,932
Education	2,212.9	2,240.2	2,275.1	2,275.1	2,065	2,112	2,120	2,117	2,122	2,125
Other State government	2,770.6	2,789.5	2,792.5	2,794.9	2,782	2,816	2,814	2,811	2,809	2,807
Local	13,569	13,789	13,870	13,859	13,285	13,518	13,529	13,549	13,583	13,584
Education	7,874.7	8,022.1	8,083.2	8,052.7	7,495	7,642	7,644	7,654	7,684	7,685
Other local government	5,694.1	5,766.6	5,786.7	5,805.8	5,790	5,876	5,885	5,895	5,899	5,899

[1] These series are not published seasonally adjusted because the seasonal component, which is small relative to the trend-cycle and irregular components, cannot be separated with sufficient precision.
[2] Includes other industries, not shown separately.
ᵖ = preliminary.

SOURCE: "Table B–1. Employees on nonfarm payrolls by industry," in *The Employment Situation: April 2002*, U.S. Department of Labor, Bureau of Labor Statistics, Washington, DC, April 2002

FIGURE 1.2

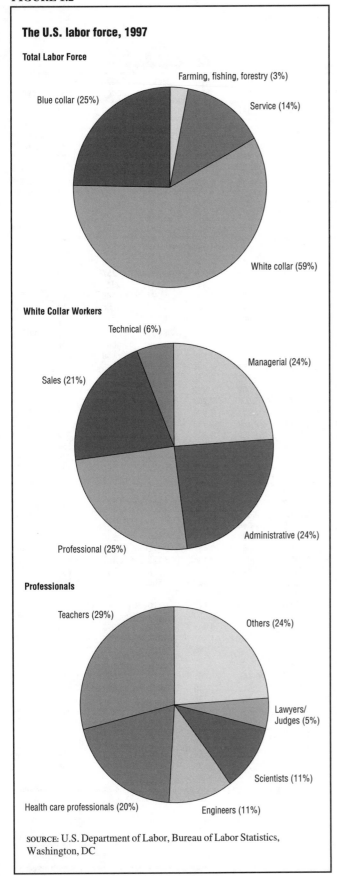

The U.S. labor force, 1997

Total Labor Force

- Farming, fishing, forestry (3%)
- Service (14%)
- White collar (59%)
- Blue collar (25%)

White Collar Workers

- Technical (6%)
- Managerial (24%)
- Sales (21%)
- Administrative (24%)
- Professional (25%)

Professionals

- Teachers (29%)
- Others (24%)
- Lawyers/Judges (5%)
- Scientists (11%)
- Engineers (11%)
- Health care professionals (20%)

SOURCE: U.S. Department of Labor, Bureau of Labor Statistics, Washington, DC

the position that best suits their interests and abilities. However, among teenagers, school enrollment appeared to limit the likelihood of searching for another job. Wage and salary workers age 16 to 19 who were not enrolled in school were twice as likely as those attending school to seek jobs. The difference was smaller among 20- to 24-year-olds. Regardless of age, men were more likely than women to search for another job while employed.

Education and Job Mismatches

In almost all occupational categories, employed persons with high levels of education had the highest job-search rates. This may be attributed to dissatisfied workers in positions not equal to their level of education. For example, in 1999 the job search rates for service workers with a bachelor's degree were 7.1 compared to 3.5 for those with a high school diploma. (See Table 1.24.)

Among the major occupational groups, workers with sales occupations had the highest job-search rates in 1995, 1997, and 1999. Workers in precision production, craft, and repair occupations had the lowest job-search rates, while rates for workers in executive, administrative, and managerial positions; professional specialties; and technical occupations were slightly below the overall average.

UNIONS

In 2001 the proportion of workers who were union members stayed the same as 2000 but continued an overall decline from 1996. Union members accounted for 13.5 percent of wage and salary workers in 2000 and 2001. (See Table 1.25.) It should be noted that a worker may be represented by a union but may not be a dues-paying member. In a "right-to-work" state, a worker is allowed to join a unionized company and not be forced to join the union. By law, the nonunion worker, working in a unionized company, must benefit from any union contract. A total of 14.8 percent of workers were represented by unions in 2001, down from 14.9 percent the year before. Almost one-half (41.8 percent) of government workers were represented by unions in 2001. (See Table 1.26.)

Union membership in general fell steadily from 20.1 percent in 1983, the first year for which comparable data were available, to 12.8 percent for all workers in 2001. (See Table 1.26.) The recession of the early 1980s, the movement of jobs overseas, the decline in traditionally unionized heavy industry, management's desire to eliminate union power, the threat of job loss, and unimaginative union leadership all contributed to the decline in union membership.

Instead of demanding better hours, more pay, and improved working conditions—the traditional union demands—most unions agreed to "give backs" (surrendering existing benefits) and lower salaries in exchange for job

TABLE 1.17

Employed persons by occupation, race, and sex, 2000–01

(Percent distribution)

Occupation and race	Total		Men		Women	
	2000	2001	2000	2001	2000	2001
TOTAL						
Total, 16 years and over (thousands)	135,208	135,073	72,293	72,080	62,915	62,992
Percent	100.0	100.0	100.0	100.0	100.0	100.0
Managerial and professional specialty	30.2	31.0	28.4	29.1	32.3	33.2
Executive, administrative, and managerial	14.6	15.1	15.0	15.2	14.2	14.8
Professional specialty	15.6	16.0	13.5	13.8	18.1	18.4
Technical, sales, and administrative support	29.2	28.9	19.8	19.7	40.0	39.5
Technicians and related support	3.2	3.3	2.9	2.9	3.6	3.8
Sales occupations	12.1	11.9	11.4	11.3	12.9	12.6
Administrative support, including clerical	13.8	13.7	5.4	5.5	23.5	23.1
Service occupations	13.5	13.6	10.0	10.1	17.5	17.6
Private household	.6	.5	(1)	(1)	1.2	1.1
Protective service	1.8	1.8	2.7	2.7	.7	.8
Service, except private household and protective	11.2	11.2	7.3	7.3	15.6	15.7
Precision production, craft, and repair	11.0	11.0	18.7	18.8	2.1	2.0
Operators, fabricators, and laborers	13.5	13.1	19.3	18.8	6.9	6.6
Machine operators, assemblers, and inspectors	5.4	5.0	6.4	5.9	4.3	3.9
Transportation and material moving occupations	4.1	4.2	6.9	7.0	.9	.9
Handlers, equipment cleaners, helpers, and laborers	4.0	3.9	6.0	5.9	1.7	1.7
Farming, forestry, and fishing	2.5	2.4	3.7	3.6	1.1	1.1
White						
Total, 16 years and over (thousands)	113,475	113,220	61,696	61,411	51,780	51,810
Percent	100.0	100.0	100.0	100.0	100.0	100.0
Managerial and professional specialty	31.1	31.9	29.2	29.8	33.4	34.4
Executive, administrative, and managerial	15.3	15.7	15.8	16.0	14.8	15.4
Professional specialty	15.8	16.2	13.4	13.8	18.6	19.0
Technical, sales, and administrative support	29.2	28.9	19.7	19.6	40.5	39.9
Technicians and related support	3.2	3.3	2.9	2.9	3.5	3.8
Sales occupations	12.5	12.2	11.9	11.7	13.2	12.8
Administrative support, including clerical	13.5	13.4	5.0	5.1	23.7	23.3
Service occupations	12.4	12.4	9.1	9.1	16.4	16.4
Private household	.6	.5	(1)	(1)	1.2	1.1
Protective service	1.6	1.7	2.5	2.5	.6	.7
Service, except private household and protective	10.2	10.2	6.5	6.5	14.6	14.6
Precision production, craft, and repair	11.6	11.6	19.5	19.7	2.1	2.0
Operators, fabricators, and laborers	12.9	12.5	18.4	17.9	6.4	6.1
Machine operators, assemblers, and inspectors	5.1	4.7	6.1	5.7	3.9	3.5
Transportation and material moving occupations	3.9	4.0	6.6	6.7	.8	.9
Handlers, equipment cleaners, helpers, and laborers	3.9	3.8	5.8	5.5	1.6	1.7
Farming, forestry, and fishing	2.8	2.6	4.0	3.8	1.3	1.2
Black						
Total, 16 years and over (thousands)	15,334	15,270	7,180	7,127	8,154	8,143
Percent	100.0	100.0	100.0	100.0	100.0	100.0
Managerial and professional specialty	21.8	22.6	18.5	18.8	24.8	26.0
Executive, administrative, and managerial	9.9	10.5	8.9	9.5	10.7	11.4
Professional specialty	12.0	12.1	9.6	9.3	14.1	14.6
Technical, sales, and administrative support	29.3	29.2	18.8	18.8	38.6	38.3
Technicians and related support	3.2	3.0	2.6	2.3	3.7	3.7
Sales occupations	9.4	9.6	7.6	8.1	10.9	10.9
Administrative support, including clerical	16.8	16.6	8.5	8.5	24.0	23.7
Service occupations	21.5	21.5	17.4	17.8	25.2	24.8
Private household	.8	.6	(1)	(1)	1.4	1.0
Protective service	3.1	3.2	4.7	5.0	1.6	1.7
Service, except private household and protective	17.7	17.7	12.6	12.7	22.1	22.0
Precision production, craft, and repair	7.8	7.5	14.2	14.1	2.1	1.8
Operators, fabricators, and laborers	18.5	18.1	29.0	28.4	9.1	9.0
Machine operators, assemblers, and inspectors	7.0	6.5	8.8	7.9	5.5	5.3
Transportation and material moving occupations	6.0	6.0	11.1	11.2	1.4	1.5
Handlers, equipment cleaners, helpers, and laborers	5.4	5.5	9.1	9.4	2.2	2.1
Farming, forestry, and fishing	1.1	1.1	2.1	2.0	.2	.2

[1]Less than 0.05 percent.

SOURCE: "10. Employed persons by occupation, race and sex," in *Employment and Earnings*, vol. 49, no. 1, January 2002

TABLE 1.18

Employed white, black, and Hispanic-origin workers by sex, occupation, class of worker, and full- or part-time status, 2000–01

(In thousands)

Category	Total		White		Black		Hispanic origin	
	2000	2001	2000	2001	2000	2001	2000	2001
Sex								
Total (all civilian workers)	135,208	135,073	113,475	113,220	15,334	15,270	14,492	14,714
Men	72,293	72,080	61,696	61,411	7,180	7,127	8,478	8,556
Women	62,915	62,992	51,780	51,810	8,154	8,143	6,014	6,159
Occupation								
Managerial and professional specialty	40,887	41,894	35,304	36,125	3,349	3,457	2,036	2,150
Executive, administrative, and managerial	19,774	20,338	17,372	17,803	1,512	1,603	1,072	1,148
Professional specialty	21,113	21,556	17,932	18,323	1,836	1,854	964	1,002
Technical, sales, and administrative support	39,442	39,044	33,146	32,718	4,497	4,461	3,504	3,556
Technicians and related support	4,385	4,497	3,611	3,731	492	463	303	338
Sales occupations	16,340	16,044	14,169	13,807	1,436	1,464	1,385	1,402
Administrative support, including clerical	18,717	18,503	15,366	15,180	2,570	2,533	1,816	1,816
Service occupations	18,278	18,359	14,066	14,083	3,301	3,281	2,867	3,000
Private household	792	715	631	593	118	87	251	234
Protective service	2,399	2,478	1,860	1,908	471	492	208	244
Service, except private household and protective	15,087	15,166	11,575	11,582	2,712	2,702	2,408	2,521
Precision production, craft, and repair	14,882	14,833	13,133	13,128	1,191	1,152	2,075	2,176
Mechanics and repairers	4,875	4,807	4,293	4,274	399	374	522	547
Construction trades	6,120	6,253	5,540	5,643	431	440	1,004	1,088
Other precision production, craft, and repair	3,887	3,772	3,300	3,210	360	337	550	541
Operators, fabricators, and laborers	18,319	17,698	14,680	14,167	2,830	2,758	3,202	3,134
Machine operators, assemblers, and inspectors	7,319	6,734	5,802	5,336	1,080	997	1,416	1,320
Transportation and material moving occupations	5,557	5,638	4,476	4,553	915	922	662	697
Handlers, equipment cleaners, helpers, and laborers	5,443	5,326	4,402	4,278	835	838	1,125	1,118
Construction laborers	1,015	1,024	876	895	113	103	281	300
Other handlers, equipment cleaners, helpers, and laborers	4,428	4,302	3,526	3,383	722	735	844	818
Farming, forestry, and fishing	3,399	3,245	3,146	3,000	166	161	807	698
Class of worker								
Agriculture:								
Wage and salary workers	2,034	1,884	1,883	1,762	107	81	685	559
Self-employed workers	1,233	1,233	1,179	1,181	31	33	59	79
Unpaid family workers	38	27	38	25	–	–	1	1
Nonagricultural industries:								
Wage and salary workers	123,128	123,235	102,595	102,524	14,611	14,607	13,114	13,404
Government	19,053	19,127	15,293	15,344	2,935	2,941	1,446	1,536
Private industries	104,076	104,108	87,302	87,181	11,676	11,667	11,669	11,867
Private households	890	803	705	655	140	106	267	255
Other industries	103,186	103,305	86,597	86,525	11,536	11,560	11,402	11,612
Self-employed workers	8,674	8,594	7,692	7,639	583	544	616	659
Unpaid family workers	101	101	89	89	2	4	17	12
Full- or part-time status								
Full-time workers	112,291	111,832	93,581	93,097	13,279	13,162	12,547	12,674
Part-time workers	22,917	23,241	19,894	20,123	2,055	2,107	1,945	2,040

Note: Detail for the above race and Hispanic-origin groups will not sum to totals because data for the "other races" group are not presented and Hispanics are included in both the white and black population groups.

SOURCE: "12. Employed white, black, and Hispanic-origin workers by sex, occupation, class of worker, and full- or part-time status," in *Employment and Earnings*, vol. 49, no. 1, January 2002

guarantees during the 1980s. Nonetheless, many companies continued to develop factories overseas or to purchase heavily from foreign producers, which resulted in fewer jobs for American workers and more plant shutdowns.

In the mid- to late-1990s, concerned about their declining membership, many unions became more aggressive in recruiting members. They attempted to gain new members in different types of occupations, such as bookstore clerks, limousine drivers, Catholic schoolteachers, and fashion models. In the New York area during the late 1990s, unions organized 2,200 asbestos-removal workers, 1,500 demolition workers, 1,400 podiatrists, 300 Red Cross workers, and 300 workers at Sony movie theaters. In Miami, Florida, unions were trying to organize nursing-home workers. In Las Vegas, Nevada, unions recruited hotel, hospital, and construction workers.

Although concerned about eroding benefits, wages, and jobs, some workers are still wary of unions—fearing the loss of their jobs if they become involved in union activities. However, the 1997 UPS strike led to a more positive public view of unions. In addition, Phil Wheeler, director of the United Automobile Workers in New York and New England, claims that workers have reached the point where they are fed up. He notes that while CEOs are

TABLE 1.19

Median years of tenure with current employer for employed wage and salary workers by age and sex, selected years, 1983–2000

Age and sex	January 1983	January 1987	January 1991	February 1996	February 1998	February 2000
Total						
16 years and over	3.5	3.4	3.6	3.8	3.6	3.5
16 to 17 years	.7	.6	.7	.7	.6	.6
18 to 19 years	.8	.7	.8	.7	.7	.7
20 to 24 years	1.5	1.3	1.3	1.2	1.1	1.1
25 years and over	5.0	5.0	4.8	5.0	4.7	4.7
25 to 34 years	3.0	2.9	2.9	2.8	2.7	2.6
35 to 44 years	5.2	5.5	5.4	5.3	5.0	4.8
45 to 54 years	9.5	8.8	8.9	8.3	8.1	8.2
55 to 64 years	12.2	11.6	11.1	10.2	10.1	10.0
65 years and over	9.6	9.5	8.1	8.4	7.8	9.5
Men						
16 years and over	4.1	4.0	4.1	4.0	3.8	3.8
16 to 17 years	.7	.6	.7	.6	.6	.6
18 to 19 years	.8	.7	.8	.7	.7	.7
20 to 24 years	1.5	1.3	1.4	1.2	1.2	1.2
25 years and over	5.9	5.7	5.4	5.3	4.9	5.0
25 to 34 years	3.2	3.1	3.1	3.0	2.8	2.7
35 to 44 years	7.3	7.0	6.5	6.1	5.5	5.4
45 to 54 years	12.8	11.8	11.2	10.1	9.4	9.5
55 to 64 years	15.3	14.5	13.4	10.5	11.2	10.2
65 years and over	8.3	8.3	7.0	8.3	7.1	9.1
Women						
16 years and over	3.1	3.0	3.2	3.5	3.4	3.3
16 to 17 years	.7	.6	.7	.7	.7	.6
18 to 19 years	.8	.7	.8	.7	.7	.7
20 to 24 years	1.5	1.3	1.3	1.2	1.1	1.0
25 years and over	4.2	4.3	4.3	4.7	4.4	4.4
25 to 34 years	2.8	2.6	2.7	2.7	2.5	2.5
35 to 44 years	4.1	4.4	4.5	4.8	4.5	4.3
45 to 54 years	6.3	6.8	6.7	7.0	7.2	7.3
55 to 64 years	9.8	9.7	9.9	10.0	9.6	9.9
65 years and over	10.1	9.9	9.5	8.4	8.7	9.7

SOURCE: "Table 1. Median years of tenure with current employer for employed wage and salary workers by age and sex, selected years,1983–2000," in *Employer Tenure,* U.S. Department of Labor, Bureau of Labor Statistics, Washington, DC, August 2000 [Online] http://www.bls.gov/new.release/tenure.t01.htm [accessed June 13, 2002]

making astronomical amounts of money, the workers under them are getting less and less. Wheeler feels that workers can correct the situation by organizing.

Industry and Occupation

In 2001 there were 16.3 million union members in the United States. Of those in private nonagricultural industries, union members made up 9.1 percent of wage and salary employment. About 7.2 million union members worked in government (federal, state, and local), accounting for 41.8 percent of government employment. (See Table 1.26.)

Among the private nonagricultural industries, transportation and public utilities had the highest unionization rate (24.7 percent), followed by construction (19 percent). Manufacturing (15.5 percent) and mining (12.9 percent) also had an above-average unionization rate. Conversely, only 2 percent of agricultural workers and 2.8 percent of those in finance, insurance, and real estate were unionized. (See Table 1.26.)

In regard to the occupational groups, the unionization rate was highest among those working in protective service jobs (40.6 percent), which include many government workers, such as police officers, firefighters, and teachers. Union membership rates also were high in precision production, craft, and repair (22.5 percent); operators, fabricators, and laborers (20.9 percent); and professional specialty (21.8 percent). Rates were low in sales (4 percent) and in farming, forestry, and fishing occupations (5.2 percent). (See Table 1.26.)

Characteristics of Union Members

In 2001 union membership was higher among white men (14.8 percent) than white women (11.1 percent) and higher among blacks (17 percent) than either whites (13.1 percent) or Hispanics (11.3 percent). Within these groups, black men continued to have the highest union membership rate (18.9 percent), while white and Hispanic women had the lowest rates (both under 12 percent). Blacks were more likely to be working in blue-collar manufacturing positions, which tend to be

TABLE 1.20

Distribution of employed wage and salary workers by tenure with current employer, age, sex, race, and Hispanic origin, February 2000

Age, sex, race, and Hispanic origin	Number employed (in thousands)	Total	Percent distribution by tenure with current employer							
			12 months or less	13 to 23 months	2 years	3 to 4 years	5 to 9 years	10 to 14 years	15 to 19 years	20 years or more
Total										
16 years and over	120,303	100.0	26.8	8.0	5.3	16.1	17.1	11.0	6.1	9.5
16 to 19 years	6,713	100.0	75.1	11.9	6.9	5.8	.3	-	-	-
20 years and over	113,590	100.0	24.0	7.7	5.3	16.7	18.1	11.7	6.4	10.1
20 to 24 years	12,535	100.0	54.7	13.0	9.3	17.5	5.5	(1)	-	-
25 to 34 years	28,560	100.0	31.1	10.3	7.1	21.9	21.2	7.4	.9	(1)
35 to 44 years	32,625	100.0	19.4	6.9	4.5	16.9	21.2	15.5	9.5	6.1
45 to 54 years	25,650	100.0	13.7	5.4	3.3	13.0	17.7	14.9	10.0	21.8
55 to 64 years	11,326	100.0	11.2	3.9	3.3	11.7	16.8	15.8	9.8	27.5
65 years and over	2,893	100.0	12.9	4.9	2.7	12.6	16.9	15.4	9.2	25.5
Men										
16 years and over	62,306	100.0	25.6	7.7	5.3	15.8	17.3	10.9	6.5	11.0
16 to 19 years	3,401	100.0	73.8	12.2	7.7	6.0	.4	-	-	-
20 years and over	58,905	100.0	22.9	7.4	5.2	16.4	18.2	11.5	6.8	11.6
20 to 24 years	6,499	100.0	52.0	12.7	9.2	19.8	6.1	.1	-	-
25 to 34 years	15,222	100.0	29.4	10.0	7.3	21.8	22.1	8.4	.9	(1)
35 to 44 years	17,023	100.0	17.9	6.4	4.2	15.7	20.9	16.4	11.1	7.3
45 to 54 years	12,858	100.0	13.1	5.0	3.2	11.7	16.8	13.0	10.8	26.3
55 to 64 years	5,841	100.0	11.2	3.9	3.2	11.4	16.9	14.5	8.2	30.6
65 years and over	1,461	100.0	14.4	3.4	2.5	12.2	18.5	12.7	8.1	28.0
Women										
16 years and over	57,997	100.0	28.1	8.3	5.4	16.4	17.0	11.1	5.7	8.0
16 to 19 years	3,312	100.0	76.5	11.7	6.0	5.6	.1	-	-	-
20 years and over	54,685	100.0	25.2	8.1	5.3	17.1	18.0	11.8	6.0	8.5
20 to 24 years	6,037	100.0	57.6	13.3	9.4	15.0	4.8	-	-	-
25 to 34 years	13,338	100.0	33.0	10.7	6.8	22.0	20.2	6.3	1.0	-
35 to 44 years	15,601	100.0	21.0	7.4	4.9	18.2	21.5	14.4	7.8	4.8
45 to 54 years	12,791	100.0	14.4	5.9	3.5	14.3	18.7	16.8	9.2	17.3
55 to 64 years	5,485	100.0	11.3	3.8	3.4	11.9	16.6	17.2	11.6	24.3
65 years and over	1,432	100.0	11.5	6.4	2.8	12.9	15.3	18.0	10.3	22.8
White										
16 years and over	100,624	100.0	26.2	8.0	5.2	16.0	17.1	11.2	6.3	9.8
Men	52,890	100.0	24.9	7.6	5.3	15.7	17.2	11.0	6.6	11.5
Women	47,735	100.0	27.6	8.5	5.2	16.4	17.0	11.4	6.0	7.9
Black										
16 years and over	14,199	100.0	29.3	7.0	6.1	15.6	17.6	10.0	5.3	9.2
Men	6,546	100.0	29.0	7.2	6.0	15.1	17.8	10.1	6.2	8.6
Women	7,653	100.0	29.5	6.8	6.1	16.1	17.4	9.8	4.5	9.8
Hispanic origin										
16 years and over	13,767	100.0	30.7	8.3	7.7	18.1	16.6	8.8	4.3	5.5
Men	7,971	100.0	28.7	8.0	7.6	17.7	17.6	9.6	4.8	6.0
Women	5,796	100.0	33.4	8.6	7.9	18.7	15.3	7.7	3.7	4.7

¹Less than 0.05 percent.

Note: Detail for the above race and Hispanic-origin groups will not sum to totals because data for the "other races" groups are not presented and Hispanics are included in both the white and black population groups. Detail may not sum to totals because of rounding. Data exclude the incorporated and unincorporated self-employed. Dash represents zero.

SOURCE: "Table 3. Distribution of employed wage and salary workers by tenure with current employer, age, sex, race, and Hispanic origin, February 2000," in *Employee Tenure*, U.S. Department of Labor, Bureau of Labor Statistics, Washington, DC, August 2000 [Online] http://www.bls.gov/new.release/tenure.t03.htm [accessed June 13, 2002]

more heavily unionized. Workers age 35 to 64 were more likely to be members of unions than either their younger or older counterparts. Full-time workers were more than twice as likely as part-timers to be union members. (See Table 1.25.)

In regard to 2001 earnings, union members garnered a median weekly salary of $718, compared with $575 for wage and salary employees not represented by unions. The union versus nonunion earnings difference was greater for women than for men and greater for blacks and Hispanics than for whites. (See Table 1.27.)

OCCUPATIONS AND INDUSTRIES. In nearly all occupations, people represented by unions earned more than those who were not. The differences were small among managerial and professional specialties and much larger among operators, fabricators, and laborers; farming, forestry, and fishing; and service occupations. In all industries (except finance, insurance, and real estate as

TABLE 1.21

Median years of tenure with current employer for employed wage and salary workers by industry, selected years, 1983–2000

Industry	January 1983	January 1987	January 1991	February 1996	February 1998	February 2000
Total, 16 years and over	3.5	3.4	3.6	3.8	3.6	3.5
Agriculture	2.2	2.4	2.6	3.4	2.9	3.1
Nonagricultural industries	3.6	3.4	3.6	3.8	3.6	3.5
Government	5.8	6.5	6.5	6.9	7.3	7.2
Private industries	3.2	3.0	3.2	3.3	3.2	3.2
Mining	3.4	6.1	5.8	6.1	5.6	6.5
Construction	2.0	2.0	2.6	2.9	2.7	2.8
Manufacturing	5.4	5.5	5.2	5.4	4.9	5.0
Durable goods[1]	5.6	6.0	5.8	5.3	4.9	4.9
Lumber and wood products	4.0	3.2	3.6	3.3	3.8	4.0
Furniture and fixtures	4.2	3.2	4.0	4.2	3.9	4.1
Stone, clay, and glass products	7.0	6.8	6.3	5.1	6.1	5.4
Primary metal industries	10.0	10.2	9.7	8.1	8.0	7.0
Fabricated metal products	5.7	5.5	5.5	5.1	4.0	4.7
Machinery and computing equipment	5.8	6.7	5.9	5.2	4.4	4.5
Electrical machinery, equipment, and supplies	4.7	4.8	5.5	4.9	5.0	4.7
Transportation equipment[1]	8.8	8.0	7.6	8.3	7.8	6.4
Motor vehicles and equipment	13.0	11.2	11.7	7.8	6.4	5.8
Aircraft and parts	6.4	6.8	6.3	9.8	9.6	9.7
Professional and photographic equipment and watches	4.7	5.9	5.1	5.1	5.5	5.2
Toys, amusements, and sporting goods	3.6	5.8	3.2	2.7	3.6	3.7
Nondurable goods[1]	5.1	4.9	4.7	5.4	4.9	5.1
Food and kindred products	5.2	4.4	4.2	5.1	5.1	5.0
Textile mill products	7.0	7.0	5.6	5.4	6.7	7.4
Apparel and other finished textile products	3.8	3.2	3.8	3.8	3.8	3.3
Paper and allied products	7.6	8.6	7.6	8.4	7.5	6.1
Printing and publishing	3.2	3.2	3.5	4.3	4.0	4.4
Chemicals and allied products	7.0	7.2	5.7	6.9	5.4	5.8
Petroleum and coal products	6.0	11.7	8.4	10.3	9.4	7.5
Rubber and miscellaneous plastics products	5.4	4.4	4.7	4.7	4.6	4.9
Transportation and public utilities	5.8	5.7	5.8	5.2	4.8	4.4
Transportation	4.6	3.9	4.2	4.1	3.8	3.9
Communications and other public utilities	8.3	8.4	9.9	8.2	8.2	5.2
Wholesale trade	3.8	3.7	3.4	3.9	4.1	3.9
Retail trade	1.9	1.8	1.9	1.9	1.8	2.0
Finance, insurance, and real estate	3.2	3.0	3.4	4.1	3.5	3.6
Banking and other finance	3.3	3.1	3.6	3.9	3.7	3.3
Insurance and real estate	3.0	2.9	3.2	4.2	3.4	3.9
Services[1]	2.5	2.5	2.7	3.0	2.9	2.9
Private households	1.8	1.7	1.9	2.3	2.3	2.9
Services, except private households	2.5	2.5	2.7	3.0	2.9	2.9
Business services	1.5	1.6	1.8	2.0	1.9	c1.8
Automobile and repair services	2.3	2.0	2.2	2.9	2.4	2.7
Personal services, except private households	2.0	2.0	2.1	2.3	2.3	2.7
Entertainment and recreation services	1.8	1.8	2.3	1.9	1.9	2.3
Hospitals	3.5	4.6	4.2	5.2	5.2	5.2
Health services, except hospitals	2.5	2.4	2.7	2.9	2.9	3.2
Educational services	2.7	3.1	3.5	3.8	3.5	3.3
Social services	2.2	2.3	2.3	2.8	2.7	2.6
Other professional services	2.9	2.8	3.3	3.5	3.3	c3.2

[1]Includes other industries, not shown separately.
c = corrected.

Note: Data for 1996, 1998, and 2000 are not strictly comparable with data for 1991 and earlier years because population controls from the 1990 census, adjusted for the estimated undercount, are used beginning in 1996. Figures for the 1983-91 period are based on population controls from the 1980 census. Also, beginning in 1996, the figures incorporate the effects of the redesign of the Current Population Survey introduced in January 1994. Data exclude the incorporated and unincorporated self-employed.

SOURCE: "Table 5. Median years of tenure with current employer for employed wage and salary workers by industry, selected years,1983–2000," *Employee Tenure*, U.S. Department of Labor, Bureau of Labor Statistics, Washington, DC, August 2000 [Online] http://www.bls.gov/news.release/tenure.t05.htm [accessed May 28, 2002]

well as federal government work), union-represented workers earned more than nonunion workers. The differences in construction, transportation, and local government were particularly large. (See Table 1.28.)

WORK STOPPAGES (STRIKES)

According to the BLS *Major Work Stoppages in 2001* (March 22, 2002), the number of work stoppages (strikes) has decreased dramatically since the 1980s. In 1974, 424

TABLE 1.22

Number of jobs held by individuals from age 18 to 34 in 1978–98 by educational attainment, sex, race, Hispanic origin, and age

| Characteristic | Total[1] | Average number of jobs for persons age 18 to 34 in 1978-98 | | |
		Age 18-24	Age 25-29	Age 30-34
Total	**9.2**	**5.6**	**3.0**	**2.4**
Less than a high school diploma	9.3	5.2	3.0	2.4
High school grad., no college	8.7	5.2	2.8	2.4
Less than a bachelor's degree	9.6	5.8	3.2	2.5
Bachelor's degree or more	9.7	6.3	3.0	2.4
Men	9.6	5.8	3.2	2.6
Less than a high school diploma	10.7	6.1	3.5	2.8
High school grad., no college	9.1	5.5	3.1	2.5
Less than a bachelor's degree	10.0	6.0	3.4	2.6
Bachelor's degree or more	9.3	6.0	2.9	2.4
Women	8.8	5.4	2.8	2.3
Less than a high school diploma	7.4	4.0	2.2	2.0
High school grad., no college	8.2	4.8	2.5	2.3
Less than a bachelor's degree	9.2	5.6	3.0	2.4
Bachelor's degree or more	10.1	6.6	3.1	2.3
White	9.4	5.8	3.0	2.4
Less than a high school diploma	9.8	5.6	3.1	2.6
High school grad., no college	8.7	5.3	2.8	2.4
Less than a bachelor's degree	9.9	6.0	3.2	2.5
Bachelor's degree or more	9.8	6.4	3.0	2.3
Black	8.5	4.7	2.9	2.5
Less than a high school diploma	8.0	3.9	2.7	2.2
High school grad., no college	8.4	4.5	2.9	2.5
Less than a bachelor's degree	8.5	5.0	2.9	2.4
Bachelor's degree or more	9.4	6.0	3.1	2.7
Hispanic origin	8.7	5.0	2.9	2.4
Less than a high school diploma	8.8	4.9	2.8	2.2
High school grad., no college	8.6	5.0	2.8	2.4
Less than a bachelor's degree	8.6	5.1	3.0	2.3
Bachelor's degree or more	8.9	5.3	2.7	2.6

[1]Jobs that were held in more than one of the age categories were counted in each appropriate column, but only once in the total column.

Note: The first two columns exclude individuals who turned age 18 before Jan. 1, 1978. The first and last columns exclude individuals who had not yet turned age 35 when interviewed in 1998.

The National Longitudinal Survey of Youth 1979 consists of men and women who were born in the years 1957-64 and were age 14 to 22 when first interviewed in 1979. These individuals were age 33 to 41 in 1998. Educational attainment is defined as of the 1998 survey. Race and Hispanic-origin groups are mutually exclusive. Totals include American Indians, Alaskan Natives, and Asian and Pacific Islanders, not shown separately.

SOURCE: *Number of Jobs Held, Labor Market Activity, and Earnings, Growth Over Two Decades: Results from a Longitudinal Survey,* U.S. Department of Labor, Bureau of Labor Statistics, Washington, DC, [Online] http://www.bls.gov/news.release/nlsoy.t01.htm [accessed June 17, 2002]

work stoppages resulted in 31.8 million days idle. (This figure is calculated by multiplying the number of workers times the number of days they were on strike.) For most of the remainder of the 1970s, there were about 200 to 300 work stoppages a year.

This changed significantly during the 1980s. The BLS report states that the number fell from 187 in 1980 to only 40 in 1988, rising slightly to 44 in 1990, with just 5.9 million days idle. In 1995 the number of strikes again tumbled to 31, involving 5.87 million idle days. In 1996 the number of stoppages rose to 37, involving 4.9 million days. By October 1997, 27 strikes had begun, with 4.37

million days idle. The UPS strike in August 1997 accounted for more than 2 million days. By 1998, 34 strikes had begun, with 5.11 million days idle, and affected 387,000 workers. There were only 17 strikes in 1999, with 73,000 workers, the lowest numbers since the government began keeping records on strikes in 1947. The figure rose again to 39 strikes in 2000, affecting 394,000 workers.

OCCUPATIONAL INJURIES, ILLNESSES, AND FATALITIES

The annual rate of occupational injuries and illnesses in full-time workers has fluctuated. There were 8.9 cases per 100 workers in 1992, dropping to 6.7 in 1998, 6.3 in 1999, and to a low of 6.1 in 2000. (See Table 1.29.) Manufacturing durable goods (9.8) and construction (8.3) had the most cases per 100 workers in 2000. These figures were all down from the prior three years. Finance, insurance, and real estate (1.9), and service occupations (4.9) had the lowest number of cases per 100 workers in 2000.

In 1998 there were 3.1 cases of lost workdays due to occupational injuries or illnesses per 100 workers. This dropped slightly to 3 cases per 100 workers in 1999 and 2000. (See Table 1.29.) The number of lost workday cases varied by the type of industry and occupation. In 2000 the manufacturing of durable goods industry had 4.7 cases of lost workdays per 100 workers, while finance, insurance, and real estate occupations had only 0.8 lost workday cases per 100 workers.

Fatalities

According to the BLS *Census of Fatal Occupational Injuries, 1995-2000,* approximately 6,000 workers died each year between 1995 and 2000. (See Table 1.30.) On average, about 16 workers were fatally injured each day during 2000.

Highway traffic incidents and homicides caused most fatal work injuries. These two events totaled more than a third of the work injury deaths that occurred in 2000. Work-related highway deaths accounted for 23 percent of the 5,915 total work injuries. More than half of the highway fatality victims (51 percent) died as a result of vehicle collision. Off-road transport-related incidents (such as tractors or forklifts overturning) and workers being struck by vehicles each accounted for between 6 to 7 percent of total worker fatalities. (See Table 1.30.)

Homicide accounted for 11 percent of fatal work injuries in 2000. Of all occupational homicides, 79 percent were caused by shooting, with 10 percent caused by stabbing, and 12 percent caused by other methods (including bombing). Falls made up 12 percent of fatal work injuries. Seventeen percent of the fatally injured workers were struck by various objects, such as falling trees,

TABLE 1.23

Wage and salary workers who actively searched for a new job in the prior 3 months, by age and sex, February 1995, 1997, and 1999

[Numbers in thousands]

Age and sex	1995		1997		1999	
	Total who responded	Percent who searched for a new job in the prior 3 months	Total who responded	Percent who searched for a new job in the prior 3 months	Total who responded	Percent who searched for a new job in the prior 3 months
Total						
Total, 16 years and older	107,031	5.6	110,546	5.0	114,898	4.5
16 to 19 years	5,351	8.1	5,828	6.9	6,360	5.9
20 to 24 years	11,842	9.2	11,326	8.4	11,692	7.3
25 years and older	89,837	5.0	93,392	4.5	96,845	4.0
25 to 34 years	29,147	7.1	28,590	6.4	28,126	5.8
35 to 44 years	29,292	5.1	30,579	4.6	31,649	4.4
45 to 54 years	19,950	3.7	22,078	3.3	23,966	2.8
55 to 64 years	9,119	2.1	9,698	2.1	10,475	1.7
65 years and older	2,329	.9	2,447	.9	2,629	1.2
Men						
Total, 16 years and older	55,897	6.0	57,655	5.3	59,541	4.6
16 to 19 years	2,641	7.9	2,978	7.3	3,187	5.1
20 to 24 years	6,264	9.5	5,932	9.0	6,049	7.8
25 years and older	46,992	5.4	48,745	4.8	50,305	4.1
25 to 34 years	15,807	7.7	15,281	7.1	14,937	6.0
35 to 44 years	15,206	5.3	16,011	4.6	16,558	4.6
45 to 54 years	10,119	3.9	11,197	3.3	12,016	2.7
55 to 64 years	4,678	2.5	5,008	2.3	5,502	1.6
65 years and older	1,182	1.1	1,249	1.0	1,292	1.3
Women						
Total, 16 years and older	51,134	5.3	52,891	4.6	55,357	4.4
16 to 19 years	2,711	8.4	2,850	6.4	3,173	6.8
20 to 24 years	5,578	8.9	5,394	7.7	5,643	6.8
25 years and older	42,845	4.6	44,647	4.2	46,540	3.9
25 to 34 years	13,340	6.4	13,309	5.5	13,189	5.6
35 to 44 years	14,086	4.9	14,568	4.5	15,092	4.2
45 to 54 years	9,831	3.6	10,882	3.4	11,950	2.9
55 to 64 years	4,441	1.8	4,690	1.8	4,973	1.8
65 years and older	1,147	.8	1,198	.9	1,337	1.2

SOURCE: Joseph R. Meisenheimer II and Randy E. Ilg, "Table 1. Wage and salary workers who actively searched for a new job in the prior 3 months, by age and sex, February 1995, 1997, and 1999," in "Looking for a 'better' job: job-search activity of the employed," *Monthly Labor Review*, vol. 123, no. 9, September 2000

machinery, or vehicles that had slipped into gear, or building materials. (See Table 1.30.)

In 2000 occupations with large numbers of fatal injuries included truck drivers, farm occupations, sales occupations, and construction trades. (See Figure 1.3.) The specific events or exposures responsible for workers' deaths varied considerably among occupations. Highway crashes and jackknifings together accounted for about two-thirds of the truck drivers' deaths, while homicides were the cause of about one-half of the fatalities among workers in sales occupations. Slightly more than one-third of the deaths in farm occupations occurred in tractor-related events.

One out of every five fatal work injuries (20 percent) occurred in the construction industry during 2000. Industries with large numbers of fatalities relative to the number of employees include agriculture, forestry, and fishing; construction; transportation and public utilities; and manufacturing. (See Table 1.31.)

According to the BLS data, 54 percent of the fatalities in 2000 were of men. Whites accounted for 74 percent of the workplace fatalities; blacks, 11 percent; Hispanics, 11 percent; and other races less than 0.5 percent. Of those killed, 23 percent were 25 to 34 years old; 27 percent were 35 to 44 years old; and 22 percent were 45 to 54 years old.

WORKPLACE VIOLENCE

In April 1996 the Society of Human Resource Management surveyed its members on issues of workplace violence. Approximately half (48 percent) of those who responded said that since January 1, 1994, a violent incident had occurred at their workplace. An earlier 1992 survey reported only 33 percent of the respondents having a violent event between 1988 and 1993. Incidents of assaults and shootings were relatively rare. In 1996, four of ten (39 percent) reported that verbal threats were the most common form of violence, followed by pushing and shoving (22 percent) and fistfights (13 percent).

TABLE 1.24

Percent of wage and salary workers age 25 and older who actively searched for a new job in the prior 3 months, by major occupation and educational attainment, February 1995, 1997, and 1999

Occupation	Total	Less than a high school diploma	High school graduates, no college	Some college or associate degree	College graduates, total
1995					
Total, 25 years and older	5.0	3.2	3.9	5.9	6.2
Executive, administrative, and managerial	5.1	1.2	3.0	4.6	6.3
Professional specialty	5.1	2.6	3.1	4.6	5.4
Technicians and related support	5.2	–	2.3	5.7	6.4
Sales occupations	5.7	2.0	4.3	7.2	6.6
Administrative support, including clerical	4.8	1.5	3.5	5.4	7.7
Service occupations	5.4	3.2	5.0	6.9	9.1
Precision production, craft, and repair	4.0	2.6	3.2	5.6	5.8
Operators, fabricators, and laborers	5.0	3.6	4.3	7.4	8.8
Farming, forestry, and fishing	5.8	5.9	4.3	10.3	1.3
1997					
Total, 25 years and older	4.5	3.3	3.2	4.9	5.9
Executive, administrative, and managerial	4.6	3.6	2.8	4.0	5.7
Professional specialty	5.0	–	3.2	4.2	5.4
Technicians and related support	5.2	–	4.7	5.2	5.9
Sales occupations	5.4	4.4	3.3	6.9	6.4
Administrative support, including clerical	4.3	2.4	2.7	4.4	8.8
Service occupations	3.9	4.2	3.0	4.7	5.6
Precision production, craft, and repair	3.6	2.1	3.0	5.2	4.9
Operators, fabricators, and laborers	4.3	3.5	3.7	5.9	8.3
Farming, forestry, and fishing	3.8	2.5	4.2	6.4	4.3
1999					
Total, 25 years and older	4.0	2.7	2.9	4.6	5.0
Executive, administrative, and managerial	4.1	2.7	2.1	3.7	5.0
Professional specialty	4.4	2.2	2.2	5.2	4.3
Technicians and related support	4.0	10.5	3.0	3.9	4.6
Sales occupations	4.4	5.1	3.5	4.4	5.2
Administrative support, including clerical	4.2	4.0	2.6	4.7	7.1
Service occupations	4.0	2.3	3.5	5.1	7.1
Precision production, craft, and repair	3.5	2.1	2.8	4.6	6.5
Operators, fabricators, and laborers	3.5	2.3	3.3	4.9	6.2
Farming, forestry, and fishing	4.1	3.8	1.2	7.4	16.2

Note: Dash indicates data not available.

SOURCE: Joseph R. Meisenheimer II and Randy E. Ilg, "Table 6. Percent of wage and salary workers age 25 and older who actively searched for a new job in the prior 3 months by major occupation and educational attainment, February 1995, 1997, and 1999," in "Looking for a better job," *Monthly Labor Review,* vol. 123, no. 9, September 2000

By 1999 the Society of Human Resource Management found that workplace violence had increased since 1996 for its members. Fifty-six percent of human resource professionals that were surveyed reported incidents of workplace violence between 1996 and 1999. As with earlier surveys, shootings and stabbings accounted for a very low proportion of the violence that human resource professionals reported. Verbal threats were the most prominent (41 percent), followed by pushing and shoving (19 percent). The most common motivator of workplace violence reported in this survey was personality conflict, though marital issues and work-related stress also played a role. The survey found that employers were responding to rising violence on the job with increased security and related training and prevention.

According to the BLS, from 1993 to 1999, U.S. residents experienced 1.7 million violent victimizations annually while they were working or on duty. The most common type of violent crime in the workplace was sim-ple assault, with an estimated average of 1.3 million victimizations occurring each year. While at work, U.S. residents also suffered 325,000 aggravated assaults, 36,500 rapes and sexual assaults, 70,100 robberies, and 900 homicides. (See Table 1.32.)

Of the occupations examined, law enforcement had the highest rates of workplace violence, while teaching had the lowest. Police officers experienced 260.8 victimizations for every 1,000 officers. College or university teaching was the occupation with the lowest rate of violence at work—1.6 victimizations per 1,000 teachers. (See Table 1.33.)

In 2000 the Occupational Safety and Health Administration (OSHA) reported that homicide remained the second leading cause of job-related deaths in the United States. The BLS reported 677 workers were murdered annually, accounting for 11 percent of fatal work injuries in 2000. (See Table 1.30.)

TABLE 1.25

Union affiliation of employed wage and salary workers by selected characteristics, 2000 and 2001

(Numbers in thousands)

Characteristic	Total em- ployed	2000 Members of unions[1] Total	2000 Members of unions[1] Percent of em- ployed	2000 Represented by unions[2] Total	2000 Represented by unions[2] Percent of em- ployed	Total em- ployed	2001 Members of unions[1] Total	2001 Members of unions[1] Percent of em- ployed	2001 Represented by unions[2] Total	2001 Represented by unions[2] Percent of em- ployed
Sex and Age										
Total, 16 years and over	120,786	16,258	13.5	17,944	14.9	120,760	16,275	13.5	17,875	14.8
16 to 24 years	20,166	1,010	5.0	1,152	5.7	19,819	1,034	5.2	1,188	6.0
25 years and over	100,620	15,248	15.2	16,792	16.7	100,941	15,241	15.1	16,688	16.5
25 to 34 years	28,406	3,369	11.9	3,720	13.1	27,710	3,180	11.5	3,539	12.8
35 to 44 years	32,470	4,822	14.9	5,293	16.3	32,124	4,807	15.0	5,242	16.3
45 to 54 years	25,651	4,815	18.8	5,305	20.7	26,503	5,015	18.9	5,455	20.6
55 to 64 years	11,204	1,998	17.8	2,193	19.6	11,609	1,997	17.2	2,185	18.8
65 years and over	2,889	243	8.4	281	9.7	2,995	242	8.1	267	8.9
Men, 16 years and over	62,853	9,578	15.2	10,355	16.5	62,727	9,502	15.1	10,268	16.4
16 to 24 years	10,440	618	5.9	697	6.7	10,165	617	6.1	705	6.9
25 years and over	52,412	8,960	17.1	9,657	18.4	52,562	8,885	16.9	9,562	18.2
25 to 34 years	15,197	2,030	13.4	2,207	14.5	14,856	1,913	12.9	2,082	14.0
35 to 44 years	17,028	2,871	16.9	3,077	18.1	16,832	2,881	17.1	3,075	18.3
45 to 54 years	12,898	2,739	21.2	2,956	22.9	13,359	2,808	21.0	3,018	22.6
55 to 64 years	5,770	1,191	20.6	1,268	22.0	5,935	1,152	19.4	1,241	20.9
65 years and over	1,519	129	8.5	148	9.8	1,580	132	8.4	147	9.3
Women, 16 years and over	57,933	6,680	11.5	7,590	13.1	58,033	6,773	11.7	7,608	13.1
16 to 24 years	9,726	392	4.0	455	4.7	9,654	417	4.3	483	5.0
25 years and over	48,207	6,288	13.0	7,135	14.8	48,379	6,356	13.1	7,125	14.7
25 to 34 years	13,209	1,340	10.1	1,513	11.5	12,855	1,267	9.9	1,457	11.3
35 to 44 years	15,441	1,951	12.6	2,215	14.3	15,292	1,927	12.6	2,167	14.2
45 to 54 years	12,752	2,077	16.3	2,348	18.4	13,145	2,208	16.8	2,437	18.5
55 to 64 years	5,434	807	14.9	925	17.0	5,673	846	14.9	944	16.6
65 years and over	1,370	114	8.3	133	9.7	1,415	109	7.7	120	8.5
Race, Hispanic Origin, and Sex										
White, 16 years and over	100,455	13,094	13.0	14,453	14.4	100,384	13,125	13.1	14,400	14.3
Men	53,105	7,911	14.9	8,541	16.1	52,970	7,849	14.8	8,474	16.0
Women	47,350	5,183	10.9	5,912	12.5	47,414	5,276	11.1	5,926	12.5
Black, 16 years and over	14,544	2,489	17.1	2,744	18.9	14,515	2,465	17.0	2,705	18.6
Men	6,701	1,282	19.1	1,388	20.7	6,660	1,256	18.9	1,357	20.4
Women	7,843	1,208	15.4	1,356	17.3	7,855	1,209	15.4	1,347	17.2
Hispanic origin, 16 years and over	13,,609	1,554	11.4	1,740	12.8	13,782	1,559	11.3	1,729	12.5
Men	7,884	972	12.3	1,063	13.5	7,950	935	11.8	1,024	12.9
Women	5,725	582	10.2	677	11.8	5,832	624	10.7	705	12.1
Full- or Part-time Status										
Full-time workers	99,917	14,822	14.8	16,306	16.3	99,599	14,809	14.9	16,218	16.3
Part-time workers	20,619	1,395	6.8	1,593	7.7	20,926	1,437	6.9	1,625	7.8

[1]Data refer to members of a labor union or an employee association similar to a union.
[2]Data refer to members of a labor union or an employee association similar to a union as well as workers who report no union affiliation but whose jobs are covered by a union or an employee association contract.
[3]The distinction between full- and part-time workers is based on hours usually worked. Beginning in 1994, these data will not sum to totals because full- or part-time status on the principal job is not identifiable for a small number of multiple jobholders.

Note: Data refer to the sole or principal job of full- and part-time workers. Excluded are all self-employed workers regardless of whether or not their businesses are incorporated. Detail for the above race and Hispanic-origin groups will not sum to totals because data for the "other races" group are not presented and Hispanics are included in both the white and black population groups.

SOURCE: "Table 1. Union affiliation of employed wage and salary workers by selected characteristics," in *Union Members in 2001,* U.S. Department of Labor, Bureau of Labor Statistics, Washington, DC, January, 17, 2002

In the National Institute for Occupational Safety and Health's HHS Press Release, *NIOSH Report Addresses Problem of Workplace Violence, Suggests Strategies for Preventing Risks* (July 8, 1996), the number of workplace circumstances that put an employee at risk for being the victim of violence are identified. These include public contact, money exchange, delivery jobs, working alone or late at night, and working in areas with high crime.

TABLE 1.26

Union affiliation of employed wage and salary workers by occupation and industry, 2000 and 2001

(Numbers in thousands)

	2000					2001				
		Members of unions[1]		Represented by unions[2]			Members of unions[1]		Represented by unions[2]	
Occupation and industry	Total em-ployed	Total	Percent of em-ployed	Total	Percent of em-ployed	Total em-ployed	Total	Percent of em-ployed	Total	Percent of em-ployed
Occupation										
Managerial and professional specialty	35,378	4,536	12.8	5,277	14.9	36,276	4,654	12.8	5,355	14.8
Executive, administrative, and managerial	16,434	875	5.3	1,075	6.5	16,916	949	5.6	1,133	6.7
Professional specialty	18,944	3,661	19.3	4,202	22.2	19,360	3,705	19.1	4,222	21.8
Technical, sales, and administrative support	36,124	3,119	8.6	3,521	9.7	35,953	3,193	8.9	3,587	10.0
Technicians and related support	4,279	431	10.1	500	11.7	4,393	474	10.8	533	12.1
Sales occupations	13,677	481	3.5	533	3.9	13,639	481	3.5	545	4.0
Administrative support, including clerical	18,167	2,207	12.1	2,487	13.7	17,921	2,239	12.5	2,509	14.0
Service occupations	16,953	2,234	13.2	2,441	14.4	17,156	2,274	13.3	2,464	14.4
Protective service	2,384	938	39.4	1,003	42.1	2,460	935	38.0	998	40.6
Service, except protective service	14,569	1,295	8.9	1,438	9.9	14,695	1,339	9.1	1,466	10.0
Precision production, craft, and repair	12,716	2,783	21.9	2,910	22.9	12,635	2,716	21.5	2,839	22.5
Operators, fabricators, and laborers	17,642	3,498	19.8	3,687	20.9	16,888	3,353	19.9	3,534	20.9
Machine operators, assemblers, and inspectors	7,043	1,366	19.4	1,442	20.5	6,502	1,317	20.3	1,383	21.3
Transportation and material moving occupations	5,182	1,195	23.1	1,260	24.3	5,153	1,202	23.3	1,276	24.8
Handlers, equipment cleaners, helpers, and laborers	5,417	938	17.3	984	18.2	5,233	834	15.9	875	16.7
Farming, forestry, and fishing	1,974	89	4.5	109	5.5	1,853	85	4.6	96	5.2
Industry										
Private wage and salary workers	101,810	9,148	9.0	9,969	9.8	101,605	9,113	9.0	9,871	9.7
Agriculture	1,821	38	2.1	45	2.5	1,667	27	1.6	33	2.0
Nonagricultural industries	99,989	9,110	9.1	9,924	9.9	99,938	9,086	9.1	9,838	9.8
Mining	499	54	10.9	57	11.4	531	65	12.3	69	12.9
Construction	6,666	1,220	18.3	1,268	19.0	6,881	1,264	18.4	1,305	19.0
Manufacturing	19,167	2,832	14.8	2,999	15.6	18,149	2,657	14.6	2,807	15.5
Durable goods	11,688	1,791	15.3	1,894	16.2	11,059	1,666	15.1	1,757	15.9
Nondurable goods	7,480	1,041	13.9	1,105	14.8	7,091	990	14.0	1,050	14.8
Transportation and public utilities	7,508	1,805	24.0	1,920	25.6	7,422	1,743	23.5	1,834	24.7
Transportation	4,573	1,135	24.8	1,203	26.3	4,441	1,069	24.1	1,126	25.4
Communications and public utilities	2,935	670	22.8	717	24.4	2,981	674	22.6	708	23.7
Wholesale and retail trade	25,133	1,194	4.7	1,315	5.2	25,045	1,174	4.7	1,284	5.1
Wholesale trade	4,766	243	5.1	265	5.6	4,540	249	5.5	268	5.9
Retail trade	20,366	951	4.7	1,049	5.2	20,505	926	4.5	1,016	5.0
Finance, insurance, and real estate	7,488	121	1.6	156	2.1	7,648	158	2.1	211	2.8
Services	33,528	1,884	5.6	2,208	6.6	34,261	2,026	5.9	2,328	6.8
Government workers	18,976	7,110	37.5	7,976	42.0	19,155	7,162	37.4	8,004	41.8
Federal	3,233	1,033	32.0	1,186	36.7	3,284	1,037	31.6	1,201	36.6
State	5,464	1,641	30.0	1,867	34.2	5,677	1,732	30.5	1,957	34.5
Local	10,278	4,436	43.2	4,923	47.9	10,195	4,393	43.1	4,847	47.5

[1]Data refer to members of a labor union or an employee association similar to a union.
[2]Data refer to members of a labor union or an employee association similar to a union as well as workers who report no union affiliation but whose jobs are covered by a union or an employee association contract.

Note: Data refer to the sole or principal job of full- and part-time workers. Excluded are all self-employed workers regardless of whether or not their businesses are incorporated.

SOURCE: "Table 3. Union affiliation of employed wage and salary workers by occupation and industry," in *Union Members in 2001*, U.S. Department of Labor, Bureau of Labor Statistics, Washington, DC, January 17, 2002

TABLE 1.27

Median weekly earnings of full-time wage and salary workers by union affiliation and selected characteristics, 2000 and 2001

Characteristic	2000				2001			
	Total	Members of unions[1]	Represented by unions[2]	Non-union	Total	Members of unions[1]	Represented by unions[2]	Non-union
Sex and Age								
Total, 16 years and over	$576	$696	$691	$542	$597	$718	$712	$575
16 to 24 years	361	437	436	355	376	473	475	370
25 years and over	611	709	705	592	632	733	728	612
25 to 34 years	550	627	624	529	579	654	646	563
35 to 44 years	631	716	712	614	658	743	738	637
45 to 54 years	671	755	752	639	693	776	774	663
55 to 64 years	617	727	723	592	640	744	744	613
65 years and over	442	577	565	422	472	607	605	440
Men, 16 years and over	646	739	737	620	672	765	761	647
16 to 24 years	376	458	457	370	392	482	488	387
25 years and over	700	753	752	682	722	781	779	705
25 to 34 years	603	678	675	591	621	699	691	610
35 to 44 years	731	776	774	718	755	799	794	744
45 to 54 years	777	801	799	769	799	814	813	790
55 to 64 years	738	755	757	729	766	801	807	748
65 years and over	537	613	613	514	548	686	705	520
Women, 16 years and over	491	616	613	472	511	643	639	494
16 to 24 years	342	406	405	339	354	458	456	348
25 years and over	515	627	623	497	542	656	652	519
25 to 34 years	493	579	578	483	514	600	597	503
35 to 44 years	520	605	604	506	545	643	641	523
45 to 54 years	565	697	692	522	588	721	715	554
55 to 64 years	505	659	647	481	539	656	659	512
65 years and over	378	485	484	365	372	497	487	358
Race, Hispanic Origin, and Sex								
White, 16 years and over	591	716	711	565	612	741	736	591
Men	669	757	755	641	694	784	781	669
Women	500	631	627	482	521	667	661	503
Black, 16 years and over	468	596	590	436	487	603	599	463
Men	503	619	614	479	518	649	637	498
Women	429	564	555	408	451	563	564	424
Hispanic origin, 16 years and over	396	584	580	377	414	578	578	398
Men	414	631	620	394	438	611	612	414
Women	364	489	492	346	385	503	501	372

[1]Data refer to members of a labor union or an employee association similar to a union.

[2]Data refer to members of a labor union or an employee association similar to a union as well as workers who report no union affiliation but whose jobs are covered by a union or an employee association contract.

Note: Data refer to the sole or principal job of full-time workers. Excluded are all self-employed workers regardless of whether or not their businesses are incorporated. Detail for the above race and Hispanic-origin groups will not sum to totals because data for the "other races" group are not presented and Hispanics are included in both the white and black population groups.

SOURCE: "Table 2. Median weekly earnings of full-time wage and salary workers by union affiliation and selected characteristics," in *Union Members in 2001*, U.S. Department of Labor, Bureau of Labor Statistics, Washington, DC, January 17, 2002

TABLE 1.28

Median weekly earnings of full-time wage and salary workers by union affiliation, occupation, and industry, 2000 and 2001

	2000				2001			
Occupation and industry	Total	Members of unions[1]	Repre-sented by unions[2]	Non-union	Total	Members of unions[1]	Repre-sented by unions[2]	Non-union
Occupation								
Managerial and professional specialty	$836	$840	$834	$836	$859	$865	$860	$859
Executive, administrative, and managerial	840	834	854	839	867	869	880	865
Professional specialty	832	841	829	832	854	864	855	853
Technical, sales, and administrative support	506	598	590	497	521	613	606	513
Technicians and related support	648	748	741	635	673	731	738	662
Sales occupations	550	526	522	552	574	559	556	575
Administrative support, including clerical	469	588	579	453	486	597	588	472
Service occupations	355	554	542	327	377	556	550	352
Protective service	623	786	771	502	629	809	797	518
Service, except protective service.	324	423	419	16	345	426	424	333
Precision production, craft, and repair	613	784	778	570	629	822	817	590
Operators, fabricators, and laborers	446	605	602	411	467	620	613	425
Machine operators, assemblers, and inspectors	436	575	572	408	457	587	582	421
Transportation and material moving occupations	540	694	690	502	573	724	715	521
Handlers, equipment cleaners, helpers, and laborers	378	555	551	355	389	530	523	369
Farming, forestry, and fishing	334	516	506	325	354	587	582	345
Industry								
Private wage and salary workers	549	663	656	530	580	684	676	566
Agriculture	347	(3)	(3)	344	371	(3)	(3)	370
Nonagricultural industries	555	664	657	537	583	685	677	572
Mining	768	746	748	774	795	816	816	789
Construction	584	814	810	529	609	864	854	569
Manufacturing	595	630	628	587	613	645	641	607
Durable goods	618	662	659	610	634	675	669	625
Nondurable goods	553	594	594	537	583	607	606	577
Transportation and public utilities	679	768	762	639	705	796	792	669
Transportation	615	744	741	582	644	781	776	609
Communications and public utilities	776	808	798	766	794	816	813	782
Wholesale and retail trade	444	518	514	439	468	540	528	464
Wholesale trade	595	607	608	593	624	654	660	621
Retail trade	403	495	490	399	421	497	488	418
Finance, insurance, and real estate	620	596	593	621	655	584	600	658
Services	543	567	574	540	580	599	597	579
Government workers	665	730	726	609	684	753	749	620
Federal	745	736	738	755	772	762	767	777
State	633	685	681	606	649	718	712	610
Local	650	746	738	562	667	764	756	580

[1]Data refer to members of a labor union or an employee association similar to a union.
[2]Data refer to members of a labor union or an employee association similar to a union as well as workers who report no union affiliation but whose jobs are covered by a union or an employee association contract.
[3]Data not shown where base is less than 50,000.

Note: Data refer to the sole or principal job of full-time workers. Excluded are all self-employed workers regardless of whether or not their businesses are incorporated.

SOURCE: "Table 4. Median weekly earnings of full-time wage and salary workers by union affiliation, occupation, and industry," in *Union Members in 2001*, U.S. Department of Labor, Bureau of Labor Statistics, Washington, DC, January 17, 2002

TABLE 1.29

Incidence rates[1] of nonfatal occupational injuries and illnesses by industry division and selected case types, 1998–2000

				Lost workday cases											
	Total cases			Total[2]			With days away from work[3]			With days of restricted work activity only			Cases without lost work days		
Industry division	1998	1999	2000	1998	1999	2000	1998	1999	2000	1998	1999	2000	1998	1999	2000
Private industry[4]	6.7	6.3	6.1	3.1	3.0	3.0	2.0	1.9	1.8	1.2	1.2	1.2	3.5	3.3	3.2
Agriculture, forestry, and fishing[4]	7.9	7.3	7.1	3.9	3.4	3.6	3.0	2.4	2.5	1.0	1.0	1.1	4.0	3.9	3.5
Mining[5]	4.9	4.4	4.7	2.9	2.7	3.0	2.2	2.0	2.4	.6	.6	.6	2.0	1.7	1.7
Construction	8.8	8.6	8.3	4.0	4.2	4.1	3.3	3.3	3.2	.8	.9	.9	4.8	4.4	4.2
Manufacturing	9.7	9.2	9.0	4.7	4.6	4.5	2.3	2.2	2.0	2.5	2.4	2.5	5.0	4.6	4.5
Durable goods	10.7	10.1	9.8	5.0	4.8	4.7	2.5	2.4	2.2	2.5	2.4	2.5	5.7	5.3	5.1
Nondurable goods	8.2	7.8	7.8	4.3	4.2	4.2	2.0	1.9	1.8	2.3	2.3	2.4	3.9	3.6	3.5
Transportation and public utilities[5]	7.3	7.3	6.9	4.3	4.4	4.3	3.2	3.1	3.1	1.1	1.4	1.1	3.0	2.8	2.6
Wholesale and retail trade	6.5	6.1	5.9	2.8	2.7	2.7	1.8	1.8	1.7	1.0	.9	1.0	3.6	3.4	3.3
Wholesale trade	6.5	6.3	5.8	3.3	3.3	3.1	2.1	2.0	1.9	1.2	1.2	1.2	3.2	3.0	2.7
Retail trade	6.5	6.1	5.9	2.7	2.5	2.5	1.8	1.7	1.6	.9	.8	.9	3.8	3.6	3.4
Finance, insurance, and real estate	1.9	1.8	1.9	.7	.8	.8	.5	.6	.6	.1	.2	.2	1.2	1.1	1.1
Services	5.2	4.9	4.9	2.4	2.2	2.2	1.5	1.5	1.4	.8	.8	.9	2.9	2.6	2.6

[1]The incidence rates represent the number of injuries and illnesses per 100 full-time workers and were calculated as: (N/EH) x 200,000, where

      N = number of injuries and illnesses
      EH = total hours worked by all employees during the calendar year
   200,000 = base for 100 equivalent full-time workers (working 40 hours per week, 50 weeks per year)

[2]Total lost workday cases involve days away from work, days of restricted work activity, or both.
[3]Days-away-from-work cases include those which result in days away from work with or without restricted work activity.
[4]Excludes farms with fewer than 11 employees.
[5]Independent mining contractors are excluded from the coal, metal, and nonmetal mining industries.

Note: Because of rounding, components may not add to totals.

SOURCE: "Table 7. Incidence rates[1] of nonfatal occupational injuries and illnesses by industry division and selected case types, 1998–2000," in *Injuries, Illnesses, and Fatalities,* U.S. Department of Labor, Bureau of Labor Statistics, Washington, DC, 2001

TABLE 1.30

Fatal occupational injuries by event or exposure, 1995–2000

Event or exposure[1]	Fatalities			
	1995-99 average	1999[2] Number	2000 Number	2000 Percent
Total	**6,165**	**6,054**	**5,915**	**100**
Transportation incidents	2,611	2,618	2,571	43
Highway	1,405	1,496	1,363	23
Collision between vehicles, mobile equipment	674	714	694	12
Moving in same direction	115	129	136	2
Moving in opposite directions, oncoming	248	270	243	4
Moving in intersection	140	161	153	3
Vehicle struck stationary object or equipment	288	334	279	5
Noncollision	371	390	356	6
Jackknifed or overturned— no collision	290	322	304	5
Nonhighway (farm, industrial premises)	376	352	399	7
Overturned	211	206	213	4
Aircraft	264	228	280	5
Worker struck by a vehicle	380	377	370	6
Water vehicle	106	102	84	1
Rail vehicle	73	56	71	1
Assaults and violent acts	1,085	909	929	16
Homicides	837	651	677	11
Shooting	663	509	533	9
Stabbing	69	62	66	1
Other, including bombing	106	80	78	1
Self-inflicted injuries	216	218	220	4
Contact with objects and equipment	987	1,030	1,005	17
Struck by object	563	585	570	10
Struck by falling object	361	358	357	6
Struck by flying object	58	55	61	1
Caught in or compressed by equipment or objects	286	302	294	5
Caught in running equipment or machinery	152	163	157	3
Caught in or crushed in collapsing materials	123	129	123	2
Falls	697	721	734	12
Fall to lower level	620	634	659	11
Fall from ladder	103	96	110	2
Fall from roof	151	153	150	3
Fall from scaffold	89	92	85	1
Fall on same level	54	70	56	1
Exposure to harmful substances or environments	561	533	480	8
Contact with electric current	308	280	256	4
Contact with overhead powerlines	134	125	128	2
Contact with temperature extremes	46	51	29	-
Exposure to caustic, noxious, or allergenic substances	113	108	100	2
Inhalation of substance	60	55	48	1
Oxygen deficiency	92	92	93	2
Drowning, submersion	74	75	74	1
Fires and explosions	202	216	177	3
Other events or exposures[3]	21	27	19	-

[1] Based on the 1992 BLS Occupational Injury and Illness Classification Structures.
[2] The BLS news release issued Aug. 17, 2000, reported a total of 6,023 fatal work injuries for calendar year 1999. Since then, an additional 31 job-related fatalities were identified, bringing the total job-related fatality count for 1999 to 6,054.
[3] Includes the category "Bodily reaction and exertion."

Note: Totals for major categories may include subcategories not shown separately. Percentages may not add to totals because of rounding. Dashes indicate less than 0.5 percent.

SOURCE: "Table 1. Fatal occupational injuries by event or exposure, 1995–2000," in *National Census of Fatal Occupational Injuries in 2000*, U.S. Department of Labor, Bureau of Labor Statistics, Washington, DC, 2001

FIGURE 1.3

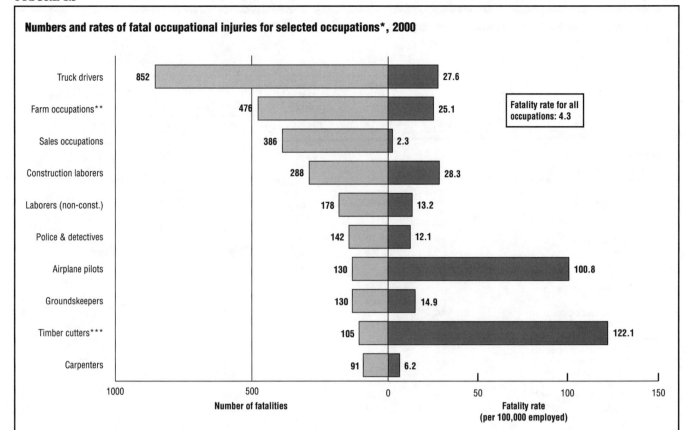

Numbers and rates of fatal occupational injuries for selected occupations*, 2000

Fatality rate for all occupations: 4.3

Occupation	Number of fatalities	Fatality rate (per 100,000 employed)
Truck drivers	852	27.6
Farm occupations**	476	25.1
Sales occupations	386	2.3
Construction laborers	288	28.3
Laborers (non-const.)	178	13.2
Police & detectives	142	12.1
Airplane pilots	130	100.8
Groundskeepers	130	14.9
Timber cutters***	105	122.1
Carpenters	91	6.2

*Selected occupations had a minimum of 40 fatalities and 45,000 employed workers in 2000.
**Farm occupations include the following: non-horticultural farmers, non-horticultural farm managers, farm workers, and farm worker supervisors.
***Timber cutters include the following: timber cutting and logging occupations; supervisors, forestry, and logging workers.
Rate = (Fatal work injuries/Employment) x 100,000 workers. Employment data extracted from the 2000 Current Population Survey (CPS).
The fatality rates were calculated using employment as the denominator; employment-based rates measure the risk for those employed during a given period of time, regardless of exposure hours.

SOURCE: "Chart 3. Numbers and rates of fatal occupational injuries for selected occupations*, 2000," in *National Census of Fatal Occupational Injuries in 2000,* U.S. Department of Labor, Bureau of Labor Statistics, Washington, DC, 2001

TABLE 1.31

Fatal occupational injuries and employment by industry, 2000

| Industry | SIC Code[1] | Fatalities | | | | Employment[3] (in thousands) | |
| | | 1995-1999 average | 1999 (revised)[2] | 2000 | | | |
		Number	Number	Number	Percent	Number	Percent
Total		6,165	6,054	5,915	100	136,377	100
Private industry		5,530	5,488	5,344	90	116,134	85
Agriculture, forestry, and fishing		819	814	720	12	3,380	2
Agricultural production – crops	01	362	356	277	5	987	1
Agricultural production – livestock	02	168	164	132	2	990	1
Agricultural services	07	168	164	213	4	1,306	1
Mining		147	122	156	3	520	-
Coal mining	12	36	35	40	1	76	-
Oil and gas extraction	13	74	50	83	1	313	-
Construction		1,115	1,191	1,154	20	8,949	7
General building contractors	15	190	183	175	3	-	-
Heavy construction, except building	16	260	280	284	5	-	-
Special trades contractors	17	652	710	672	11	-	-
Manufacturing		720	722	668	11	19,868	15
Food and kindred products	20	76	83	68	1	1,661	1
Lumber and wood products	24	190	190	186	3	782	1
Transportation and public utilities		960	1,008	957	16	8,084	6
Local and interurban passenger transportation	41	98	102	84	1	574	-
Trucking and warehousing	42	548	607	566	10	2,733	2
Transportation by air	45	85	74	97	2	889	1
Electric, gas, and sanitary services	49	88	86	84	1	1,007	1
Wholesale trade		247	238	230	4	5,407	4
Retail trade		624	513	594	10	22,315	16
Food stores	54	163	118	145	2	3,385	2
Automotive dealers and service stations	55	108	83	95	2	2,246	2
Eating and drinking places	58	148	146	138	2	6,836	5
Finance, insurance, and real estate		107	107	79	1	8,538	6
Services		750	736	768	13	39,170	29
Business services	73	184	161	199	3	9,602	7
Automotive repair, services, and parking	75	119	133	132	2	1,622	1
Government[4]		634	566	571	10	20,243	15
Federal (including resident armed forces)		191	148	149	3	4,461	3
State		125	109	108	2	5,468	4
Local		312	303	310	5	10,314	8
Police protection	9221	99	91	112	2	-	-

[1] Standard Industrial Classification Manual, 1987 Edition.

[2] The BLS news release issued Aug. 17, 2000, reported a total of 6,023 fatal work injuries for calendar year 1999. Since then, an additional 31 job-related fatalities were identified, bringing the total job-related fatality count for 1999 to 6,054.

[3] Employment is an annual average of employed civilians 16 years of age and older from the Current Population Survey, 2000, adjusted to include data for resident armed forces from the Department of Defense.

[4] Includes fatalities to workers employed by government organizations regardless of industry.

Note: Totals for major categories may include subcategories not shown separately. Percentages may not add to totals because of rounding. There were 17 fatalities for which there was insufficient information to determine a specific industry classification, although a distinction between private sector and government was made for each. Dashes indicate less than 0.5 percent or data that are not available or that do not meet publication criteria.

SOURCE: "Table 2. Fatal occupational injuries and employment by industry, 2000," in *National Census of Fatal Occupational Injuries in 2000,* U.S. Department of Labor, Bureau of Labor Statistics, Washington, DC, 2001

TABLE 1.32

Average annual number, rate, and percent of workplace victimization by type of crime, 1993–99

Crime category	Average annual workplace victimization	Rate per 1,000 persons in the workforce	Percent of workplace victimization
All violent crime	1,744,300	12.5	100%
Homicide	900	0.01	0.1
Rape/Sexual assault	36,500	0.3	2.1
Robbery	70,100	0.5	4.0
Aggravated assault	325,000	2.3	18.6
Simple assault	1,311,700	9.4	75.2

Note: Homicide data are obtained from the Bureau of Labor Statistics Census of Fatal Occupational Injuries. Rape and sexual assault, robbery, aggravated assault, and simple assault data are from the National Crime Victimization Survey (NCVS).

SOURCE: Detis T. Duhart, "Table 1. Average annual number, rate, and percent of workplace victimization by type of crime, 1993–99," in *Violence in the Workplace, 1993–99,* U.S. Department of Justice, Bureau of Justice Statistics, Washington, DC, 2001

TABLE 1.33

Average annual rate of violent victimization in the workplace, by occupation of the victim, 1993–99

Occupational field of victim	Violent victimizations in the workplace		
	Number	Rate per 1,000 workers	Percent of total
Total	12,328,000	12.6	100%
Medical			
Physician	71,300	16.2	0.6%
Nurse	429,100	21.9	3.5
Technician	97,600	12.7	0.8
Other	315,000	8.5	2.6
Mental health			
Professional	290,900	68.2	2.4%
Custodial	60,400	69.0	0.5
Other	186,700	40.7	1.5
Teaching			
Preschool	32,900	7.1	0.3%
Elementary	262,700	16.8	2.1
Junior high	321,300	54.2	2.6
High school	314,500	38.1	2.6
College/university	41,600	1.6	0.3
Technical/industrial	7,400	12.2*	0.1*
Special education	102,000	68.4	0.8
Other	169,800	16.7	1.4
Law enforcement			
Police	1,380,400	260.8	11.2%
Corrections	277,100	155.7	2.3
Private security	369,300	86.6	3.0
Other	359,800	48.3	2.9
Retail sales			
Convenience store	336,800	53.9	2.7%
Gas station	86,900	68.3	0.7
Bartender	170,600	81.6	1.4
Other	1,383,100	15.3	11.2
Transportation			
Bus driver	105,800	38.2	0.9%
Taxi cab driver	84,400	128.3	0.7
Other	350,500	11.7	2.8
Other	4,720,100	7.0	38.3%

Note: Rates are calculated using population estimates from the National Crime Victimization Survey (NCVS) for occupations, 1993–99. The total number of victimizations in this table and all other tables with detail for occupation differs from the total in tables without occupational detail because of the way teacher victimization was computed. Details may not add to total because of rounding.
*Estimate based on 10 or fewer sample cases.

SOURCE: Detis T. Duhart, "Table 6. Average annual rate of violent victimization in the workplace, by occupation of the victim, 1993–99," in *Violence in the Workplace, 1993–99,* U.S. Department of Justice, Bureau of Justice Statistics, Washington, DC, 2001

CHAPTER 2
THE CHANGING AMERICAN WORKFORCE

A WORKPLACE IN TRANSITION

Throughout most of the 1990s, the rapid increase in the labor force (those working part- or full-time or unemployed but actively looking for a job) put a severe strain on the economic system to produce more jobs. At the same time, multinational companies shifted many tasks overseas, worldwide competition became more intense, and significant economic activity became international. American companies responded to these changes in many ways:

• Greater use of technologically advanced machinery designed to replace human workers;

• Greater pressure on workers to limit wage and benefit demands (especially for new entrants into the job market), or to "give back" already existing benefits;

• Management programs designed to accomplish more per worker so that the economy could remain competitive with international economies (which often have considerably lower standards of living);

• Employee reductions through layoffs or early retirement; and

• Increased attempts to become part of an international economy.

Downsizing the labor force to become more competitive in the international market became the management style of many companies in the late 1980s and early 1990s. Many companies laid off older workers to cut expenses. Many of these laid-off workers, however, returned to their firms as contract workers. Some began working for less money than they had earned when they were employees. Even if the firm pays the contract worker at the same rate, the companies do not have to pay for health or retirement benefits.

In 1997 and 1998 a booming economy led to the creation of hundreds of thousands of new jobs. This led to a tight labor market in which there was a demand for workers. Earlier in the decade, workers worried about losing their jobs and tended not to ask for raises. The changing economy, with many areas having a shortage of workers, changed some workers' outlooks on job possibilities and wage increases. College graduates at the end of the 1990s were finding jobs more easily than in the past, and many received signing bonuses.

At the same time the economy was producing many thousands of jobs, the U.S. Conference of Mayors, in its survey of 13 cities, feared a shortage of low-skilled jobs. For example, in 1997 Detroit officials estimated that more than 93,000 people, including welfare recipients participating in workfare, would compete for a projected 18,447 jobs. The problem, however, was that most of the low-skilled jobs were in the suburbs, and many of the people in need of low-skill jobs were in the inner cities. Public transportation between the two places was not always available.

According to the Bureau of Labor Statistics (BLS) through the 1990s, the average unemployment rate gradually declined from a decade-high 7.5 percent in 1992 to 4.0 percent in 2000. With a weakening economy in 2001, the average unemployment rate rose somewhat to 4.8 percent. The September 11, 2001 terrorist attacks on the United States in New York City and Washington, D.C., further affected the weakening economy and unemployment rates. At mid-2002, the rate (unadjusted seasonally) stood at 5.9 percent.

SERVICE ECONOMY

The American economy has moved away from producing goods to providing services. From about 1970 to 2001, the service-producing sector has accounted for an increasing proportion of workers. In 1960 for every goods-producing worker, there were about 1.7 service-producing workers. By 1970 the ratio was 1 goods-producing worker

TABLE 2.1

Employees on nonfarm payrolls by major industry, 1951–2001

(In thousands)

Year and month	Total	Total private	Goods-producing				Service-producing						Government		
			Total	Mining	Construc-tion	Manufac-turing	Total	Transpor-tation and public utilities	Whole-sale trade	Retail trade	Finance, insurance, and real estate	Services	Federal	State	Local
							Annual averages								
1951	47,819	41,430	19,959	929	2,637	16,393	27,860	4,226	2,735	7,007	1,956	5,547	2,302	(1)	(1)
1952	48,793	42,185	20,198	898	2,668	16,632	28,595	4,248	2,821	7,184	2,035	5,699	2,420	(1)	(1)
1953	50,202	43,556	21,074	866	2,659	17,549	29,128	4,290	2,862	7,385	2,111	5,835	2,305	(1)	(1)
1954	48,990	42,238	19,751	791	2,646	16,314	29,239	4,084	2,875	7,360	2,200	5,969	2,188	(1)	(1)
1955	50,641	43,727	20,513	792	2,839	16,882	30,128	4,141	2,934	7,601	2,298	6,240	2,187	1,168	3,558
1956	52,369	45,091	21,104	822	3,039	17,243	31,264	4,244	3,027	7,831	2,389	6,497	2,209	1,250	3,819
1957	52,855	45,239	20,967	828	2,962	17,176	31,889	4,241	3,037	7,848	2,438	6,708	2,217	1,328	4,071
1958	51,322	43,483	19,513	751	2,817	15,945	31,811	3,976	2,989	7,761	2,481	6,765	2,191	1,415	4,232
1959[2]	53,270	45,186	20,411	732	3,004	16,675	32,857	4,011	3,092	8,035	2,549	7,087	2,233	1,484	4,366
1960	54,189	45,836	20,434	712	2,926	16,796	33,755	4,004	3,153	8,238	2,628	7,378	2,270	1,536	4,547
1961	53,999	45,404	19,857	672	2,859	16,326	34,142	3,903	3,142	8,195	2,688	7,619	2,279	1,607	4,708
1962	55,549	46,660	20,451	650	2,948	16,853	35,098	3,906	3,207	8,359	2,754	7,982	2,340	1,668	4,881
1963	56,653	47,429	20,640	635	3,010	16,995	36,013	3,903	3,258	8,520	2,830	8,277	2,358	1,747	5,121
1964	58,283	48,686	21,005	634	3,097	17,274	37,278	3,951	3,347	8,812	2,911	8,660	2,348	1,856	5,392
1965	60,763	50,689	21,926	632	3,232	18,062	38,839	4,036	3,477	9,239	2,977	9,036	2,378	1,996	5,700
1966	63,901	53,116	23,158	627	3,317	19,214	40,743	4,158	3,608	9,637	3,058	9,498	2,564	2,141	6,080
1967	65,803	54,413	23,308	613	3,248	19,447	42,495	4,268	3,700	9,906	3,185	10,045	2,719	2,302	6,371
1968	67,897	56,058	23,737	606	3,350	19,781	44,158	4,318	3,791	10,308	3,337	10,567	2,737	2,442	6,660
1969	70,384	58,189	24,361	619	3,575	20,167	46,023	4,442	3,919	10,785	3,512	11,169	2,758	2,533	6,904
1970	70,880	58,325	23,578	623	3,588	19,367	47,302	4,515	4,006	11,034	3,645	11,548	2,731	2,664	7,158
1971	71,211	58,331	22,935	609	3,704	18,623	48,276	4,476	4,014	11,338	3,772	11,797	2,696	2,747	7,437
1972	73,675	60,341	23,668	628	3,889	19,151	50,007	4,541	4,127	11,822	3,908	12,276	2,684	2,859	7,790
1973	76,790	63,058	24,893	642	4,097	20,154	51,897	4,656	4,291	12,315	4,046	12,857	2,663	2,923	8,146
1974	78,265	64,095	24,794	697	4,020	20,077	53,471	4,725	4,447	12,539	4,148	13,441	2,724	3,039	8,407
1975	76,945	62,259	22,600	752	3,525	18,323	54,345	4,542	4,430	12,630	4,165	13,892	2,748	3,179	8,758
1976	79,382	64,511	23,352	779	3,576	18,997	56,030	4,582	4,562	13,193	4,271	14,551	2,733	3,273	8,865
1977	82,471	67,344	24,346	813	3,851	19,682	58,125	4,713	4,723	13,792	4,467	15,302	2,727	3,377	9,023
1978	86,697	71,026	25,585	851	4,229	20,505	61,113	4,923	4,985	14,556	4,724	16,252	2,753	3,474	9,446
1979	89,823	73,876	26,461	958	4,463	21,040	63,363	5,136	5,221	14,972	4,975	17,112	2,773	3,541	9,633
1980	90,406	74,166	25,658	1,027	4,346	20,285	64,748	5,146	5,292	15,018	5,160	17,890	2,866	3,610	9,765
1981	91,152	75,121	25,497	1,139	4,188	20,170	65,655	5,165	5,375	15,171	5,298	18,615	2,772	3,640	9,619
1982	89,544	73,707	23,812	1,128	3,904	18,780	65,732	5,081	5,295	15,158	5,340	19,021	2,739	3,640	9,458
1983	90,152	74,282	23,330	952	3,946	18,432	66,821	4,952	5,283	15,587	5,466	19,664	2,774	3,662	9,434
1984	94,408	78,384	24,718	966	4,380	19,372	69,690	5,156	5,568	16,512	5,684	20,746	2,807	3,734	9,482
1985	97,387	80,992	24,842	927	4,668	19,248	72,544	5,233	5,727	17,315	5,948	21,927	2,875	3,832	9,687
1986	99,344	82,651	24,533	777	4,810	18,947	74,811	5,247	5,761	17,880	6,273	22,957	2,899	3,893	9,901
1987	101,958	84,948	24,674	717	4,958	18,999	77,284	5,362	5,848	18,422	6,533	24,110	2,943	3,967	10,100
1988	105,209	87,823	25,125	713	5,098	19,314	80,084	5,512	6,030	19,023	6,630	25,504	2,971	4,076	10,339
1989	107,884	90,105	25,254	692	5,171	19,391	82,630	5,614	6,187	19,475	6,668	26,907	2,988	4,182	10,609
1990	109,403	91,098	24,905	709	5,120	19,076	84,497	5,777	6,173	19,601	6,709	27,934	3,085	4,305	10,914
1991	108,249	89,847	23,745	689	4,650	18,406	84,504	5,755	6,081	19,284	6,646	28,336	2,966	4,355	11,081
1992	108,601	89,956	23,231	635	4,492	18,104	85,370	5,718	5,997	19,356	6,602	29,052	2,969	4,408	11,267
1993	110,713	91,872	23,352	610	4,668	18,075	87,361	5,811	5,981	19,773	6,757	30,197	2,915	4,488	11,438
1994	114,163	95,036	23,908	601	4,986	18,321	90,256	5,984	6,162	20,507	6,896	31,579	2,870	4,576	11,682
1995	117,191	97,885	24,265	581	5,160	18,524	92,925	6,132	6,378	21,187	6,806	33,117	2,822	4,635	11,849
1996	119,608	100,189	24,493	580	5,418	18,495	95,115	6,253	6,482	21,597	6,911	34,454	2,757	4,606	12,056
1997	122,690	103,133	24,962	596	5,691	18,675	97,727	6,408	6,648	21,966	7,109	36,040	2,699	4,582	12,276
1998	125,865	106,042	25,414	590	6,020	18,805	100,451	6,611	6,800	22,295	7,389	37,533	2,686	4,612	12,525
1999	128,916	108,709	25,507	539	6,415	18,552	103,409	6,834	6,911	22,848	7,555	39,055	2,669	4,709	12,829
2000	131,759	111,079	25,709	543	6,698	18,469	106,050	7,019	7,024	23,307	7,560	40,460	2,777	4,785	13,119
2001	132,213	111,341	25,122	563	6,861	17,698	107,092	7,070	7,014	23,488	7,624	41,024	2,616	4,880	13,377

[1]Not available.

[2]Data include Alaska and Hawaii beginning in 1959. This inclusion resulted in an increase of 212,000 (0.4 percent) in the nonfarm total for the March 1959 benchmark month.

Note: Establishment survey estimates are currently projected from March 2000 benchmark levels. When more recent benchmark data are introduced, all unadjusted data (beginning April 2000) and all seasonally adjusted data (beginning January 1997) are subject to revision.

SOURCE: Adapted from "B-1. Employees on nonfarm payrolls by major industry, 1951 to date," in *Historical Payroll Data*, U.S. Department of Labor, Bureau of Labor Statistics, Washington, DC, 2002

to every 2 service-producing workers, and by 2001 it was more than 1 to 4. (See Table 2.1.)

From 1990 to 2001 only the construction industry in the goods-producing area has consistently employed more workers each year, while the numbers working in mining have fallen significantly. The amount of workers in manufacturing has stayed relatively level from 1970 to 2000, but the proportion of manufacturing jobs fell from 34 percent of all jobs in 1951 to just 13 percent in 2001. (See Table 2.1.)

Indeed, in 1945, at the conclusion of World War II, the services industry accounted for 10 percent of nonfarm employment, compared with 38 percent for manufacturing. (See Figure 2.1.) In 1982 services surpassed manufacturing as the largest employer among major industry groups. By 1996 the services industry accounted for 29 percent of nonfarm employment, and manufacturing, at 15 percent, was actually somewhat smaller than retail trade.

Service-producing industries include jobs in transportation, wholesale and retail trade, services, finance, and more. Within the service-producing industry, service industry jobs are found in legal services, hotels, health services, educational services, and social services, among others. However, all jobs within the service industry are not necessarily service occupations. For example, while hotels are part of the services industry within the service-producing sector, they employ workers who are not only in service occupations, but also secretaries, managers, and accountants whose occupations are not considered service occupations.

About 20.8 million persons (about 16 percent of the nonfarm working population) worked in government positions in 2001. Between 1990 and 2001, the federal government lost 15 percent of its workers, while state and local governments increased their workforce by 13 percent and nearly 23 percent, respectively. (See Table 2.1.)

Because average wages are higher in manufacturing than in services, some observers view employment shifts to services as a change from "good" to "bad" jobs. In "The Services Industry in the 'Good' Versus 'Bad' Jobs Debate" (*Monthly Labor Review,* February 1998), Joseph R. Meisenheimer II found that many service industries equal or exceed manufacturing and other industries on measures of job quality, while some service industries could be viewed as less desirable by these measures.

Meisenheimer stresses the importance of examining more than just average pay when assessing the quality of jobs in each industry. Within each industry, there are jobs at a variety of different quality levels. The quality of service-industry jobs is especially diverse, encompassing many of the "best" jobs in the economy and a substantial share of the "worst." Thus, employment shifts away from manufacturing and toward services do not necessarily signal deterioration in overall job quality in the United States, although, in many cases, they certainly can.

FIGURE 2.1

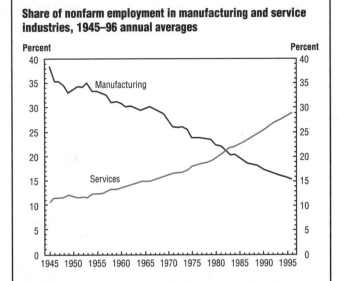

Share of nonfarm employment in manufacturing and service industries, 1945–96 annual averages

SOURCE: Joseph R. Meisenheimer II, "Share of Nonfarm Employment in Manufacturing and Services Industries, 1945–1996 Annual Averages," in "The Services Industry in the 'Good' Versus 'Bad' Jobs Debate," *Monthly Labor Review,* vol. 121, no. 2, February 1998

HOW LONG DO AMERICANS WORK?

Between 1990 and 1995 the United States stood out among all nations as a country with an advanced economy that had the longest work year. Japan's average work year, however, declined during that time period. The United States has a long work year, due in part to a lack of legally mandated, employer-paid vacation time. Such paid vacation time is common in many countries in Europe.

In 2001 about 76 percent of nonfarm American laborers were working full-time (35 hours or more), while the remaining 24 percent were working part-time (less than 35 hours). The average worker labored 39.2 hours per week (average hours of part-time and full-time), while the average full-time employee worked 42.8 hours per week. Women (32 percent) were more likely to work part-time than men (17 percent). As a result, men worked an average of 41.9 hours per week, and women worked an average of 36.1 hours per week. (See Table 2.2.) Almost 20 percent of all nonfarm workers spent more than 49 hours a week on the job. Almost one-third (31.2 percent) of agricultural workers labored more than 49 hours per week. (See Table 2.3.)

Studies vary in assessing Americans' work hours over time. A study in the BLS *Monthly Labor Review,* July 2000, indicates that data from the Current Employment Statistics (CES) program showed a long-term decline in the number of hours worked per week from 38.7 hours in 1964 to 34.5 hours in 1999, an 11 percent reduction over that period. Reflected in these figures is a large decrease in hours for certain industries, particularly retail.

TABLE 2.2

Persons at work in nonfarm occupations by sex and usual full- or part-time status, 2001

(Numbers in thousands)

Occupation and sex	Total at work	Worked 1 to 34 hours Total	For economic reasons	For noneconomic reasons Usually work full time	For noneconomic reasons Usually work part time	Worked 35 hours or more	Average hours Total at work	Average hours Persons who usually work full time
Total, 16 years and over[1]	126,412	30,323	3,515	8,612	18,196	96,089	39.2	42.8
Managerial and professional specialty	39,872	7,553	485	3,015	4,053	32,318	41.5	44.2
Executive, administrative, and managerial	19,662	2,906	183	1,378	1,345	16,755	43.2	45.0
Professional specialty	20,210	4,647	302	1,636	2,708	15,563	39.9	43.3
Technical, sales, and administrative support	37,586	10,379	865	2,593	6,921	27,207	37.5	41.9
Technicians and related support	4,343	932	59	359	515	3,410	39.1	41.7
Sales occupations	15,489	4,423	469	804	3,150	11,066	38.6	44.0
Administrative support, including clerical	17,754	5,024	337	1,431	3,256	12,730	36.2	40.2
Service occupations	17,597	6,818	944	948	4,927	10,779	34.7	41.7
Private household	690	389	62	36	292	300	28.8	40.1
Protective service	2,379	381	38	139	204	1,999	42.7	45.3
Service, except private household and protective	14,528	6,048	845	773	4,431	8,480	33.7	41.0
Precision production, craft, and repair	14,324	2,037	463	987	587	12,287	41.6	42.7
Operators, fabricators, and laborers	17,034	3,535	758	1,069	1,708	13,499	39.8	42.5
Machine operators, assemblers, and inspectors	6,506	1,030	253	448	330	5,476	40.1	41.4
Transportation and material moving occupations	5,383	957	184	299	475	4,425	42.9	45.5
Handlers, equipment cleaners, helpers, and laborers	5,145	1,548	321	323	904	3,597	36.3	40.8
Men, 16 years and over[1]	67,217	11,430	1,744	4,103	5,583	55,787	41.9	44.2
Managerial and professional specialty	20,224	2,646	219	1,322	1,105	17,578	44.4	46.0
Executive, administrative, and managerial	10,665	1,131	95	628	408	9,534	45.7	46.8
Professional specialty	9,559	1,515	124	694	697	8,044	43.0	45.1
Technical, sales, and administrative support	13,771	2,533	242	779	1,512	11,238	41.4	44.4
Technicians and related support	2,032	317	28	167	121	1,716	41.2	42.8
Sales occupations	7,907	1,421	140	344	937	6,486	42.7	46.1
Administrative support, including clerical	3,832	796	74	267	455	3,036	38.9	41.8
Service occupations	7,021	2,014	319	333	1,363	5,007	37.8	43.2
Private household	27	13	3	1	9	14	(2)	(2)
Protective service	1,899	248	25	103	120	1,651	44.2	46.2
Service, except private household and protective	5,095	1,753	291	228	1,234	3,342	35.4	41.7
Precision production, craft, and repair	13,099	1,771	421	907	443	11,328	41.9	42.8
Operators, fabricators, and laborers	13,102	2,465	543	762	1,160	10,637	40.7	43.2
Machine operators, assemblers, and inspectors	4,164	542	136	265	142	3,622	41.2	42.0
Transportation and material moving occupations	4,837	740	155	254	331	4,097	43.7	45.8
Handlers, equipment cleaners, helpers, and laborers	4,102	1,183	252	243	688	2,919	36.8	41.1
Women, 16 years and over[1]	59,195	18,893	1,771	4,509	12,613	40,302	36.1	40.9
Managerial and professional specialty	19,647	4,907	266	1,692	2,948	14,740	38.5	42.0
Executive, administrative, and managerial	8,997	1,775	88	750	937	7,222	40.2	42.6
Professional specialty	10,651	3,132	179	942	2,012	7,519	37.1	41.5
Technical, sales, and administrative support	23,815	7,846	623	1,814	5,408	15,969	35.3	40.2
Technicians and related support	2,310	616	31	191	393	1,694	37.2	40.6
Sales occupations	7,582	3,002	329	459	2,214	4,580	34.4	41.3
Administrative support, including clerical	13,922	4,227	262	1,164	2,801	9,695	35.4	39.6
Service occupations	10,576	4,804	625	615	3,564	5,772	32.7	40.5
Private household	663	376	59	34	283	287	28.8	40.0
Protective service	481	132	13	36	83	348	37.0	41.5
Service, except private household and protective	9,433	4,296	553	544	3,198	5,137	32.8	40.5
Precision production, craft, and repair	1,225	266	42	80	144	959	38.5	41.3
Operators, fabricators, and laborers	3,932	1,070	215	308	548	2,861	36.9	40.1
Machine operators, assemblers, and inspectors	2,342	488	117	183	188	1,854	38.2	40.0
Transportation and material moving occupations	546	218	29	44	144	329	35.4	41.7
Handlers, equipment cleaners, helpers, and laborers	1,043	365	69	80	216	679	34.7	39.4

[1]Excludes farming, forestry, and fishing occupations.
[2]Data not shown where base is less than 35,000.

SOURCE: "23. Persons at work in nonfarm occupations by sex and usual full- or part-time status," in *Employment and Earnings*, vol. 49, no. 1, January 2002

Some occupations require more time than others. Transportation and material-moving workers labored 42.9 hours per week (45.5 hours for workers on full-time schedules). Executive, administrative, and managerial people averaged about 43.2 hours (45.0 hours a week for full-time). Conversely, private household workers averaged only 28.8 hours a week (40.1 hours for full-time). (See Table 2.2.)

TABLE 2.3

Persons at work in agriculture and nonagricultural industries by hours of work, 2001

	2001					
	Thousands of persons			Percent distribution		
Hours of work	All industries	Agriculture	Nonagricultural industries	All industries	Agriculture	Nonagricultural industries
Total, 16 years and over	129,517	3,004	126,513	100.0	100.0	100.0
1 to 34 hours	31,175	838	30,337	24.1	27.9	24.0
1 to 4 hours	1,336	61	1,275	1.0	2.0	1.0
5 to 14 hours	4,819	197	4,622	3.7	6.6	3.7
15 to 29 hours	15,305	389	14,917	11.8	12.9	11.8
30 to 34 hours	9,715	191	9,524	7.5	6.4	7.5
35 hours and over	98,342	2,166	96,176	75.9	72.1	76.0
35 to 39 hours	8,703	169	8,534	6.7	5.6	6.7
40 hours	51,822	831	50,991	40.0	27.7	40.3
41 hours and over	37,817	1,166	36,651	29.2	38.8	29.0
41 to 48 hours	13,665	228	13,437	10.6	7.6	10.6
49 to 59 hours	14,067	360	13,706	10.9	12.0	10.8
60 hours and over	10,085	577	9,507	7.8	19.2	7.5
Average hours, total at work	39.2	41.6	39.2	–	–	–
Average hours, persons who usually work full time	42.9	47.6	42.8	–	–	–

Note: Detail on persons at work may not sum to the totals shown because of minor editing problems associated with the redesigned survey.

SOURCE: "19. Persons at work in agriculture and nonagricultural industries by hours of work," in *Employment and Earnings,* vol. 49, no. 1, January 2002

According to another report, "Trends in the Hours of Work Since the Mid-1970s," that was published in the BLS *Monthly Labor Review,* April 1997, the average number of hours worked each week has changed little since the mid-1970s, but the proportion of people working very long work weeks has risen. Figure 2.2 shows that the proportion of nonagricultural wage and salary workers who worked exactly 40 hours per week declined between 1976 and 1993, while the share working 49 hours or more rose. The proportions working fewer than 40 hours and 41 to 48 hours remained fairly stable.

From 1976 to 1993 average hours at work increased only 1 hour, from 41 to 42 hours, for men, and 2 hours, from 34 to 36 hours, for women. Part of these increases can be attributed to the changing age profile of the American workforce. By 1993 baby boomers—those born between 1946 and 1964—had all moved into the middle working ages of 25 to 54. Meanwhile, younger and older workers made up a declining share of employment. Work weeks typically are longer for workers age 25 to 54, and part-time employment is more common among younger and older workers. This pattern continued in 1995, with men working 42.1 hours overall, but men in the 25 to 54 age category worked 44.1 hours. (See Table 2.4.)

Table 2.5 shows the calculation as if the age distribution of those at work had remained unchanged between 1976 and 1993. After removing the effect of age, the work week for men was virtually unchanged, and women's weekly hours rose by only a single hour.

Many employees are working longer hours by skipping or shortening their lunch breaks. In 1996 the National Restaurant Association reported that 40 percent of the surveyed workers said they did not leave the office for a lunch break. Forty-five percent reported they had less time for lunch than they ever had. Many workers say they stay on the job to get things done because they fear being downsized. Fewer workers often means those remaining have to do more.

Who Is Working the Longer Work Weeks?

The growth in the share of workers reporting very long work weeks is often attributed to a shift in employment toward high-hour occupations, such as managers, professionals, and certain sales workers. (See Figure 2.3.) This may reflect the considerable responsibilities associated with many of these types of jobs. In addition, employers are often not required by law to pay overtime premiums to workers in these occupations, as they must for most hourly paid workers. However, salaried workers tend to be better paid.

The changes in number of hours worked varies in different employment sectors. For example, between 1964 and 1999, mining, construction, and manufacturing jobs increased in the number of hours worked weekly. The service-producing industries, including transportation, all decreased the number of hours worked. Retail trade had a dramatic decrease in hours worked weekly. (See Table 2.6.)

For specific segments of the population, the work week showed a tendency to increase at the end of the twentieth

FIGURE 2.2

Distribution of hours at work of nonagricultural wage and salary workers, selected years 1976–93 annual averages

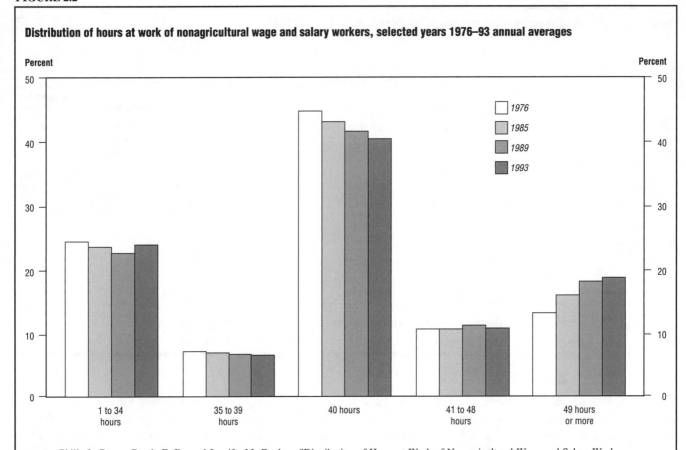

SOURCE: Philip L. Rones, Randy E. Ilg, and Jennifer M. Gardner, "Distribution of Hours at Work of Nonagricultural Wage and Salary Workers, Selected Years 1976–93 Annual Averages," in "Trends in the Hours of Work Since the Mid-1970s," *Monthly Labor Review,* vol. 120, no. 4, April 1997

century. According to the BLS, women who had children worked more hours each week in 1998 than they did in 1969. The increase was most pronounced in women with children between the ages of 6 and 17. Between 1969 and 1998 hours worked per week for these women increased by 2.5 hours. Women with children between 3 and 5 years of age increased their work week by 1.4 hours between 1969 and 1998. Men with children, however, decreased the length of their work week between 1969 and 1998; men with children under 3 years worked 0.8 hours less, and men with children between 3 and 5 years worked 0.3 hours less.

Another study by the BLS looked at welfare recipients who were able to obtain jobs. The study showed that this population segment usually worked a relatively high number of hours per week—usually over 30 hours—for relatively low pay. Such jobs usually paid between $8,000 to $10,000 per year.

Increases in average hours worked per week can have peripheral effects. A study by the insurance industry estimated that for each 1 percent increase in average hours worked per week, a 3.4 percent increase can be expected in injury and illness rates. Increases in work hours per

week can lead to job-related tiredness and stress, which can in turn result in injury and illness.

In 1997 many trade organizations reported that their members were working a lot of overtime because of the economic expansion. Professional Secretaries International (Kansas City, Missouri) found that the proportion of its 27,000 members putting in 40 to 44 hours per week rose from 64.7 percent in 1992 to 68.4 percent in 1997. According to the National Restaurant Association, its members increased their average hours from 51.2 in 1992 to 56 hours in 1997. The BLS reported that the weekly hours for temporaries rose from 27.1 in 1982 to 32.3 in 1997. Manufacturing jobs reached a high of 41.7 hours worked per week in 1999. The figure for mining jobs was even higher, at 43.8 hours per week. (See Table 2.6.)

Part-Time Work

People work part-time for various reasons. Nearly 12 percent of part-time workers took part-time work due to economic conditions. These economic reasons, usually caused by employers' circumstances, included slack work, material shortages, or the availability of only part-time

TABLE 2.4

Nonagricultural wage and salary workers at work and their average hours by selected characteristics, 1995 annual averages

[Numbers in thousands]

Characteristic	Total at work	Average hours	
		Total at work	Persons who usually work full time
Age and sex			
Total, 16 years and older	107,656	39.2	43.0
16 to 24 years	17,282	32.6	41.3
25 to 54 years	78,682	41.0	43.3
55 years and older	11,692	36.7	42.3
Men, 16 years and older	57,362	42.1	44.5
16 to 24 years	8,989	34.7	42.3
25 to 54 years	42,124	44.1	44.9
55 years and older	6,250	39.6	43.7
Women, 16 years and older	50,294	35.8	40.8
16 to 24 years	8,293	30.4	40.0
25 to 54 years	36,558	37.4	41.0
55 years and older	5,442	33.3	40.3
Race and Hispanic origin			
White, 16 years and older	90,997	39.3	43.2
Men	49,114	42.4	44.8
Women	41,883	35.6	40.9
Black, 16 years and older	12,162	38.3	41.2
Men	5,826	40.0	42.3
Women	6,336	36.7	40.1
Hispanic origin, 16 years and older	9,645	38.5	41.5
Men	5,688	40.5	42.4
Women	3,956	35.6	39.9

SOURCE: Philip L. Rones, Randy E. Ilg, and Jennifer M. Gardner, "Table 1. Nonagricultural wage and salary workers at work and their annual average hours by age, sex, race, and Hispanic origin, 1995 annual averages," in "Trends in the Hours of Work Since the Mid-1970s," *Monthly Labor Review,* vol. 120, no. 4, April 1997

TABLE 2.5

Average workweek, 1976 and 1993

	Average hours		Age-adjusted hours
	1976	1993	1993
Men, 16 years and older	41.0	42.0	41.2
Women, 16 years and older	34.0	36.0	35.0

SOURCE: "Average Workweek," in "How Long Is the Workweek?" in *Issues in Labor Statistics,* U.S. Department of Labor, Bureau of Labor Statistics, Washington, DC, 1997

work. Most workers (88 percent) who usually worked part-time did so for noneconomic reasons. They did not want to work full-time or were unavailable, perhaps because they were going to school, were taking care of children, or had other family or personal obligations. (See Table 2.7.)

MULTIPLE JOBS

In 2001, 5.4 percent of workers held multiple jobs. The multiple job-holding rate among men declined from 7 percent in 1970 to 5.3 in 2001. However, the proportion of women holding more than one job increased significantly from 2 percent in 1970 to 5.6 percent in 2001. Single women (6.3 percent) and widowed, divorced, and separated women (6.4 percent) were most likely to have more than one job. Married women (4.9 percent) and single men (4.8 percent) were the least likely. (See Table 2.8.)

CONTINGENT WORKERS AND ALTERNATIVE WORK ARRANGEMENTS

According to the BLS, even though most studies have found no change in workers' overall job tenure, reports of corporate downsizing, production streamlining, and the increasing use of temporary workers have caused many workers to question employers' commitment to long-term, stable employment relationships. There is also a growing sense that employers, in their attempts to reduce costs, have increased their use of "employment intermediaries," such as temporary help services and contract companies, and are relying more on alternative staffing arrangements, such as on-call workers and independent contractors/free-lancers. Permanent workers sometimes fear they will be replaced by these alternatives.

Workers may take employment in a nonstandard arrangement, such as working for a temporary agency, for a number of reasons, including inability to find a permanent job, wanting to work fewer hours when they have a young child at home, or wanting to learn about a number of different jobs or fields. In addition, some nonstandard work arrangements, such as consulting or contracting, may provide workers with relatively more flexible and lucrative employment opportunities.

Contingent Workers

The BLS defines contingent work as any job in which an individual does not have an explicit or implicit contract for long-term employment. This includes independent contractors, on-call workers, and those working for temporary help services. The February 1995 *Current Population Survey* estimated that between 2.7 and 6 million workers (2.2 to 4.9 percent of total employment) were in contingent positions. By 1999 a temporary employment agency in Milwaukee estimated that 2.5 percent of the U.S. workforce consisted of contingent workers.

The reason the estimates ran from 2.2 percent to 4.9 percent of total employment is due to alternative definitions. Estimate 1, the narrowest estimate, included wage and salary workers who had held their jobs for one year or less and expected to be employed for an additional year or less. Estimate 2, the middle estimate, added the self-employed and independent contractors. Estimate 3, the broadest estimate, dropped the time limit on wage and

FIGURE 2.3

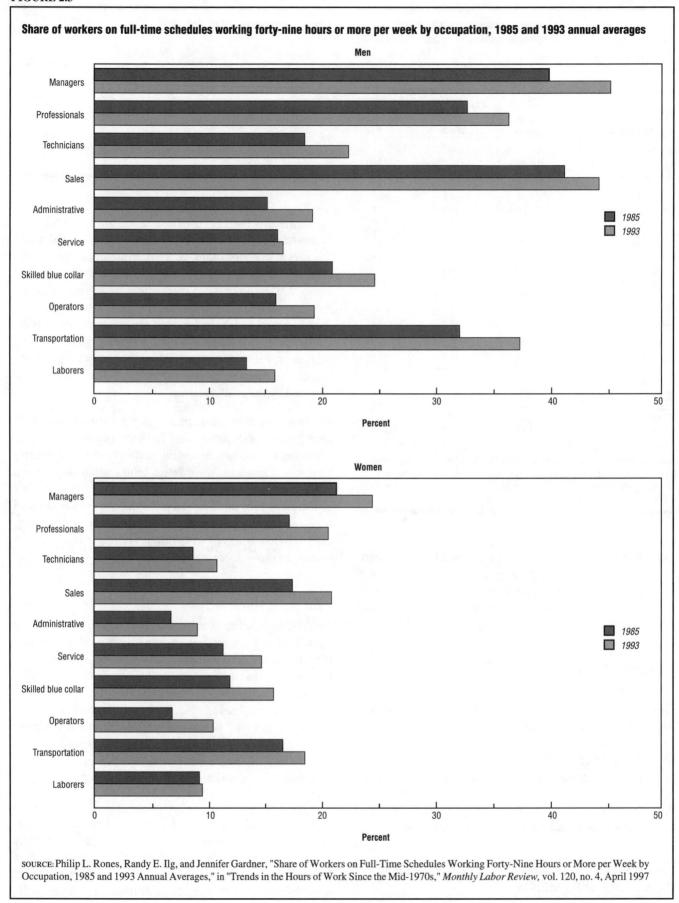

Share of workers on full-time schedules working forty-nine hours or more per week by occupation, 1985 and 1993 annual averages

Men

Women

SOURCE: Philip L. Rones, Randy E. Ilg, and Jennifer Gardner, "Share of Workers on Full-Time Schedules Working Forty-Nine Hours or More per Week by Occupation, 1985 and 1993 Annual Averages," in "Trends in the Hours of Work Since the Mid-1970s," *Monthly Labor Review,* vol. 120, no. 4, April 1997

TABLE 2.6

Average weekly hours and employment of production/nonsupervisory workers by major industry division, 1964–99

| | Average weekly hours | | | | Production/nonsupervisory workers | | | |
| | | | Change | | | | Change | |
Industry	1964	1999	Level	Percent	1964	1999	Level	Percent
Total private	**38.7**	**34.5**	**−4.2**	**−10.9**	**40,560**	**88,911**	**48,351**	**119.2**
Goods producing								
Mining	41.9	43.8	1.9	4.5	497	402	−95	−19.1
Construction	37.2	39.1	1.9	5.1	2,637	4,953	2,316	87.8
Manufacturing	40.7	41.7	1.0	2.5	12,781	12,739	−42	−.3
Service producing								
Transportation								
and public utilities	41.1	38.7	−2.4	−5.8	3,490	5,660	2,170	62.2
Wholesale trade	40.7	38.3	−2.4	−5.9	2,832	5,538	2,706	95.6
Retail trade	37.0	29.0	−8.0	−21.6	8,037	20,046	12,009	149.4
Finance, insurance,								
and real estate	37.3	36.2	−1.1	−2.9	2,346	5,546	3,200	136.4
Services	36.1	32.6	−3.5	−9.7	7,939	34,027	26,088	328.6

Note: Levels of production/nonsupervisory workers are in thousands.

SOURCE: Katie Kirkland, "Table 1. Average weekly hours and employment of production/nonsupervisory workers by major industry division, W1964–1999," in "On the Decline in Average Weekly Hours Worked," *Monthly Labor Review,* Vol. 123, No. 7, July 2000

TABLE 2.7

Persons at work in all and nonagricultural industries by reason for working less than 35 hours and usual full- or part-time status, 2001

(Numbers in thousands)

| | 2001 | | | | | |
| | All industries | | | Nonagricultural industries | | |
Reason for working less than 35 hours	Total	Usually work full time	Usually work part time	Total	Usually work full time	Usually work part time
Total, 16 years and over	31,175	10,312	20,863	30,337	10,067	20,270
Economic reasons	3,672	1,516	2,156	3,529	1,436	2,093
Slack work or business conditions	2,355	1,256	1,099	2,266	1,203	1,063
Could only find part-time work	1,007	–	1,007	989	–	989
Seasonal work	160	111	50	130	88	42
Job started or ended during week	149	149	–	144	144	–
Noneconomic reasons	27,503	8,797	18,707	26,808	8,632	18,177
Child-care problems	785	87	699	772	85	686
Other family or personal obligations	5,659	772	4,887	5,515	757	4,758
Health or medical limitations	759	–	759	734	–	734
In school or training	6,264	95	6,169	6,138	92	6,045
Retired or Social Security limit on earnings	1,896	–	1,896	1,780	–	1,780
Vacation or personal day	3,520	3,520	–	3,471	3,471	–
Holiday, legal or religious	1,162	1,162	–	1,151	1,151	–
Weather-related curtailment	294	294	–	259	259	–
All other reasons	7,164	2,868	4,296	6,990	2,816	4,174
Average hours:						
Economic reasons	23.2	24.1	22.6	23.3	24.2	22.7
Noneconomic reasons	21.5	25.3	19.7	21.6	25.3	19.8

Note: Details on persons at work may not sum to totals shown because of minor editing problems associated with the redesigned survey.

SOURCE: "20. Persons at work 1 to 34 hours in all agricultural and nonagricultural industries by reason for working less than 35 hours and usual full- or part-time status," in *Employment and Earnings,* vol. 49, no. 1, January 2002

---

salary workers and included any worker who believed his or her job was temporary. (See Table 2.9.)

Contingent workers were more likely to be in professional specialties; administrative support; service; and farming, forestry, and fishing; and less likely to be in executive, administrative, and managerial; technical; or sales occupations. (See Table 2.9.) It might seem surprising that contingent workers appear to be overrepresented in professional specialty occupations. However, this category includes teachers, who had an above average rate of contingency.

TABLE 2.8

Multiple jobholders by selected demographic and economic characteristics, 2000–01

(Numbers in thousands)

	Both sexes				Men				Women			
	Number		Rate[1]		Number		Rate[1]		Number		Rate[1]	
Characteristic	2000	2001	2000	2001	2000	2001	2000	2001	2000	2001	2000	2001
Age												
Total, 16 years and over[2]	7,556	7,319	5.6	5.4	3,968	3,808	5.5	5.3	3,588	3,511	5.7	5.6
16 to 19 years	346	318	4.8	4.6	145	130	3.9	3.7	201	188	5.6	5.5
20 years and over	7,210	7,000	5.6	5.5	3,822	3,677	5.6	5.4	3,388	3,323	5.7	5.6
20 to 24 years	752	756	5.6	5.7	337	345	4.8	5.0	415	411	6.6	6.4
25 years and over	6,458	6,244	5.6	5.4	3,485	3,333	5.7	5.4	2,972	2,912	5.6	5.5
25 to 54 years	5,614	5,412	5.8	5.6	3,011	2,868	5.8	5.6	2,604	2,544	5.8	5.7
55 years and over	843	833	4.8	4.5	474	465	4.9	4.6	369	368	4.6	4.4
55 to 64 years	695	686	5.1	4.9	379	372	5.1	4.9	317	314	5.1	4.8
65 years and over	148	146	3.6	3.5	95	92	4.1	3.8	52	54	3.1	3.0
Race and Hispanic origin												
White	6,462	6,281	5.7	5.5	3,433	3,275	5.6	5.3	3,029	3,006	5.8	5.8
Black	818	759	5.3	5.0	396	390	5.5	5.5	422	369	5.2	4.5
Hispanic origin	490	504	3.4	3.4	298	290	3.5	3.4	192	214	3.2	3.5
Marital status												
Married, spouse present	4,156	4,028	5.4	5.2	2,499	2,380	5.8	5.5	1,656	1,648	4.9	4.9
Widowed, divorced, or separated	1,299	1,297	6.1	6.0	469	472	5.3	5.4	830	824	6.6	6.4
Single (never married)	2,101	1,994	5.7	5.4	1,000	956	5.0	4.8	1,102	1,038	6.6	6.3
Full- or part-time status												
Primary job full time, secondary job part time	4,173	3,992	–	–	2,409	2,311	–	–	1,764	1,681	–	–
Primary and secondary jobs both part time	1,595	1,581	–	–	518	507	–	–	1,077	1,073	–	–
Primary and secondary jobs both full time	317	280	–	–	210	181	–	–	106	100	–	–
Hours vary on primary or secondary job	1,429	1,425	–	–	811	787	–	–	618	639	–	–

[1] Multiple jobholders as a percent of all employed persons in specified group.

[2] Includes a small number of persons who work part time on their primary job and full time on their secondary jobs(s), not shown separately.

Note: Detail for the above race and Hispanic-origin groups will not sum to totals because data for the "other races" group are not presented and Hispanics are included in both the white and black population groups.

SOURCE: "36. Multiple jobholders by selected demographic and economic characteristics," in *Employment and Earnings*, vol. 49, no. 1, January 2002

Colleges and universities use many adjunct or temporary teachers with short-term contracts. College and university instructors have, according to a 2001 BLS report, the highest contingency rate, at 29 percent, of all workers in the professional specialty category. Other professionals with high rates of contingency are physicians (12.3 percent), biological and life scientists (11.8 percent), and photographers (9.1 percent). Those with the highest rates of contingency in the administrative support category include library clerks (24.1 percent), interviewers (19.2 percent), general office clerks (14 percent), and receptionists (8.9 percent).

CONTINGENT WORKER CHARACTERISTICS. Black and Hispanic laborers were more likely to be contingent workers, whereas, whites were more likely to be noncontingent workers. Those between the ages of 20 and 24 years were more than twice as likely to be contingent workers as noncontingent workers. Contingent workers were also more likely to be enrolled in school but not have a high school diploma than noncontingent workers. (See Table 2.10.)

Alternative Work Arrangements

Employees in alternative work arrangements are individuals whose place, time, and quantity of work are potentially unpredictable or individuals whose employment is arranged through an employment intermediary. By 1999 these included workers such as independent contractors (6.3 percent of total employed), on-call workers (1.5 percent), workers paid by temporary help firms (0.9 percent), and workers whose services are provided through contract firms (0.6 percent). (See Table 2.11.)

Some of the alternative arrangements have been in existence for decades; however, there is a lack of data analyzing the number of workers in these arrangements. The ranks of independent contractors include construction workers and farmhands whose working situations did not change much in the twentieth century. Similarly, on-call workers such as substitute teachers, registered nurses, and performance artists did not see much change in the manner of obtaining work. However, temporary help agencies can only trace their widespread existence in the United States to shortly after World War II, and there is evidence that providing employees to fulfill the administrative or business needs of other companies is a spreading phenomenon.

By 1999 the BLS found that approximately 12.2 million persons, or 9.3 percent of the workforce, fell into at

TABLE 2.9

Contingency rates by occupation and industry, February 1995–99

[In percent]

Occupation and industry	Contingency rates[1]								
	Estimate 1			Estimate 2			Estimate 3		
	1995	1997	1999	1995	1997	1999	1995	1997	1999
Occupation									
Total, 16 years and older	2.2	1.9	1.9	2.8	2.4	2.3	4.9	4.4	4.3
Managerial and professional specialty	1.7	1.4	1.5	2.1	1.7	1.8	4.8	4.2	4.4
Executive, administrative, and managerial	.8	.7	.5	1.1	1.0	.8	2.7	2.2	2.0
Professional specialty	2.6	2.0	2.4	3.1	2.4	2.7	6.8	6.0	6.7
Technical, sales, and administrative support	2.1	2.1	2.1	2.5	2.6	2.6	4.4	4.3	4.3
Technicians and related support	1.3	1.8	2.0	1.9	2.7	2.5	4.2	4.7	4.4
Sales occupations	1.2	1.1	1.2	1.6	1.5	1.7	2.6	2.1	2.4
Administrative support, including clerical	3.1	3.0	2.9	3.4	3.5	3.3	5.8	6.0	5.8
Service occupations	3.0	2.3	2.3	4.1	3.2	3.1	5.8	5.0	4.7
Precision, production, craft, and repair	2.3	1.8	1.4	2.9	2.3	1.8	4.6	4.1	3.3
Operators, fabricators, and laborers	2.7	2.2	2.0	3.1	3.0	2.4	5.4	4.4	4.0
Farming, forestry, and fishing	2.2	2.0	2.9	3.2	3.0	3.3	5.6	5.9	7.3
Industry									
Total, 16 years and older	2.2	1.9	1.9	2.8	2.4	2.3	4.9	4.4	4.3
Agriculture	2.4	1.6	2.6	3.3	2.6	3.2	5.0	5.2	6.1
Mining	1.0	1.1	.7	1.0	1.8	.7	2.6	4.0	2.6
Construction	4.5	3.7	2.3	5.7	4.7	2.9	8.4	7.2	5.2
Manufacturing	1.3	.8	.8	1.6	1.1	1.0	3.1	2.1	2.2
Durable goods	1.3	.7	.9	1.6	1.0	1.1	3.4	2.0	2.4
Nondurable goods	1.3	1.0	.6	1.5	1.1	.9	2.8	2.3	2.0
Transportation	1.1	.7	.6	1.1	1.4	1.0	2.3	2.7	1.7
Communications and public utilities	1.4	.6	1.6	1.6	1.0	1.6	4.0	2.3	2.7
Wholesale trade	.7	.8	1.1	1.0	1.3	1.5	2.3	2.1	2.8
Retail trade	1.6	1.5	1.6	2.0	1.7	1.8	3.0	2.6	2.7
Finance, insurance, and real estate	.7	1.1	.6	.8	1.3	1.0	2.0	2.1	1.9
Services	3.4	2.8	2.9	4.3	3.7	3.6	7.5	6.7	6.9
Private household	8.2	6.1	8.8	11.9	9.8	11.8	17.9	15.7	16.8
Business, auto, and repair services	5.3	3.8	3.2	7.3	5.8	4.7	9.6	8.0	7.5
Personal services	3.6	2.5	3.6	3.9	3.3	4.3	5.6	5.7	6.2
Entertainment and recreation services	4.3	3.6	3.9	5.3	4.0	4.3	8.2	6.8	5.7
Professional services	2.7	2.4	2.6	3.3	3.0	3.1	6.7	6.3	6.6
Hospitals	.8	1.1	1.0	.8	1.2	1.0	2.2	3.8	3.7
Health services, excluding hospitals	1.2	1.0	.7	1.5	1.3	.9	2.7	2.4	1.7
Educational services	5.3	4.6	5.0	5.5	4.8	5.1	12.3	11.4	11.6
Social services	2.3	1.6	2.1	5.6	4.5	5.2	7.8	6.2	7.3
Other professional services	1.1	1.7	1.5	2.1	2.4	2.0	4.2	3.6	4.1
Public administration	1.2	1.2	1.2	1.2	1.2	1.4	3.6	4.2	3.1

[1]Contingency rates are calculated by dividing the number of contingent workers in a specified worker group by total employment for the same worker group. Estimate 1 above is calculated using the narrowest definition of contingent work; estimate 3 uses the broadest definition.

SOURCE: Steven Hipple, "Table 3. Contingency rates by occupation and industry, February 1995–99," in "Contingent work in the late 1990s," *Monthly Labor Review*, vol. 124, no. 3, March 2001

least 1 of 4 categories. The largest category was independent contractors, with 8.3 million, followed by on-call workers (almost 2 million), temporary help agency workers (1.2 million), and contract company employees (769,000). (See Table 2.12 and Table 2.13 for selected characteristics of workers in alternative work arrangements.)

TEMPORARY WORKFORCE. In its 1997 survey, the National Association of Temporary and Staffing Services (NATSS) found that many of those who enter the workforce for the first time see temporary work as an "entry level transitional form of employment." One-fifth (21 percent) of those who became temporary employees had been students prior to their employment.

The survey asked the respondents why they became temporary workers. Three-quarters (74 percent) saw working as a temporary employee as "a way to get full-time work," and 73 percent wanted additional income. Two-thirds (64 percent) wanted to improve skills and have flexible work time. Only one-fifth (19 percent) worked at temporary jobs because they could not work full-time. (See Table 2.14.)

NATSS projects an increase in hiring temporary workers in industrial, construction, technical, and professional worker categories as businesses reduce staff. According to the U.S. Census Bureau (*Service Annual Survey: 1997,* Washington, DC, 1999), in 1993 office

TABLE 2.10

Contingent and noncontingent workers by selected characteristics, February 1995–99

[Percent distribution]

| | Contingent workers[1] | | | | | | | | | Noncontingent workers[2] | | |
| | Estimate 1 | | | Estimate 2 | | | Estimate 3 | | | | | |
Characteristic	1995	1997	1999	1995	1997	1999	1995	1997	1999	1995	1997	1999
Age and sex												
Total, 16 years and older (thousands)	2,739	2,385	2,444	3,422	3,096	3,038	6,034	5,574	5,641	117,174	121,168	125,853
Percent	100.0	100.0	100.0	100.0	100.0	100.0	100.0	100.0	100.0	100.0	100.0	100.0
16 to 19 years	16.6	19.2	20.9	15.2	16.0	17.8	10.7	12.4	13.2	4.3	4.4	4.7
20 to 24 years	25.0	23.9	23.5	22.2	21.0	22.1	19.8	17.9	19.8	9.6	9.0	9.0
25 to 34 years	26.0	23.7	23.1	27.5	24.4	24.7	26.3	24.8	24.4	26.1	25.0	23.5
35 to 44 years	18.5	17.5	15.6	19.8	20.6	17.5	21.0	20.9	18.8	28.0	28.2	28.1
45 to 54 years	8.2	8.3	11.0	9.5	10.8	11.8	12.6	13.6	13.2	19.8	21.0	21.8
55 to 64 years	3.8	5.3	3.9	3.7	5.4	3.9	5.9	7.3	6.4	9.4	9.6	10.1
65 years and older	1.8	2.1	1.9	2.1	1.9	2.1	3.7	3.1	4.1	2.8	2.9	2.8
Men	49.3	49.5	46.9	49.4	48.4	46.6	49.6	49.3	48.7	54.0	53.8	53.5
Women	50.7	50.5	53.1	50.6	51.6	53.4	50.4	50.7	51.3	46.0	46.2	46.5
Race and Hispanic origin												
White	80.0	79.5	80.9	80.1	80.6	80.5	80.9	81.9	80.2	85.6	85.3	84.5
Black	13.9	13.3	11.8	13.6	13.0	12.7	13.3	11.1	12.2	10.5	10.6	11.1
Hispanic origin	13.6	12.2	13.8	12.9	12.8	13.6	11.3	12.4	13.2	8.3	9.4	10.0
Country of birth and U.S. citizenship status												
U.S. born	87.5	87.6	85.2	87.3	87.1	85.3	86.8	85.3	84.0	91.0	89.4	89.0
Foreign born	12.5	12.4	14.8	12.7	13.0	14.7	13.2	14.7	16.0	9.0	10.6	11.0
U.S. citizen	1.6	3.2	3.0	1.7	3.7	3.1	2.2	3.9	3.9	3.2	4.2	4.4
Not a U.S. citizen	10.9	9.1	11.8	11.0	9.2	11.7	11.0	10.7	12.1	5.8	6.4	6.6
Full- or part-time status												
Full-time workers	52.9	53.5	48.4	53.6	54.8	52.0	57.1	57.5	55.9	81.8	82.2	83.0
Part-time workers	47.1	46.6	51.6	46.4	45.2	48.0	42.9	42.5	44.1	18.2	17.8	17.0
School enrollment												
Total, 16 to 24 years (thousands)	1,142	1,029	1,086	1,279	1,143	1,212	1,841	1,690	1,863	16,215	16,299	17,261
Percent	100.0	100.0	100.0	100.0	100.0	100.0	100.0	100.0	100.0	100.0	100.0	100.0
Enrolled	55.3	61.4	63.8	53.7	57.7	62.1	58.1	63.7	65.9	38.4	40.0	41.4
Not enrolled	44.7	38.6	36.2	46.3	42.3	37.9	41.9	36.3	34.1	61.6	60.0	58.6
Educational attainment												
Total, 25 to 64 years (thousands)	1,547	1,308	1,311	2,070	1,893	1,762	3,968	3,710	3,546	97,633	101,397	105,043
Percent	100.0	100.0	100.0	100.0	100.0	100.0	100.0	100.0	100.0	100.0	100.0	100.0
Less than a high school diploma	14.0	10.0	12.7	13.6	11.0	12.6	12.0	10.4	11.9	9.6	9.6	9.1
High school graduates, no college	27.9	27.9	27.8	27.5	28.5	28.5	27.3	26.8	25.8	32.4	32.8	31.4
Some college, no degree	22.8	21.9	19.1	23.3	20.2	18.5	19.6	18.8	17.0	19.9	18.9	19.3
Associate degree	8.4	10.7	7.7	8.0	10.1	8.0	7.9	8.2	6.9	9.1	9.1	9.2
College graduates	27.0	29.4	32.6	27.7	30.1	32.4	33.2	35.8	38.5	28.9	29.5	31.0
Advanced degree	9.4	10.5	11.6	10.0	9.3	11.4	14.9	14.7	16.0	9.9	10.0	10.3

[1]Contingent workers are defined as individuals who do not perceive themselves as having an explicit or implicit contract with their employers for ongoing employment. Estimate 1 is calculated using the narrowest definition of contingent work; estimate 3 uses the broadest definition.
[2]Noncontingent workers are those who do not meet the criteria for any of the three definitions of contingent work.

Note: Detail for the above race and Hispanic-origin groups will not sum to totals because data for the "other races" group are not presented and Hispanics are included in both the white and black population groups. Detail for other characteristics may not sum to totals due to rounding.

SOURCE: Steven Hipple, "Table 1. Contingent and noncontingent workers by selected characteristics, February 1995–99," in "Contingent work in the late 1990s," *Monthly Labor Review*, vol. 124, no. 3, March 2001

support temporary workers accounted for 37 percent ($10.7 billion) of total receipts for temporary help agencies. By 1997 office support receipts were 35 percent ($18.0 billion) of the total revenue, the biggest proportion of the receipts to the temporary agencies. Industrial and construction temporary employees brought in 19 percent ($8.0 billion) of the total revenue in 1993; by 1997 they were 24 percent ($12.3 billion). The temporary employment of technical and professional workers increased as well. Total revenues more than doubled from $6.7 billion in 1993 to $15.5 billion in 1997.

The hiring of temporary workers has steadily increased in the overall job market. Temporary jobs accounted for about 0.5 percent of all jobs in 1983. That rose to nearly 3 percent of jobs in 1999, according to the BLS data. As of mid-2002 the effects of the terrorist attacks on the United States on September 11, 2001 on the temporary workforce were not yet known.

AT-HOME WORK

Between 1960 and 1980 the number of Americans working at home steadily declined, largely reflecting a drop in the number of family farmers who gave up farming. In addition, many professionals, such as doctors and lawyers, left their home offices and joined group practices or larger firms in office buildings. This trend was reversed in the 1990 census, which showed a dramatic increase in the number of people who worked at home, up 56 percent from 1980 to 3.4 million people in 1990. (See Figure 2.4.)

In 1990 more than half the workers who worked in their homes (54 percent) were self-employed. Only 36 percent of those who worked at home were employed by private sector companies. (See Figure 2.5.) According to the Census Bureau, the proportion of women who worked at home (52 percent) was greater than those who worked away from home (45 percent). Those who worked at home were also older on average than those who did not. Forty-four percent of the at-home workers were 45 years old or older, compared with only 29 percent over this age working away from home.

Almost half of the workers whose workplace was home (46 percent) worked in the service industries, which include businesses and repair services, personal services, entertainment and recreation services, and other professional and related services.

Work at Home as Part of Primary Job

In May 2001 the BLS reported that more than 19 million persons did some work at home as part of their primary job. While the number of persons reporting they worked at home is approximately the same as it was in 1991, there was a sharp increase in the number of persons who were paid for working at home. In 2001, 3.4 million wage and salary workers—about 2.6 percent of all wage and salary workers—were paid for the work they did at home. In 1991 only 1.9 million wage and salary workers—1.9 percent of the total—were doing work at home for pay.

More than half (52 percent) of those working at home were wage and salary workers who were not paid expressly for their time. About 17.4 percent, however, were wage and salary workers who were paid for the hours they put in at home. Virtually all the remainder were self-employed workers. (See Table 2.15.)

Of the 3.4 million wage and salary workers doing paid work at home, more than 80 percent were in white-collar occupations. Nearly a million of these workers were in

TABLE 2.11

Workers in alternative arrangements as a percent of total employment, February 1995, 1997, and 1999

Alternative arrangement	February 1995	February 1997	February 1999
Independent contractors Workers identified as independent contractors, independent consultants, or freelance workers, whether they were self-employed or wage and salary workers	6.7	6.7	6.3
On-call workers Workers called to work only as needed, although they can be scheduled to work for several days or weeks in a row	1.7	1.6	1.5
Temporary help agency workers Workers paid by a temporary help agency, whether or not their job actually was temporary	1.0	1.0	.9
Contract company workers Workers employed by a company that provides them or their services to others under contract and who are usually assigned to only one customer and usually work at the customer's worksite	.5	.6	.6

SOURCE: Marisa DiNatale, "Exhibit 1. Workers in alternative arrangements as a percent of total employment, February 1995, 1997, and 1999" in "Characteristics of and preferences for alternative work arrangements,1999," *Monthly Labor Review,* vol. 124, no. 3, March 2001

professional specialty occupations, while 880,000 were executives and managers. A large number of paid home workers were in sales and administrative occupations. Almost half (48 percent) of those doing paid work at home were in the services industry. More than half a million in manufacturing were paid for work at home. (See Table 2.16.)

The BLS went on to report that about 11.1 million workers were simply "taking work home from the office" (wage and salary workers who were not being officially compensated for the work they did at home). As with those who were paid, persons not paid for the work they did at home were overwhelmingly employed in white-collar occupations. Teachers were especially likely to do unpaid work at home: 2.8 million teachers reported doing so in 1997.

From an industry perspective, half (51.5 percent) of the unpaid home laborers worked in services (6.1 million), followed by manufacturing (1.5 million). About 6.5 million of self-employed persons did some work at home in May 1997, more than half of all the self-employed who were at work during the survey reference week. More than 4.1 million of the self-employed indicated that they were working in home-based businesses.

Telecommuting

As of 2002 the BLS has figures for workers who are paid for work done at home, but does not currently track numbers specifically for telecommuting workers. However, there is a trend in some work sectors for employees to work

TABLE 2.12

Incidence of alternative and traditional work arrangements by selected characteristics, February 1999

[Percent distribution]

| Characteristic | Total employed (thousands) | Workers with alternative arrangements | | | | Workers with traditional arrangements[1] |
		Independent contractors	On-call workers	Temporary help agency workers	Contract company workers	
Age and sex						
Total, 16 years and older[2]	131,494	6.3	1.5	.9	.6	90.6
16 to 19	6,662	1.1	2.7	1.0	.6	94.0
20 to 24	12,462	2.0	1.6	2.0	.7	93.4
25 to 34	30,968	4.8	1.5	1.1	.8	91.7
35 to 44	36,415	6.8	1.4	.6	.6	90.5
45 to 54	28,144	7.7	1.1	.6	.5	90.0
55 to 64	13,062	9.3	1.6	.6	.4	88.1
65 and older	3,781	14.8	4.4	.9	.4	79.3
Men, 16 years and older	70,040	7.8	1.4	.7	.8	89.2
16 to 19	3,339	1.4	2.8	1.1	.9	93.3
20 to 24	6,489	2.4	1.8	1.8	1.1	92.5
25 to 34	16,617	5.4	1.2	.9	1.0	91.3
35 to 44	19,603	8.7	1.2	.4	.8	88.9
45 to 54	14,684	9.6	1.1	.5	.5	88.3
55 to 64	7,186	11.3	1.4	.4	.5	86.3
65 and older	2,122	20.1	4.0	.8	.6	74.2
Women, 16 years and older	61,454	4.5	1.7	1.1	.4	92.2
16 to 19	3,323	.9	2.6	.9	.2	94.8
20 to 24	5,973	1.6	1.4	2.2	.3	94.3
25 to 34	14,351	4.0	1.9	1.4	.5	92.2
35 to 44	16,812	4.7	1.6	.9	.4	92.4
45 to 54	13,459	5.7	1.1	.8	.4	91.9
55 to 64	5,876	6.8	1.8	.9	.2	90.2
65 and older	1,659	8.0	5.0	.9	.1	86.0
Race and Hispanic origin[3]						
White	110,887	6.7	1.5	.8	.5	90.2
Black	14,620	3.3	1.8	1.7	.7	92.6
Hispanic origin	13,356	3.8	1.8	1.2	.3	92.5
Full- or part-time status						
Full-time workers	107,630	5.8	.9	.9	.6	91.8
Part-time workers	23,864	8.6	4.3	1.1	.4	85.2
Educational attainment (aged 25 to 64)						
Less than a high school diploma	10,027	5.5	2.0	1.2	.4	90.6
High school graduates, no college	33,867	6.4	1.3	.8	.4	90.9
Less than a bachelor's degree	20,842	7.1	1.4	1.0	.6	89.9
College graduates	33,930	7.4	1.2	.5	.7	90.1

[1] Workers with traditional arrangements are those who do not fall into any of the "alternative arrangements" categories.
[2] Detail may not sum to total employed because a small number of workers are both "on call" and "provided by contract firms," and total employed includes day laborers, an alternative arrangement not shown separately.
[3] Detail for the above race and Hispanic-origin groups will not sum to totals because data for "other races" group are not presented and Hispanics are included in both the white and black population groups.

SOURCE: Marisa DiNatale, "Table 1. Incidence of alternative and traditional work arrangements by selected characteristics, February 1999" in "Characteristics of and preferences for alternative work arrangements, 1999," *Monthly Labor Review,* vol. 124, no. 3, March 2001

one or more days per month at home, during regular work hours, communicating with the office through the Internet, fax, and telephone. The fall 2000 *Occupational Outlook Quarterly,* published by the BLS, notes certain types of jobs that work well for telecommuting. Service industries have by far the most telecommuters, particularly in the professional specialties. Executive and managerial, sales, and clerical support positions also have telecommuters.

FLEXIBLE SCHEDULES

In May 2001 about 29 percent of full-time wage and salary workers had flexible work schedules that allowed them to vary the time they began or ended work. The increase in flexible work schedules was widespread across demographic groups, occupations, and industries. Whites (30.0 percent) were more likely to work flexible schedules than blacks (21.2 percent) or Hispanics (19.8 percent). (See Table 2.17.) Parents (29.8 percent) were somewhat more likely than workers with no children under 18 (28.2 percent) to work a flexible schedule.

In 2001 about 45.5 percent of executives, administrators, and managers and 40.7 percent of sales workers were able to vary their work hours. However, fewer than one-quarter of

TABLE 2.13

Employed persons with alternative and traditional work arrangements by age and sex, race and Hispanic origin, and educational attainment, February 1999

[Percent distribution]

| | | Workers with alternative arrangements | | | Workers with traditional arrangements[1] |
Characteristic	Independent contractors	On-call workers	Temporary help agency workers	Contract company workers	
Age and sex[2]					
Total, 16 years and older (thousands)	8,247	2,032	1,188	769	119,109
Percent	100.0	100.0	100.0	100.0	100.0
16 to 19	.9	8.8	5.8	4.8	5.3
20 to 24	3.1	9.9	20.9	11.3	9.8
25 to 34	17.9	23.1	29.3	30.5	23.9
35 to 44	30.2	24.9	19.4	28.1	27.7
45 to 54	26.4	14.9	15.4	17.2	21.3
55 to 64	14.7	10.1	6.5	6.1	9.7
65 and older	6.8	8.2	2.8	1.9	2.5
Men, 16 years and older	66.2	48.8	42.2	70.5	52.4
16 to 19	0.6	4.6	3.2	3.8	2.6
20 to 24	1.9	5.9	9.6	9.2	5.0
25 to 34	10.9	10.0	12.2	21.8	12.7
35 to 44	20.7	11.6	7.0	20.1	14.6
45 to 54	17.0	7.6	6.3	9.4	10.9
55 to 64	9.9	5.0	2.2	4.6	5.2
65 and older	5.2	4.2	1.6	1.6	1.3
Women, 16 years and older	33.8	51.2	57.8	29.5	47.6
16 to 19	0.4	4.2	2.5	1.0	2.6
20 to 24	1.1	4.0	11.3	2.0	4.7
25 to 34	7.0	13.1	17.1	8.8	11.1
35 to 44	9.5	13.4	12.4	8.0	13.0
45 to 54	9.4	7.3	9.0	7.8	10.4
55 to 64	4.8	5.1	4.2	1.6	4.5
65 years and older	1.6	4.1	1.3	0.3	1.2
Race and Hispanic origin[3]					
White	90.6	84.2	74.3	79.2	84.0
Black	5.8	12.7	21.2	12.6	11.4
Hispanic origin	6.1	11.6	13.6	6.0	10.4
Educational attainment[2]					
Total, 25 to 64 years					
Thousands	7,359	1,485	838	631	98,207
Percent	100.0	100.0	100.0	100.0	100.0
Less than a high school diploma	7.5	13.4	14.6	6.4	9.2
High school graduates, no college	29.7	29.6	30.5	22.7	31.4
Less than a bachelor's degree	28.5	29.1	33.7	31.9	28.3
College graduates	34.3	27.9	21.2	38.9	31.1
Men, 25 to 64 years					
Thousands	4,826	695	330	430	51,769
Percent	100.0	100.0	100.0	100.0	100.0
Less than a high school diploma	9.5	16.7	19.7	8.4	10.4
High school graduates, no college	30.7	38.1	33.6	23.7	30.8
Less than a bachelor's degree	26.8	25.0	25.2	31.6	26.8
College graduates	33.0	20.3	21.5	36.0	32.0
Women, 25 to 64 years					
Thousands	2,533	790	508	201	46,439
Percent	100.0	100.0	100.0	100.0	100.0
Less than a high school diploma	3.8	10.5	11.2	2.0	7.9
High school graduates, no college	27.6	22.2	28.3	20.9	32.0
Less than a bachelor's degree.	31.7	32.8	39.4	31.8	29.9
College graduates	36.9	34.7	20.9	45.3	30.1

[1]Workers with traditional arrangements are those who do not fall into any of the "alternative arrangements" categories.
[2]Detail for other characteristics may not sum to totals because of rounding.
[3]Detail for race and Hispanic-origin groups will not sum to totals because data for the "other races" group are not presented and Hispanics are included in both the white and black population groups.

SOURCE: Marisa DiNatale, "Table 3. Employed persons with alternative and traditional work arrangements by age and sex, race and Hispanic origin, and educational attainment, February 1999," in "Characteristics of and preferences for alternative work arrangements, 1999," *Monthly Labor Review,* vol. 124, no. 3, March 2001

TABLE 2.14

How important were each of the following factors in your decision to become a temporary employee?

(Percentage represents those answering very and somewhat important)

	1994	1997
A way to get full time work	76 %	74 %
Additional income	78	73
Improve skills	67	64
Flexible work time	63	64
Between full time jobs	59	55
Less stress	45	46
Need time for family	44	43
New to area	33	30
Can't work full-time	21	19

SOURCE: Bruce Steinberg, "Profile of the Temporary Work Force," in *Contemporary Times,* vol. 17, issue 63, 1998

those employed in administrative support roles or as service workers had such flexibility. Operators, fabricators, and laborers, as well as workers in precision production, craft, and repair, were also less likely to have flexible work schedules. (See Table 2.18.)

Among private-sector employees, the proportion of workers with flexible schedules was much higher in service-producing industries (33.3 percent) than in goods-producing industries (23.1 percent). In the public sector, flexible schedules were more common among federal government employees (34.4 percent) than workers in state (29.7 percent) or local (14 percent) government, which includes public elementary and secondary schools. (See Table 2.18.)

SHIFT SCHEDULES

In May 2001 among full-time wage and salary workers, 85.5 percent were on regular daytime schedules; alternative schedules worked included evening shifts (4.8 percent), employer-arranged irregular schedules (2.8 percent), night shifts (3.3 percent), and rotating shifts (2.3 percent). Men (16.4 percent) were more likely than women (12.1 percent) to work an alternative shift.

Shift work was most common among workers in service-oriented occupations, such as protective service (49 percent—which includes police, firefighters, and guards) and food service (40.4 percent), and among those employed as operators, fabricators, and laborers (25.4 percent). It was lowest for managers and professionals (6.7 percent) and those in administrative support occupations (8.4 percent).

In private sector industries, the percent of workers on alternative shifts was highest in eating and drinking establishments (46.2 percent) and lowest in construction (2.5 percent). Although shift work was generally less common in the public sector, nearly half the local government workers employed in "justice, public order, and safety," the category that includes police and fire departments, were shift workers.

FIGURE 2.4

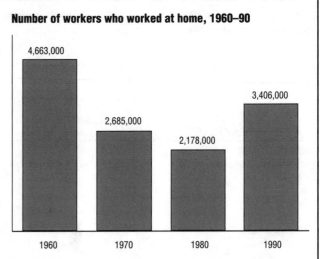

Number of workers who worked at home, 1960–90

SOURCE: "Increase in At-Home Workers Reverse Earlier Trend," in *Census Brief,* U.S. Department of Commerce, U.S. Census Bureau, Washington, DC, 1998

FIGURE 2.5

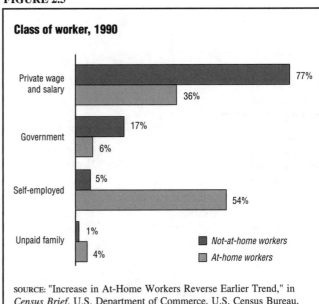

Class of worker, 1990

SOURCE: "Increase in At-Home Workers Reverse Earlier Trend," in *Census Brief,* U.S. Department of Commerce, U.S. Census Bureau, Washington, DC, 1998

WORKER DISPLACEMENT

Displaced workers are persons 20 years and older who lost or left jobs because their plant or company closed or moved, there was insufficient work for them to do, or their position or shift was abolished. A total of 3.3 million workers were displaced between January 1997 and December 1999 from jobs they had held for at least three years.

Of the nearly 3.3 million displaced workers, 73.5 percent were reemployed and 10.4 percent were unemployed when surveyed in February 2000. (See Table 2.19.) The February 2000 survey found the reemployment rate highest for workers 20 to 24, with 87.7 percent working again.

TABLE 2.15

Job-related work at home on primary job by sex, occupation, industry, race, Hispanic origin, class of worker, and pay status, May 2001

(Numbers in thousands)

		Persons who usually worked at home[2]					
					Percent distribution by class of worker[3]		
					Wage and salary		
Characteristic	Total employed[1]	Total	Percent of total employed	Total	Paid work at home	Unpaid work at home	Self-employed[4]
Total, 16 years and over	131,803	19,759	15.0	100.0	17.4	52.0	29.7
Men	69,659	10,291	14.8	100.0	16.0	50.5	32.6
Women	62,144	9,468	15.2	100.0	18.9	53.7	26.5
Occupation							
Managerial and professional specialty	42,442	12,628	29.8	100.0	14.2	62.8	22.4
Executive, administrative, and managerial	20,484	5,262	25.7	100.0	16.7	52.5	30.0
Professional specialty	21,958	7,366	33.5	100.0	12.5	70.1	17.0
Technical, sales, and administrative support	38,203	4,669	12.2	100.0	24.7	40.2	33.9
Technicians and related support	4,392	305	6.9	100.0	36.0	48.4	14.3
Sales occupations	15,636	3,133	20.0	100.0	20.3	40.3	38.9
Administrative support, including clerical	18,174	1,231	6.8	100.0	33.4	37.8	25.8
Service occupations	18,189	972	5.3	100.0	24.1	18.4	55.1
Precision production, craft, and repair	14,737	1,050	7.1	100.0	15.7	19.4	64.4
Operators, fabricators, and laborers	17,553	381	2.2	100.0	19.4	24.3	49.3
Farming, forestry, and fishing	678	59	8.7	100.0	(5)	(5)	(5)
Industry							
Mining	590	65	11.1	100.0	(5)	(5)	(5)
Construction	9,153	1,134	12.4	100.0	11.6	20.5	65.2
Manufacturing	19,466	1,806	9.3	100.0	28.7	54.9	15.7
Transportation and public utilities	10,072	898	8.9	100.0	22.8	49.4	26.0
Wholesale trade	5,207	1,009	19.4	100.0	24.4	47.9	25.6
Retail trade	21,963	1,529	7.0	100.0	12.8	36.4	49.8
Finance, insurance, and real estate	8,693	1,810	20.8	100.0	18.8	48.2	33.0
Services	50,374	10,926	21.7	100.0	14.8	57.2	27.1
Public administration	6,285	581	9.2	100.0	29.6	69.8	-
Race and Hispanic origin							
White	110,109	17,947	16.3	100.0	17.5	51.6	30.0
Black	15,116	1,152	7.6	100.0	14.9	57.9	26.0
Hispanic origin	13,946	937	6.7	100.0	20.4	49.2	28.4

[1]Includes persons who did not provide information on work at home.
[2]Persons who usually work at home are defined as those who work at home at least once per week as part of their primary job.
[3]Unpaid family workers and wage and salary workers who did not report pay status are included in total but not shown separately.
[4]Includes both the incorporated and unincorporated self-employed.
[5]Data not shown where the base is less than 75,000.

Note: Data refer to employed persons in nonagricultural industries. Detail for the above race and Hispanic-origin groups will not sum to totals because data for the "other races" group are not presented and Hispanics are included in both the white and black population groups. Dash represents zero.

SOURCE: "Table 1. Job-related work at home on primary job by sex, occupation, industry, race, Hispanic origin, class of worker, pay status, May 2001," *Work At Home,* U.S. Department of Labor, Bureau of Labor Statistics, Washington, DC, March 2002 [Online] http://www.bls.gov/news.release/homey.t01.htm [accessed May 24, 2002]

The reemployment rates for older workers age 55 to 64 and 65 and older were 56 percent and 26.3 percent, respectively. There were 78.9 percent of men working in a new job, compared with 67.3 percent of women. Among those not reemployed at the time of the survey, women were slightly more likely (11.3 percent) than men (9.6 percent) to be unemployed. The proportion of displaced women who left the labor force (21.4 percent) was nearly twice that of men (11.5 percent). (See Table 2.19.)

Industry and Occupation

Manufacturing continued to account for the largest proportion of displacements in 2000 (31 percent). (See Table 2.20.) Approximately 61.7 percent occurred among workers in the durable goods manufacturing industries. These industries tend to be among those most affected by cyclical changes in economic conditions. About 72.9 percent of workers displaced from manufacturing were reemployed at the time of the survey. This compared with 74.7 percent of the workers displaced from the services industries and 77.9 percent of the workers displaced from construction. (See Table 2.20.)

Managerial and professional specialty employees (30 percent) and technical, sales, and administrative support (29 percent) accounted for 59 percent of the displaced workers by occupation. More than three-fourths (78.5 percent) of the

TABLE 2.16

Hours of paid job-related work at home on primary job among wage and salary workers by selected characteristics, May 2001

(Numbers in thousands)

| Characteristic | Paid work at home[1] | Total | Percent distribution by hours worked home[2] | | 8 hours or more | | Mean weekly hours usually worked at home |
			Hours vary	Less than 8 hours	Total	35 hours or more	
Total, 16 years and over	3,436	100.0	27.4	24.5	47.6	15.7	18.0
Men	1,642	100.0	30.9	23.3	45.1	14.8	17.8
Women	1,794	100.0	24.2	25.7	49.9	16.5	18.1
Occupation							
Managerial and professional specialty	1,798	100.0	28.0	24.1	47.4	13.9	17.0
Executive, administrative, and managerial	880	100.0	25.8	24.3	49.3	12.9	16.8
Professional specialty	918	100.0	30.1	23.9	45.6	14.9	17.2
Technical, sales, and administrative support	1,155	100.0	27.3	22.1	50.3	16.7	19.1
Technicians and related support	110	100.0	40.2	24.6	35.3	21.2	21.3
Sales occupations	635	100.0	27.8	18.9	53.0	13.0	18.5
Administrative support, including clerical	411	100.0	23.3	26.5	50.3	21.0	19.5
Service occupations	234	100.0	25.6	19.6	54.7	33.1	26.9
Precision production, craft, and repair	165	100.0	29.1	47.2	22.1	2.7	7.8
Operators, fabricators, and laborers	74	100.0	(3)	(3)	(3)	(3)	(3)
Farming, forestry, and fishing	10	100.0	(3)	(3)	(3)	(3)	
Industry							
Mining	9	100.0	(3)	(3)	(3)	(3)	(3)
Construction	131	100.0	31.8	36.5	31.7	5.1	13.2
Manufacturing	518	100.0	27.0	21.5	51.2	12.5	16.7
Transportation and public utilities	205	100.0	14.1	29.7	54.8	25.3	19.1
Wholesale trade	247	100.0	28.1	15.0	56.0	12.9	17.8
Retail trade	196	100.0	23.7	32.5	43.9	10.3	14.2
Finance, insurance, and real estate.	340	100.0	30.7	24.0	45.3	9.5	15.1
Services	1,618	100.0	28.0	24.3	47.5	19.0	19.9
Public administration	172	100.0	33.7	27.1	37.7	12.8	15.7
Race and Hispanic origin							
White	3,138	100.0	27.2	24.4	48.0	15.0	17.7
Black	172	100.0	29.7	22.1	48.1	28.9	23.2
Hispanic origin	191	100.0	32.3	15.9	51.8	27.6	23.2

[1]Includes persons who worked at home at least once per week but did not report the number of hours usually worked.
[2]Persons who did not report the number of hours worked are included in total but not shown separately.
[3]Data not shown where the base is less than 75,000.

Note: Data refer to employed persons in nonagricultural industries who reported that they usually work at home at least once per week as part of their primary job and exclude the incorporated and unincorporated self-employed. Detail for the above race and Hispanic-origin groups will not sum to totals because data for the "other races" group are not presented and Hispanics are included in both the white and black population groups.

SOURCE: "Table 3. Hours of paid job-related work at home on primary job among wage and salary workers by selected characteristics, May 2001," *Work At Home,* U.S. Department of Labor, Bureau of Labor Statistics, Washington, DC, March 2002 [Online] http://www.bls.gov/news.release/homey.t03.htm [accessed May 24, 2002]

managerial and professional specialty group and 73 percent of the technical, sales, and administrative support force were employed at the time of the survey. However, only 66.4 percent of the machine operators, assemblers, and inspectors were working again. In fact 17.9 percent of this occupation had left the labor force. (See Table 2.21.)

Earnings

Of the 2.2 million reemployed displaced workers who had lost full-time wage and salary jobs from 1997 to 1999, 1.9 million were again working in similar jobs in February 2000. The remainder were holding part-time wage and salary jobs, were self-employed, or working as unpaid workers in family businesses. More than one-half of those reemployed in full-time wage and salary jobs were earning as much or

more than they did prior to their job loss. About one-fourth, however, suffered earnings losses of 20 percent or more.

JOB SECURITY

The Society for Human Resource Management (SHRM; *1996 Job Security and Layoffs Survey,* Alexandria, VA, August 1996), surveyed its members on the issues of layoffs and job security. About 65 percent of the businesses responding reported that their employees felt very secure, secure, or somewhat secure. Smaller firms were more likely to report secure employees than were larger firms.

Firms that had not had layoffs since 1994 were also more likely to report that their employees felt secure (86 percent) than did firms who had laid off workers (47

TABLE 2.17

Flexible schedules and shift work of full-time wage and salary workers by sex, race, and Hispanic origin, May, selected years, 1985–2001

Characteristic	Percent with flexible Schedules				Percent with alternate shifts			
	May 1985	May 1991	May 1997	May 2001	May 1985	May 1991	May 1997	May 2001
Sex								
Total, 16 years and over	12.4	15.0	27.6	28.8	16.0	18.0	16.9	14.5
Men	13.1	15.4	28.6	30.0	17.9	20.4	19.2	16.4
Women	11.3	14.5	26.2	27.4	13.2	14.8	13.7	12.1
Race and Hispanic origin								
White	12.8	15.4	28.6	30.0	15.5	17.2	16.2	13.6
Black	9.1	12.0	20.1	21.2	20.0	23.3	21.0	19.7
Hispanic origin	8.9	10.6	18.2	19.8	15.5	19.2	16.2	14.8

Note: Data are tabulated for all employed persons. Estimates for years prior to 2001 may differ slightly from those previously published, which were tabulated only for persons at work. Data exclude the incorporated and unincorporated self- employed.

SOURCE: "Table A. Flexible schedules and shift work of full–time wage and salary workers by sex, race, and Hispanic origin, May, selected years, 1985–2001," in *Workers on Flexible and Shift Schedules in 2001,* U.S. Department of Labor, Bureau of Labor Statistics,Washington, DC, April 2002 [Online] http://www.bls.gov/news.release/flex.nr0.htm [accessed May 24, 2002]

percent). Companies planning future layoffs reported that 61 percent of their employees felt very insecure, insecure, or somewhat insecure, while only 9 percent of firms who did not plan layoffs reported such insecurity among their workforce. The SHRM concluded that the majority of survey respondents thought their employees felt secure in their jobs. About one-third believed their employees felt insecure and agreed that the employees' views were justified.

Almost half of all the responding companies (49 percent) reported that employees felt more insecure since January 1, 1994; 14 percent, more secure; and 37 percent, no change. Again larger firms reported more feelings of insecurity than did smaller companies.

According to a Gallup Poll, more people surveyed in 1998 (60 percent) felt that they were "not at all likely" to lose their jobs than did in 1996 (51 percent). Twelve percent indicated they were very likely or fairly likely to lose their jobs in 1998, compared to 16 percent in July 1982. (See Figure 2.6.)

However, in February 1997, Alan Greenspan, chairperson of the Federal Reserve (the central bank of the United States), thought that downsizing and job insecurity must have been rising because workers in a booming economy were not pressing for wage increases. He believes that changing technology makes workers feel insecure. Citing a survey taken of 444 large companies by the International Survey Research Corporation in Chicago, Greenspan observed that between 1979 and 1990, no more than 24 percent of respondents felt insecure. In the 1990s the proportion increased, reaching 46 percent in 1995 and 1996. Other economists disagreed. For example, Henry Farber at

Princeton University asserted that there was no direct evidence to indicate that job insecurity was higher.

In a 1999 statement to the Joint Economic Committee of the U.S. Congress, Alan Greenspan reiterated his concerns about the effects of "an impressive proliferation of new technologies" and the pace of change in the economy.

Following the terrorist attacks on New York City and Washington, D.C., on September 11, 2001, the BLS reported significant disruptions to local economies and an increase in layoffs, particularly in the last quarter of that year. (See Table 2.22.) The rate of layoffs tapered off by the first quarter of 2002 to lower than 2001 levels. Beyond the initial effects of layoffs directly related to the tragedies, certain job sectors have continued to suffer. The travel industry, particularly the airlines and hotels, have experienced greatly reduced business, due to a reluctance on the part of many Americans to travel.

A weakening economy in 2001 and the first half of 2002 resulted in numerous mass layoffs (a mass layoff is considered to be a layoff of 50 or more employees). BLS reported more mass layoffs in May 2002 than in any May since 1995, when the data were first gathered. More than 180,000 workers were laid off in May 2002. The accounting scandals involving huge corporations, beginning with Enron in October 2001, and resulting in layoffs, have also shaken the confidence of many in the stability of the American economy and job security.

However, due to the corporate scandals' negative impact on investors' confidence in the stock market and the threatened U.S. economy, lawmakers decided to take

TABLE 2.18

Flexible schedules, full-time wage and salary workers by sex, occupation, and industry, May 2001

(Numbers in thousands)

Occupation and industry	Both sexes Total[1]	With flexible schedules Number	Percent of total	Men Total[1]	With flexible schedules Number	Percent of total	Women Total[1]	With flexible schedules Number	Percent of total
Total, 16 years and over	99,631	28,724	28.8	56,066	16,792	30.0	43,566	11,931	27.4
Occupation									
Managerial and professional specialty	32,960	13,326	40.4	16,785	7,954	47.4	16,175	5,372	33.2
Executive, administrative, and managerial	16,279	7,404	45.5	8,748	4,277	48.9	7,531	3,128	41.5
Professional specialty	16,681	5,922	35.5	8,037	3,678	45.8	8,644	2,244	26.0
Mathematical and computer scientists	1,930	1,134	58.7	1,308	770	58.9	623	364	58.4
Natural scientists	461	241	52.4	289	154	53.4	172	87	50.7
Teachers, college and university	661	395	59.8	386	251	65.1	275	144	52.3
Technical, sales, and administrative support	27,607	8,617	31.2	10,493	3,840	36.6	17,113	4,777	27.9
Technicians and related support	3,757	1,181	31.4	1,863	683	36.7	1,894	498	26.3
Sales occupations	9,852	4,011	40.7	5,424	2,404	44.3	4,428	1,607	36.3
Sales workers, retail and personal services	3,146	901	28.6	1,346	419	31.1	1,800	482	26.8
Administrative support, including clerical	13,997	3,426	24.5	3,206	753	23.5	10,791	2,672	24.8
Service occupations	12,382	2,572	20.8	6,463	1,283	19.9	5,919	1,289	21.8
Private household	377	132	35.0	5	3	(2)	371	129	34.8
Protective service	2,144	343	16.0	1,773	291	16.4	371	52	14.0
Service, except private household and protective	8,207	1,755	21.4	3,324	698	21.0	4,883	1,057	21.6
Food service	3,036	696	22.9	1,517	367	24.2	1,518	330	21.7
Health service	1,829	304	16.6	222	45	20.5	1,608	258	16.1
Cleaning and building service	2,151	326	15.2	1,287	194	15.0	864	133	15.4
Personal service	1,192	429	36.0	299	93	31.1	893	336	37.7
Precision production, craft, and repair	12,061	2,209	18.3	11,000	2,026	18.4	1,061	183	17.3
Mechanics and repairers	4,133	827	20.0	3,937	792	20.1	195	35	17.9
Construction trades	4,333	755	17.4	4,232	726	17.2	101	29	(2)
Other precision production, craft, and repair	3,596	628	17.5	2,830	508	18.0	766	119	15.6
Operators, fabricators, and laborers	14,621	1,999	13.7	11,324	1,689	14.9	3,297	310	9.4
Machine operators, assemblers, and inspectors	6,220	614	9.9	3,994	457	11.4	2,227	157	7.1
Transportation and material moving	4,735	946	20.0	4,380	867	19.8	355	79	22.2
Handlers, equipment cleaners, helpers, and laborers	3,667	439	12.0	2,951	365	12.4	716	74	10.3
Farming, forestry, and fishing	1,653	342	20.7	1,360	291	21.4	293	51	17.5
Industry									
Private sector	83,015	24,987	30.1	48,423	14,927	30.8	34,592	10,061	29.1
Goods-producing industries	26,021	6,014	23.1	19,626	4,585	23.4	6,395	1,429	22.3
Agriculture	1,543	343	22.2	1,194	249	20.8	349	94	26.9
Mining	539	121	22.5	470	101	21.5	69	20	(2)
Construction	6,133	1,386	22.6	5,590	1,205	21.6	543	181	33.3
Manufacturing	17,805	4,163	23.4	12,372	3,030	24.5	5,433	1,133	20.9
Durable goods	11,171	2,743	24.6	8,179	2,078	25.4	2,992	666	22.3
Nondurable goods	6,635	1,420	21.4	4,193	953	22.7	2,441	468	19.2
Service-producing industries	56,995	18,974	33.3	28,797	10,342	35.9	28,197	8,632	30.6
Transportation and public utilities	6,961	2,068	29.7	5,069	1,444	28.5	1,892	624	33.0
Wholesale trade	4,319	1,528	35.4	3,123	1,121	35.9	1,196	407	34.0
Retail trade	13,038	3,989	30.6	7,042	2,154	30.6	5,995	1,835	30.6
Eating and drinking places	3,436	1,045	30.4	1,830	546	29.8	1,605	499	1.1
Finance, insurance, and real estate	6,645	2,687	40.4	2,614	1,287	49.2	4,031	1,400	34.7
Services	26,031	8,701	33.4	10,949	4,335	39.6	15,082	4,366	28.9
Private households	416	149	35.8	14 7		(2)	402	142	35.4
Business, automobile, and repair	6,646	2,473	37.2	4,344	1,640	37.8	2,301	833	36.2
Personal, except private household	1,954	609	31.2	823	244	29.6	1,130	365	32.3
Entertainment and recreation	1,215	489	40.2	762	303	39.7	453	186	41.1
Professional services	15,777	4,970	31.5	4,984	2,132	42.8	10,794	2,838	26.3
Forestry and fisheries	24	11	(2)	22	10	(2)	2	1	(2)
Government	16,616	3,736	22.5	7,642	1,865	24.4	8,974	1,871	20.8
Federal	3,140	1,079	34.4	1,817	584	32.1	1,324	495	37.4
State	4,868	1,447	29.7	2,125	669	31.5	2,743	779	28.4
Local	8,608	1,209	14.0	3,701	613	16.6	4,907	597	12.2

[1]Includes persons who did not provide information on flexible schedules.
[2]Percent not shown where base is less than 75,000.

Note: Data relate to the sole or principal job of full-time wage and salary workers and exclude all self-employed persons, regardless of whether or not their businesses were incorporated.

SOURCE: "Table 2. Flexible schedules: Full–time wage and salary workers by sex, occupation, and industry, May 2001," in *Workers on Flexible and Shift Schedules in 2001*, U.S. Department of Labor, Bureau of Labor Statistics, Washington, DC, April 2002 [Online] http://www.bls.gov/news.release/flex.t02.htm [accessed May 24, 2002]

action. On July 30, 2002, President George W. Bush signed into law a corporate fraud bill consisting of new corporate reporting and disclosure rules, plus increased penalties for fraud.

TABLE 2.19

Displaced workers by age, sex, race, Hispanic origin, and employment status, February 2000

Age, sex, race, and Hispanic origin	Total (thousands)	Percent distribution by employment status			
		Total	Employed	Un-employed	Not in the labor force
Total					
Total, 20 years and over	3,275	100.0	73.5	10.4	16.1
20 to 24 years	100	100.0	87.7	3.7	8.7
25 to 54 years	2,503	100.0	79.5	10.3	10.2
55 to 64 years	517	100.0	56.0	13.6	30.4
65 years and over	155	100.0	26.3	5.2	68.6
Men					
Total, 20 years and over	1,765	100.0	78.9	9.6	11.5
20 to 24 years	75	100.0	86.6	4.9	8.4
25 to 54 years	1,331	100.0	85.1	9.1	5.8
55 to 64 years	279	100.0	62.9	13.3	23.8
65 years and over	80	100.0	23.6	10.0	66.4
Women					
Total, 20 years and over	1,511	100.0	67.3	11.3	21.4
20 to 24 years.	25	100.0	(1)	(1)	(1)
25 to 54 years	1,172	100.0	73.2	11.7	15.1
55 to 64 years	238	100.0	47.9	14.0	38.1
65 years and over	75	100.0	29.1	-	70.9
White					
Total, 20 years and over	2,778	100.0	74.4	9.9	15.7
Men	1,522	100.0	79.0	10.0	11.0
Women	1,256	100.0	68.8	9.8	21.4
Black					
Total, 20 years and over	363	100.0	72.2	12.8	15.0
Men	188	100.0	82.0	4.7	13.4
Women	175	100.0	61.8	21.5	16.7
Hispanic origin					
Total, 20 years and over	346	100.0	69.7	13.0	17.3
Men	181	100.0	84.6	9.1	6.2
Women	165	100.0	53.4	17.2	29.5

[1]Data not shown where base is less than 75,000.

Note: Data for displaced workers refer to persons who had 3 or more years of tenure on a job they had lost or left between January 1997 and December 1999 because of plant or company closings or moves, insufficient work, or the abolishment of their positions or shifts.

Detail for the above race and Hispanic-origin groups will not sum to totals because data for the "other races" group are not presented and Hispanics are included in both the white and black population groups. Dash represents zero.

SOURCE: "Table 1. Displaced workers by age, sex, race, Hispanic origin, and employment status in February 2000," in *Worker Displacement During the Late 1990s, August 2000,* U.S. Department of Labor, Bureau of Labor Statistics, Washington, DC, 2000 [Online] http://www.bls.gov/news.release/disp.t01.htm [accessed May 24, 2002]

TABLE 2.20

Displaced workers by industry and class of worker of lost job and employment status, February 2000

Industry and class of worker of lost job	Total (thousands)	Percent distribution by employment status			
		Total	Employed	Unemployed	Not in the labor force
Total, 20 years and over[1]	3,275	100.0	73.5	10.4	16.1
Agricultural wage and salary workers	52	100.0	(2)	(2)	(2)
Nonagricultural wage and salary workers	3,162	100.0	73.5	10.3	16.2
Private wage and salary workers	3,004	100.0	73.4	10.6	16.0
Mining	55	100.0	(2)	(2)	(2)
Construction	214	100.0	77.9	10.6	11.4
Manufacturing	1,016	100.0	72.9	11.9	15.1
Durable goods	627	100.0	77.2	11.1	11.8
Lumber and wood products	43	100.0	(2)	(2)	(2)
Furniture and fixtures	19	100.0	(2)	(2)	(2)
Stone, clay, and glass products	29	100.0	(2)	(2)	(2)
Primary metal industries	24	100.0	(2)	(2)	(2)
Fabricated metal products	59	100.0	(2)	(2)	(2)
Machinery, except electrical	147	100.0	78.9	9.9	11.2
Electrical machinery	134	100.0	72.7	13.5	13.8
Transportation equipment	77	100.0	76.8	5.2	18.0
Automobiles	28	100.0	(2)	(2)	(2)
Other transportation equipment	48	100.0	(2)	(2)	(2)
Professional and photographic equipment	68	100.0	(2)	(2)	(2)
Other durable goods industries	26	100.0	(2)	(2)	(2)
Nondurable goods	389	100.0	66.1	13.3	20.5
Food and kindred products	53	100.0	(2)	(2)	(2)
Textile mill products	37	100.0	(2)	(2)	(2)
Apparel and other finished textile products	95	100.0	40.8	21.0	38.2
Paper and allied products	24	100.0	(2)		(2)
Printing and publishing	72	100.0	(2)	(2)	(2)
Chemical and allied products	73	100.0	(2)	(2)	(2)
Rubber and miscellaneous plastics products	15	100.0	(2)	(2)	(2)
Other nondurable goods industries	19	100.0	(2)	(2)	(2)
Transportation and public utilities	164	100.0	74.4	15.7	9.9
Transportation	90	100.0	75.3	22.4	2.3
Communications and other public utilities	74	100.0	(2)	(2)	(2)
Wholesale and retail trade	616	100.0	71.3	8.0	20.8
Wholesale trade	161	100.0	70.7	7.1	22.2
Retail trade	456	100.0	71.5	8.3	20.3
Finance, insurance, and real estate	245	100.0	75.8	8.5	15.7
Services	692	100.0	74.7	9.3	16.0
Professional services	385	100.0	77.0	8.9	14.1
Other service industries	307	100.0	71.9	9.7	18.3
Government workers	158	100.0	74.8	4.7	20.4

Note: Data for displaced workers refer to persons who had 3 or more years of tenure on a job they had lost or left between January 1997 and December 1999 because of plant or company closings or moves, insufficient work, or the abolishment of their positions or shifts.

[1]Total includes a small number of unpaid family workers and persons who did not report industry or class of worker.
[2]Data not shown where base is less than 75,000.

SOURCE: "Table 4. Displaced workers by industry and class of worker of lost job and employment status in Feburary 2000," in *Worker Displacement During the Late 1990s,* U.S. Department of Labor, Bureau of Labor Statistics, Washington, DC, 2000 [Online] http://www.bls.gov/news.release/disp.t04.htm [accessed May 24, 2002]

TABLE 2.21

Displaced workers by occupation of lost job and employment status, February 2000

Occupation of lost job	Total (thousands)	Total	Employed	Unemployed	Not in the labor force
Total, 20 years and over[1]	3,275	100.0	73.5	10.4	16.1
Managerial and professional specialty	982	100.0	78.5	9.2	12.3
Executive, administrative, and managerial	600	100.0	77.8	11.6	10.6
Professional specialty	382	100.0	79.6	5.3	15.0
Technical, sales, and administrative support	941	100.0	73.0	10.0	17.0
Technicians and related support	126	100.0	85.6	5.8	8.6
Sales occupations	360	100.0	72.0	11.3	16.6
Administrative support, including clerical	454	100.0	70.4	10.1	19.5
Service occupations	216	100.0	67.1	3.9	28.9
Precision production, craft, and repair	448	100.0	74.9	10.7	14.5
Mechanics and repairers	105	100.0	76.3	7.9	15.8
Construction trades	159	100.0	76.5	11.0	12.5
Other precision production, craft, and repair	184	100.0	72.6	12.0	15.4
Operators, fabricators, and laborers	590	100.0	69.4	13.6	17.1
Machine operators, assemblers, and inspectors	338	100.0	66.4	15.6	17.9
Transportation and material moving occupations	126	100.0	78.1	13.3	8.6
Handlers, equipment cleaners, helpers, and laborers	126	100.0	68.5	8.2	23.3
Farming, forestry, and fishing	52	100.0	(2)	(2)	(2)

Note: Data for displaced workers refer to persons who had 3 or more years of tenure on a job they had lost or left between January 1997 and December 1999 because of plant or company closings or moves, insufficient work, or the abolishment of their positions or shifts.

[1] Total includes a small number who did not report occupation.
[2] Data not shown where base is less than 75,000.

SOURCE: "Table 5. Displaced workers by occupation of lost job and employment status in February 2000," in *Worker Displacement During the Late 1990s,* U.S. Department of Labor, Bureau of Labor Statistics, Washington, DC, 2000 [Online] http://www.bls.gov/news.release/disp.t05.htm [accessed May 24, 2002]

FIGURE 2.6

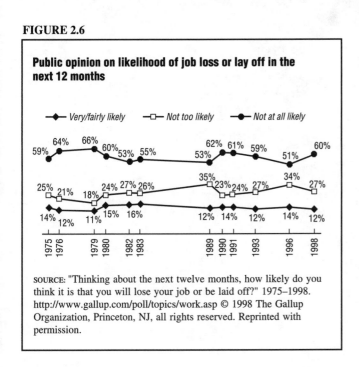

Public opinion on likelihood of job loss or lay off in the next 12 months

SOURCE: "Thinking about the next twelve months, how likely do you think it is that you will lose your job or be laid off?" 1975–1998. http://www.gallup.com/poll/topics/work.asp © 1998 The Gallup Organization, Princeton, NJ, all rights reserved. Reprinted with permission.

TABLE 2.22

Selected measures of mass layoff activity, 1998–2002

Period	Layoff events	Separations	Initial claimants
1998			
January-March	1,320	208,082	247,315
April-June	1,563	391,461	402,276
July-September	1,234	248,054	256,803
October-December	1,734	379,976	325,990
1999			
January-March	1,509	277,780	252,122
April-June	1,444	294,968	242,464
July-September	1,097	241,725	189,973
October-December	1,625	334,794	287,685
2000			
January-March	1,330	254,646	221,368
April-June	1,271	258,608	231,471
July-September	1,014	230,103	189,250
October-December r	2,005	427,070	376,611
2001			
January-March r	1,765	342,954	340,151
April-June r	2,072	481,876	401,294
July-September r	1,815	384,403	371,124
October-December r	2,700	541,410	497,136
2002			
January-March p	1,669	301,181	236,891

p=preliminary.
r=revised.

SOURCE: "Table A. Selected measure of mass layoff activity," in *Extended Mass Layoffs in the First Quarter of 2002,* U.S. Department of Labor, Bureau of Labor Statistics, Washington, DC, 2002 [Online] ftp://ftp.bls.gov/ publnews.release/History/mslo.05162002.news [accessed June 17, 2002]

CHAPTER 3

UNEMPLOYMENT

The United States unemployment rate reached a post-World War II high of 9.7 percent in 1982. It remained high at 9.6 percent in 1983 as a result of the most severe economic recession since the Great Depression of the 1930s. The unemployment rate then dropped, approaching 5 percent in 1989, but again began increasing, reaching 7 percent in 1991 and rising almost to 8 percent in 1992. As the economy improved, the rate fell to 6.9 percent in 1993. By 1998 the U.S. unemployment rate had dropped to 4.5 percent, and in 1999 reached a low of 4.2 percent. By April 2000 unemployment had declined to 3.9 percent, the lowest level in three decades.

With a creeping recession, unemployment once again began to rise in early 2001 and rose significantly following the terror attacks on the United States on September 11, 2001. As of April 2002 the rate was as high as 6 percent. (See Figure 3.1.) Not counted in the unemployment rate were some previously laid-off workers, especially those over 55 years old, who had stopped looking for work.

INTERNATIONAL UNEMPLOYMENT

In the third quarter of 2000 the United States, as compared to other countries, had the lowest unemployment rate (4.1 percent), followed by Japan at 5 percent. This was already much higher than Japan's 1991 rate of 2.1 percent. France (9.8 percent), Germany (8.4 percent), Canada (6.8 percent), and Australia (6.9 percent) all had higher rates. (See Table 3.1.)

BY STATES

Unemployment rates in the United States vary from state to state. In December 2001, Oregon (7.8 percent), Washington (7.4 percent), Nevada (6.9 percent), Louisiana (6.7 percent), Mississippi and North Carolina (both 6.5 percent), and District of Columbia (6.4 percent) had the highest unemployment rates. North Dakota (3.1

percent), Nebraska (3.4 percent), and Delaware (3.4 percent) had the lowest rates. (See Table 3.2.)

AGE

Unemployment does not occur evenly in all occupations or sectors of society. Younger workers under 25 years of age are far more likely to be unemployed than older workers. Their jobs are often more marginal, and younger workers leave their jobs more often than older ones. They also have less seniority to protect themselves against layoffs.

While the average unemployment rate was 4.8 percent in 2001, those 16 to 24 years old experienced a rate of 10.6 percent. Young adults 20 to 24 years old (8.3

FIGURE 3.1

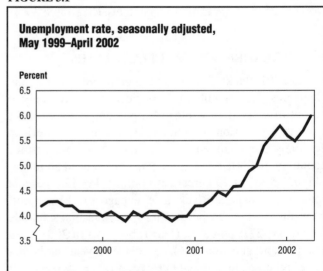

Unemployment rate, seasonally adjusted, May 1999–April 2002

SOURCE: "Chart 1. Unemployment Rate, Seasonally Adjusted, May 1999-April 2002," in "The Employment Situation: April 2002," *News, United States Department of Labor,* U.S. Department of Labor, Bureau of Labor Statistics, Washington, DC, May 3, 2002

TABLE 3.1

Civilian unemployment rates in nine countries, seasonally adjusted, 1990–2000

Year and quarter or month	United States	Canada	Australia	Japan	France	Germany[1]	Italy[2]	Sweden	United Kingdom
1990	5.6	8.1	6.9	2.1	9.1	5.0	7.0	1.8	6.9
1991	6.8	10.3	9.6	2.1	9.6	[3]5.6	[3]6.9	3.1	8.8
1992	7.5	11.2	10.8	2.2	[3]10.4	6.7	7.3	5.6	10.1
1993	6.9	11.4	10.9	2.5	11.8	7.9	[3]10.2	9.3	10.5
1994	[3]6.1	10.4	9.7	2.9	12.3	8.5	11.2	9.6	9.7
1995	5.6	9.4	8.5	3.2	11.8	8.2	11.8	9.1	8.7
1996	5.4	9.6	8.6	3.4	12.5	8.9	11.7	9.9	8.2
1997	4.9	9.1	8.6	3.4	12.4	9.9	11.9	10.1	7.0
1998	4.5	8.3	8.0	4.1	11.8	9.3	12.0	8.4	6.3
I	4.7	8.6	8.1	3.7	12.0	9.8	11.8	8.8	6.4
II	4.4	8.3	8.0	4.2	11.7	9.5	12.0	8.7	6.3
III	4.5	8.2	8.1	4.3	11.7	9.1	12.0	8.5	6.3
IV	4.4	8.1	7.7	4.5	11.5	8.9	12.0	7.6	6.3
1999	4.2	7.6	7.2	P4.7	P11.1	P8.7	11.5	7.1	P6.1
I	4.3	7.9	7.5	4.7	11.3	8.9	11.9	7.2	6.3
II	4.3	7.8	7.4	4.8	11.2	8.8	11.6	6.9	6.1
III	4.2	7.6	7.1	4.8	11.0	8.8	11.6	7.0	5.9
IV	4.1	7.0	7.0	4.7	10.6	8.7	11.1	7.1	5.9
October	4.1	7.1	7.1	4.7	10.8	8.8	11.1	7.1	5.9
November	4.1	6.9	6.8	4.6	10.6	8.7	–	7.2	5.9
December	4.1	6.8	7.0	4.7	10.4	8.5	–	7.0	5.9
2000									
I	4.1	6.8	6.8	4.9	10.0	8.4	11.3	6.9	–
January	4.0	6.8	6.9	4.7	10.3	8.4	11.3	6.9	–
February	4.1	6.8	6.7	4.9	10.0	8.4	–	6.9	–
March	4.1	6.8	6.9	5.0	9.8	8.4	–	6.8	–

[1] Unified Germany for 1991 onward. Prior to 1991, data relate to the former West Germany.
[2] Quarterly rates are for the first month of the quarter.
[3] Break in series.
P = preliminary. Dash indicates data not available.
Note: Quarterly and monthly figures for France and Germany should be viewed as less precise indicators of unemployment under U.S. concepts than the annual figures.

SOURCE: Constance Sorrentino, "Table A-1. Unemployment rates in nine countries, civilian labor force basis, approximating U.S. concepts, seasonally adjusted, 1990–2000," in "International Unemployment Rates: How Comparable Are They?," *Monthly Labor Review,* vol. 123, no. 6, June 2000

percent) had more than double the unemployment rate of workers 25 to 54 years old (3.8 percent). (See Table 3.3.)

RACE, GENDER, AND MARITAL STATUS

In 2001 blacks (8.7 percent unemployment rate) and Hispanics (6.6 percent) were considerably more likely to be out of work than whites (4.2 percent). Many blacks work in occupations that have suffered as the American economy has changed from an industrial to a service economy. In 2001 black teenagers experienced an unemployment rate of 29 percent as compared to 12.7 percent for white teenagers. Black male teenagers (30.5 percent) were more likely to be unemployed than black female teenagers (27.5 percent). (See Table 3.4.) In 2001, men (4.8 percent) and women (4.7 percent) 16 years and older had similar unemployment rates. (See Table 3.5.)

A married person was much less likely to be unemployed than a single, widowed, or divorced individual. This observation held true across all races. In 2001, single, never married males (9 percent) had more than triple the unemployment rate of married males (2.7 percent). Widowed, divorced, or separated males (5.1 percent) had nearly two times the rate of married men. While only 2.5 percent of white married men were unemployed, 7.9 percent of single white men and 4.7 percent of widowed, divorced, or separated white males were out of work. Among blacks, 4.5 percent of married men, 16 years and older were unemployed, compared to 7.5 percent of widowed, divorced, or separated and 15.6 percent of singles. (See Table 3.5.)

The same situation held true for married, single, divorced, widowed, and separated women. While 7.7 percent of single females over 16 years of age were unemployed, only 3.1 percent of married women and 4.7 percent of widowed, divorced, or separated women were unemployed. Single white women over the age of 16 (6.6 percent) were more than twice as likely to be out of work as married white women (2.8 percent) were. Single black women (12.2 percent) were almost three times as likely to be unemployed as married black women (4.4 percent). (See Table 3.5.)

TABLE 3.2

Unemployment rates by state, seasonally adjusted, December 2000–December 2001

State	Dec. 2000	Nov. 2001ᵖ	Dec. 2001ᵖ	State	Dec. 2000	Nov. 2001ᵖ	Dec. 2001ᵖ
Alabama	4.7	5.9	6.0	Missouri	4.3	5.0	4.9
Alaska	6.6	6.1	6.0	Montana	4.7	4.6	4.7
Arizona	3.8	5.6	5.8	Nebraska	2.9	3.3	3.4
Arkansas	4.6	5.4	5.5	Nevada	4.4	6.7	6.9
California	4.7	6.1	6.1	New Hampshire	2.8	4.0	3.9
Colorado	2.7	4.9	5.1	New Jersey	3.7	4.8	4.8
Connecticut	2.3	3.9	4.0	New Mexico	4.6	5.1	5.1
Delaware	4.0	3.3	3.4	New York	4.3	5.6	5.7
District of Columbia	6.3	6.8	6.4	North Carolina	4.2	6.5	6.5
Florida	3.8	5.6	6.0	North Dakota	2.9	2.9	3.1
Georgia	3.6	4.5	4.5	Ohio	3.9	4.7	4.8
Hawaii	4.2	5.7	5.6	Oklahoma	3.0	4.4	4.7
Idaho	4.8	5.3	5.5	Oregon	4.7	7.7	7.8
Illinois	4.8	5.9	6.0	Pennsylvania	4.3	5.0	5.1
Indiana	3.3	5.1	5.1	Rhode Island	4.2	4.9	6.0
Iowa	2.9	3.7	3.7	South Carolina	4.2	5.9	6.1
Kansas	4.0	4.5	4.4	South Dakota	2.6	3.6	4.0
Kentucky	4.6	6.1	6.2	Tennessee	4.1	4.8	5.0
Louisiana	6.0	6.5	6.7	Texas	3.9	5.6	5.7
Maine	3.4	4.3	4.3	Utah	3.5	5.2	5.9
Maryland	3.9	4.4	4.4	Vermont	3.0	4.2	4.3
Massachusetts	2.6	4.4	4.4	Virginia	2.2	4.5	4.5
Michigan	–	–	–	Washington	5.5	7.2	7.4
Minnesota	3.4	3.9	4.0	West Virginia	5.4	4.6	4.6
Mississippi	5.1	6.3	6.5	Wisconsin	3.9	4.9	4.9
				Wyoming	3.8	4.1	4.2

ᵖ = preliminary
Dash indicates data not available.

SOURCE: "Table 10. Unemployment rates by state, seasonally adjusted," in "Current Labor Statistics," *Monthly Labor Review,* vol. 125, no. 3, March 2002

EDUCATION

The more education an individual has, the less likely he or she will be unemployed. In 2001 while 7.3 percent of those with less then a high school diploma were unemployed, only 2.3 percent of college graduates were. High school graduates with no college had an unemployment rate of 4.2 percent, while those with some college, but no degree, faced a 3.3 percent unemployment rate. (See Table 3.4.)

OCCUPATIONS AND INDUSTRIES

Some occupations are more susceptible to unemployment than others. In 2001 people employed in managerial and professional specialties (2.3 percent) were much less likely to find themselves unemployed than those working as operators, fabricators, and laborers (7.7 percent). Within each occupational grouping, differences exist. While the overall technical, sales, and administrative support field had 4.2 percent unemployed, those in sales occupations were more likely to be unemployed (4.7 percent) than technicians (2.9 percent) and administrative support, including clerical workers (4 percent). (See Table 3.6.)

Gender also plays a role. Women in sales occupations had an unemployment rate of 5.8 percent, compared to 3.6 percent for men. While women and men had similar unemployment rates in managerial and professional specialty fields, more female operators, fabricators, and laborers were out of work than males. (See Table 3.6.)

In 2001 those working in apparel, agricultural industries, textiles, and construction were most likely to find themselves without jobs. Those in government, finance, insurance, and real estate, and certain segments of the manufacturing industry (including chemicals and allied products) were the least likely to be unemployed. (See Table 3.7.)

HOW LONG DOES UNEMPLOYMENT LAST?

In 2001 the average length of unemployment was 13.2 weeks, down from 15.8 weeks in 1997 and 16.7 weeks in 1996. The median duration of unemployment was 6.8 weeks. Almost one half (42 percent) of the unemployed had been unemployed for less than 5 weeks, and a little less than one-third (32 percent) had been out of work for 5 to 14 weeks. About 14 percent were out of work 15 to 26 weeks and 12 percent for 27 weeks and over. (See Table 3.8.)

Gender and Age

Men tended to stay unemployed somewhat longer (an average of 13.5 weeks) than women (12.7 weeks) in 2001. Generally, the older the job seeker, the longer it took to

TABLE 3.3

Unemployment rates by sex and age, monthly data seasonally adjusted, January 2001–January 2002

[Civilian workers]

Sex and age	Annual average		2001												2002
	2000	2001	Jan.	Feb.	Mar.	Apr.	May	June	July	Aug.	Sept.	Oct.	Nov.	Dec.	Jan.
Total, 16 years and over	4.0	4.8	4.2	4.2	4.3	4.5	4.4	4.6	4.6	4.9	5.0	5.4	5.6	5.8	5.6
16 to 24 years	9.3	10.6	9.5	9.5	9.9	10.3	10.0	10.4	10.2	11.3	10.8	11.5	11.7	11.9	11.9
16 to 19 years	13.1	14.7	13.7	13.5	13.8	14.2	13.8	14.4	14.8	15.8	14.9	15.4	15.7	16.2	16.1
16 to 17 years	15.4	17.1	16.6	16.9	5.9	16.7	15.8	16.5	19.0	18.6	16.6	17.4	17.5	18.8	17.0
18 to 19 years	11.5	13.2	11.5	11.0	12.2	12.6	12.5	13.0	12.4	14.4	13.9	14.2	14.8	14.8	15.2
20 to 24 years	7.1	8.3	7.2	7.3	7.7	8.2	7.9	8.2	7.7	8.9	8.6	9.3	9.5	9.6	9.7
25 years and over	3.0	3.7	3.1	3.2	3.2	3.4	3.4	3.5	3.5	3.8	3.8	4.2	4.4	4.5	4.4
25 to 54 years	3.1	3.8	3.2	3.2	3.3	3.4	3.5	3.6	3.7	3.9	3.9	4.4	4.6	4.7	4.7
55 years and over	2.6	3.0	2.7	2.8	2.7	2.7	2.6	2.8	2.9	3.1	3.2	3.4	3.5	4.0	3.5
Men, 16 years and over	3.9	4.8	4.2	4.2	4.4	4.6	4.5	4.7	4.7	5.1	5.0	5.5	5.9	5.8	5.8
16 to 24 years	9.7	11.4	10.2	10.6	10.9	10.9	11.0	11.6	10.7	12.3	1.5	12.4	13.0	12.8	12.5
16 to 19 years	14.0	15.9	14.8	15.0	14.3	15.1	15.4	15.8	15.6	17.4	16.0	17.2	17.7	17.2	16.3
16 to 17 years	16.8	18.8	19.0	18.4	16.2	18.7	17.9	18.5	19.1	21.9	18.7	20.3	20.4	20.0	17.6
18 to 19 years	12.2	14.1	11.9	12.9	12.7	12.9	13.9	14.2	13.4	15.0	14.5	15.1	16.2	15.6	15.1
20 to 24 years	7.3	8.9	7.7	8.1	8.9	8.6	8.7	9.3	8.1	9.5	9.1	9.8	10.5	10.5	10.6
25 years and over	2.8	3.6	3.1	3.0	3.2	3.4	3.3	3.4	3.6	3.8	3.7	4.2	4.5	4.5	4.4
25 to 54 years	2.9	3.7	3.1	3.1	3.2	3.5	3.4	3.5	3.6	3.9	3.8	4.3	4.6	4.5	4.7
55 years and over	2.7	3.3	2.9	2.8	3.0	2.9	2.9	3.0	3.1	3.3	3.3	3.7	4.1	4.2	3.8
Women, 16 years and over	4.1	4.7	4.1	4.1	4.2	4.3	4.3	4.4	4.6	4.8	5.0	5.3	5.4	5.8	5.4
16 to 24 years	8.9	9.7	8.8	8.3	8.9	9.7	8.8	9.2	9.7	10.3	10.1	10.5	10.3	11.0	11.3
16 to 19 years	12.1	13.4	12.5	11.9	13.3	13.2	12.1	13.0	14.0	14.1	13.6	13.6	13.7	15.1	15.8
16 to 17 years	14.0	15.3	14.0	15.3	15.6	14.5	13.8	14.4	18.8	15.4	14.3	14.5	14.5	17.6	16.4
18 to 19 years	10.8	12.2	11.1	8.8	11.6	12.2	11.0	11.8	11.3	13.7	13.3	13.3	13.3	14.0	15.2
20 to 24 years	7.0	7.5	6.7	6.3	6.4	7.8	7.0	7.0	7.3	8.2	8.1	8.7	8.3	8.7	8.7
25 years and over	3.2	3.7	3.2	3.4	3.2	3.3	3.4	3.5	3.5	3.8	4.0	4.2	4.4	4.6	4.3
25 to 54 years	3.3	3.8	3.3	3.4	3.4	3.4	3.6	3.7	3.7	3.9	4.0	4.4	4.7	4.8	4.6
55 years and over	2.6	2.7	2.4	2.7	2.3	2.5	2.4	2.6	2.6	2.8	3.2	3.2	2.8	3.7	3.0

SOURCE: "Table 9. Unemployment rates by sex and age, monthly data seasonally adjusted," in "Current Labor Statistics," *Monthly Labor Review,* vol. 125, no. 3, March 2002

find work. Young adults 16 to 19 years old were unemployed an average of 9.6 weeks, compared to 18 weeks for those 55 to 64 years old. (See Table 3.8.)

Because better-paying jobs usually take longer to find, men 45 years and older, who were more likely to be seeking higher-paying employment than either women or younger people, remained unemployed longer.

Race and Ethnicity

Whites and workers of Hispanic origin were both unemployed for an average of 11.9 weeks in 2001. Blacks were out of work longer at 16.9 weeks. (See Table 3.8.)

Marital Status

Widowed, divorced, or separated women were unemployed somewhat longer (14.3 weeks) in 2001 than those who had never been married (12 weeks) or those who were still living with their spouses (12.7 weeks). Married men living with their wives (14 weeks) and widowed, divorced, or separated (16.1 weeks) were out of work longer than never married men (12.6 weeks). (See Table 3.8.)

Occupations

In 2001 almost half (45 percent) of those unemployed in service occupations were out of work less than 5

weeks, and 24 percent were still looking for work after 15 weeks. More than one-third (39 percent) of those seeking managerial and professional positions were unemployed less than 5 weeks, and another 28 percent still lacked jobs after 15 weeks. (See Table 3.9.)

Managerial and professional specialties had among the longest average duration of unemployment (13.7 weeks). Many of these had experienced the downsizing of staff in major companies. They were often older workers looking for higher-paying jobs. Operators, fabricators, and laborers had an average duration of 13.6 weeks, and service occupations endured unemployment for an average of 13.1 weeks. (See Table 3.9.)

Industry

During 2001, 44 percent of construction workers, 39 percent of transportation and utilities laborers, and 37 percent of finance, insurance, and real estate workers found employment within 5 weeks of being jobless. Almost one-quarter (22 percent) of construction workers still needed jobs after 15 weeks. Construction workers were out of work an average of 11.9 weeks. Public administration workers had the longest average duration of unemployment (17 weeks). The manufacturing labor force took an average of 13.9 weeks to find a job. More than one-third

TABLE 3.4

Selected unemployment indicators, monthly data seasonally adjusted, January 2001–January 2002

[Unemployment rates]

Selected categories	Annual average 2000	Annual average 2001	2001 Jan.	Feb.	Mar.	Apr.	May	June	July	Aug.	Sept.	Oct.	Nov.	Dec.	2002 Jan.
Characteristic															
Total, 16 years and over	4.0	4.8	4.2	4.2	4.3	4.5	4.4	4.6	4.6	4.9	5.0	5.4	5.6	5.8	5.6
Both sexes, 16 to 19 years	13.1	14.7	13.7	13.5	13.8	14.2	13.6	14.4	14.8	15.8	14.9	15.4	15.7	16.2	16.1
Men, 20 years and over	3.3	4.2	3.6	3.5	3.8	3.9	3.9	4.1	4.0	4.4	4.3	4.8	5.2	5.2	5.2
Women, 20 years and over	3.6	4.1	3.5	3.6	3.6	3.8	3.8	3.9	4.0	4.2	4.4	4.8	4.9	52.0	4.8
White, total	3.5	4.2	3.6	3.7	3.7	3.9	3.9	4.0	4.1	4.3	4.3	4.7	5.0	5.1	5.0
Both sexes, 16 to 19 years	11.4	12.7	11.7	11.2	11.7	11.9	12.0	12.7	13.2	13.8	12.7	23.1	13.5	13.7	14.2
Men, 16 to 19 years	12.3	13.8	13.1	12.7	12.3	12.9	13.3	14.3	13.8	15.1	13.6	14.7	15.8	14.6	13.7
Women, 16 to 19 years	10.4	11.4	10.2	9.6	11.0	10.9	10.7	11.0	12.6	12.4	11.7	11.5	11.1	12.8	14.6
Men, 20 years and over	2.8	3.7	3.1	3.1	3.3	3.4	3.4	3.6	3.5	3.8	3.8	4.4	4.7	4.6	4.7
Women, 20 years and over	3.1	3.6	3.0	3.3	3.1	3.4	3.4	3.4	3.5	3.6	3.8	4.1	4.2	4.5	4.2
Black, total	7.6	8.7	8.2	7.5	8.4	8.2	8.0	8.4	8.1	9.0	8.8	9.6	9.9	10.2	9.8
Both sexes, 16 to 19 years	24.7	29.0	27.5	28.1	28.3	30.5	25.7	28.0	26.6	30.1	28.5	30.2	32.1	33.4	30.7
Men, 16 to 19 years	26.4	30.5	27.3	31.1	28.7	33.5	30/0	6.0	28.1	31.4	430.8	31.2	31.6	32.0	32.1
Women, 16 to 19 years	23.0	27.5	27.6	25.1	28.0	27.7	21.5	25.7	25.2	28.7	26.1	29.1	32.6	34.8	29.0
Men, 20 years and over	7.0	8.0	7.0	6.7	8.2	8.1	7.6	7.8	7.9	8.8	7.8	8.2	8.7	9.1	8.9
Women, 20 years and over	6.3	7.0	6.9	5.9	6.3	5.9	6.4	6.7	6.2	7.0	7.7	8.5	8.4	8.7	8.4
Hispanic origin, total	5.7	6.6	5.9	6.2	6.2	6.3	6.2	6.6	6.2	6.4	6.5	7.1	7.4	7.9	8.1
Married men, spouse present	2.0	2.7	2.3	2.3	2.4	2.5	2.6	2.6	2.7	2.8	2.8	3.1	3.3	3.4	3.5
Married women, spouse present	2.7	3.1	2.6	2.6	2.7	2.8	2.9	3.0	2.9	3.1	3.3	3.6	3.6	3.7	3.4
Women who maintain families	5.9	6.6	6.4	6.0	6.1	6.3	6.2	6.3	6.3	6.8	7.1	6.8	8.0	8.0	7.9
Full-time workers	3.9	4.7	4.0	4.0	4.1	4.3	4.3	4.5	4.5	4.8	5.0	5.4	5.6	5.8	5.7
Part-time workers	4.8	5.1	4.9	4.8	4.9	5.3	4.8	5.2	5.1	5.4	4.6	5.5	5.6	5.6	5.2
Industry															
Nonagricultural wage and salary workers	4.1	5.1	4.2	4.4	4.5	4.6	4.6	4.8	4.8	5.2	5.2	5.8	6.0	6.2	5.9
Mining	3.9	4.7	2.2	4.5	4.0	4.8	4.9	5.9	3.9	4.7	5.0	5.8	5.3	6.1	5.9
Construction	6.4	7.3	6.7	6.8	6.4	6.9	6.7	6.9	7.1	7.6	7.8	8.3	8.9	8.9	9.4
Manufacturing	3.6	5.2	4.1	4.5	4.8	4.6	4.8	5.0	5.2	5.7	5.6	6.0	6.4	6.8	6.6
Durable goods	3.4	5.3	4.0	4.1	4.7	4.4	4.8	5.0	5.0	5.8	5.8	6.5	6.9	7.2	7.0
Nondurable goods	4.0	5.1	4.4	4.9	4.9	4.9	4.8	4.9	5.5	5.4	5.4	5.3	5.5	6.1	5.9
Transportation and public utilities	3.1	4.1	2.9	3.0	3.2	4.0	3.6	4.1	3.4	3.6	3.9	6.0	6.1	6.1	6.2
Wholesale and retail trade	5.0	5.6	4.9	5.1	5.3	5.2	5.2	5.4	5.3	5.6	5.9	6.1	6.4	7.1	6.3
Finance, insurance, and real estate	2.3	2.8	2.3	2.4	2.5	2.6	2.4	2.6	3.1	2.7	2.8	2.8	3.6	3.0	2.2
Services	3.8	4.6	3.9	4.1	4.1	4.1	4.2	4.4	4.4	4.9	4.8	5.5	5.4	5.5	5.4
Government workers	2.1	2.2	2.2	1.6	2.1	2.2	2.0	2.1	2.1	2.1	2.2	2.3	2.4	2.4	2.3
Agricultural wage and salary workers	7.5	9.7	9.0	9.2	11.1	9.4	8.4	9.5	10.5	10.0	7.6	9.0	9.3	9.6	10.3
Educational attainment[1]															
Less than a high school diploma	6.4	7.3	6.7	7.4	6.8	6.7	6.7	6.9	6.8	7.3	7.7	7.8	8.1	8.8	8.1
High school graduates, no college	3.5	4.2	3.7	3.7	3.8	3.8	3.9	3.9	4.1	4.3	4.3	4.6	5.0	4.9	5.2
Some college, less than a bachelor's degree	2.7	3.3	2.9	2.7	2.7	2.9	3.0	3.1	3.1	3.3	3.5	3.9	4.2	4.3	4.2
College graduates	1.7	2.3	1.6	1.6	1.9	2.2	2.1	2.1	22.2	2.2	2.5	2.7	2.9	3.1	2.9

[1]Data refer to persons 25 years and over.

SOURCE: "Table 6. Selected unemployment indicators, monthly data seasonally adjusted," in "Current Labor Statistics," *Monthly Labor Review*, vol. 125, no. 3, March 2002

(37.6 percent) were unemployed for less than 5 weeks, and another 30 percent were unemployed more than 15 weeks. (See Table 3.9.)

REASONS FOR UNEMPLOYMENT

In 2001 most of those classified as unemployed had lost their jobs or had completed temporary jobs (50.8 percent). Slightly less than one-third (30.1 percent) had left the labor force and were returning. Only 6.7 percent were new entrants to the labor force. About 33 percent of the unemployed men and 27 percent of the unemployed women had been laid off permanently. (See Table 3.10.)

Duration by Reason of Unemployment

More than 2 of 5 (42 percent) workers who had lost their jobs or who had completed temporary jobs were unemployed less than 5 weeks. More than one-fourth (25.9 percent) were unemployed 15 weeks or more. Nearly 3 of 5 (56.1 percent) of those who were on temporary layoff were out of work for 5 weeks or less. More than one-third (33.8 percent) of those who were permanently laid off found work in 5 weeks or less. (See Table 3.11.)

Younger unemployed people and temporary workers tended to find jobs more quickly than older workers.

TABLE 3.5

Unemployed persons by marital status, race, and age, 2000–2001

Marital status, race, and age	Men				Women			
	Thousands of persons		Unemployment rates		Thousands of persons		Unemployment rates	
	2000	2001	2000	2001	2000	2001	2000	2001
Total, 16 years and over	2,954	3,663	3.9	4.8	2,701	3,079	4.1	4.7
Married, spouse present	891	1,213	2.0	2.7	923	1,058	2.7	3.1
Widowed, divorced, or separated	400	472	4.4	5.1	553	628	4.2	4.7
Single (never married)	1,663	1,979	7.6	9.0	1,224	1,393	6.9	7.7
White, 16 years and over	2,165	2,730	3.4	4.3	1,934	2,193	3.6	4.1
Married, spouse present	706	969	1.8	2.5	755	846	2.5	2.8
Widowed, divorced, or separated	304	361	4.0	4.7	412	466	4.0	4.4
Single (never married)	1,154	1,400	6.6	7.9	767	881	5.8	6.6
Black, 16 years and over	636	731	8.1	9.3	633	719	7.2	8.1
Married, spouse present	127	161	3.7	4.5	114	126	4.0	4.4
Widowed, divorced, or separated	82	91	6.7	7.5	123	136	5.5	6.1
Single (never married)	426	480	13.7	15.6	395	456	10.7	12.2
Total, 25 years and over	1,800	2,323	2.8	3.6	1,736	2,028	3.2	3.7
Married, spouse present	841	1,145	2.0	2.6	817	957	2.5	2.9
Widowed, divorced, or separated	383	450	4.3	5.0	518	586	4.1	4.5
Single (never married)	576	728	5.0	6.3	401	485	4.5	5.4
White, 25 years and over	1,343	1,753	2.5	3.2	1,266	1,477	2.8	3.3
Married, spouse present	669	913	1.8	2.4	667	762	2.3	2.7
Widowed, divorced, or separated	289	344	3.9	4.6	383	432	3.8	4.2
Single (never married)	386	496	4.3	5.4	217	283	3.6	4.6
Black, 25 years and over	360	438	5.6	6.7	380	430	5.2	5.9
Married, spouse present	119	152	3.5	4.4	101	117	3.7	4.2
Widowed, divorced, or separated	81	87	6.7	7.3	118	130	5.3	5.9
Single (never married)	160	198	8.5	10.7	161	183	7.0	7.7

SOURCE: "24. Unemployed persons by marital status, race, age, and sex," in *Employment and Earnings,* vol. 49, no. 1, January 2002

Nearly two-thirds (66 percent) of the 16- to 19-year-olds who had lost their jobs or who had completed temporary jobs had found work in 5 weeks or less. (See Table 3.11.)

JOB SEARCH

Unemployed workers use different methods to find new jobs. In 2001 most tried an average of 1.85 different techniques. Almost two-thirds (62.4 percent) approached an employer directly. Just more than one-half (51.5 percent) sent out resumes or filled out applications. Approximately 15.6 percent sought the help of friends and relatives. Just over 19 percent went to public employment agencies, and 8.6 percent visited private employment agencies. (See Table 3.12.)

New entrants to the job market were less likely to seek out employers directly (58 percent) than those who had lost their jobs or who had completed temporary jobs (64.8 percent). They were also less likely to use employment agencies than those who had been working and lost their jobs. (See Table 3.12.)

WITHDRAWN FROM THE LABOR FORCE

The labor force includes those working and those unemployed who are still looking for work. In 2001 more than half (55 percent) of those people who were not in the

labor force were 55 or older. More than 6 of 10 (62.7 percent) were women. (See Table 3.13.)

Reasons for Not Working

In 1996, 15.8 million people between the ages of 25 and 54 neither worked nor looked for work at any time during the prior year. Women accounted for about 3 out of 4 of these persons. The reasons they were not in the labor market differed markedly from those reported by men. The large majority, 69 percent, were taking care of their home or family, 20 percent were either ill or disabled, and a little more than 5 percent were in school. In contrast among the 4 million men of this age range who neither worked nor looked for work, 8 percent were taking care of their family or home, and 63 percent were either ill or disabled. (See Table 3.14.)

Income and Education

Women who neither worked nor looked for work tended to be somewhat better off economically than their male counterparts. As of March 1997, 38.2 percent of the women had family or personal income of less than $20,000, compared with 60.2 percent of the men. However, 21.3 percent of the women, but only 6.7 percent of the men, had incomes of $60,000 or more. (See Table 3.14.)

About 25 percent of women nonworkers were high school dropouts, compared with 33 percent of men. At the

TABLE 3.6

Unemployed persons by occupation and sex, 2000–2001

| Occupation | Thousands of persons Total | | Unemployment rates | | | | | |
| | | | Total | | Men | | Women | |
	2000	2001	2000	2001	2000	2001	2000	2001
Total, 16 years and over[1]	5,655	6,742	4.0	4.8	3.9	4.8	4.1	4.7
Managerial and professional specialty	725	973	1.7	2.3	1.6	2.3	1.9	2.2
Executive, administrative, and managerial	356	491	1.8	2.4	1.7	2.3	1.9	2.5
Professional specialty	369	482	1.7	2.2	1.6	2.3	1.9	2.1
Technical, sales, and administrative support	1,464	1,699	3.6	4.2	3.1	3.9	3.8	4.3
Technicians and related support	97	133	2.2	2.9	2.3	3.4	2.0	2.4
Sales occupations	684	794	4.0	4.7	2.9	3.6	5.1	5.8
Administrative support, including clerical	684	772	3.5	4.0	4.0	4.8	3.4	3.8
Service occupations	1,023	1,150	5.3	5.9	5.3	6.1	5.3	5.8
Private household	58	53	6.9	6.9	9.1	(2)	6.8	6.6
Protective service	65	74	2.6	2.9	2.3	2.7	3.9	3.9
Service, except private household and protective	900	1,023	5.6	6.3	6.3	7.3	5.3	5.8
Precision production, craft, and repair	554	711	3.6	4.6	3.5	4.4	4.3	6.3
Mechanics and repairers	129	153	2.6	3.1	2.5	3.0	4.3	4.0
Construction trades	312	391	4.9	5.9	4.8	5.8	6.8	9.5
Other precision production, craft, and repair	113	167	2.8	4.2	2.5	3.6	3.8	6.3
Operators, fabricators, and laborers	1,228	1,481	6.3	7.7	5.9	7.3	7.5	8.9
Machine operators, assemblers, and inspectors	455	573	5.9	7.8	4.9	7.1	7.4	9.1
Transportation and material moving occupations	253	298	4.4	5.0	4.2	4.9	5.8	6.0
Handlers, equipment cleaners, helpers, and laborers	520	610	8.7	10.3	8.7	10.3	8.6	10.1
Construction laborers	133	155	11.6	13.1	11.6	13.0	11.9	18.0
Other handlers, equipment cleaners, helpers, and laborers	387	455	8.0	9.6	7.9	9.5	8.5	9.8
Farming, forestry, and fishing	215	259	6.0	7.4	5.5	6.9	7.7	9.1
No previous work experience	431	453	–	–	–	–	–	–
16 to 19 years	300	311	–	–	–	–	–	–
20 to 24 years	70	67	–	–	–	–	–	–
25 years and over	62	74	–	–	–	–	–	–

[1] Includes a small number of persons whose last job was in the Armed Forces.
[2] Data not shown where base is less than 35,000.

SOURCE: "25. Unemployed persons by occupation and sex," in *Employment and Earnings,* vol. 49, no. 1, January 2002

upper educational level, 16 percent of the women versus 12 percent of the men were college graduates.

Still Wanted a Job

In 2001 only about 6.5 percent of those who were no longer part of the labor force still wanted a job, and 40.7 percent of those who wanted a job had looked for work during the previous year. Some of the reasons those who were available for work gave for not looking were discouragement over job prospects (25 percent), family responsibilities (10.3 percent), school or training (16 percent), and ill health or disability (7 percent). (See Table 3.13.)

TABLE 3.7

Unemployed persons by industry and sex, 2000–2001

Industry	Thousands of persons — Total		Unemployment rates — Total		Men		Women	
	2000	2001	2000	2001	2000	2001	2000	2001
Total, 16 years and over	5,655	6,742	4.0	4.8	3.9	4.8	4.1	4.7
Nonagricultural private wage and salary workers	4,446	5,468	4.1	5.0	4.0	5.0	4.2	4.9
Mining	21	27	3.9	4.7	4.3	4.8	1.5	4.0
Construction	499	598	6.4	7.3	6.5	7.5	5.2	5.1
Manufacturing	733	1,024	3.6	5.2	3.1	4.7	4.7	6.3
Durable goods	413	632	3.4	5.3	3.1	4.9	4.0	6.4
Lumber and wood products	30	42	4.1	6.3	4.1	6.6	3.9	4.7
Furniture and fixtures	30	32	4.6	5.1	4.2	4.7	5.5	5.8
Stone, clay, and glass products	20	30	3.2	5.4	3.3	5.3	2.9	5.8
Primary metal industries	24	44	3.1	5.6	3.3	4.9	2.2	9.1
Fabricated metal products	45	65	3.5	4.9	3.1	4.5	4.7	6.5
Machinery, except electrical	79	119	3.2	5.0	2.9	4.9	3.9	5.2
Electrical machinery, equipment, and supplies	53	113	2.7	5.9	2.2	4.7	3.5	7.8
Transportation equipment	82	98	3.5	4.4	3.1	4.0	4.6	5.8
Automobiles	50	66	3.7	5.2	3.1	4.7	5.4	6.7
Other transportation equipment	31	32	3.2	3.4	3.2	3.2	3.3	4.3
Professional and photographic equipment	16	28	2.1	3.8	2.0	3.3	2.3	4.7
Other durable goods industries	35	61	5.0	8.2	4.2	8.3	6.1	8.0
Nondurable goods	320	391	4.0	5.1	3.2	4.4	5.3	6.2
Food and kindred products	91	88	5.2	5.2	3.8	4.7	7.8	6.1
Textile mill products	22	45	4.2	8.5	3.3	7.5	5.2	9.7
Apparel and other textile products	60	61	8.0	10.0	5.7	8.0	9.3	11.2
Paper and allied products	16	25	2.6	4.0	2.0	3.1	4.2	6.6
Printing and publishing	56	69	3.1	4.0	2.8	4.2	3.5	3.8
Chemicals and allied products	30	50	2.3	3.9	2.3	3.7	2.3	4.2
Rubber and miscellaneous plastics products	30	40	3.2	4.8	2.8	4.0	4.1	6.4
Other nondurable goods industries	15	14	5.1	4.5	4.9	3.9	5.5	5.6
Transportation and public utilities	243	329	3.1	4.1	2.9	3.9	3.4	4.5
Transportation	179	221	3.7	4.5	3.6	4.4	3.9	5.0
Communications and other public utilities	65	108	2.1	3.5	1.8	3.2	2.8	3.9
Wholesale and retail trade	1,381	1,554	5.0	5.6	4.4	5.2	5.7	6.1
Wholesale trade	150	195	2.8	3.9	2.5	3.5	3.6	4.8
Retail trade	1,231	1,359	5.5	6.0	5.0	5.7	6.0	6.3
Finance, insurance, and real estate	185	226	2.3	2.8	2.0	2.7	2.5	2.8
Service industries	1,383	1,711	3.8	4.6	3.9	4.9	3.7	4.3
Professional services	503	633	2.4	2.9	2.1	2.8	2.5	2.9
Other service industries	880	1,077	5.8	7.0	5.4	6.6	6.3	7.5
Agricultural wage and salary workers	165	202	7.5	9.7	7.0	9.7	8.9	9.5
Government, self-employed, and unpaid famiy workers	613	619	2.1	2.1	2.0	2.1	2.1	2.1
No previous work experience	431	453	–	–	–	–	–	–

SOURCE: "26. Unemployed persons by industry and sex," in *Employment and Earnings,* vol. 49, no. 1, January 2002

TABLE 3.8

Unemployed persons by selected demographic characteristics and duration of unemployment, 2001

	2001							
	Thousands of persons						Weeks	
				15 weeks and over				
Characteristic	Total	Less than 5 weeks	5 to 14 weeks	Total	15 to 26 weeks	27 weeks and over	Average (mean) duration	Median duration
Total								
Total, 16 years and over	6,742	2,833	2,163	1,746	949	797	13.2	6.8
16 to 19 years	1,187	613	375	199	116	83	9.6	4.4
20 to 24 years	1,203	567	384	252	139	113	11.4	5.4
25 to 34 years	1,447	613	470	363	202	161	12.7	6.7
35 to 44 years	1,359	507	456	395	215	180	14.2	8.0
45 to 54 years	972	338	307	327	174	153	16.0	9.0
55 to 64 years	446	144	137	165	85	80	18.0	9.8
65 years and over	129	51	34	44	17	26	18.1	7.6
Men, 16 years and over	3,663	1,504	1,187	972	529	443	13.5	7.1
16 to 19 years	660	331	218	111	64	47	9.8	4.5
20 to 24 years	680	319	215	147	81	66	11.5	5.5
25 to 34 years	731	302	239	189	112	77	12.9	7.1
35 to 44 years	722	266	246	209	113	96	14.2	8.1
45 to 54 years	531	177	167	186	98	88	16.9	9.3
55 to 64 years	265	79	82	104	52	52	19.3	10.3
65 years and over	76	29	20	26	10	17	19.0	7.7
Women, 16 years and over	3,079	1,329	976	774	420	354	12.7	6.5
16 to 19 years	527	282	157	89	53	36	9.3	4.2
20 to 24 years	523	248	170	106	59	47	11.2	5.2
25 to 34 years	716	311	231	174	89	84	12.5	6.4
35 to 44 years	637	241	210	186	102	84	14.2	7.9
45 to 54 years	441	160	139	141	76	66	15.0	8.6
55 to 64 years	181	65	55	61	33	28	16.1	9.0
65 years and over	53	22	14	17	8	10	16.8	7.5
Race and Hispanic origin								
White, 16 years and over	4,923	2,187	1,580	1,156	661	496	11.9	6.1
Men	2,730	1,178	881	671	383	288	12.4	6.5
Women	2,193	1,009	699	485	278	208	11.3	5.6
Black, 16 years and over	1,450	503	457	489	235	254	16.9	8.9
Men	731	251	236	244	116	128	17.1	9.0
Women	719	252	221	245	120	126	16.8	8.9
Hispanic origin, 16 years and over	1,037	458	337	242	137	106	11.9	6.3
Men	542	245	177	121	68	53	11.7	6.0
Women	495	213	160	122	69	53	12.2	6.7
Marital status								
Men, 16 years and over:								
Married, spouse present	1,213	455	406	351	201	150	14.0	7.9
Widowed, divorced, or separated	472	185	144	143	68	75	16.1	7.7
Single (never married)	1,979	864	637	478	260	218	12.6	6.4
Women, 16 years and over:								
Married, spouse present	1,058	453	334	270	154	116	12.7	6.5
Widowed, divorced, or separated	628	242	199	187	97	89	14.3	7.9
Single (never married)	1,393	633	443	317	168	149	12.0	5.8

Note: Detail for the above race and Hispanic-origin groups will not sum to totals because data for the "other races" group are not presented and Hispanics are included in both the white and black population groups.

SOURCE: "31. Unemployed persons by selected demographic characteristics and duration of employment," in *Employment and Earnings*, vol. 49, no. 1, January 2002

TABLE 3.9

Unemployed persons by occupation, industry, and duration of unemployment, 2001

	2001							
	Thousands of persons						Weeks	
				15 weeks and over				
Occupation and industry	Total	Less than 5 weeks	5 to 14 weeks	Total	15 to 26 weeks	27 weeks and over	Average (mean) duration	Median duration
Occupation								
Managerial and professional specialty	973	377	320	276	159	117	13.7	7.8
Technical, sales, and administrative support	1,699	725	546	429	238	191	12.7	6.6
Service occupations	1,150	521	351	278	132	145	13.1	5.9
Precision production, craft, and repair	711	320	228	163	96	67	12.0	5.9
Operators, fabricators, and laborers	1,481	601	470	409	222	187	13.6	7.2
Farming, forestry, and fishing	259	104	85	70	44	25	12.5	7.3
Industry[1]								
Agriculture	202	87	65	49	32	17	11.5	6.3
Construction	609	270	207	132	72	60	11.9	6.0
Manufacturing	1,028	387	327	313	182	132	13.9	8.2
Durable goods	635	245	201	189	112	76	13.5	8.0
Nondurable goods	393	143	126	124	69	55	14.6	8.5
Transportation and public utilities	352	138	119	95	54	41	13.0	7.6
Wholesale and retail trade	1,562	699	483	379	203	176	12.5	6.1
Finance, insurance, and real estate	231	86	77	68	37	32	14.4	8.2
Services	1,949	843	616	491	261	230	13.1	6.6
Public administration	116	35	39	42	24	18	17.0	10.7
No previous work experience	453	179	155	118	55	63	14.8	7.0

[1]Includes wage and salary workers only.

SOURCE: "32. Unemployed persons by occupation, industry, and duration of unemployment," in *Employment and Earnings,* vol. 49, no. 1, January 2002

TABLE 3.10

Unemployed persons by reason for unemployment, sex, and age, 2000–2001

(Numbers in thousands)

Reason	Total, 16 years and over		Men, 20 years and over		Women, 20 years and over		Both sexes, 16 to 19 years	
	2000	2001	2000	2001	2000	2001	2000	2001
Number of unemployed								
Total unemployed	5,655	6,742	2,350	3,003	2,212	2,551	1,093	1,187
Job losers and persons who completed temporary jobs	2,492	3,428	1,398	1,977	934	1,265	160	186
On temporary layoff	842	1,049	484	613	302	367	57	70
Not on temporary layoff	1,650	2,379	914	1,364	632	898	103	117
Permanent job losers	1,108	1,737	609	993	441	681	58	63
Persons who completed temporary jobs	542	642	306	371	191	217	45	54
Job leavers	775	832	324	369	340	362	111	101
Reentrants	1,957	2,029	574	606	860	835	522	589
New entrants	431	453	54	52	78	90	300	311
Percent distribution								
Job losers and persons who completed temporary jobs	44.1	50.8	59.5	65.8	42.2	49.6	14.6	15.7
On temporary layoff	14.9	15.6	20.6	20.4	13.6	14.4	5.2	5.9
Not on temporary layoff	29.2	35.3	38.9	45.4	28.6	35.2	9.4	9.8
Job leavers	13.7	12.3	13.8	12.3	15.4	14.2	10.1	8.5
Reentrants	34.6	30.1	24.4	20.2	38.9	32.7	47.8	49.6
New entrants	7.6	6.7	2.3	1.7	3.5	3.5	27.4	26.2
Unemployed as a percent of the civilian labor force								
Job losers and persons who completed temporary jobs	1.8	2.4	2.0	2.8	1.5	2.0	1.9	2.3
Job leavers	.6	.6	.5	.5	.6	.6	1.3	1.3
Reentrants	1.4	1.4	.8	.8	1.4	1.3	6.2	7.3
New entrants	.3	.3	.1	.1	.1	.1	3.6	3.9

SOURCE: "27. Unemployed persons by reason for unemployment, sex, and age," in *Employment and Earnings,* vol. 49, no. 1, January 2002

TABLE 3.11

Unemployed persons by selected characteristics, 2001

(Percent distribution)

Reason, sex, and age	2001						
	Total unemployed		Duration of unemployment				
					15 weeks and over		
	Thousands of persons	Percent	Less than 5 weeks	5 to 14 weeks	Total	15 to 26 weeks	27 weeks and over
Total, 16 years and over	6,742	100.0	42.0	32.1	25.9	14.1	11.8
Job losers and persons who completed temporary jobs	3,428	100.0	42.0	32.2	25.7	15.5	10.3
On temporary layoff	1,049	100.0	56.1	31.0	12.9	9.8	3.1
Not on temporary layoff	2,379	100.0	35.8	32.8	31.4	18.0	13.4
Permanent job losers	1,737	100.0	33.8	32.8	33.4	19.0	14.4
Persons who completed temporary jobs	642	100.0	41.3	32.6	26.1	15.3	10.8
Job leavers	832	100.0	47.6	31.7	20.6	11.4	9.2
Reentrants	2,029	100.0	40.2	31.5	28.3	13.2	15.0
New entrants	453	100.0	39.6	34.3	26.1	12.1	14.0
Men, 20 years and over	3,003	100.0	39.0	32.3	28.7	15.5	13.2
Job losers and persons who completed temporary jobs	1,977	100.0	40.1	32.5	27.3	16.2	11.1
On temporary layoff	613	100.0	52.9	32.7	14.4	11.3	3.0
Not on temporary layoff	1,364	100.0	34.4	32.4	33.2	18.4	14.8
Permanent job losers	993	100.0	33.2	32.0	34.9	19.0	15.9
Persons who completed temporary jobs	371	100.0	37.7	33.7	28.6	16.8	11.9
Job leavers	369	100.0	43.0	33.7	23.2	12.0	11.2
Reentrants	606	100.0	34.0	30.9	35.1	15.4	19.7
New entrants	52	100.0	28.2	28.3	43.5	13.9	29.7
Women, 20 years and over	2,551	100.0	41.0	32.1	26.9	14.4	12.5
Job losers and persons who completed temporary jobs	1,265	100.0	41.4	32.7	25.8	15.9	9.9
On temporary layoff	367	100.0	57.1	30.7	12.2	8.7	3.6
Not on temporary layoff	898	100.0	35.1	33.6	31.4	18.9	12.5
Permanent job losers	681	100.0	32.5	34.3	33.2	20.2	13.0
Persons who completed temporary jobs	217	100.0	43.1	31.3	25.6	14.7	10.9
Job leavers	362	100.0	47.7	30.9	21.4	12.3	9.1
Reentrants	835	100.0	38.0	31.6	30.4	13.2	17.2
New entrants	90	100.0	36.2	33.1	30.6	12.6	18.0
Both sexes, 16 to 19 years	1,187	100.0	51.6	31.6	16.8	9.8	7.0
Job losers and persons who completed temporary jobs	186	100.0	66.0	25.8	8.2	4.7	3.4
On temporary layoff	70	100.0	78.4	17.8	3.8	2.3	1.5
Not on temporary layoff	117	100.0	58.6	30.6	10.8	6.2	4.6
Permanent job losers	63	100.0	58.3	30.8	10.9	5.2	5.6
Persons who completed temporary jobs	54	100.0	59.1	30.3	10.6	7.3	3.3
Job leavers	101	100.0	64.1	27.4	8.5	6.1	2.4
Reentrants	589	100.0	49.8	32.0	18.2	11.0	7.2
New entrants	311	100.0	42.5	35.6	22.0	11.7	10.2

SOURCE: "29. Unemployed persons by reason for unemployment, sex, age, and duration of unemployment," in *Employment and Earnings,* vol. 49, no. 1, January 2002

TABLE 3.12

Unemployed jobseekers by sex, reason for unemployment, and active jobsearch methods used, 2001

	2001									
	Thousands of persons		Methods used as a percent of total jobseekers							
Sex and reason	Total unem- ployed	Total job- seekers	Employer directly	Sent out resumes or filled out applica- tions	Placed or answered ads	Friends or relatives	Public employ- ment agency	Private employ- ment agency	Other	Average number of methods used
Total, 16 years and over	6,742	5,693	62.4	51.5	15.8	15.6	19.2	8.6	11.4	1.85
Job losers and persons who completed temporary jobs[1]	3,428	2,379	64.8	51.9	19.0	19.3	25.7	11.7	13.7	2.07
Job leavers	832	832	65.4	51.2	17.8	12.9	19.1	9.0	11.1	1.87
Reentrants	2,029	2,029	59.5	51.1	12.5	13.1	13.2	5.6	10.0	1.65
New entrants	453	453	58.0	52.1	10.1	12.8	11.7	4.3	6.8	1.56
Men, 16 years and over	3,663	3,004	63.9	50.0	15.5	17.2	19.5	8.7	12.2	1.88
Job losers and persons who completed temporary jobs[1]	2,098	1,439	65.9	49.9	18.6	20.6	25.4	11.5	14.9	2.08
Job leavers	419	419	68.1	48.6	16.0	12.6	19.4	9.4	11.3	1.86
Reentrants	929	929	60.6	50.3	11.7	14.9	12.1	5.3	9.9	1.65
New entrants	217	217	56.4	52.6	9.8	13.2	12.3	4.0	6.4	1.55
Women, 16 years and over	3,079	2,689	60.8	53.2	16.1	13.8	18.8	8.3	10.6	1.82
Job losers and persons who completed temporary jobs[1]	1,330	940	63.0	54.9	19.4	17.2	26.2	12.1	11.9	2.06
Job leavers	413	413	62.7	53.8	19.6	13.1	18.8	8.7	10.9	1.88
Reentrants	1,100	1,100	58.5	51.8	13.3	11.6	14.1	5.8	10.1	1.65
New entrants	236	236	59.4	51.6	10.3	12.4	11.2	4.6	7.1	1.57

[1] Data on the number of jobseekers and the jobsearch methods used exclude persons on temporary layoff.
Note: The jobseeker total is less than the total unemployed because it does not include persons on temporary layoff. The percent using each method will always total more than 100 because many jobseekers use more than one method.

SOURCE: "34. Unemployed jobseekers by sex, reason for unemployment, and active jobsearch methods used," in *Employment and Earnings,* vol. 49, no. 1, January 2002

TABLE 3.13

Persons not in the labor force by desire and availability for work, age, and sex, 2000–2001

(In thousands)

Category	Total 2000	Total 2001	Age 16 to 24 years 2000	Age 16 to 24 years 2001	Age 25 to 54 years 2000	Age 25 to 54 years 2001	Age 55 years and over 2000	Age 55 years and over 2001	Sex Men 2000	Sex Men 2001	Sex Women 2000	Sex Women 2001
Total not in the labor force	68,836	70,050	11,738	12,384	18,953	19,495	38,146	38,171	25,484	26,114	43,352	43,935
Do not want a job now[1]	64,459	65,483	10,107	10,629	17,007	17,509	37,345	37,345	23,627	24,119	40,832	41,363
Want a job[1]	4,377	4,567	1,631	1,755	1,945	1,986	801	826	1,856	1,995	2,521	2,572
Did not search for work in previous year	2,675	2,705	903	946	1,143	1,130	629	629	1,068	1,130	1,607	1,575
Searched for work in previous year[2]	1,703	1,862	728	809	802	856	172	197	788	865	914	997
Not available to work now	550	591	280	306	237	248	33	36	217	227	334	364
Available to work now	1,152	1,271	448	503	565	608	139	161	572	638	581	634
Reason not currently looking:												
Discouragement over job prospects[3]	260	319	79	105	143	165	39	49	160	191	100	128
Reasons other than discouragement	892	952	369	398	422	443	101	112	412	447	481	505
Family responsibilities	118	131	26	31	83	87	10	13	23	30	96	101
In school or training	185	208	158	174	26	32	1	2	97	112	88	96
Ill health or disability	95	95	15	16	58	55	22	24	49	45	46	50
Other[4]	493	518	171	177	255	268	68	74	243	260	250	258

[1] Includes some persons who are not asked if they want a job.
[2] Persons who had a job in the prior 12 months must have searched since the end of that job.
[3] Includes believes no work available, could not find work, lacks necessary schooling or training, employer thinks too young or old, and other types of discrimination.
[4] Includes those who did not actively look for work in the prior 4 weeks for such reasons as child-care and transportation problems, as well as a small number for which reason for nonparticipation was not ascertained.

SOURCE: "35. Persons not in the labor force by desire and availability for work, age, and sex," in *Employment and Earnings,* vol. 49, no. 1, January 2002

TABLE 3.14

Persons 25–54 years old who did not work or look for work in 1996 by selected characteristics, March 1997

(Numbers in thousands)

Characteristic	Total nonworkers Number	Total nonworkers Percent	Percent distribution by income Under $20,000	Percent distribution by income $20,000 to $39,999	Percent distribution by income $40,000 to $59,999	Percent distribution by income $60,000 or more
Men, 25 to 54 years	4,038	100.0	60.2	22.1	10.9	6.7
Ill or disabled	2,527	62.6	61.9	21.2	11.6	5.4
Retired	188	4.7	33.8	28.5	19.4	18.2
Home responsibilities	341	8.4	54.8	28.8	8.8	7.6
Going to school	398	9.9	60.0	21.7	6.4	11.9
Could not find work	217	5.4	61.6	15.9	17.1	5.4
Other	367	9.1	67.1	22.7	5.5	4.7
Women, 25 to 54 years	11,717	100.0	38.2	24.5	16.0	21.3
Ill or disabled	2,291	19.6	62.1	20.1	8.1	9.7
Retired	371	3.2	29.0	19.8	20.0	31.2
Home responsibilities	8,064	68.8	30.3	26.3	18.6	24.8
Going to school	607	5.2	48.5	23.4	9.9	18.3
Could not find work	114	.7	81.3	7.9	5.1	5.8
Other	269	1.7	44.2	22.1	16.5	17.2

Note: Income refers to family income for those who were living with their families or to personal income for those not in families. Income refers to earnings, disability or unemployment benefits, interest income, and other sources. Detail may not sum to totals due to rounding.

SOURCE: "Persons 25–54 Years Old Who Did Not Work or Look For Work in 1996 by Reason, Income, and Sex, March 1997," in "Who's Not Working?" *Issues in Labor Statistics,* U.S. Department of Labor, Bureau of Labor Statistics, Washington, DC, 1998

CHAPTER 4
THE EDUCATION OF AMERICAN WORKERS

Education is an investment in skills, and like all investments, it involves both costs and returns. The cost of finishing high school to the student is quite low. However, the cost to the student of attending college is higher because it includes tuition, books, fees, and the earnings a student gives up either by not working at all during college or by working part-time. It is important to remember that while the returns from a high school or college education can be measured economically, there are invaluable social, emotional, and intellectual returns.

While some returns from education accrue for the individual, others benefit society and the nation in general. Returns related to the economy, specifically the labor market, include better job opportunities and jobs that are less sensitive to general economic conditions. Other societal returns often attributed to education include a greater interest and participation in civil affairs.

A BETTER-EDUCATED NATION

American workers are better educated than ever before. Before the end of World War II (1939–45), with the exception of doctors, lawyers, engineers, teachers, and some other professionals, very few people earned higher degrees for the purpose of preparing for a career or vocation. For the most part, a person who wanted training for a job or occupation went to a vocational high school or became an apprentice, one who learns a trade from a highly skilled person.

The GI Bill of Rights, introduced after World War II, changed the way Americans looked at higher education. The soldiers, sailors, and pilots returning to civilian life wanted to make better lives for themselves, and the U.S. government was willing to pay to give them the chance. Federal money paid to America's returning veterans opened up and enlarged trade and vocational schools and filled college classrooms across the nation. Since then, American colleges

and universities have been graduating more and more engineers, accountants, scientists, businesspeople, technicians, nurses, and others with similar technical careers.

How Well Educated Are Americans?

From approximately 1925 to 2000 the median number of school years completed had risen from 8.4 years in 1930 to 13 years. As late as 1930 fewer than 1 in 5 Americans had completed 4 or more years of high school. Since that time the proportion has steadily increased, reaching 84.2 percent of those 25 years and older in 2000. Among young people 25 to 29 years of age, 88.1 percent completed 4 or more years of high school. (See Table 4.1.) By 2000 almost 25 percent of people 25 years and older had completed 4 or more years of college, compared to roughly 2 percent in 1940. People 25 years and older who had less than 12 years of education have decreased steadily since 1940; roughly 15 percent of these people had less than 12 years of education in 2000, compared to almost 80 percent in 1940. (See Figure 4.1.)

More High School Graduates in College

At the end of the 2000 to 2001 school year, 2.8 million students graduated from high school, representing about 70.5 percent of all 17-year-olds. In 1996 about 1.7 million or 65 percent of high school graduates were enrolled in college. In 1960 only 45 percent of high school graduates enrolled in college.

GENDER. Increased female enrollment has contributed to the growth in college enrollment. From 1980 to 1999 male enrollment increased by only 10.5 percent, while the number of females rose by 33 percent. (See Table 4.2.) Between 1999 and 2011 female enrollment is projected to increase another 24 percent, while male enrollment is thought to only rise 14 percent.

OLDER STUDENTS. Between the school years 1990 and 1999 the number of older students attending

TABLE 4.1

Years of education completed by persons age 25 and over and 25–29, by race/ethnicity and sex, 1910–2000

	Percent, by years of school completed											
	All races			White, non-Hispanic[1]			Black, non-Hispanic[1]			Hispanic		
Age and year	Less than 5 years of elementary school	High school completion or higher[2]	4 or more years of college[3]	Less than 5 years of elementary school	High school completion or higher[2]	4 or more years of college[3]	Less than 5 years of elementary school	High school completion or higher[2]	4 or more years of college[3]	Less than 5 years of elementary school	High school completion or higher[2]	4 or more years of college[3]
1	2	3	4	5	6	7	8	9	10	11	12	13

Males and females

25 and over

1910[4]	23.8	13.5	2.7	—	—	—	—	—	—	—	—	—
1920[4]	22.0	16.4	3.3	—	—	—	—	—	—	—	—	—
1930[4]	17.5	19.1	3.9	—	—	—	—	—	—	—	—	—
April 1940	13.7	24.5	4.6	10.9	26.1	4.9	41.8	7.7	1.3	—	—	—
April 1950	11.1	34.3	6.2	8.9	36.4	6.6	32.6	13.7	2.2	—	—	—
April 1960	8.3	41.1	7.7	6.7	43.2	8.1	23.5	21.7	3.5	—	—	—
March 1970	5.3	55.2	11.0	4.2	57.4	11.6	14.7	36.1	6.1	—	—	—
March 1980	3.4	68.6	17.0	1.9	71.9	18.4	9.1	51.4	7.9	15.8	44.5	7.6
March 1985	2.7	73.9	19.4	1.4	77.5	20.8	6.1	59.9	11.1	13.5	47.9	8.5
March 1989	2.5	76.9	21.1	1.2	80.7	22.8	5.2	64.7	11.7	12.2	50.9	9.9
March 1990	2.5	77.6	21.3	1.1	81.4	23.1	5.1	66.2	11.3	12.3	50.8	9.2
March 1991	2.4	78.4	21.4	1.1	82.4	23.3	4.7	66.8	11.5	12.5	51.3	9.7
March 1992	2.1	79.4	21.4	0.9	83.4	23.2	3.9	67.7	11.9	11.8	52.6	9.3
March 1993	2.1	80.2	21.9	0.8	84.1	23.8	3.7	70.5	12.2	11.8	53.1	9.0
March 1994	1.9	80.9	22.2	0.8	84.9	24.3	2.7	73.0	12.9	10.8	53.3	9.1
March 1995	1.9	81.7	23.0	0.7	85.9	23.4	2.5	73.8	13.3	10.6	53.4	9.3
March 1996	1.8	81.7	23.6	0.6	86.0	25.9	2.2	74.6	13.8	10.4	53.1	9.3
March 1997	1.7	82.1	23.9	0.6	86.3	26.2	2.0	75.3	13.3	9.4	54.7	10.3
March 1998	1.7	82.8	24.4	0.6	87.1	26.6	1.7	76.4	14.8	9.3	55.5	11.0
March 1999	1.6	83.4	25.2	0.6	87.7	27.7	1.8	77.4	15.5	9.0	56.1	10.9
March 2000	1.6	84.1	25.6	0.5	88.4	28.1	1.6	78.9	16.6	8.7	57.0	10.6

25 to 29

1920[4]	—	—	—	12.9	22.0	4.5	44.6	6.3	1.2	—	—	—
April 1940	5.9	38.1	5.9	3.4	41.2	6.4	27.0	12.3	1.6	—	—	—
April 1950	4.6	52.8	7.7	3.3	56.3	8.2	16.1	23.6	2.8	—	—	—
April 1960	2.8	60.7	11.0	2.2	63.7	11.8	7.2	38.6	5.4	—	—	—
March 1970	1.1	75.4	16.4	0.9	77.8	17.3	2.2	58.4	10.0	—	—	—
March 1980	0.8	85.4	22.5	0.3	89.2	25.0	0.7	76.7	11.6	6.7	58.0	7.7
March 1985	0.7	86.1	22.2	0.2	89.5	24.4	0.4	80.5	11.6	6.0	60.9	11.1
March 1989	1.0	85.5	23.4	0.3	89.3	26.3	0.5	82.3	12.7	5.4	61.0	10.1
March 1990	1.2	85.7	23.2	0.3	90.1	26.4	1.0	81.7	13.4	7.3	58.2	8.2
March 1991	1.0	85.4	23.2	0.3	89.8	26.7	0.5	81.8	11.0	5.8	56.7	9.2
March 1992	0.9	86.3	23.6	0.3	90.7	27.2	0.8	80.9	11.1	5.2	60.9	9.5
March 1993	0.7	86.7	23.7	0.3	91.2	27.2	0.2	82.7	13.3	4.0	60.9	8.3
March 1994	0.8	86.1	23.3	0.3	91.1	27.1	0.6	84.1	13.6	3.6	60.3	8.0
March 1995	1.0	86.9	24.7	0.3	92.5	28.8	0.2	86.7	15.4	4.9	57.2	8.9
March 1996	0.8	87.3	27.1	0.2	92.6	31.6	0.4	86.0	14.6	4.3	61.1	10.0
March 1997	0.8	87.4	27.8	0.1	92.9	32.6	0.6	86.9	14.2	4.2	61.8	11.0
March 1998	0.7	88.1	27.3	0.1	93.6	32.3	0.4	88.3	15.8	3.7	62.8	10.4
March 1999	0.6	87.8	28.2	0.1	93.0	33.6	0.2	88.7	15.0	3.2	61.6	8.9
March 2000	0.7	88.1	29.1	0.1	94.0	34.0	—	86.8	17.8	3.8	62.8	9.7

Males

25 and over

April 1940	15.1	22.7	5.5	12.0	24.2	5.9	46.2	6.9	1.4	—	—	—
April 1950	12.2	32.6	7.3	9.8	34.6	7.9	36.9	12.6	2.1	—	—	—
April 1960	9.4	39.5	9.7	7.4	41.6	10.3	27.7	20.0	3.5	—	—	—
March 1970	5.9	55.0	14.1	4.5	57.2	15.0	17.9	35.4	6.8	—	—	—
March 1980	3.6	69.2	20.9	2.0	72.4	22.8	11.3	51.2	7.7	16.5	44.9	9.2
March 1990	2.7	77.7	24.4	1.3	81.6	26.7	6.4	65.8	11.9	12.9	50.3	9.8
March 1994	2.1	81.1	25.1	0.8	85.1	27.8	3.9	71.8	12.7	11.4	53.4	9.6
March 1995	2.0	81.7	26.0	0.8	86.0	28.9	3.4	73.5	13.7	10.8	52.9	10.1
March 1996	1.9	81.9	26.0	0.7	86.1	28.8	2.9	74.6	12.5	10.2	53.0	10.3
March 1997	1.8	82.0	26.2	0.6	86.3	29.0	2.9	73.8	12.5	9.2	54.9	10.6
March 1998	1.7	82.8	26.5	0.7	87.1	29.3	2.3	75.4	14.0	9.3	55.7	11.1
March 1999	1.6	83.5	27.5	0.6	87.7	30.6	2.1	77.2	14.3	9.0	56.0	10.7
March 2000	1.6	84.2	27.8	0.6	88.5	30.8	2.1	79.1	16.4	8.2	56.6	10.7

colleges grew faster than the number of younger students. However, this is beginning to change. During that period, enrollment of students under age 24 increased by almost 12 percent, while enrollment of persons 35 and over increased by a little over 12 percent. (See Figure 4.2 and Table 4.2.) From 1999 to 2011 the National Center for Education Statistics projects a rise of 22.2 percent in enrollments of persons 24 and under and only a 5.4 percent increase in the number of those 35 and over.

TABLE 4.1

Years of education completed by persons age 25 and over and 25–29, by race/ethnicity and sex, 1910–2000 [CONTINUED]

	All races			White, non-Hispanic[1]			Black, non-Hispanic[1]			Hispanic		
Age and year	Less than 5 years of elementary school	High school completion or higher[2]	4 or more years of college[3]	Less than 5 years of elementary school	High school completion or higher[2]	4 or more years of college[3]	Less than 5 years of elementary school	High school completion or higher[2]	4 or more years of college[3]	Less than 5 years of elementary school	High school completion or higher[2]	4 or more years of college[3]
1	2	3	4	5	6	7	8	9	10	11	12	13
						Females						
25 and over												
April 1940	12.4	26.3	3.8	9.8	28.1	4.0	37.5	8.4	1.2	—	—	—
April 1950	10.0	36.0	5.2	8.1	38.2	5.4	28.6	14.7	2.4	—	—	—
April 1960	7.4	42.5	5.8	6.0	44.7	6.0	19.7	23.1	3.6	—	—	—
March 1970	4.7	55.4	8.2	3.9	57.7	8.6	11.9	36.6	5.6	—	—	—
March 1980	3.2	68.1	13.6	1.8	71.5	14.4	7.4	51.5	8.1	15.3	44.2	6.2
March 1990	2.2	77.5	18.4	1.0	81.3	19.8	4.1	66.5	10.8	11.7	51.3	8.7
March 1994	1.7	80.8	19.6	0.7	84.7	21.1	1.8	73.9	13.1	10.3	53.2	8.6
March 1995	1.7	81.6	20.2	0.6	85.8	22.2	1.8	74.1	13.0	10.4	53.8	8.4
March 1996	1.7	81.6	21.4	0.5	85.9	23.2	1.6	74.6	14.8	10.6	53.3	8.3
March 1997	1.6	82.2	21.7	0.5	86.3	23.7	1.3	76.5	14.0	9.5	54.6	10.1
March 1998	1.6	82.9	22.4	0.6	87.1	24.1	1.2	77.1	15.5	9.2	55.3	10.9
March 1999	1.6	83.4	23.1	0.5	87.7	25.0	1.5	77.5	16.5	9.0	56.3	11.0
March 2000	1.5	84.0	23.6	0.4	88.4	25.5	1.1	78.7	16.8	9.3	57.5	10.6

—Not available.

[1] Includes persons of Hispanic origin for years prior to 1980.

[2] Data for years prior to 1993 include all persons with at least 4 years of high school.

[3] Data for 1993 and later years are for persons with a bachelor's or higher degree.

[4] Estimates based on Bureau of the Census retrojection of 1940 Census data on education by age.

Note: Data for 1980 and subsequent years are for the noninstitutional population.

SOURCE: "Table 8. Years of school completed by persons age 25 and over and 25 to 29, by race/ethnicity and sex: 1910 to 2000," in *Digest of Education Statistics, 2001,* U.S. Department of Education, National Center for Education Statistics, Washington, DC, 2001 [Online] http://nces.ed.gov/pubs2002/digest2001/tables/PDF /table008.pdf [accessed May 31, 2002]

FIGURE 4.1

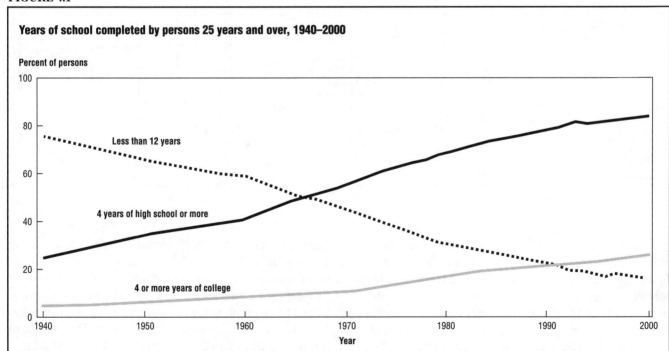

Years of school completed by persons 25 years and over, 1940–2000

SOURCE: "Figure 3. Years of school completed by persons 25 years and over: 1940–2000," in *Digest of Education Statistics, 2001,* U.S. Department of Education, National Center for Education Statistics, Washington, DC, 2001 [Online] http://nces.ed.gov/pubs2002/digest2001/ch1.asp [accessed May 31, 2002]

TABLE 4.2

Total fall enrollment in institutions of higher education, by gender and age, 1970–2011

[In thousands]

Sex and age	1970[1]	1975[1]	1980[1]	1990[1]	1995[1]	1996[1]	1997[1]	1998[2]	1999[2]	Projected[2]			
										2000	2001	2010	2011
1	2	3	4	5	6	7	8	9	10	11	12	13	14
Men and women, total	**8,581**	**11,185**	**12,097**	**13,819**	**14,262**	**14,300**	**14,345**	**14,507**	**14,791**	**14,979**	**15,300**	**17,457**	**17,688**
14 to 17 years old	259	278	247	177	148	229	168	119	143	172	170	224	224
18 and 19 years old	2,600	2,786	2,901	2,950	2,894	3,004	3,014	3,382	3,414	3,458	3,543	4,136	4,111
20 and 21 years old	1,880	2,243	2,424	2,761	2,705	2,643	2,843	2,811	2,989	3,017	3,101	3,615	3,716
22 to 24 years old	1,457	1,753	1,989	2,144	2,411	2,316	2,453	2,377	2,435	2,395	2,457	2,862	2,928
25 to 29 years old	1,074	1,774	1,871	1,982	2,120	2,124	1,981	1,991	1,870	1,867	1,863	2,316	2,355
30 to 34 years old	487	967	1,243	1,322	1,236	1,194	1,098	1,195	1,145	1,185	1,223	1,356	1,405
35 years old and over	823	1,383	1,421	2,484	2,747	2,790	2,790	2,632	2,796	2,885	2,943	2,948	2,948
Men	**5,044**	**6,149**	**5,874**	**6,284**	**6,343**	**6,344**	**6,330**	**6,369**	**6,491**	**6,538**	**6,644**	**7,325**	**7,401**
14 to 17 years old	130	126	99	87	61	92	55	45	72	94	89	109	108
18 and 19 years old	1,349	1,397	1,375	1,421	1,338	1,342	1,392	1,535	1,541	1,551	1,585	1,797	1,783
20 and 21 years old	1,095	1,245	1,259	1,368	1,282	1,224	1,359	1,374	1,392	1,420	1,450	1,625	1,665
22 to 24 years old	964	1,047	1,064	1,107	1,153	1,175	1,190	1,127	1,090	1,091	1,136	1,319	1,346
25 to 29 years old	783	1,122	993	940	962	993	964	908	874	865	861	1,038	1,051
30 to 34 years old	308	557	576	537	561	480	439	463	517	521	531	543	559
35 years old and over	415	654	507	824	986	1,039	931	917	1,005	997	992	894	889
Women	**3,537**	**5,036**	**6,223**	**7,535**	**7,919**	**7,956**	**8,015**	**8,138**	**8,301**	**8,441**	**8,656**	**10,132**	**10,287**
14 to 17 years old	129	152	148	90	87	137	113	74	72	78	81	115	116
18 and 19 years old	1,250	1,389	1,526	1,529	1,557	1,662	1,622	1,847	1,874	1,907	1,958	2,338	2,328
20 and 21 years old	786	998	1,165	1,392	1,424	1,419	1,484	1,437	1,597	1,597	1,651	1,990	2,052
22 to 24 years old	493	706	925	1,037	1,258	1,141	1,263	1,250	1,344	1,305	1,321	1,543	1,583
25 to 29 years old	291	652	878	1,043	1,159	1,131	1,017	1,083	995	1,002	1,002	1,278	1,304
30 to 34 years old	179	410	667	784	675	714	659	732	627	664	692	813	846
35 years old and over	409	729	914	1,659	1,760	1,752	1,859	1,715	1,791	1,888	1,951	2,054	2,059
Full-time, total	**5,816**	**6,841**	**7,098**	**7,821**	**8,129**	**8,213**	**8,322**	**8,563**	**8,786**	**8,797**	**9,035**	**10,586**	**10,747**
14 to 17 years old	242	253	223	144	123	164	120	93	129	136	143	188	189
18 and 19 years old	2,406	2,619	2,669	2,548	2,387	2,516	2,492	2,794	2,848	2,857	2,956	3,556	3,540
20 and 21 years old	1,647	1,910	2,075	2,151	2,109	2,098	2,248	2,271	2,362	2,400	2,492	2,962	3,049
22 to 24 years old	881	924	1,121	1,350	1,517	1,586	1,590	1,564	1,662	1,613	1,642	1,890	1,937
25 to 29 years old	407	630	577	770	908	902	886	890	854	811	795	960	980
30 to 34 years old	100	264	251	387	430	379	371	367	338	372	391	427	445
35 years old and over	134	241	182	471	653	568	616	584	593	608	615	602	606
Men	**3,505**	**3,927**	**3,689**	**3,808**	**3,807**	**3,816**	**3,839**	**3,934**	**4,026**	**4,005**	**4,091**	**4,627**	**4,682**
14 to 17 years old	124	114	87	71	54	71	46	39	63	69	74	90	90
18 and 19 years old	1,265	1,329	1,270	1,230	1,091	1,111	1,134	1,240	1,271	1,271	1,308	1,523	1,513
20 and 21 years old	990	1,074	1,109	1,055	999	961	1,061	1,129	1,125	1,144	1,171	1,321	1,354
22 to 24 years old	650	633	665	742	789	853	762	777	788	761	779	895	914
25 to 29 years old	327	445	360	401	454	440	470	424	416	401	396	461	468
30 to 34 years old	72	181	124	156	183	143	158	141	149	155	162	167	172
35 years old and over	75	149	74	152	238	237	207	184	213	204	201	171	171
Women	**2,311**	**2,915**	**3,409**	**4,013**	**4,321**	**4,398**	**4,483**	**4,630**	**4,761**	**4,792**	**4,945**	**5,959**	**6,065**
14 to 17 years old	117	138	136	73	69	93	74	54	66	67	69	98	100
18 and 19 years old	1,140	1,290	1,399	1,318	1,296	1,405	1,358	1,555	1,577	1,585	1,648	2,033	2,027
20 and 21 years old	657	835	966	1,096	1,111	1,137	1,187	1,142	1,237	1,256	1,321	1,642	1,695
22 to 24 years old	231	291	456	608	729	734	828	787	875	852	864	995	1,023
25 to 29 years old	80	185	217	369	455	462	416	466	437	410	399	500	513
30 to 34 years old	28	83	127	231	247	236	213	226	190	218	229	261	272
35 years old and over	59	92	108	319	415	331	409	400	380	403	414	431	435

Observers attribute the enrollment of older students to the higher education levels required by many occupations and the growing number of students who leave school to work and return later to complete their education. It has been found that the main reasons older students begin or return to degree programs are career transitions and the need for new skills to obtain different jobs.

MINORITY ENROLLMENT. The enrollment of minority students (non-Hispanic blacks, Hispanics, Asians or Pacific Islanders, and American Indians/ Alaskan Natives) in higher education has been rising steadily. In 1976 some 15.7 percent of college students were from minority groups, compared to 28.1 percent in 1999. (See Table 4.3.) Much of the increase can be traced to larger numbers of Hispanic and Asian/Pacific Islander students, who made up about 55 percent of minority enrollment in institutions of higher education during 1999.

While white students still comprise the large majority of college students, the trend is toward more racial and ethnic diversity on campuses. In 1976 white

TABLE 4.2

Total fall enrollment in institutions of higher education, by gender and age, 1970–2011 [CONTINUED]

[In thousands]

Sex and age	1970[1]	1975[1]	1980[1]	1990[1]	1995[1]	1996[1]	1997[1]	1998[2]	1999[2]	Projected[2] 2000	2001	2010	2011
1	2	3	4	5	6	7	8	9	10	11	12	13	14
Part-time, total	**2,765**	**4,344**	**4,999**	**5,998**	**6,133**	**6,087**	**6,023**	**5,944**	**6,005**	**6,182**	**6,265**	**6,871**	**6,942**
14 to 17 years old	17	42	38	32	25	65	47	26	14	36	27	35	35
18 and 19 years old	194	340	418	402	507	488	522	588	566	602	587	580	571
20 and 21 years old	233	447	441	610	596	544	595	540	627	617	609	653	667
22 to 24 years old	576	717	844	794	894	729	863	813	772	782	815	973	991
25 to 29 years old	668	1,032	1,209	1,213	1,212	1,222	1,095	1,101	1,016	1,055	1,067	1,356	1,374
30 to 34 years old	388	670	905	935	805	815	727	828	806	813	831	928	961
35 years old and over	689	1,098	1,145	2,012	2,093	2,222	2,174	2,048	2,203	2,278	2,328	2,346	2,342
Men	**1,540**	**2,222**	**2,185**	**2,476**	**2,535**	**2,528**	**2,491**	**2,436**	**2,465**	**2,533**	**2,554**	**2,698**	**2,719**
14 to 17 years old	5	18	17	16	7	21	9	5	8	25	15	19	19
18 and 19 years old	84	153	202	191	246	231	258	296	269	280	278	274	270
20 and 21 years old	105	219	201	313	283	263	298	245	267	276	279	304	311
22 to 24 years old	314	358	392	365	365	323	427	350	302	330	357	424	431
25 to 29 years old	456	631	594	539	508	553	494	485	458	464	465	577	583
30 to 34 years old	236	361	397	381	378	337	281	322	369	366	369	376	387
35 years old and over	340	486	382	672	748	801	724	733	791	793	791	723	718
Women	**1,225**	**2,121**	**2,814**	**3,521**	**3,598**	**3,558**	**3,532**	**3,508**	**3,540**	**3,648**	**3,711**	**4,173**	**4,222**
14 to 17 years old	12	24	20	17	18	45	39	21	6	11	12	16	16
18 and 19 years old	110	188	215	211	261	257	264	292	297	322	309	306	301
20 and 21 years old	128	228	240	297	313	282	297	295	360	341	330	349	357
22 to 24 years old	262	359	452	429	529	407	436	463	470	452	458	549	560
25 to 29 years old	212	401	616	674	704	669	601	617	558	591	603	779	791
30 to 34 years old	151	309	507	554	427	478	446	506	438	446	462	552	574
35 years old and over	349	612	762	1,340	1,345	1,421	1,450	1,315	1,411	1,485	1,537	1,623	1,623

[1] Institutions that were accredited by an agency or association that was recognized by the U.S. Department of Education, or recognized directly by the Secretary of Education.
[2] Four-year and 2-year degree-granting institutions that were participating in Title IV federal financial aid programs. Some data have been revised from previously published figures.

Note: Distributions by age are estimates based on samples of the civilian noninstitutional population. Data for 1999 imputed using alternative methods. Some data have been revised from previously published figures. Detail may not sum to totals due to rounding.

SOURCE: "Table 174.—Total fall enrollment in degree-granting institutions, by attendance status, sex, and age: 1970 to 2011," in *Digest of Education Statistics, 2001,* U.S. Department of Education, National Center for Education Statistics, Washington, DC, 2002

FIGURE 4.2

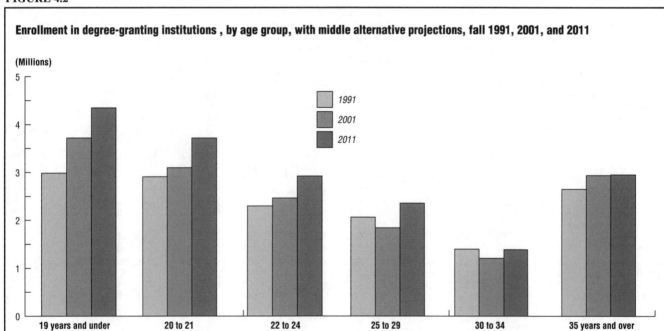

Enrollment in degree-granting institutions , by age group, with middle alternative projections, fall 1991, 2001, and 2011

(Millions)

Legend: 1991, 2001, 2011

Age groups: 19 years and under, 20 to 21, 22 to 24, 25 to 29, 30 to 34, 35 years and over

SOURCE: "Figure 31. Enrollment in degree-granting institutions , by age group, with middle alternative projections, Fall 1991, 2001, and 2011," in *Projections of Education Statistics to 2011,* U.S. Department of Education, National Center for Education Statistics, Washington, DC, August 2001 [Online] http://nces.ed.gov/pubs2001/proj01/figures/figure31.asp [accessed June 13, 2001]

TABLE 4.3

Total fall enrollment in degree-granting institutions, by level of study, sex, and race/ethnicity of student, 1976–99

Level of study, sex, and race/ethnicity of student	Institutions of higher education, in thousands[1]				Degree-granting institutions, in thousands[2]				Percentage distribution of students[3]							
									Institutions of higher education[1]				Degree-granting institutions[2]			
	1976	1980	1990	1995	1996	1997	1998	1999	1976	1980	1990	1995	1996	1997	1998	1999
1	2	3	4	5	6	7	8	9	10	11	12	13	14	15	16	17
All students																
Total	10,985.6	12,086.8	13,818.6	14,261.8	14,367.5	14,502.3	14,507.0	14,791.2	100.0	100.0	100.0	100.0	100.0	100.0	100.0	100.0
White, non-Hispanic	9,076.1	9,833.0	10,722.5	10,311.2	10,263.9	10,266.1	10,178.8	10,262.5	84.3	83.5	79.9	74.7	73.8	73.1	72.4	71.9
Total minority	1,690.8	1,948.8	2,704.7	3,496.2	3,637.4	3,771.2	3,884.7	4,012.3	15.7	16.5	20.1	25.3	26.2	26.9	27.6	28.1
Black, non-Hispanic	1,033.0	1,106.8	1,247.0	1,473.7	1,505.6	1,551.0	1,582.9	1,640.7	9.6	9.4	9.3	10.7	10.8	11.0	11.3	11.5
Hispanic	383.8	471.7	782.4	1,093.8	1,166.1	1,218.5	1,257.1	1,316.6	3.6	4.0	5.8	7.9	8.4	8.7	8.9	9.2
Asian or Pacific Islander	197.9	286.4	572.4	797.4	828.2	859.2	900.5	909.7	1.8	2.4	4.3	5.8	6.0	6.1	6.4	6.4
American Indian/Alaskan Native	76.1	83.9	102.8	131.3	137.6	142.5	144.2	145.3	0.7	0.7	0.8	1.0	1.0	1.0	1.0	1.0
Nonresident alien	218.7	305.0	391.5	454.4	466.3	465.0	443.5	516.4	(4)	(4)	(4)	(4)	(4)	(4)	(4)	(4)
Men	5,794.4	5,868.1	6,283.9	6,342.5	6,352.8	6,396.0	6,369.3	6,490.6	100.0	100.0	100.0	100.0	100.0	100.0	100.0	100.0
White, non-Hispanic	4,813.7	4,772.9	4,861.0	4,594.1	4,552.2	4,548.8	4,499.4	4,539.9	85.3	84.4	80.5	75.6	74.8	74.2	73.6	73.2
Total minority	826.6	884.4	1,176.6	1,484.2	1,533.4	1,582.3	1,615.2	1,659.1	14.7	15.6	19.5	24.4	25.2	25.8	26.4	26.8
Black, non-Hispanic	469.9	463.7	484.7	555.9	564.1	579.8	584.0	603.0	8.3	8.2	8.0	9.1	9.3	9.5	9.6	9.7
Hispanic	209.7	231.6	353.9	480.2	506.6	525.8	538.6	562.3	3.7	4.1	5.9	7.9	8.3	8.6	8.8	9.1
Asian or Pacific Islander	108.4	151.3	294.9	393.3	405.5	417.7	433.6	435.3	1.9	2.7	4.9	6.5	6.7	6.8	7.1	7.0
American Indian/ Alaskan Native	38.5	37.8	43.1	54.8	57.2	59.0	59.0	58.5	0.7	0.7	0.7	0.9	0.9	1.0	1.0	0.9
Nonresident alien	154.1	210.8	246.3	264.3	267.2	264.9	254.6	291.6	(4)	(4)	(4)	(4)	(4)	(4)	(4)	(4)
Women	5,191.2	6,218.7	7,534.7	7,919.2	8,014.7	8,106.3	8,137.7	8,300.6	100.0	100.0	100.0	100.0	100.0	100.0	100.0	100.0
White, non-Hispanic	4,262.4	5,060.1	5,861.5	5,717.2	5,711.7	5,717.4	5,679.4	5,722.6	83.1	82.6	79.3	74.0	73.1	72.3	71.4	70.9
Total minority	864.2	1,064.4	1,528.1	2,012.0	2,104.0	2,188.9	2,269.4	2,353.2	16.9	17.4	20.7	26.0	26.9	27.7	28.6	29.1
Black, non-Hispanic	563.1	643.0	762.3	917.8	941.4	971.3	999.0	1,037.7	11.0	10.5	10.3	11.9	12.0	12.3	12.6	12.8
Hispanic	174.1	240.1	428.5	613.7	659.5	692.7	718.5	754.4	3.4	3.9	5.8	7.9	8.4	8.8	9.0	9.3
Asian or Pacific Islander	89.4	135.2	277.5	404.1	422.6	441.5	466.9	474.4	1.7	2.2	3.8	5.2	5.4	5.6	5.9	5.9
American Indian/ Alaskan Native	37.6	46.1	59.7	76.5	80.4	83.4	85.1	86.8	0.7	0.8	0.8	1.0	1.0	1.1	1.1	1.1
Nonresident alien	64.6	94.2	145.2	190.1	199.0	200.1	188.9	224.8	(4)	(4)	(4)	(4)	(4)	(4)	(4)	(4)
Full-time	6,703.6	7,088.9	7,821.0	8,128.8	8,303.0	8,438.1	8,563.3	8,786.5	100.0	100.0	100.0	100.0	100.0	100.0	100.0	100.0
White, non-Hispanic	5,512.6	5,717.0	6,016.5	5,833.8	5,906.1	5,960.1	6,022.8	6,133.9	84.2	83.4	79.9	74.9	74.3	73.8	73.3	73.1
Total minority	1,030.9	1,137.5	1,514.9	1,955.3	2,046.8	2,118.7	2,193.6	2,257.5	15.8	16.6	20.1	25.1	25.7	26.2	26.7	26.9
Black, non-Hispanic	659.2	685.6	718.3	840.4	871.9	896.6	917.5	946.4	10.1	10.0	9.5	10.8	11.0	11.1	11.2	11.3
Hispanic	211.1	247.0	394.7	553.2	588.8	614.0	636.3	666.7	3.2	3.6	5.2	7.1	7.4	7.6	7.7	7.9
Asian or Pacific Islander	117.7	162.0	347.4	488.7	508.5	526.6	557.0	561.4	1.8	2.4	4.6	6.3	6.4	6.5	6.8	6.7
American Indian/ Alaskan Native	43.0	43.0	54.4	73.0	77.5	81.5	82.8	83.1	0.7	0.6	0.7	0.9	1.0	1.0	1.0	1.0
Nonresident alien	160.0	234.4	289.6	339.7	350.1	359.2	347.0	395.1	(4)	(4)	(4)	(4)	(4)	(4)	(4)	(4)
Part-time	4,282.1	4,997.9	5,997.7	6,133.0	6,064.6	6,064.3	5,943.6	6,004.7	100.0	100.0	100.0	100.0	100.0	100.0	100.0	100.0
White, non-Hispanic	3,563.5	4,116.0	4,706.0	4,477.4	4,357.8	4,306.0	4,156.0	4,128.6	84.4	83.5	79.8	74.4	73.3	72.3	71.1	70.2
Total minority	659.9	811.3	1,189.8	1,540.9	1,590.6	1,652.5	1,691.1	1,754.8	15.6	16.5	20.2	25.6	26.7	27.7	28.9	29.8
Black, non-Hispanic	373.8	421.2	528.7	633.3	633.6	654.5	665.4	694.3	8.9	8.5	9.0	10.5	10.7	11.0	11.4	11.8
Hispanic	172.7	224.8	387.7	540.7	577.3	604.5	620.8	649.9	4.1	4.6	6.6	9.0	9.7	10.1	10.6	11.0
Asian or Pacific Islander	80.2	124.4	225.1	308.6	319.6	332.6	343.5	348.3	1.9	2.5	3.8	5.1	5.4	5.6	5.9	5.9
American Indian/ Alaskan Native	33.1	40.9	48.4	58.3	60.0	61.0	61.3	62.2	0.8	0.8	0.8	1.0	1.0	1.0	1.0	1.1
Nonresident alien	58.7	70.6	101.8	114.7	116.2	105.8	96.5	121.4	(4)	(4)	(4)	(4)	(4)	(4)	(4)	(4)
Undergraduate																
Total	9,419.0	10,469.1	11,959.1	12,231.7	12,326.9	12,450.6	12,436.9	12,681.2	100.0	100.0	100.0	100.0	100.0	100.0	100.0	100.0
White, non-Hispanic	7,740.5	8,480.7	9,272.6	8,805.6	8,769.5	8,783.9	8,703.6	8,796.7	83.4	82.7	79.0	73.6	72.8	72.1	71.4	71.0
Total minority	1,535.3	1,778.5	2,467.7	3,158.5	3,282.1	3,398.5	3,492.1	3,600.4	16.6	17.3	21.0	26.4	27.2	27.9	28.6	29.0
Black, non-Hispanic	943.4	1,018.8	1,147.2	1,333.6	1,358.6	1,398.1	1,421.7	1,470.5	10.2	9.9	9.8	11.1	11.3	11.5	11.7	11.9
Hispanic	352.9	433.1	724.6	1,012.0	1,079.4	1,125.9	1,159.8	1,212.3	3.8	4.2	6.2	8.5	9.0	9.2	9.5	9.8
Asian or Pacific Islander	169.3	248.7	500.5	692.2	717.6	743.7	778.3	784.3	1.8	2.4	4.3	5.8	6.0	6.1	6.4	6.3
American Indian/Alaskan Native	69.7	77.9	95.5	120.7	126.5	130.8	132.2	133.3	0.8	0.8	0.8	1.0	1.0	1.1	1.1	1.1
Nonresident alien	143.2	209.9	218.7	267.6	275.3	268.2	241.3	284.2	(4)	(4)	(4)	(4)	(4)	(4)	(4)	(4)
Men	4,896.8	4,997.4	5,379.8	5,401.1	5,420.7	5,468.5	5,446.1	5,559.5	100.0	100.0	100.0	100.0	100.0	100.0	100.0	100.0
White, non-Hispanic	4,052.2	4,054.9	4,184.4	3,918.1	3,890.8	3,899.3	3,861.8	3,914.9	84.4	83.5	79.6	74.5	73.8	73.2	72.6	72.4
Total minority	748.2	802.7	1,069.3	1,339.3	1,384.1	1,427.9	1,455.5	1,495.6	15.6	16.5	20.4	25.5	26.2	26.8	27.4	27.6
Black, non-Hispanic	430.7	428.2	448.0	506.8	513.6	527.7	530.2	547.8	9.0	8.8	8.5	9.6	9.7	9.9	10.0	10.1
Hispanic	191.7	211.2	326.9	444.2	469.2	486.7	498.2	519.8	4.0	4.3	6.2	8.4	8.9	9.1	9.4	9.6
Asian or Pacific Islander	91.1	128.5	254.5	338.1	348.8	359.4	373.0	374.1	1.9	2.6	4.8	6.4	6.6	6.7	7.0	6.9
American Indian/ Alaskan Native	34.8	34.8	39.9	50.2	52.4	54.1	54.2	53.9	0.7	0.7	0.8	1.0	1.0	1.0	1.0	1.0
Nonresident alien	96.4	139.8	126.1	143.8	145.8	141.4	128.8	149.0	(4)	(4)	(4)	(4)	(4)	(4)	(4)	(4)

TABLE 4.3

Total fall enrollment in degree-granting institutions, by level of study, sex, and race/ethnicity of student, 1976–99 [CONTINUED]

Level of study, sex, and race/ethnicity of student	Institutions of higher education, in thousands[1]				Degree-granting institutions, in thousands[2]				Percentage distribution of students[3]							
									Institutions of higher education[1]				Degree-granting institutions[2]			
	1976	1980	1990	1995	1996	1997	1998	1999	1976	1980	1990	1995	1996	1997	1998	1999
1	2	3	4	5	6	7	8	9	10	11	12	13	14	15	16	17
Women	4,522.1	5,471.7	6,579.3	6,830.6	6,906.3	6,982.1	6,990.8	7,121.8	100.0	100.0	100.0	100.0	100.0	100.0	100.0	100.0
White, non-Hispanic	3,688.3	4,425.8	5,088.2	4,887.5	4,878.7	4,884.6	4,841.8	4,881.7	82.4	81.9	78.4	72.9	72.0	71.3	70.4	69.9
Total minority	787.0	975.8	1,398.5	1,819.2	1,898.1	1,970.6	2,036.5	2,104.9	17.6	18.1	21.6	27.1	28.0	28.7	29.6	30.1
Black, non-Hispanic	512.7	590.6	699.2	826.9	845.0	870.3	891.5	922.7	11.5	10.9	10.8	12.3	12.5	12.7	13.0	13.2
Hispanic	161.2	221.8	397.6	567.8	610.1	639.3	661.6	692.5	3.6	4.1	6.1	8.5	9.0	9.3	9.6	9.9
Asian or Pacific Islander	78.2	120.2	246.0	354.1	368.8	384.4	405.3	410.2	1.7	2.2	3.8	5.3	5.4	5.6	5.9	5.9
American Indian/ Alaskan Native	34.9	43.1	55.5	70.5	74.1	76.7	78.1	79.4	0.8	0.8	0.9	1.1	1.1	1.1	1.1	1.1
Nonresident alien	46.8	70.1	92.6	123.8	129.5	126.8	112.5	135.2	(4)	(4)	(4)	(4)	(4)	(4)	(4)	(4)
Graduate																
Total	1,322.5	1,340.9	1,586.2	1,732.5	1,742.3	1,753.5	1,767.6	1,806.8	100.0	100.0	100.0	100.0	100.0	100.0	100.0	100.0
White, non-Hispanic	1,115.6	1,104.7	1228.4	1,282.3	1,272.6	1,261.8	1,254.3	1,246.2	89.2	88.5	86.6	82.6	81.6	80.7	79.8	78.7
Total minority	134.5	144.0	190.5	270.7	286.3	302.3	318.5	336.4	10.8	11.5	13.4	17.4	18.4	19.3	20.2	21.3
Black, non-Hispanic	78.5	75.1	83.9	118.6	125.5	131.6	138.7	147.8	6.3	6.0	5.9	7.6	8.0	8.4	8.8	9.3
Hispanic	26.4	32.1	47.2	68.0	72.8	78.7	82.9	89.6	2.1	2.6	3.3	4.4	4.7	5.0	5.3	5.7
Asian or Pacific Islander	24.5	31.6	53.2	75.6	79.1	82.6	87.0	89.2	2.0	2.5	3.8	4.9	5.1	5.3	5.5	5.6
American Indian/Alaskan Native	5.1	5.2	6.2	8.5	8.9	9.4	9.8	9.9	0.4	0.4	0.4	0.5	0.6	0.6	0.6	0.6
Nonresident alien	72.4	92.2	167.3	179.5	183.3	189.4	194.8	224.2	(4)	(4)	(4)	(4)	(4)	(4)	(4)	(4)
Men	707.9	672.2	737.4	767.5	759.4	757.9	754.3	766.1	100.0	100.0	100.0	100.0	100.0	100.0	100.0	100.0
White, non-Hispanic	589.1	538.5	538.8	541.6	529.0	520.4	510.4	501.1	90.2	89.2	86.8	83.1	82.3	81.4	80.6	79.7
Total minority	63.7	65.0	82.1	110.4	114.0	118.8	122.8	127.3	9.8	10.8	13.2	16.9	17.7	18.6	19.4	20.3
Black, non-Hispanic	32.0	28.2	29.3	39.8	41.2	42.8	44.2	46.1	4.9	4.7	4.7	6.1	6.4	6.7	7.0	7.3
Hispanic	14.6	15.7	20.6	28.2	29.6	31.5	32.6	34.7	2.2	2.6	3.3	4.3	4.6	4.9	5.1	5.5
Asian or Pacific Islander	14.4	18.6	29.7	39.0	39.7	40.7	42.3	42.8	2.2	3.1	4.8	6.0	6.2	6.4	6.7	6.8
American Indian/ Alaskan Native	2.7	2.5	2.6	3.4	3.6	3.7	3.7	3.6	0.4	0.4	0.4	0.5	0.6	0.6	0.6	0.6
Nonresident alien	55.1	68.7	116.4	115.6	116.4	118.7	121.1	137.7	(4)	(4)	(4)	(4)	(4)	(4)	(4)	(4)
Women	614.6	668.7	848.8	965.0	982.8	995.6	1,013.3	1,040.7	100.0	100.0	100.0	100.0	100.0	100.0	100.0	100.0
White, non-Hispanic	526.5	566.2	689.5	740.7	743.6	741.4	743.9	745.0	88.1	87.8	86.4	82.2	81.2	80.2	79.2	78.1
Total minority	70.8	79.0	108.3	160.3	172.3	183.5	195.6	209.1	11.9	12.2	13.6	17.8	18.8	19.8	20.8	21.9
Black, non-Hispanic	46.5	46.9	54.6	78.8	84.3	88.8	94.5	101.6	7.8	7.3	6.8	8.7	9.2	9.6	10.1	10.7
Hispanic	11.8	16.4	26.6	39.9	43.2	47.2	50.4	54.9	2.0	2.5	3.3	4.4	4.7	5.1	5.4	5.8
Asian or Pacific Islander	10.1	13.0	23.6	36.6	39.4	41.8	44.8	46.4	1.7	2.0	3.0	4.1	4.3	4.5	4.8	4.9
American Indian/ Alaskan Native	2.4	2.7	3.6	5.0	5.3	5.7	6.0	6.3	0.4	0.4	0.5	0.6	0.6	0.6	0.6	0.7
Nonresident alien	17.3	23.5	50.9	63.9	66.9	70.7	73.7	86.6	(4)	(4)	(4)	(4)	(4)	(4)	(4)	(4)
First-professional																
Total	244.1	276.8	273.4	297.6	298.3	298.3	302.5	303.2	100.0	100.0	100.0	100.0	100.0	100.0	100.0	100.0
White, non-Hispanic	220.0	247.7	221.5	223.3	221.7	220.4	220.9	219.7	91.3	90.4	82.6	76.9	76.3	75.8	74.9	74.4
Total minority	21.1	26.3	46.5	67.0	69.0	70.4	74.1	75.5	8.7	9.6	17.4	23.1	23.7	24.2	25.1	25.6
Black, non-Hispanic	11.2	12.8	15.9	21.4	21.5	21.4	22.5	22.5	4.6	4.7	5.9	7.4	7.4	7.3	7.6	7.6
Hispanic	4.5	6.5	10.7	13.8	13.9	13.9	14.4	14.7	1.9	2.4	4.0	4.8	4.8	4.8	4.9	5.0
Asian or Pacific Islander	4.1	6.1	18.7	29.6	31.4	32.9	35.1	36.2	1.7	2.2	7.0	10.2	10.8	11.3	11.9	12.3
American Indian/Alaskan Native	1.3	0.8	1.1	2.1	2.2	2.3	2.2	2.1	0.5	0.3	0.4	0.7	0.7	0.8	0.7	0.7
Nonresident alien	3.1	2.9	5.4	7.3	7.6	7.5	7.4	8.0	(4)	(4)	(4)	(4)	(4)	(4)	(4)	(4)
Men	189.6	198.5	166.8	173.9	172.7	169.6	168.8	165.1	100.0	100.0	100.0	100.0	100.0	100.0	100.0	100.0
White, non-Hispanic	172.4	179.5	137.8	134.4	132.3	129.1	127.2	123.9	92.1	91.5	84.5	79.5	78.9	78.3	77.5	77.4
Total minority	14.7	16.7	25.3	34.6	35.4	35.7	36.9	36.3	7.9	8.5	15.5	20.5	21.1	21.7	22.5	22.6
Black, non-Hispanic	7.2	7.4	7.4	9.4	9.4	9.2	9.5	9.1	3.9	3.8	4.5	5.5	5.6	5.6	5.8	5.7
Hispanic	3.5	4.6	6.4	7.8	7.7	7.6	7.8	7.7	1.9	2.4	3.9	4.6	4.6	4.6	4.8	4.8
Asian or Pacific Islander	2.9	4.1	10.8	16.2	17.1	17.6	18.4	18.4	1.6	2.1	6.6	9.6	10.2	10.7	11.2	11.5
American Indian/ Alaskan Native	1.0	0.5	0.6	1.2	1.2	1.2	1.1	1.1	0.6	0.3	0.4	0.7	0.7	0.7	0.7	0.7
Nonresident alien	2.5	2.3	3.8	4.9	5.1	4.9	4.8	5.0	(4)	(4)	(4)	(4)	(4)	(4)	(4)	(4)

students made up 84.3 percent of higher education enrollment. (See Table 4.3.) In 1999 whites accounted for 71.9 percent of those attending college; blacks, 11.5 percent; Hispanics, 9.2 percent; Asian or Pacific Islanders, 6.4 percent; and American Indians and Alaskan Natives, 1 percent.

Between 1976 and 1999 the number of white students grew by 13 percent and the number of black students by 59 percent. Other minority groups increased by even higher proportions: American Indians/Alaskan Natives more than doubled, Hispanics more than tripled, and Asian/Pacific Islanders more than quadrupled. Women in general

TABLE 4.3

Total fall enrollment in degree-granting institutions, by level of study, sex, and race/ethnicity of student, 1976–99 [CONTINUED]

Level of study, sex, and race/ethnicity of student	Institutions of higher education, in thousands[1]				Degree-granting institutions, in thousands[2]				Percentage distribution of students[3]								
									Institutions of higher education[1]				Degree-granting institutions[2]			
	1976	1980	1990	1995	1996	1997	1998	1999	1976	1980	1990	1995	1996	1997	1998	1999
1	2	3	4	5	6	7	8	9	10	11	12	13	14	15	16	17
Women	54.5	78.4	106.6	123.7	125.6	128.6	133.6	138.1	100.0	100.0	100.0	100.0	100.0	100.0	100.0	100.0
White, non-Hispanic	47.6	68.1	83.7	88.9	89.4	91.3	93.7	95.8	88.2	87.6	79.7	73.3	72.7	72.5	71.6	71.0
Total minority	6.4	9.6	21.3	32.4	33.6	34.7	37.3	39.2	11.8	12.4	20.3	26.7	27.3	27.5	28.4	29.0
Black, non-Hispanic	3.9	5.5	8.5	12.1	12.1	12.1	12.9	13.4	7.3	7.0	8.1	10.0	9.8	9.6	9.9	9.9
Hispanic	1.0	1.9	4.3	6.0	6.2	6.2	6.5	7.0	1.9	2.4	4.1	5.0	5.0	4.9	5.0	5.2
Asian or Pacific Islander	1.1	2.0	7.9	13.4	14.4	15.3	16.8	17.9	2.1	2.6	7.6	11.0	11.7	12.1	12.8	13.2
American Indian/ Alaskan Native	0.2	0.3	0.5	0.9	1.0	1.1	1.0	1.0	0.4	0.3	0.5	0.8	0.8	0.8	0.8	0.8
Nonresident alien	0.5	0.6	1.6	2.4	2.6	2.6	2.6	3.1	(4)	(4)	(4)	(4)	(4)	(4)	(4)	(4)

[1] Institutions that were accredited by an agency or association that was recognized by the U.S. Department of Education, or recognized directly by the Secretary of Education.
[2] Data are for 4-year and 2-year degree-granting higher education institutions that participated in Title IV federal financial aid programs.
[3] Distribution for U.S. citizens only.
[4] Not applicable.
Note: Because of underreporting and nonreporting of racial/ethnic data, some figures are slightly lower than corresponding data in other tables. Data for 1998 revised from previously published figures. Data for 1999 imputed using alternative methods. Detail may not sum to totals due to rounding.

SOURCE: "Table 208. Total fall enrollment in degree-granting institutions, by level of study, sex, and race/ethnicity of student: 1976 to 1999," in *Digest of Education Statistics, 2001,* U.S. Department of Education, National Center for Education Statistics, Washington, DC, 2001 [Online] http://nces.ed.gov/pubs2002/digest2001/tables/PDF/table208.pdf [accessed May 31, 2002]

---

increased enrollment by 60 percent between 1976 and 1999, compared to a 12 percent increase for men. (See Table 4.3.)

Types of Degrees

Students can earn a variety of vocational certifications and college degrees. Associate degrees are usually awarded by junior colleges or community colleges after about two years of course work. Private institutions, as well as community and junior colleges, award vocational degrees. These degrees prepare people for specific jobs, such as court reporter, legal assistant, or computer programmer. Bachelor's degrees usually take a minimum of four years to complete. Private and public universities also award advanced master's, doctoral, or professional (doctor or lawyer) degrees.

HOW MANY? At the end of the 1999 to 2000 school year, about 565,000 associate degrees, 1.24 million bachelor's, 457,000 master's, 80,000 first-professional, and 44,800 doctoral degrees were awarded. (See Table 4.4.) While more women than men earned associate, bachelor's, and master's degrees, more men than women earned first-professional and doctoral degrees. This trend is projected to remain similar through 2011. In some cases, the total amount of each type of degree awarded is projected to increase through 2011: 625,000 associate degrees are expected to be awarded, as well as 1.4 million bachelor's degrees. Other degree types are expected to increase. (See Table 4.4.)

Despite the growth in enrollment, non-Hispanic black and Hispanic students were underrepresented in attaining college degrees. In the 1999 to 2000 school year, for example, while black and Hispanic students made up 21

percent of the undergraduate student body, they earned only about 15.3 percent of all bachelor's degrees for that year. (See Table 4.3 and Table 4.5.) Similarly, minorities were underrepresented at the master's, doctoral, and first-professional degree levels.

Of the 1.24 million bachelor's degrees conferred in the 1999 to 2000 school year, 21 percent were for business and management, while 10.3 percent were awarded for social sciences and 9 percent for education. Computer and information sciences, virtually unknown a generation ago, accounted for 3 percent of bachelor's degrees. (See Table 4.6 for the kinds of associate, master's, and doctoral degrees.)

LABOR FORCE PARTICIPATION

Adults with higher levels of education were more likely to participate in the labor force than those with less education. About 79.5 percent of adults 25 years of age and over with a bachelor's degree participated in the labor force in 2000, compared to 64.6 percent of high school graduates and just 43.1 percent of those who had not graduated. The labor force participation rates for blacks age 25 and older with high school diplomas and bachelor's degrees were higher in 1998 than the average for each ethnic group with similar levels of education. However, by 2000 Hispanics in the labor force with high school diplomas exceeded the number of blacks, but the number of blacks in the labor force with bachelor's degrees still exceeded the number of Hispanics. (See Table 4.7.)

Persons with lower levels of education were more likely to be unemployed than those with higher levels of

TABLE 4.4

Earned degrees conferred by degree-granting institutions, by level of degree and sex of student, 1869–70 to 2010–11

Year	Associate degrees			Bachelor's degrees			Master's degrees			First-professional degrees			Doctor's degrees [1]		
	Total	Men	Women	Total	Men	Women	Total	Men	Women	Total	Men	Women	Total	Men	Women
1	2	3	4	5	6	7	8	9	10	11	12	13	14	15	16
1869–70	—	—	—	[2]9,371	[2]7,993	[2]1,378	0	0	0	([3])	([3])	([3])	1	1	0
1879–80	—	—	—	[2]12,896	[2]10,411	[2]2,485	879	868	11	([3])	([3])	([3])	54	51	3
1889–90	—	—	—	[2]15,539	[2]12,857	[2]2,682	1,015	821	194	([3])	([3])	([3])	149	147	2
1899–1900	—	—	—	[2]27,410	[2]22,173	[2]5,237	1,583	1,280	303	([3])	([3])	([3])	382	359	23
1909–10	—	—	—	[2]37,199	[2]28,762	[2]8,437	2,113	1,555	558	([3])	([3])	([3])	443	399	44
1919–20	—	—	—	[2]48,622	[2]31,980	[2]16,642	4,279	2,985	1,294	([3])	([3])	([3])	615	522	93
1929–30	—	—	—	[2]122,484	[2]73,615	[2]48,869	14,969	8,925	6,044	([3])	([3])	([3])	2,299	1,946	353
1939–40	—	—	—	[2]186,500	[2]109,546	[2]76,954	26,731	16,508	10,223	([3])	([3])	([3])	3,290	2,861	429
1949–50	—	—	—	[2]432,058	[2]328,841	[2]103,217	58,183	41,220	16,963	([3])	([3])	([3])	6,420	5,804	616
1959–60	—	—	—	[2]392,440	[2]254,063	[2]138,377	74,435	50,898	23,537	([3])	([3])	([3])	9,829	8,801	1,028
1960–61	—	—	—	365,174	224,538	140,636	84,609	57,830	26,779	25,253	24,577	676	10,575	9,463	1,112
1961–62	—	—	—	383,961	230,456	153,505	91,418	62,603	28,815	25,607	24,836	771	11,622	10,377	1,245
1962–63	—	—	—	411,420	241,309	170,111	98,684	67,302	31,382	26,590	25,753	837	12,822	11,448	1,374
1963–64	—	—	—	461,266	265,349	195,917	109,183	73,850	35,333	27,209	26,357	852	14,490	12,955	1,535
1964–65	—	—	—	493,757	282,173	211,584	121,167	81,319	39,848	28,290	27,283	1,007	16,467	14,692	1,775
1965–66	111,607	63,779	47,828	520,115	299,287	220,828	140,602	93,081	47,521	30,124	28,982	1,142	18,237	16,121	2,116
1966–67	139,183	78,356	60,827	558,534	322,711	235,823	157,726	103,109	54,617	31,695	30,401	1,294	20,617	18,163	2,454
1967–68	159,441	90,317	69,124	632,289	357,682	274,607	176,749	113,552	63,197	33,939	32,402	1,537	23,089	20,183	2,906
1968–69	183,279	105,661	77,618	728,845	410,595	318,250	193,756	121,531	72,225	35,114	33,595	1,519	26,158	22,722	3,436
1969–70	206,023	117,432	88,591	792,316	451,097	341,219	208,291	125,624	82,667	34,918	33,077	1,841	29,866	25,890	3,976
1970–71	252,311	144,144	108,167	839,730	475,594	364,136	230,509	138,146	92,363	37,946	35,544	2,402	32,107	27,530	4,577
1971–72	292,014	166,227	125,787	887,273	500,590	386,683	251,633	149,550	102,083	43,411	40,723	2,688	33,363	28,090	5,273
1972–73	316,174	175,413	140,761	922,362	518,191	404,171	263,371	154,468	108,903	50,018	46,489	3,529	34,777	28,571	6,206
1973–74	343,924	188,591	155,333	945,776	527,313	418,463	277,033	157,842	119,191	53,816	48,530	5,286	33,816	27,365	6,451
1974–75	360,171	191,017	169,154	922,933	504,841	418,092	292,450	161,570	130,880	55,916	48,956	6,960	34,083	26,817	7,266
1975–76	391,454	209,996	181,458	925,746	504,925	420,821	311,771	167,248	144,523	62,649	52,892	9,757	34,064	26,267	7,797
1976–77	406,377	210,842	195,535	919,549	495,545	424,004	317,164	167,783	149,381	64,359	52,374	11,985	33,232	25,142	8,090
1977–78	412,246	204,718	207,528	921,204	487,347	433,857	311,620	161,212	150,408	66,581	52,270	14,311	32,131	23,658	8,473
1978–79	402,702	192,091	210,611	921,390	477,344	444,046	301,079	153,370	147,709	68,848	52,652	16,196	32,730	23,541	9,189
1979–80	400,910	183,737	217,173	929,417	473,611	455,806	298,081	150,749	147,332	70,131	52,716	17,415	32,615	22,943	9,672
1980–81	416,377	188,638	227,739	935,140	469,883	465,257	295,739	147,043	148,696	71,956	52,792	19,164	32,958	22,711	10,247
1981–82	434,526	196,944	237,582	952,998	473,364	479,634	295,546	145,532	150,014	72,032	52,223	19,809	32,707	22,224	10,483
1982–83	449,620	203,991	245,629	969,510	479,140	490,370	289,921	144,697	145,224	73,054	51,250	21,804	32,775	21,902	10,873
1983–84	452,240	202,704	249,536	974,309	482,319	491,990	284,263	143,595	140,668	74,468	51,378	23,090	33,209	22,064	11,145
1984–85	454,712	202,932	251,780	979,477	482,528	496,949	286,251	143,390	142,861	75,063	50,455	24,608	32,943	21,700	11,243
1985–86	446,047	196,166	249,881	987,823	485,923	501,900	288,567	143,508	145,059	73,910	49,261	24,649	33,653	21,819	11,834
1986–87	436,304	190,839	245,465	991,264	480,782	510,482	289,349	141,269	148,080	71,617	46,523	25,094	34,041	22,061	11,980
1987–88	435,085	190,047	245,038	994,829	477,203	517,626	299,317	145,163	154,154	70,735	45,484	25,251	34,870	22,615	12,255
1988–89	436,764	186,316	250,448	1,018,755	483,346	535,409	310,621	149,354	161,267	70,856	45,046	25,810	35,720	22,648	13,072
1989–90	455,102	191,195	263,907	1,051,344	491,696	559,648	324,301	153,653	170,648	70,988	43,961	27,027	38,371	24,401	13,970
1990–91	481,720	198,634	283,086	1,094,538	504,045	590,493	337,168	156,482	180,686	71,948	43,846	28,102	39,294	24,756	14,538
1991–92	504,231	207,481	296,750	1,136,553	520,811	615,742	352,838	161,842	190,996	74,146	45,071	29,075	40,659	25,557	15,102
1992–93	514,756	211,964	302,792	1,165,178	532,881	632,297	369,585	169,258	200,327	75,387	45,153	30,234	42,132	26,073	16,059
1993–94	530,632	215,261	315,371	1,169,275	532,422	636,853	387,070	176,085	210,985	75,418	44,707	30,711	43,185	26,552	16,633
1994–95	539,691	218,352	321,339	1,160,134	526,131	634,003	397,629	178,598	219,031	75,800	44,853	30,947	44,446	26,916	17,530
1995–96	555,216	219,514	335,702	1,164,792	522,454	642,338	406,301	179,081	227,220	76,734	44,748	31,986	44,652	26,841	17,811
1996–97	571,226	223,948	347,278	1,172,879	520,515	652,364	419,401	180,947	238,454	78,730	45,564	33,166	45,876	27,146	18,730
1997–98	558,555	217,613	340,942	1,184,406	519,956	664,450	430,164	184,375	245,789	78,598	44,911	33,687	46,010	26,664	19,346
1998–99	559,954	218,417	341,537	1,200,303	518,746	681,557	439,986	186,148	253,838	78,439	44,339	34,100	44,077	25,146	18,931
1999–2000	564,933	224,721	340,212	1,237,875	530,367	707,508	457,056	191,792	265,264	80,057	44,239	35,818	44,808	25,028	19,780
2000–01[4]	562,000	214,000	348,000	1,209,000	524,000	685,000	428,000	178,000	250,000	81,900	44,700	37,200	46,700	26,900	19,800
2001–02[4]	569,000	216,000	353,000	1,227,000	529,000	698,000	432,000	179,000	253,000	80,400	44,000	36,400	46,500	26,500	20,000
2002–03[4]	574,000	217,000	357,000	1,241,000	527,000	714,000	436,000	180,000	256,000	80,400	43,600	36,800	46,700	26,600	20,100
2003–04[4]	582,000	218,000	364,000	1,251,000	535,000	716,000	442,000	181,000	261,000	81,300	43,900	37,400	47,100	26,700	20,400
2004–05[4]	587,000	219,000	368,000	1,275,000	538,000	737,000	448,000	182,000	266,000	82,300	44,100	38,200	47,500	26,900	20,600

education. In 2000, 6.4 percent of adults (25 years and older) who had not completed high school were unemployed, compared to 3.5 percent for those with four years of high school and 1.7 percent for those with a bachelor's degree or higher. Among whites, blacks, and Hispanics 25 years or older, blacks in 2000 who had not completed high school had the highest percent of unemployment (10.7 percent). (See Table 4.8 and Figure 4.3.)

Labor Force Participation for Bachelor's Degree Recipients

The U.S. Department of Education conducted a longitudinal study of people who had received bachelor's degrees in the 1992 to 1993 school year. By April 1997, 76.3 percent of these people were employed and not enrolled in college. Gender specific percentages were very similar; 78.5 percent of men and 74.4 percent of women were employed and not enrolled in a degree

TABLE 4.4
Earned degrees conferred by degree-granting institutions, by level of degree and sex of student, 1869–70 to 2010–11 [CONTINUED]

Year	Associate degrees			Bachelor's degrees			Master's degrees			First-professional degrees			Doctor's degrees [1]		
	Total	Men	Women	Total	Men	Women	Total	Men	Women	Total	Men	Women	Total	Men	Women
1	2	3	4	5	6	7	8	9	10	11	12	13	14	15	16
2005–06[4]	594,000	220,000	374,000	1,294,000	544,000	750,000	453,000	183,000	270,000	83,500	44,400	39,100	47,800	27,000	20,800
2006–07[4]	600,000	221,000	379,000	1,318,000	549,000	769,000	458,000	184,000	274,000	84,700	44,900	39,800	48,100	27,100	21,000
2007–08[4]	605,000	222,000	383,000	1,337,000	553,000	784,000	464,000	186,000	278,000	85,700	45,200	40,500	48,400	27,200	21,200
2008–09[4]	611,000	223,000	388,000	1,355,000	558,000	797,000	468,000	187,000	281,000	86,500	45,400	41,100	48,700	27,400	21,300
2009–10[4]	617,000	224,000	393,000	1,373,000	562,000	811,000	472,000	188,000	284,000	87,500	45,800	41,700	48,800	27,500	21,300
2010–11[4]	625,000	226,000	399,000	1,392,000	568,000	824,000	477,000	190,000	287,000	88,300	46,100	42,200	49,100	27,600	21,500

—Not available.

[1] Includes Ph.D., Ed.D., and comparable degrees at the doctoral level. Excludes first-professional, such as M.D., D.D.S., and law degrees.

[2] Includes first-professional degrees.

[3] First-professional degrees are included with bachelor's degrees.

[4] Projected.

Note: Data for 1869–70 to 1994–95 are for institutions of higher education. Institutions of higher education were accredited by an agency or association that was recognized by the U.S. Department of Education, or recognized directly by the Secretary of Education. The new degree-granting classification is very similar to the earlier higher education classification, except that it includes some additional institutions, primarily 2-year colleges, and excludes a few higher education institutions that did not award associate or higher degrees. Data for 1998–99 imputed using alternative procedures. Detail may not sum to totals due to rounding.

SOURCE: "Table 247. Earned degrees conferred by degree-granting institutions, by level of degree and sex of student: 1869–70 to 2010–11," in *Digest of Education Statistics, 2001*, U.S. Department of Education, National Center for Education Statistics, Washington, DC, 2001 [Online] http://nces.ed.gov/pubs2002/digest2001/tables/PDF/table247.pdf [accessed June 3, 2002]

program in 1997. For ethnic groups, blacks had the highest percentage of people employed and not enrolled (79.4 percent), and Asian/Pacific Islanders had the lowest rate (69.7 percent). Of the entire group, the majority received bachelor's degrees in business and management (85.8 percent), and public affairs/social services (80.4 percent). The biological sciences had the least degree recipients from this group (50.7 percent). (See Table 4.9.)

DROPOUTS AND HIGH SCHOOL GRADUATES

In general, high school dropouts and youth find it difficult to enter the job market. Only 48.9 percent of 1999 to 2000 dropouts were in the labor force (employed or looking for work), 19.2 percent were unemployed, and 32 percent were not in the labor force. In contrast, 69.7 percent of high school graduates were employed in 2000, and 30.2 percent were either unemployed or not in the labor force. (See Figure 4.4.)

Penalties of Not Graduating from High School

Without prior job experience or specialized training, dropouts often have difficulty finding jobs. In 2000, 48.9 percent of high school dropouts were employed. (See Table 4.10.) Employment rates vary by gender and race/ethnicity. For example, male high school dropouts were more likely to be employed (56.2 percent) than female dropouts (39.1 percent). White high school dropouts were more likely to be employed (54.8 percent) than black dropouts (27.5 percent). In 2000 the rate of unemployment for high school dropouts was 28.1 percent.

The disadvantage of not having a high school diploma persists well into a person's thirties. For example, in 1998, 79 percent of males age 25 to 34 who completed 9

to 11 years of school were working, compared to 84 percent of males in this age group who graduated from high school. Among females age 25 to 34, less than half (47.3 percent) of high school dropouts were employed, compared to 69.5 percent of their female peers with a high school diploma. (See Figure 4.5.)

Of those who were working, there was a clear economic advantage to finishing high school. Among workers age 25 to 34, those who attended 9 to 11 years of school earned substantially less than those who completed high school. In 2000, for example, the median annual salary of males with 9 to 11 years of schooling was 27 percent less than high school graduates. The median annual salary of female high school dropouts was only 70 percent of that of female high school graduates. (See Table 4.11.)

EDUCATION AND EARNINGS

Many people decide to attend college because they think a college degree will get them a better job and more earnings. Individuals with a higher level of education are generally more likely to be working. In 1998 male (92 percent) and female (84 percent) college graduates age 25 to 34 were more likely to be employed than male (88 percent) and female (70 percent) high school graduates of the same age. (See Figure 4.5.)

The financial returns of attending and graduating from college become even more evident when comparing the median annual earnings of those who attended and graduated from college to the median annual earnings of high school graduates. In 2000 males age 25 to 34 who had completed a bachelor's degree earned 60 percent more than their male peers who had only a high school

TABLE 4.5

Bachelor's degrees conferred by degree-granting institutions, by racial/ethnic group and sex of student, 1976–77 to 1999–2000

	Number of degrees conferred							Percentage distribution of degrees conferred to U.S. citizens					
Year	Total	White, non-Hispanic	Black, non-Hispanic	Hispanic	Asian/Pacific Islander	American Indian/Alaskan Native	Non-resident alien	Total	White, non-His-panic	Black, non-His-panic	His-panic	Asian/ Pacific Is-lander	American Indian/ Alaskan Native
1	2	3	4	5	6	7	8	9	10	11	12	13	14
					Total						Total		
1976–77 [1]	917,900	807,688	58,636	18,743	13,793	3,326	15,714	100.0	89.5	6.5	2.1	1.5	0.4
1978–79 [2]	919,540	802,542	60,246	20,096	15,407	3,410	17,839	100.0	89.0	6.7	2.2	1.7	0.4
1980–81 [3]	934,800	807,319	60,673	21,832	18,794	3,593	22,589	100.0	88.5	6.7	2.4	2.1	0.4
1984–85 [4]	968,311	826,106	57,473	25,874	25,395	4,246	29,217	100.0	88.0	6.1	2.8	2.7	0.5
1986–87	991,264	841,818	56,560	26,988	32,624	3,968	29,306	100.0	87.5	5.9	2.8	3.4	0.4
1988–89 [5]	1,016,350	859,703	58,078	29,918	37,674	3,951	27,026	100.0	86.9	5.9	3.0	3.8	0.4
1989–90 [6]	1,048,631	884,376	61,063	32,844	39,248	4,392	26,708	100.0	86.5	6.0	3.2	3.8	0.4
1990–91 [7]	1,081,280	904,062	65,341	36,612	41,618	4,513	29,134	100.0	85.9	6.2	3.5	4.0	0.4
1991–92 [8]	1,129,833	936,771	72,326	40,761	46,720	5,176	28,079	100.0	85.0	6.6	3.7	4.2	0.5
1992–93 [9]	1,159,931	947,309	77,872	45,376	51,463	5,671	32,240	100.0	84.0	6.9	4.0	4.6	0.5
1993–94 [10]	1,165,973	936,227	83,576	50,241	55,660	6,189	34,080	100.0	82.7	7.4	4.4	4.9	0.5
1994–95 [11]	1,158,788	913,377	87,203	54,201	60,478	6,606	36,923	100.0	81.4	7.8	4.8	5.4	0.6
1995–96 [12]	1,163,036	904,709	91,166	58,288	64,359	6,970	37,544	100.0	80.4	8.1	5.2	5.7	0.6
1996–97 [13]	1,168,023	898,224	94,053	61,941	67,969	7,409	38,427	100.0	79.5	8.3	5.5	6.0	0.7
1997–98 [14]	1,183,033	900,317	98,132	65,937	71,592	7,894	39,161	100.0	78.7	8.6	5.8	6.3	0.7
1998–99	1,200,303	906,305	102,106	70,008	74,102	8,418	39,364	100.0	78.1	8.8	6.0	6.4	0.7
1999–2000	1,237,875	928,013	107,891	74,963	77,793	8,711	40,504	100.0	77.5	9.0	6.3	6.5	0.7
					Men						Men		
1976–77 [1]	494,424	438,161	25,147	10,318	7,638	1,804	11,356	100.0	90.7	5.2	2.1	1.6	0.4
1978–79 [2]	476,065	418,215	24,659	10,418	8,261	1,736	12,776	100.0	90.3	5.3	2.2	1.8	0.4
1980–81 [3]	469,625	406,173	24,511	10,810	10,107	1,700	16,324	100.0	89.6	5.4	2.4	2.2	0.4
1984–85 [4]	476,148	405,085	23,018	12,402	13,554	1,998	20,091	100.0	88.8	5.0	2.7	3.0	0.4
1986–87	480,782	406,749	22,501	12,865	17,253	1,817	19,597	100.0	88.2	4.9	2.8	3.7	0.4
1988–89 [5]	481,946	407,154	22,370	13,950	19,260	1,730	17,482	100.0	87.7	4.8	3.0	4.1	0.4
1989–90 [6]	490,317	413,573	23,262	14,941	19,721	1,859	16,961	100.0	87.4	4.9	3.2	4.2	0.4
1990–91 [7]	496,424	415,505	24,328	16,158	20,678	1,901	17,854	100.0	86.8	5.1	3.4	4.3	0.4
1991–92 [8]	516,976	429,842	26,956	17,976	23,248	2,182	16,772	100.0	85.9	5.4	3.6	4.6	0.4
1992–93 [9]	530,541	435,084	28,883	19,865	25,293	2,449	18,967	100.0	85.0	5.6	3.9	4.9	0.5
1993–94 [10]	530,804	429,121	30,648	21,807	26,938	2,616	19,674	100.0	84.0	6.0	4.3	5.3	0.5
1994–95 [11]	525,174	417,006	31,775	23,600	28,973	2,736	21,084	100.0	82.7	6.3	4.7	5.7	0.5
1995–96 [12]	521,439	408,829	32,852	24,994	30,630	2,885	21,249	100.0	81.7	6.6	5.0	6.1	0.6
1996–97 [13]	517,901	401,878	33,509	26,007	32,111	2,988	21,408	100.0	80.9	6.7	5.2	6.5	0.6
1997–98 [14]	519,360	399,105	34,469	27,648	33,405	3,148	21,585	100.0	80.2	6.9	5.6	6.7	0.6
1998–99	518,746	396,476	34,827	28,624	34,172	3,320	21,327	100.0	79.7	7.0	5.8	6.9	0.7
1999–2000	530,367	402,368	36,972	30,255	35,789	3,459	21,524	100.0	79.1	7.3	5.9	7.0	0.7

diploma. For females in the same age group, the earnings premium was even greater. Females who completed a bachelor's degree earned 95 percent more than females with only a high school diploma. Since 1971 the earnings advantage for 25- to 34-year-olds who attended some college or earned a bachelor's degree was generally greater for females than for males. (See Table 4.11.)

Choosing a Field of Study

When most students decide what to study in college, they often consider what type of job they can get with their major and how much they will earn. In 1994 about three-fourths (77.6 percent) of 1992 to 1993 graduates who were working reported having a job related to their major. A similar proportion (75.7 percent) believed that their jobs had career potential. Only 59.9 percent thought that a college degree was required to get their job. (See Table 4.12.) About two-thirds of the college graduates of the class of 1992 to 1993 had jobs in professional, managerial, and

technical areas in 1994. The remainder worked in nonprofessional, nonmanagerial, and nontechnical areas.

Starting Salaries

According to the most recent data available, the median starting salary (in 1997 constant dollars) for 1993 graduates who worked full-time was $24,156. Graduates who majored in computer sciences and engineering had higher starting salaries than average, while students who majored in education, the humanities, and social and behavioral sciences had the lowest starting salaries. (See Table 4.13.)

The majors that both sexes choose account for some of the salary differences between male and female college graduates. In 1993 females were more likely than males to major in education, and males were more likely to major in computer sciences and engineering. (See Table 4.13.) Nevertheless, among college graduates working full-time, females earned less than males in social and

TABLE 4.5

Bachelor's degrees conferred by degree-granting institutions, by racial/ethnic group and sex of student, 1976–77 to 1999–2000 [CONTINUED]

	Number of degrees conferred							Percentage distribution of degrees conferred to U.S. citizens					
Year	Total	White, non-Hispanic	Black, non-Hispanic	Hispanic	Asian/Pacific Islander	American Indian/Alaskan Native	Non-resident alien	Total	White, non-Hispanic	Black, non-Hispanic	Hispanic	Asian/Pacific Islander	American Indian/Alaskan Native
1	2	3	4	5	6	7	8	9	10	11	12	13	14
	Women								Women				
1976–77 [1]	423,476	369,527	33,489	8,425	6,155	1,522	4,358	100.0	88.2	8.0	2.0	1.5	0.4
1978–79 [2]	443,475	384,327	35,587	9,678	7,146	1,674	5,063	100.0	87.7	8.1	2.2	1.6	0.4
1980–81 [3]	465,175	401,146	36,162	11,022	8,687	1,893	6,265	100.0	87.4	7.9	2.4	1.9	0.4
1984–85 [4]	492,163	421,021	34,455	13,472	11,841	2,248	9,126	100.0	87.2	7.1	2.8	2.5	0.5
1986–87	510,482	435,069	34,059	14,123	15,371	2,151	9,709	100.0	86.9	6.8	2.8	3.1	0.4
1988–89 [5]	534,404	452,549	35,708	15,968	18,414	2,221	9,544	100.0	86.2	6.8	3.0	3.5	0.4
1989–90 [6]	558,314	470,803	37,801	17,903	19,527	2,533	9,747	100.0	85.8	6.9	3.3	3.6	0.5
1990–91 [7]	584,856	488,557	41,013	20,454	20,940	2,612	11,280	100.0	85.2	7.2	3.6	3.7	0.5
1991–92 [8]	612,857	506,929	45,370	22,785	23,472	2,994	11,307	100.0	84.3	7.5	3.8	3.9	0.5
1992–93 [9]	629,390	512,225	48,989	25,511	26,170	3,222	13,273	100.0	83.1	8.0	4.1	4.2	0.5
1993–94 [10]	635,169	507,106	52,928	28,434	28,722	3,573	14,406	100.0	81.7	8.5	4.6	4.6	0.6
1994–95 [11]	633,614	496,371	55,428	30,601	31,505	3,870	15,839	100.0	80.3	9.0	5.0	5.1	0.6
1995–96 [12]	641,597	495,880	58,314	33,294	33,729	4,085	16,295	100.0	79.3	9.3	5.3	5.4	0.7
1996–97 [13]	650,122	496,346	60,544	35,934	35,858	4,421	17,019	100.0	78.4	9.6	5.7	5.7	0.7
1997–98 [14]	663,673	501,212	63,663	38,289	38,187	4,746	17,576	100.0	77.6	9.9	5.9	5.9	0.7
1998–99	681,557	509,829	67,279	41,384	39,930	5,098	18,037	100.0	76.8	10.1	6.2	6.0	0.8
1999–2000	707,508	525,645	70,919	44,708	42,004	5,252	18,980	100.0	76.3	10.3	6.5	6.1	0.8

[1] Excludes 1,121 men and 528 women whose racial/ethnic group was not available.
[2] Excludes 1,279 men and 571 women whose racial/ethnic group was not available.
[3] Excludes 258 men and 82 women whose racial/ethnic group was not available.
[4] Excludes 6,380 men and 4,786 women whose racial/ethnic group was not available.
[5] Excludes 1,400 men and 1,005 women whose racial/ethnic group was not available.
[6] Excludes 1,379 men and 1,334 women whose racial/ethnic group was not available.
[7] Excludes 7,621 men and 5,637 women whose racial/ethnic group was not available.
[8] Excludes 3,835 men and 2,885 women whose racial/ethnic group was not available.
[9] Excludes 2,340 men and 2,907 women whose racial/ethnic group was not available.
[10] Excludes 1,618 men and 1,684 women whose racial/ethnic group was not available.
[11] Excludes 957 men and 389 women whose racial/ethnic group was not available.
[12] Excludes 1,015 men and 741 women whose racial/ethnic group was not available.
[13] Excludes 2,614 men and 2,242 women whose racial/ethnic group was not available.
[14] Excludes 596 men and 777 women whose racial/ethnic group was not available.
Note: For years 1984–85 to 1999–2000, reported racial/ethnic distributions of students by level of degree, field of degree, and sex were used to estimate race/ethnicity for students whose race/ethnicity was not reported. Data for 1998–99 imputed using alternative procedures. Detail may not sum to totals due to rounding.

SOURCE: Thomas D. Snyder and Charlene M. Hoffman, "Table 268. Bachelor's degrees conferred by degree-granting institutions, by racial/ethnic group and sex of student: 1976–77 to 1999–2000," in *Digest of Education Statistics, 2001*, U.S. Department of Education, Office of Educational Research and Improvement, National Center for Education Statistics, Washington, DC, May 14, 2002

behavioral sciences, natural sciences, and business and management; the latter had the greatest disparity between male and female starting incomes. (See Figure 4.6.)

Median Incomes

There is a long-term difference between the earnings of males and females with the same educational background. Among full-time, year-round workers, males earned more than females across all levels of education. In 1999, for instance, the median income for male college graduates (in 2000 constant dollars) was $42,341 compared to $32,145 for female college graduates. (See Table 4.14.)

Between 1989 and 1999, median annual income of male full-time workers, when adjusted for inflation, declined about 1.5 percent, compared to an over 4 percent increase for female full-time workers. Income of men who

were year-round full-time workers with four or more years of college increased by almost 7 percent, compared to an 11.5 percent drop for men with one to three years of high school. Income for men who had completed high school dropped by about 7 percent. (See Table 4.15.)

Women's incomes were much lower than men's incomes, even after adjusting for level of education. (See Table 4.15 and Figure 4.7.) Similarly, a far greater percentage of men with a bachelor's degree or more (21.9 percent) earned more than $75,000 annually than did women (5.2 percent). (See Table 4.16.)

Women fare better when their major fields are taken into account because women's distribution of employment by field of study differs significantly from men's. What is highly significant is that almost all of the major fields in which men were concentrated had above-average median earnings (one-half earn more than this

TABLE 4.6

Degrees conferred by degree-granting institutions, by control of institution, level of degree, and discipline division, 1999–2000

Discipline division	Public institutions				Private institutions			
	Associate degrees	Bachelor's degrees	Master's degrees	Doctor's degrees[1]	Associate degrees	Bachelor's degrees	Master's degrees	Doctor's degrees[1]
1	2	3	4	5	6	7	8	9
Total	448,446	810,855	243,157	28,408	116,487	427,020	213,899	16,400
Agriculture and natural resources [2]	6,278	21,975	3,830	1,159	389	2,272	545	22
Architecture and related programs	308	6,444	2,848	76	84	2,018	1,420	53
Area, ethnic, and cultural studies	106	3,652	817	114	153	2,729	774	103
Biological sciences/life sciences	1,376	41,663	4,274	3,223	58	21,869	1,924	1,644
Business [3]	71,139	150,637	43,905	717	36,262	107,072	68,353	479
Communications	1,475	38,579	2,635	280	1,279	17,181	2,534	67
Communications technologies	1,270	448	9	0	439	702	346	10
Computer and information sciences	10,961	21,095	7,510	512	9,489	15,100	6,754	265
Construction trades	1,950	40	0	0	387	146	12	0
Education	6,936	77,997	72,754	4,801	1,290	30,171	51,486	2,029
Engineering	1,435	44,093	17,317	3,784	317	14,334	8,279	1,600
Engineering-related technologies	18,147	10,219	746	5	17,248	3,653	168	1
English language and literature/letters	870	34,277	5,247	1,213	77	16,643	1,983	415
Foreign languages and literatures	400	9,755	2,090	560	101	5,213	690	355
Health professions and related sciences	69,051	51,376	23,512	1,869	15,030	27,082	18,944	807
Home economics and vocational home economics	7,960	15,292	1,649	245	421	2,487	1,181	112
Law and legal studies	4,093	1,051	714	11	3,172	874	3,036	63
Liberal arts and sciences, general studies, and humanities	178,725	25,037	1,361	38	8,729	11,067	1,895	45
Library science	98	151	3,663	62	0	3	914	6
Mathematics	639	7,784	2,599	781	36	4,286	813	325
Mechanics and repairers	8,264	55	0	0	3,350	15	0	0
Multi/interdisciplinary studies	11,544	21,006	1,898	238	240	6,454	1,166	146
Parks, recreation, leisure, and fitness studies	691	14,115	1,943	123	164	4,996	535	11
Philosophy and religion	35	3,357	446	243	28	5,009	883	343
Physical sciences and science technologies	2,320	11,984	3,569	2,869	140	6,401	1,272	1,149
Precision production trades	7,147	331	0	0	4,667	62	5	0
Protective services	15,275	18,889	1,351	50	1,023	5,988	1,258	2
Psychology	1,291	48,856	5,581	1,869	164	25,204	8,884	2,441
Public administration and services	3,311	13,921	15,657	289	345	6,264	9,937	248
R.O.T.C. and military technologies	65	7	0	0	0	0	0	0
Social sciences and history	4,805	81,922	8,785	2,534	331	45,179	5,281	1,561
Theological studies/religious vocations	1	0	0	0	635	6,809	5,576	1,643
Transportation and material moving workers	711	1,387	94	0	310	2,008	603	0
Visual and performing arts	7,232	32,743	5,471	743	9,868	26,048	5,447	384
Not classified by field of study	2,537	717	801	0	261	1,681	1,001	71

[1] Includes Ph.D., Ed.D., and comparable degrees at the doctoral level. Excludes first-professional degrees such as M.D., D.D.S., and law degrees.
[2] Includes "Agricultural business and production," "Agricultural sciences," and "Conservation and renewable natural resources."
[3] Includes "Business management and administrative services," "Marketing operations/marketing and distribution," and "Consumer and personal services."

SOURCE: "Table 261. Degrees conferred by degree-granting institutions, by control of institution, level of degree, and discipline division: 1999–2000," in *Digest of Education Statistics, 2001*, U.S. Department of Education, National Center for Education Statistics, Washington, DC, 2001 [Online] http://nces.ed.gov/pubs2002/digest2001/tables/PDF/table261.pdf [accessed June 3, 2002]

figure, and one-half earn less than this figure), while the majors in which women were concentrated were characterized by below-average medians. Men were more likely to have degrees in engineering, computer science, architecture, mathematics, economics, theology, and business. Women were more likely to have degrees in social work, psychology, nursing, physical therapy, and education.

EDUCATION AND POVERTY

In general, as individuals attain higher educational levels, the risk of living in poverty falls rapidly. Of all those in the labor force for at least half of 1999, those with less than a high school diploma had a much higher poverty rate (14.3 percent) than high school graduates (6 percent). Workers with an associate (2.9 percent) or col-

lege degree (1.3 percent) reported the lowest poverty rates. (See Table 4.17.)

Poverty rates are higher for black workers than for white workers at almost all educational levels. Black men had lower or equal poverty rates with white men at the less than one year of high school level or if they had college degrees. Poverty rates for white men and women were fairly similar at all education levels. Among black men and women, however, there were marked differences, especially at lower educational levels. The poverty rate for black women workers with less than a high school diploma (32.3 percent) was higher than for black men (14.9 percent). Moreover, among high school graduates, the poverty rate of black women (17 percent) was more than twice that of black men (6.5 percent). (See Table 4.17.)

TABLE 4.7

Labor force participation of persons 16 years old and over, by selected characteristics, 2000

Age, sex, and race/ethnicity	Labor force participation rate[1]						Employment/population ratio[2]					
				College						College		
	Total	Less than high school graduate[3]	High school graduate	Some college, no degree	Associate degree	Bachelor's degree or higher	Total	Less than high school graduate[3]	High school graduate	Some college, no degree	Associate degree	Bachelor's degree or higher
1	2	3	4	5	6	7	8	9	10	11	12	13
16 to 19 years old [4]	52.2	45.1	69.6	61.9	68.9	—	45.4	38.0	61.6	57.8	65.7	—
Men	53.0	46.3	73.1	60.3	76.8	—	45.6	38.6	64.6	56.0	70.1	—
Women	51.3	43.7	66.2	63.1	64.2	—	45.2	37.3	58.6	59.1	63.1	—
White[5]	55.7	48.7	72.5	65.1	72.0	—	49.3	41.9	65.6	61.1	68.6	—
Black[5]	39.2	32.5	58.4	49.0	43.9	—	29.5	23.3	44.4	43.5	40.7	—
Hispanic[6]	46.3	38.6	67.9	65.8	72.9	—	38.5	30.9	59.4	58.9	72.9	—
20 to 24 years old [4]	77.9	69.5	82.3	74.2	84.9	84.4	72.4	59.5	75.5	70.4	82.2	80.8
Men	82.6	83.0	88.2	75.0	88.3	86.5	76.6	72.8	80.9	71.0	85.6	82.7
Women	73.3	52.4	75.7	73.4	82.1	83.0	68.2	42.7	69.2	69.8	79.3	79.4
White[5]	79.9	72.0	84.4	75.9	86.1	86.6	75.3	63.8	78.8	72.6	83.7	83.1
Black[5]	71.8	59.7	75.6	71.1	80.9	80.7	61.0	41.6	63.2	64.4	75.9	75.7
Hispanic[6]	77.7	72.8	82.1	77.6	80.0	86.3	71.8	65.8	75.6	73.7	78.4	82.6
25 and older	67.4	43.1	64.6	72.2	78.1	79.5	65.4	40.4	62.3	70.1	76.3	78.2
Men	76.0	55.1	75.0	79.4	84.6	84.4	73.8	52.1	72.5	77.3	82.7	83.1
Women	59.7	32.4	55.8	65.7	73.2	74.2	57.8	29.8	53.8	63.7	71.4	72.9
White[5]	67.2	43.8	63.8	71.1	77.8	79.1	65.4	41.3	61.9	69.2	76.2	77.9
Black[5]	68.3	39.1	69.9	78.4	81.8	84.4	64.6	34.9	65.4	75.2	78.9	82.3
Hispanic[6]	70.2	60.3	74.0	79.4	81.6	82.9	67.1	56.5	71.1	76.9	79.3	81.1

—Too few sample cases for a reliable estimate.
[1] Percent of the civilian population who are employed or seeking employment.
[2] Number of persons employed as a percent of civilian population.
[3] Includes persons reporting no school years completed.
[4] Excludes persons enrolled in school.
[5] Includes persons of Hispanic origin.
[6] Hispanics may be of any race.

SOURCE: "Table 379. Labor force participation of persons 16 years old and over, by age, sex, race/ethnicity, and highest level of education: 2000," in *Digest of Education Statistics, 2001*, U.S. Department of Education, National Center for Education Statistics, Washington, DC, 2001 [Online] http://nces.ed.gov/pubs2002 /digest2001/tables/PDF/table381.pdf [accessed June 3, 2002]

TABLE 4.8

Unemployment rate of persons 16 years old and over, by selected characteristics, 1998–2000

Sex, race/ethnicity, and highest degree attained	Percent unemployed,[1] 1998				Percent unemployed,[1] 1999				Percent unemployed, 2000			
	16- to 24-year-olds[2]			25 years old and over	16- to 24-year-olds[2]			25 years old and over	16- to 24-year-olds[2]			25 years old and over
	Total	16 to 19 years	20 to 24 years		Total	16 to 19 years	20 to 24 years		Total	16 to 19 years	20 to 24 years	
1	2	3	4	5	6	7	8	9	10	11	12	13
All persons												
All education levels	10.4	14.6	7.9	3.4	9.9	13.9	7.5	3.1	9.3	13.1	7.1	3.0
Less than a high school graduate	14.0	13.2	16.1	7.1	16.0	16.5	14.6	6.7	15.3	15.6	14.4	6.4
High school graduate, no college	10.1	12.5	9.1	4.0	9.7	12.3	8.6	3.5	9.3	11.6	8.3	3.5
Some college, no degree	6.3	7.7	5.9	3.2	5.9	7.3	5.4	3.0	5.5	6.7	5.1	2.9
Associate degree	4.3	—	4.1	2.5	4.7	6.7	4.6	2.5	3.2	3.2	3.2	2.3
Bachelor's degree or higher	4.0	—	4.1	1.8	4.7	—	4.8	1.8	4.2	—	4.2	1.7
Men												
All education levels	11.1	16.2	8.1	3.2	10.3	14.7	7.7	3.0	9.7	14.0	7.3	2.8
Less than a high school graduate	17.4	18.7	14.2	6.1	15.6	17.0	12.2	5.8	15.2	16.5	12.2	5.5
High school graduate, no college	10.0	13.6	8.5	3.9	9.7	12.3	8.6	3.3	9.2	11.7	8.2	3.4
Some college, no degree	6.7	8.7	6.2	3.0	6.2	8.2	5.7	2.8	5.7	7.2	5.4	2.7
Associate degree	4.2	—	—	2.3	5.3	9.1	5.2	2.5	3.2	7.7	3.0	2.3
Bachelor's degree or higher	4.3	—	4.3	1.6	5.6	—	5.7	1.8	4.2	—	4.2	1.5
Women												
All education levels	9.8	12.9	7.8	3.6	9.5	13.2	7.2	3.3	8.9	12.1	7.0	3.2
Less than a high school graduate	16.6	15.8	20.0	8.6	16.6	15.9	19.1	8.2	15.4	14.5	18.6	7.8
High school graduate, no college	10.3	11.4	9.8	4.1	9.8	12.3	8.6	3.7	9.5	11.5	8.5	3.5
Some college, no degree	5.9	7.0	5.6	3.4	5.6	6.8	5.2	3.2	5.2	6.3	4.9	3.0
Associate degree	4.5	—	4.2	2.7	4.2	5.3	4.2	2.5	3.2	—	3.3	2.4
Bachelor's degree or higher	3.8	—	3.9	2.0	4.1	—	4.1	1.8	4.2	—	4.3	1.8
White[3]												
All education levels	8.8	12.6	6.5	3.0	8.5	12.0	6.3	2.8	7.9	11.4	5.8	2.6
Less than a high school graduate	14.3	14.9	12.6	6.3	13.7	14.3	12.1	5.9	13.2	13.8	11.4	5.6
High school graduate, no college	8.4	10.8	7.2	3.4	8.0	10.3	7.0	3.0	7.5	9.5	6.6	3.0
Some college, no degree	5.5	6.9	5.1	2.8	5.0	6.4	4.6	2.7	4.7	6.1	4.3	2.6
Associate degree	3.9	—	3.7	2.2	4.4	8.0	4.2	2.3	2.9	3.7	2.8	2.1
Bachelor's degree or higher	3.9	—	3.9	1.7	4.6	—	4.6	1.7	4.0	—	4.0	1.6
Black[3]												
All education levels	20.7	27.6	16.8	6.4	19.2	27.9	14.6	5.7	18.2	24.7	15.0	5.4
Less than a high school graduate	33.1	33.1	33.2	11.6	31.2	32.3	28.7	11.6	29.1	28.4	30.3	10.7
High school graduate, no college	19.5	22.8	18.2	7.4	18.6	24.6	16.4	6.3	18.3	23.9	16.4	6.5
Some college, no degree	11.2	14.0	10.6	5.5	10.8	15.4	10.0	4.7	9.7	11.1	9.4	4.2
Associate degree	8.1	—	—	4.0	8.0	20.0	7.4	3.8	6.3	—	6.4	3.5
Bachelor's degree or higher	4.6	—	4.6	2.9	5.7	—	5.7	2.7	5.6	—	5.7	2.5
Hispanic origin[4]												
All education levels	13.2	21.3	9.3	5.5	11.8	18.7	8.3	5.0	10.6	16.7	7.5	4.4
Less than a high school graduate	17.9	24.3	11.9	7.2	16.1	21.3	11.1	7.1	14.4	19.9	9.6	6.3
High school graduate, no college	11.6	17.3	9.6	5.5	10.2	15.4	8.3	4.7	9.1	12.6	7.9	3.9
Some college, no degree	7.9	12.4	7.0	4.0	7.2	11.4	6.1	3.4	6.4	10.4	5.1	3.2
Associate degree	—	—	—	3.4	4.3	—	4.4	3.1	2.4	—	2.5	2.9
Bachelor's degree or higher	—	—	—	3.2	4.1	—	4.1	2.5	4.6	—	4.7	2.2

—Not available.

[1] The unemployment rate is the percent of individuals in the labor force who are not working and who made specific efforts to find employment sometime during the prior 4 weeks. The labor force includes both employed and unemployed persons.
[2] Excludes persons enrolled in school.
[3] Includes persons of Hispanic origin.
[4] Persons of Hispanic origin may be of any race.

SOURCE: "Table 381. Unemployment rate of persons 16 years old and over, by age, sex, race/ethnicity, and highest degree attained: 1998, 1999, and 2000," in *Digest of Educational Statistics, 2001*, U.S. Department of Education, National Center for Educational Statistics, Washington, DC, 2001 [Online] http://www.nces.ed.gov /pubs2002/digest2001/tables/PDF/table381.pdf [accessed June 3, 2002]

FIGURE 4.3

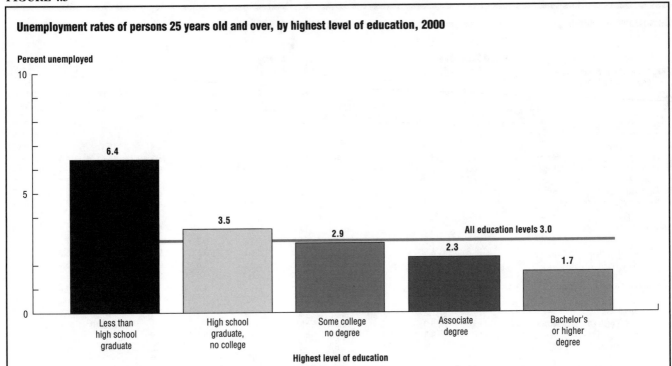

Unemployment rates of persons 25 years old and over, by highest level of education, 2000

SOURCE: "Figure 24. Unemployment rates of persons 25 years old and over, by highest level of education, 2000," in *Digest of Educational Statistics, 2001,* U.S. Department of Education, National Center for Education Statistics, Washington, DC, 2001 [Online] http://nces.ed.gov/pubs2002/digest2001/ch5. asp#f24 [accessed June 3, 2002]

TABLE 4.9

Percentage distribution of 1992–93 bachelor's degree recipients according to employment and enrollment status in April 1997, by selected characteristics

Selected student characteristics	Employment and enrollment status in April 1997			
	Employed and not enrolled	Enrolled and employed	Enrolled and not employed	Not employed and not enrolled
Total	**76.3**	**13.0**	**4.7**	**6.1**
Sex				
Male	78.5	12.1	5.4	4.1
Female	74.4	13.8	4.1	7.7
Race–ethnicity				
White	76.8	13.1	4.3	5.8
Black	79.4	11.3	4.6	4.7
Hispanic	70.5	15.0	6.0	8.5
Asian/Pacific Islander	69.7	11.9	10.0	8.4
American Indian/Alaskan Native	76.4	6.5	6.2	10.9
Marital status in April 1997				
Never married	74.5	14.1	6.6	4.9
Married/cohabit as married	77.6	12.1	3.0	7.3
Divorced/separated/widowed	78.1	13.3	4.3	4.3
Number of children				
No children	76.0	13.8	5.7	4.5
One	79.0	9.6	2.6	8.9
Two or more children	74.6	12.2	1.0	12.2
Baccalaureate degree major				
Professional fields	80.2	12.0	2.4	5.4
Arts and sciences	68.6	15.1	9.1	7.2
Other	79.9	11.9	2.4	5.9
Baccalaureate degree major				
Business and management	85.8	7.4	1.8	4.9
Education	71.0	20.1	2.3	6.7
Engineering	80.0	14.1	3.6	2.3
Health professions	79.2	9.8	4.2	6.8
Public affairs/social services	80.4	12.4	0.7	6.5
Biological sciences	50.7	16.6	25.4	7.3
Mathematics and other sciences	74.5	13.1	7.7	4.7
Social sciences	71.1	16.7	6.1	6.2
History	72.8	11.8	11.1	4.3
Humanities	71.7	13.6	5.2	9.5
Psychology	63.9	18.2	8.4	9.5
Other	79.9	11.9	2.4	5.9

NOTE: Details may not add to 100.0 due to rounding.

SOURCE: *The Condition of Education 1999*, National Center for Education Statistics, U.S. Department of Education, Office of Educational Research and Improvement, Washington, DC, 1999

FIGURE 4.4

Labor force status of 1999–2000 high school dropouts and graduates not enrolled in college, October 2000

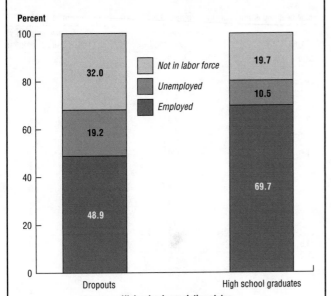

NOTE: Detail may not sum to totals due to rounding.

SOURCE: "Figure 25. Labor Force status of 1999–2000 high school dropouts and graduates not enrolled in college: October 2000," in *Digest of Education Statistics, 2001,* National Center for Education Statistics, U.S. Department of Education, Washington, DC, 2001 [Online] http://www.nces.ed.gov/pubs2002/digest2001/ch5.asp#f25 [accessed June 17, 2002]

TABLE 4.10

Labor force status of high school dropouts, by sex and race/ethnicity, October 1980–October 2000

(Number in thousands)

Year, sex, and race	Dropouts		Dropouts in civilian labor force[1]						Not in labor force	
				Labor force par-ticipation rate	Employed		Unemployed			
	Number	Percent of total	Number		Number	Percent of dropouts	Number	Unem-ployment rate	Number	Percent of population
1	2	3	4	5	6	7	8	9	10	11
All dropouts [2]										
1980	739	100.0	471	63.7	322	43.6	149	31.6	268	36.3
1985	612	100.0	413	67.5	266	43.5	147	35.6	199	32.5
1990	405	100.0	280	69.0	189	46.7	90	32.3	125	31.0
1994	510	100.0	311	61.1	219	42.9	93	29.8	198	38.9
1995	604	100.0	409	67.7	288	47.7	121	29.6	195	32.3
1996	496	100.0	289	58.4	210	42.3	80	27.6	206	41.6
1997	502	100.0	302	60.2	225	44.9	77	25.4	200	39.8
1998	505	100.0	308	60.9	221	43.7	87	28.2	197	39.1
1999	524	100.0	300	57.3	222	42.4	78	26.1	224	42.7
2000	515	100.0	350	68.0	252	48.9	99	28.1	165	32.0
Men										
1980	422	57.1	305	72.3	212	50.2	93	30.5	117	27.7
1985	321	52.5	261	81.3	163	50.8	98	37.5	60	18.7
1990	215	53.1	173	80.2	110	51.2	63	36.2	42	19.8
1994	259	50.8	198	76.5	151	58.2	47	23.9	61	23.5
1995	339	56.1	251	74.0	179	52.8	72	28.7	88	26.0
1996	241	48.6	178	74.0	123	51.0	56	31.1	63	26.0
1997	289	57.6	207	71.8	165	57.2	42	20.3	81	28.2
1998	257	50.9	164	63.9	133	51.8	31	19.0	93	36.1
1999	243	46.4	162	66.8	120	49.5	42	25.8	81	33.2
2000	295	57.3	220	74.4	166	56.2	54	24.5	76	25.6
Women										
1980	317	42.9	166	52.4	110	34.7	56	33.7	151	47.6
1985	291	47.5	152	52.2	103	35.4	49	32.2	139	47.8
1990	190	46.9	107	56.3	79	41.6	28	26.1	83	43.7
1994	251	49.2	113	45.2	68	27.1	45	40.0	137	54.8
1995	265	43.9	157	59.5	109	41.1	49	30.9	107	40.5
1996	255	51.4	111	43.6	87	34.1	24	21.8	144	56.4
1997	213	42.4	95	44.4	60	28.1	35	36.6	119	55.6
1998	248	49.1	143	57.8	88	35.4	56	38.7	105	42.2
1999	282	53.8	139	49.2	102	36.2	37	26.4	143	50.8
2000	220	42.7	131	59.4	86	39.1	45	34.2	90	40.6
White [3]										
1980	580	78.5	392	67.6	286	49.3	106	27.0	188	32.4
1985	458	74.8	330	72.1	214	46.7	116	35.2	128	27.9
1990	303	74.8	211	69.8	156	51.4	56	26.3	92	30.2
1994	382	74.9	252	66.0	177	46.3	75	29.8	130	34.0
1995	448	74.2	312	69.8	227	50.8	85	27.2	135	30.2
1996	365	73.6	238	65.1	178	48.6	60	25.3	127	34.9
1997	386	76.9	250	64.8	199	51.5	51	20.5	136	35.2
1998	384	76.0	257	67.0	194	50.6	63	24.5	127	33.0
1999	377	71.9	227	60.3	174	46.1	54	23.6	150	39.7
2000	384	74.6	280	73.0	210	54.8	70	24.9	104	27.0
Black [3]										
1980	146	19.8	73	50.0	33	22.6	40	(4)	73	50.0
1985	132	21.6	69	52.3	39	29.5	30	(4)	63	47.7
1990	86	21.2	56	65.3	26	29.9	30	(4)	30	34.7
1994	100	19.6	48	47.9	34	34.1	14	(4)	52	52.1
1995	109	18.0	66	61.0	40	36.4	27	(4)	42	39.0
1996	111	22.4	40	35.7	23	20.7	17	(4)	71	64.3
1997	90	17.9	41	45.1	18	20.4	22	(4)	49	54.9
1998	98	19.4	46	47.2	24	24.2	23	(4)	52	52.8
1999	118	22.5	59	50.0	39	33.0	20	(4)	59	50.0
2000	111	21.5	58	51.9	31	27.5	27	(4)	53	48.1
Hispanic [5]										
1980	91	12.3	60	65.9	43	47.3	17	(4)	31	34.1
1985	106	17.3	73	68.9	40	37.7	33	(4)	33	31.1
1990	67	16.5	32	(4)	22	(4)	10	(4)	35	(4)
1994	108	21.2	51	47.5	31	28.6	20	(4)	57	52.5

TABLE 4.10

Labor force status of high school dropouts, by sex and race/ethnicity, October 1980–October 2000 [CONTINUED]

Year, sex, and race	Dropouts		Dropouts in civilian labor force[1]						Not in labor force	
				Labor force participation rate	Employed		Unemployed			
	Number	Percent of total	Number		Number	Percent of dropouts	Number	Unemployment rate	Number	Percent of population
	1	2	3	4	5	6	7	8	9	10	11
1995	174	28.8	119	68.6	84	48.5	35	29.3	55	31.4
1996	105	21.2	71	67.7	57	54.5	14	(4)	34	32.3
1997	121	24.1	88	73.1	73	60.4	15	17.4	32	26.9
1998	120	23.8	82	68.5	60	50.0	22	27.1	38	31.5
1999	119	22.7	85	71.4	75	62.8	10	12.0	34	28.6
2000	101	19.6	62	61.1	39	39.0	22	(4)	39	38.9

[1] The labor force includes all employed persons plus those seeking employment. The labor force participation rate is the percentage of persons either employed or seeking employment. The unemployment rate is the percent of persons in the labor force who are seeking employment.

[2] Persons 16 to 24 years old who dropped out of school in the 12-month period ending in October of years shown.

[3] Includes persons of Hispanic origin.

[4] Data not shown where base is less than 75,000.

[5] Persons of Hispanic origin may be of any race.

Note: Data are based upon sample surveys of the civilian noninstitutional population. Includes dropouts from any grade, including a small number from elementary and middle schools. Percents are only shown when the base is 75,000 or greater. Even though the standard errors are large, smaller estimates are shown to permit users to combine categories in various ways. Detail for the above race and Hispanic-origin groups will not sum to totals because data for the "other races" group are not presented and Hispanics are included in both the white and black population groups. Detail may not sum to totals due to rounding.

SOURCE: Thomas D. Snyder and Charlene M. Hoffman, "Table 385. Labor force status of 1979–80 to 1999–2000 high school dropouts, by sex and race/ethnicity: October 1980 to October 2000," in *Digest of Education Statistics, 2001,* U.S. Department of Education, Office of Educational Research and Improvement, National Center for Education Statistics, Washington, DC, May 14, 2002

FIGURE 4.5

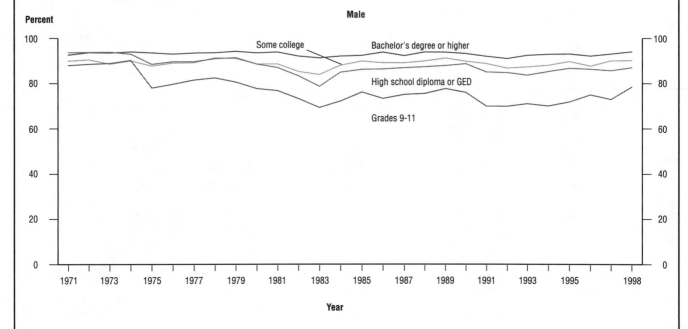

Employment rate of 25- to 34-year olds, by gender and educational attainment, March 1971–98

Male

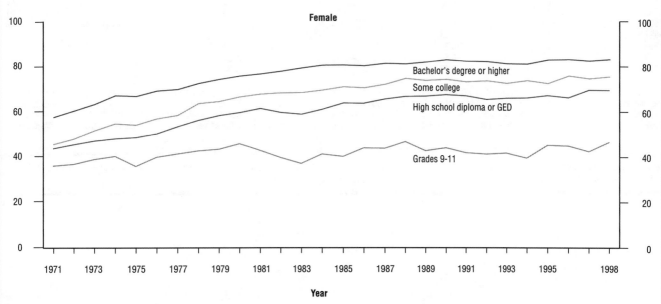

Female

Note: The employment rate represents the number of employed individuals as a percentage of the total population.

SOURCE: *The Condition of Education 1999*, National Center for Education Statistics, U.S. Department of Education, Office of Educational Research and Improvement, Washington, DC, 1999

TABLE 4.11

Ratio of median annual earnings of all wage and salary workers ages 25–34 whose highest education level was grades 9–11, some college, or a bachelor's degree or higher, compared with those with a high school diploma or GED, by sex, 1971–2000

Year	Grades 9–11		Some college		Bachelor's degree or higher	
	Male	Female	Male	Female	Male	Female
1971	0.84	0.64	1.05	1.15	1.22	1.87
1972	0.79	0.63	1.01	1.18	1.18	1.79
1973	0.83	0.70	0.99	1.27	1.16	1.78
1974	0.81	0.62	1.02	1.19	1.14	1.74
1975	0.78	0.64	1.07	1.24	1.17	1.72
1976	0.78	0.61	1.03	1.14	1.19	1.58
1977	0.77	0.63	1.02	1.23	1.18	1.53
1978	0.77	0.54	1.05	1.17	1.18	1.55
1979	0.76	0.70	1.06	1.19	1.16	1.55
1980	0.73	0.65	1.04	1.24	1.19	1.52
1981	0.73	0.61	1.07	1.23	1.29	1.54
1982	0.71	0.66	1.12	1.21	1.34	1.63
1983	0.70	0.66	1.13	1.24	1.35	1.67
1984	0.63	0.56	1.15	1.21	1.36	1.61
1985	0.70	0.63	1.19	1.18	1.50	1.69
1986	0.69	0.65	1.18	1.21	1.50	1.78
1987	0.72	0.67	1.13	1.25	1.49	1.78
1988	0.68	0.56	1.10	1.31	1.42	1.81
1989	0.70	0.63	1.12	1.32	1.45	1.93
1990	0.71	0.58	1.14	1.34	1.48	1.92
1991	0.64	0.64	1.14	1.32	1.53	1.90
1992	0.68	0.76	1.13	1.34	1.60	2.00
1993	0.67	0.59	1.12	1.31	1.57	1.99
1994	0.67	0.58	1.14	1.20	1.52	1.86
1995	0.74	0.61	1.11	1.28	1.55	1.91
1996	0.69	0.64	1.14	1.27	1.56	1.88
1997	0.71	0.63	1.11	1.22	1.50	1.91
1998	0.70	0.69	1.16	1.31	1.56	2.00
1999	0.69	0.61	1.16	1.25	1.58	1.92
2000	0.73	0.70	1.19	1.30	1.60	1.95

Note: This ratio is most useful when compared with 1.0. For example, the ratio of 1.60 for males in 2000 whose highest education level was a bachelor's degree or higher means that they earned 60 percent more than males who had a high school diploma or GED. The ratio of 0.73 for males in 2000 whose highest education level was grades 9–11 means that they earned 27 percent less than males who had a high school diploma or GED. The Current Population Survey (CPS) questions used to obtain educational attainment were changed in 1992. In 1994, the survey methodology for the CPS was changed and weights were adjusted. Table derived from U.S. Department of Commerce, Bureau of the Census. March Current Population Surveys, 1972–2001.

SOURCE: "Table 16-2: Ratio of median annual earnings of all wage and salary workers ages 25–34 whose highest education level was grades 9–11, some college, or a bachelor's degree or higher, compared with those with a high school diploma or GED, by sex: March 1971–2000," in *The Condition of Education 2002*, U.S. Department of Education, National Center for Education Statistics, Washington, DC, 2002

TABLE 4.12

Percentage of 1992–93 college graduates, by employment and enrollment status, relatedness of jobs to education, and selected characteristics, April 1994

Selected characteristics	Employment and enrollment status					Relatedness of job to education[1]		
	Employed full time, not enrolled	Employed part time, not enrolled	In labor force, enrolled[2]	Not in labor force, enrolled	Not employed, not enrolled[3]	Job related to field of study	Job required college degree	Job had career potential
Total	67.1	8.7	12.4	5.5	6.3	77.6	59.9	75.7
Field of study								
Business and management	80.0	5.3	7.9	1.9	4.9	87.1	54.1	79.6
Education	59.9	16.1	14.4	4.8	4.8	80.4	72.1	78.1
Engineering	69.2	3.4	13.7	7.2	6.5	90.0	83.0	85.8
Health professions	68.6	8.4	12.9	4.5	5.6	94.4	77.4	84.6
Public affairs/social services	70.3	9.0	9.2	5.0	6.5	73.5	53.0	71.6
Biological sciences	44.3	8.4	17.4	18.3	11.5	69.5	54.7	62.1
Mathematics and science	60.8	8.5	14.9	9.9	5.9	87.1	71.0	80.8
Social sciences	66.6	7.0	13.1	6.l	7.2	57,7	48.8	72.3
History	64.9	8.1	16.4	6.6	4.0	40.6	43.4	69.3
Humanities	59.2	12.8	13.5	5.9	8.5	58.2	50.1	69.1
Psychology	56.5	6.9	19.5	8.8	8.3	59.2	54.5	54.1
Other	69.4	9.0	11.4	3.6	6.6	75.2	55.0	70.5
Sex								
Male	69.2	6.8	11.9	6.3	5.7	76.6	59.l	78.0
Female	65.3	10.3	12.8	4.7	6.9	78.4	60.5	73.6
College grade point average								
Less than 3.0	71.7	8.9	11.1	2.2	6.1	73.2	54.6	74.2
3.0 to 3.49	68.2	7.9	12.7	5.0	6.3	78.7	63.0	74.7
3.5 and higher	61.l	9.3	14.1	9.4	6.0	81.5	61.6	79.2

[1] Includes only those who worked full time and who were not enrolled in postsecondary education.

[2] Includes persons who worked full time or part time or who were unemployed.

[3] Includes persons who were not in the work force or who were unemployed.

SOURCE: *The Condition of Education 1999,* National Center for Education Statistics, U.S. Department of Education, Office of Educational Research and Improvement, Washington, DC, 1999

TABLE 4.13

Annual median starting salaries (in 1997 constant dollars) of 1993 college graduates, by gender and major field of study, and the percentage difference between male and female starting salaries

Major field of study	All graduates	Male		Female		Female/male percentage difference
		Percentage in field	Median starting salary	Percentage in field	Median starting salary	
Total	$24,156	100	$26,738	100	$22,508	*(15.8)
Humanities	21,469	9	22,307	12	21,100	(5.4)
Social and behavioral sciences	21,984	13	23,885	15	21,061	*(11.8)
Natural sciences	22,347	7	24,798	6	20,991	*(15.3)
Computer sciences and engineering	32,802	16	33,148	3	30,866	(6.9)
Education	20,456	6	21,737	17	20,114	(7.5)
Business and management	26,658	32	28,382	23	24,363	*(14.2)
Other professional or technical	24,959	17	24,938	23	24,974	0.1

*Male starting salaries were greater than female salaries (p< 0.05).

Note: Data presented are for bachelor's degree recipients who were working full time and who were not enrolled in postsecondary education 1 year after graduation. Details may not add to totals due to rounding.

SOURCE: "Annual Median Starting Salaries (in 1997 Constant Dollars) of 1993 College Graduates, by Gender and Major Field of Study, and the Percentage Difference Between Male and Female Starting Salaries," part of "Economic and Other Outcomes of Education," *Digest of Education Statistics,* U.S. Department of Education, Office of Educational Research & Improvement, National Center for Education Statistics, Washington, DC, 1999

FIGURE 4.6

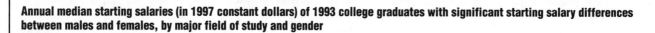

Annual median starting salaries (in 1997 constant dollars) of 1993 college graduates with significant starting salary differences between males and females, by major field of study and gender

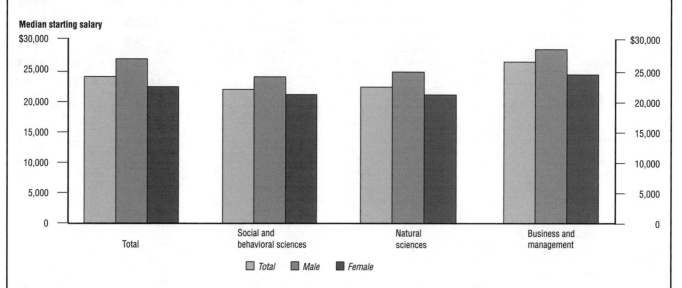

Median starting salary

Note: Data presented are for bachelor's degree recipients who were working full time and who were not enrolled in postsecondary education 1 year after graduation.

SOURCE: "Annual Median Starting Salaries (in 1997 Constant Dollars) of 1993 College Graduates with Significant Starting Salary Differences Between Males and Females, by Major Field of Study and Gender," part of "Economic and Other Outcomes of Education," in *Digest of Education Statistics,* U.S. Department of Education, Office of Educational Research & Improvement, National Center for Education Statistics, Washington, DC, 1999

TABLE 4.14

Annual median earnings (in 2000 constant dollars) of all wage and salary workers ages 25–34, by sex and educational attainment level, March 1970–99

Year	Male				Female			
	Grades 9–11	High school diploma or equivalent	Some college including vocational/ technical	Bachelor's degree or higher	Grades 9–11	High school diploma or equivalent	Some college including vocational/ technical	Bachelor's degree or higher
1970	$30,346	$36,726	$40,074	$45,484	$8,925	$15,166	$18,150	$27,656
1971	31,039	36,935	38,947	45,219	10,045	15,656	17,942	29,345
1972	30,845	38,951	39,342	46,065	10,235	16,217	19,188	29,047
1973	32,579	39,326	39,118	45,610	11,122	15,929	20,301	28,401
1974	29,965	37,122	37,765	42,491	9,833	15,815	18,885	27,463
1975	26,882	34,318	36,681	40,089	10,161	15,810	19,594	27,249
1976	27,191	34,740	35,920	41,279	10,080	16,544	18,815	26,170
1977	26,970	34,968	35,779	41,175	10,527	16,820	20,613	25,757
1978	26,928	35,197	36,802	41,422	8,839	16,424	19,139	25,460
1979	26,214	34,533	36,455	40,033	11,687	16,585	19,788	25,770
1980	23,575	32,100	33,459	38,242	10,624	16,469	20,454	25,042
1981	21,939	29,898	31,849	38,691	9,842	16,055	19,776	24,777
1982	19,773	27,785	31,030	37,253	10,427	15,680	18,905	25,551
1983	19,598	27,945	31,622	37,809	10,542	15,857	19,662	26,438
1984	18,111	28,622	32,995	38,864	9,341	16,564	20,072	26,702
1985	19,395	27,536	32,707	41,276	10,415	16,618	19,582	28,053
1986	19,204	27,660	32,602	41,608	10,690	16,534	20,075	29,437
1987	20,305	28,082	31,804	41,743	11,404	16,932	21,171	30,164
1988	19,469	28,759	31,570	40,720	9,305	16,640	21,780	30,131
1989	19,559	28,040	31,479	40,656	10,037	16,020	21,118	30,889
1990	18,628	26,259	30,051	38,770	9,139	15,872	21,223	30,503
1991	16,471	25,563	29,161	39,019	9,910	15,539	20,534	29,516
1992	16,596	24,389	27,668	39,070	11,724	15,339	20,575	30,684
1993	16,201	24,231	27,218	38,014	8,905	15,172	19,909	30,245
1994	16,588	24,589	28,149	37,437	9,248	15,993	19,244	29,822
1995	17,847	24,213	26,891	37,553	9,436	15,346	19,603	29,328
1996	16,926	24,663	28,233	38,593	9,789	15,366	19,579	28,940
1997	18,191	25,618	28,453	38,410	10,279	16,276	19,817	31,024
1998	18,569	26,717	31,118	41,695	10,989	15,863	20,736	31,789
1999	18,582	26,842	31,208	42,341	10,174	16,770	21,008	32,145

SOURCE: Table 18-1. "Median Annual Earnings (in Constant 2000 Dollars) of All Wage and Salary Workers Ages 25-34, by sex and educational attainment level: March 1970–1999," in *Condition of Education, 2001,* U.S. Department of Education, Office of Educational Research & Improvement, National Center for Education Statistics, Washington DC, 2001

TABLE 4.15

Annual median income of year-round, full-time workers 25 years old and over, by level of education completed and sex, 1989–99

| | | Elementary/secondary | | | | | College | | | | |
| | | | | | Some | | | Bachelor's degree or higher[5] | | | |
Sex and year	Total	Less than 9th grade	9th to 12th grade, no diploma[1]	High school graduate[2]	college, no degree[3]	Associate degree[4]	Total[5]	Bachelor's[6]	Master's[4]	Professional[4]	Doctorate[4]
1	2	3	4	5	6	7	8	9	10	11	12
Current dollars											
Men											
1989	$30,465	$17,555	$21,065	$26,609	$31,308	—	$41,892	$38,565	—	—	—
1990	30,733	17,394	20,902	26,653	31,734	—	42,671	39,238	—	—	—
1991	31,613	17,623	21,402	26,779	31,663	$33,817	45,138	40,906	$49,734	$73,996	$57,187
1992	32,057	17,294	21,274	27,280	32,103	33,433	45,802	41,355	49,973	76,220	57,418
1993	32,359	16,863	21,752	27,370	32,077	33,690	47,740	42,757	51,867	80,549	63,149
1994	33,440	17,532	22,048	28,037	32,279	35,794	49,228	43,663	53,500	75,009	61,921
1995	34,551	18,354	22,185	29,510	33,883	35,201	50,481	45,266	55,216	79,667	65,336
1996	35,622	17,962	22,717	30,709	34,845	37,131	51,436	45,846	60,508	85,963	71,227
1997	36,678	19,291	24,726	31,215	35,945	38,022	53,450	48,616	61,690	85,011	76,234
1998	37,906	19,380	23,958	31,477	36,934	40,274	56,524	51,405	62,244	94,737	75,078
1999	40,333	20,429	25,035	33,184	39,221	41,638	60,201	52,985	66,243	100,000	81,687
Women											
1989	20,570	12,188	13,923	17,528	21,631	—	28,799	26,709	—	—	—
1990	21,372	12,251	14,429	18,319	22,227	—	30,377	28,017	—	—	—
1991	22,043	12,066	14,455	18,836	22,143	25,000	31,310	29,079	34,949	46,742	43,303
1992	23,139	12,958	14,559	19,427	23,157	25,624	32,304	30,326	36,037	46,257	45,790
1993	23,629	12,415	15,386	19,963	23,056	25,883	34,307	31,197	38,612	50,211	47,248
1994	24,399	12,430	15,133	20,373	23,514	25,940	35,378	31,741	39,457	50,615	51,119
1995	24,875	13,577	15,825	20,463	23,997	27,311	35,259	32,051	40,263	50,000	48,141
1996	25,808	14,414	16,953	21,175	25,167	28,083	36,461	33,525	41,901	57,624	56,267
1997	26,974	14,161	16,697	22,067	26,335	28,812	38,038	35,379	44,949	61,051	53,037
1998	27,956	14,467	16,482	22,780	27,420	29,924	39,786	36,559	45,283	57,565	57,796
1999	28,844	15,098	17,015	23,061	27,757	30,919	41,747	37,993	48,097	59,904	60,079
Constant 1999 dollars											
Men											
1989	$40,931	$23,586	$28,302	$35,750	$42,064	—	$56,284	$51,814	—	—	—
1990	39,175	22,172	26,643	33,974	40,451	—	54,392	50,016	—	—	—
1991	38,669	21,556	26,179	32,756	38,730	$41,365	55,213	50,036	$60,835	$90,512	$69,951
1992	38,066	20,536	25,262	32,394	38,121	39,700	54,388	49,107	59,341	90,508	68,181
1993	37,308	19,442	25,079	31,556	36,983	38,843	55,041	49,296	59,800	92,868	72,807
1994	37,592	19,709	24,785	31,518	36,287	40,238	55,340	49,084	60,142	84,322	69,609
1995	37,770	20,064	24,252	32,260	37,040	38,481	55,185	49,484	60,361	87,090	71,424
1996	37,824	19,072	24,121	32,608	36,999	39,427	54,616	48,680	64,249	91,277	75,630
1997	38,072	20,024	25,666	32,401	37,311	39,467	55,481	50,464	64,035	88,242	79,131
1998	38,743	19,808	24,487	32,172	37,750	41,163	57,772	52,540	63,619	96,829	76,736
1999	40,333	20,429	25,035	33,184	39,221	41,638	60,201	52,985	66,243	100,000	81,687
Women											
1989	27,637	16,375	18,706	23,550	29,062	—	38,693	35,885	—	—	—
1990	27,242	15,616	18,392	23,351	28,332	—	38,721	35,713	—	—	—
1991	26,963	14,759	17,681	23,040	27,085	30,580	38,298	35,569	42,750	57,175	52,968
1992	27,477	15,387	17,288	23,069	27,498	30,427	38,360	36,011	42,792	54,928	54,374
1993	27,243	14,314	17,739	23,016	26,582	29,842	39,554	35,968	44,517	57,890	54,474
1994	27,428	13,973	17,012	22,902	26,433	29,161	39,770	35,682	44,356	56,899	57,466
1995	27,193	14,842	17,300	22,370	26,233	29,856	38,544	35,037	44,015	54,659	52,627
1996	27,404	15,305	18,001	22,484	26,723	29,819	38,715	35,598	44,491	61,186	59,746
1997	27,999	14,699	17,332	22,906	27,336	29,907	39,484	36,724	46,657	63,371	55,053
1998	28,573	14,787	16,846	23,283	28,026	30,585	40,665	37,366	46,283	58,836	59,072
1999	28,844	15,098	17,015	23,061	27,757	30,919	41,747	37,993	48,097	59,904	60,079
Number with income (in thousands)											
Men											
1989	44,596	2,425	3,312	16,392	9,028	—	13,439	7,473	—	—	—
1990	44,406	2,250	3,315	16,394	9,113	—	13,334	7,569	—	—	—
1991	44,199	1,807	3,083	15,025	8,034	2,899	13,350	8,456	3,073	1,147	674
1992	44,752	1,815	3,009	14,722	8,067	3,203	13,937	8,719	3,178	1,295	745
1993	45,873	1,790	3,083	14,604	8,493	3,557	14,346	9,178	3,131	1,231	808
1994	47,566	1,895	3,057	15,109	8,783	3,735	14,987	9,636	3,225	1,258	868
1995	48,500	1,946	3,335	15,331	8,908	3,926	15,054	9,597	3,395	1,208	853
1996	49,764	2,041	3,441	15,840	9,173	3,931	15,339	9,898	3,272	1,277	893
1997	50,807	1,914	3,548	16,225	9,170	4,086	15,864	10,349	3,228	1,321	966
1998	52,381	1,870	3,613	16,442	9,375	4,347	16,733	11,058	3,414	1,264	998
1999	53,062	1,993	3,295	16,589	9,684	4,359	17,142	11,142	3,725	1,267	1,008

TABLE 4.15

Annual median income of year-round, full-time workers 25 years old and over, by level of education completed and sex, 1989–99

[CONTINUED]

Sex and year	Total	Elementary/secondary					College				
		Less than 9th grade	9th to 12th grade, no diploma[1]	High school grad-uate[2]	Some college, no de-gree[3]	Associate degree[4]	Total[5]	Bachelor's degree or higher[5]			
								Bach-elor's[6]	Master's[4]	Profes-sional[4]	Doc-torate[4]
1	2	3	4	5	6	7	8	9	10	11	12
					Number with income (in thousands)						
Women											
1989	28,056	906	1,830	11,785	6,217	—	7,318	4,465	—	—	—
1990	28,636	847	1,861	11,810	6,462	—	7,655	4,704	—	—	—
1991	29,474	733	1,819	10,959	5,633	2,523	7,807	5,263	2,025	312	206
1992	30,346	734	1,659	11,039	5,904	2,655	8,355	5,604	2,192	334	225
1993	30,683	765	1,576	10,513	6,279	3,067	8,483	5,735	2,166	323	260
1994	31,379	696	1,675	10,785	6,256	3,210	8,756	5,901	2,174	398	283
1995	32,673	774	1,763	11,064	6,329	3,336	9,406	6,434	2,268	421	283
1996	33,549	750	1,751	11,363	6,582	3,468	9,636	6,689	2,213	413	322
1997	34,624	791	1,765	11,475	6,628	3,538	10,427	7,173	2,448	488	318
1998	35,628	814	1,878	11,613	7,070	3,527	10,725	7,288	2,639	468	329
1999	37,091	886	1,883	11,824	7,453	3,804	11,242	7,607	2,818	470	346

—Not available.
[1] Includes 1 to 3 years high school for 1989 and 1990.
[2] Includes 4 years of high school for 1989 and 1990, and equivalency certificates for the other years.
[3] Includes 1 to 3 years of college and associate degrees for 1989 and 1990.
[4] Not reported separately for 1989 and 1990.
[5] Includes 4 or more years of college for 1989 and 1990.
[6] Includes 4 years of college for 1989 and 1990.
Note: Data for 1992 and later years are based on 1990 Census counts. Detail may not sum to totals due to rounding.

SOURCE: Table 382. "Median annual income of year-round full-time workers 25 years old and over, by level of education completed and sex: 1989-1999," in *Digest of Education Statistics, 2001,* U.S. Department of Education, Office of Educational Research & Improvement, National Center for Education Statistics, Washington DC, 2001

FIGURE 4.7

Annual median income of persons with income 25 years old and over, by sex and highest level of education, 1999

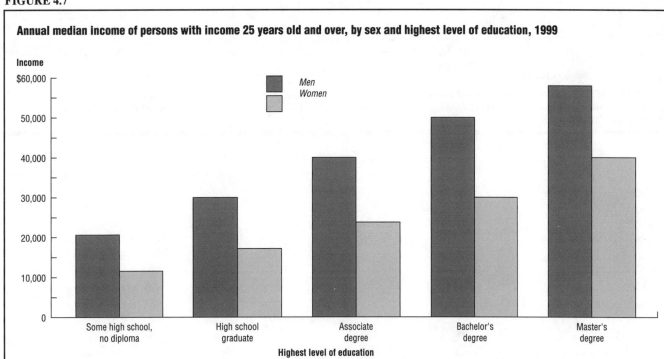

SOURCE: "Figure 26. Median annual income of persons with income 25 years old and over, by highest level of education and sex: 1999," in *Digest of Education Statistics, 2001,* U.S. Department of Education, Office of Educational Research & Improvement, National Center for Education Statistics, Washington, DC, 2001

TABLE 4.16

Total annual money income and median income of persons 25 years old and over, by educational attainment and sex: 1999

1	Total	Less than 9th grade	Some high school (no diploma)	High school graduate (includes equivalency)	Some college, no degree	Associate degree	College — Bachelor's or higher degree — Total	Bachelor's degree	Master's degree	Profes-sional degree	Doctor's degree
	2	3	4	5	6	7	8	9	10	11	12

					Number, in thousands						
Men, 25 years old and over											
Total	83,611	5,918	7,298	26,651	14,540	5,952	23,251	14,909	5,166	1,752	1,425
With income	65,412	2,833	4,608	20,656	11,908	5,175	20,232	13,057	4,462	1,480	1,233
					Percentage distribution of men with income						
Total	100.0	100.0	100.0	100.0	100.0	100.0	100.0	100.0	100.0	100.0	100.0
$1 to $4,999 or loss	5.0	9.9	9.3	5.3	5.2	4.0	3.1	2.9	4.0	2.5	3.3
$5,000 to $9,999	4.4	13.0	8.6	5.1	4.1	3.2	2.1	2.4	2.0	1.0	1.1
$10,000 to $14,999	6.4	19.1	14.5	7.2	5.2	4.7	3.1	3.6	2.0	2.0	2.0
$15,000 to $24,999	16.8	32.9	28.4	21.7	17.0	14.7	7.5	8.6	5.9	4.6	4.6
$25,000 to $34,999	17.5	13.7	19.9	22.0	19.4	18.0	11.7	13.5	9.9	5.5	6.6
$35,000 to $49,999	20.4	7.5	13.0	22.2	24.0	25.6	18.5	21.4	14.7	10.2	11.7
$50,000 to $74,999	17.1	2.8	4.9	12.4	16.8	21.6	25.9	25.8	29.9	15.7	24.1
$75,000 and over	12.3	1.1	1.5	4.1	8.3	8.2	28.2	21.9	31.5	58.4	46.6
Median income	$34,850	$16,704	$20,604	$29,917	$34,270	$36,885	$51,815	$47,419	$57,841	$86,523	$71,531
					Number, in thousands						
Women, 25 years old and over											
Total	91,620	6,261	8,377	31,435	16,213	7,740	21,595	14,931	5,230	834	599
With income	58,225	1,673	3,489	18,756	11,483	5,844	16,980	11,548	4,238	687	507
					Percentage distribution of women with income						
Total	100.0	100.0	100.0	100.0	100.0	100.0	100.0	100.0	100.0	100.0	100.0
$1 to $4,999 or loss	11.2	22.7	20.9	12.9	11.0	9.3	7.1	7.9	5.7	5.4	5.3
$5,000 to $9,999	10.4	22.2	21.1	12.7	9.9	8.4	5.5	5.9	5.2	2.3	1.8
$10,000 to $14,999	12.3	26.6	22.1	16.0	11.9	10.4	5.6	6.7	3.3	3.6	3.6
$15,000 to $24,999	23.5	21.5	24.5	29.8	26.2	24.6	14.3	16.7	8.6	9.5	11.6
$25,000 to $34,999	18.1	4.1	8.1	17.2	20.2	22.4	19.5	21.8	16.0	11.1	8.3
$35,000 to $49,999	14.1	2.0	2.4	8.6	13.3	17.3	23.4	21.7	28.7	22.6	20.9
$50,000 to $74,999	7.5	0.7	0.7	2.3	5.5	5.9	17.3	14.1	24.6	18.6	26.2
$75,000 and over	2.9	0.4	0.4	0.6	2.0	1.8	7.3	5.2	8.1	26.8	22.1
Median income	$21,417	$10,754	$11,432	$17,126	$21,426	$23,760	$33,370	$30,730	$40,553	$45,926	$46,949

Note: Detail may not sum to totals due to rounding.

SOURCE: Table 383. Total annual money income and median income of persons 25 years old and over, by educational attainment and sex: 1999, in *Digest of Education Statistics, 2001,* U.S. Department of Education, Office of Educational Research & Improvement, National Center for Education Statistics, Washington, DC, 2001

TABLE 4.17

Persons in the labor force for 27 weeks or more: poverty status by educational attainment, race, and sex, 1999

Educational attainment and race	Total	Men	Women	Below poverty level			Poverty rate[1]		
				Total	Men	Women	Total	Men	Women
Total, 16 years and older	133,651	71,790	61,861	6,796	3,165	3,631	5.1	4.4	5.9
Less than a high school diploma	15,991	9,728	6,263	2,287	1,257	1,030	14.3	12.9	16.4
Less than 1 year of high school	4,589	2,999	1,591	701	446	255	15.3	14.9	16.1
1-3 years of high school	9,914	5,861	4,054	1,412	720	692	14.2	12.3	17.1
4 years of high school, no diploma	1,487	868	619	174	91	83	11.7	10.5	13.3
High school graduates, no college	42,601	22,904	19,697	2,535	1,042	1,493	6.0	4.6	7.6
Some college, no degree	27,294	13,840	13,454	1,192	486	706	4.4	3.5	5.2
Associate degree	11,146	5,334	5,812	319	122	196	2.9	2.3	3.4
College graduates	36,619	19,984	16,635	463	257	206	1.3	1.3	1.2
White, 16 years and older	111,714	61,163	50,551	4,830	2,526	2,303	4.3	4.1	4.6
Less than a high school diploma	13,046	8,160	4,887	1,650	1,019	632	12.6	12.5	12.9
Less than 1 year of high school	3,967	2,660	1,307	592	410	182	14.9	15.4	13.9
1-3 years of high school	7,954	4,822	3,132	944	545	399	11.9	11.3	12.8
4 years of high school, no diploma	1,126	678	448	114	64	50	10.1	9.4	11.3
High school graduates, no college	35,536	19,448	16,088	1,758	816	942	4.9	4.2	5.9
Some college, no degree	22,412	11,605	10,807	844	377	467	3.8	3.2	4.3
Associate degree	9,507	4,646	4,861	213	93	119	2.2	2.0	2.5
College graduates	31,213	17,304	13,908	365	222	143	1.2	1.3	1.0
Black, 16 years and older	15,698	7,260	8,438	1,596	447	1,149	10.2	6.2	13.6
Less than a high school diploma	2,206	1,126	1,080	517	168	349	23.4	14.9	32.3
Less than 1 year of high school	365	213	151	74	17	57	20.2	7.8	37.7
1-3 years of high school	1,585	785	800	399	134	264	25.2	17.1	33.0
4 years of high school, no diploma	257	128	128	44	17	27	17.3	13.5	21.1
High school graduates, no college	5,632	2,733	2,899	668	177	491	11.9	6.5	17.0
Some college, no degree	3,790	1,644	2,146	276	71	205	7.3	4.3	9.6
Associate degree	1,172	457	715	81	14	67	6.9	3.1	9.4
College graduates	2,898	1,299	1,598	54	17	37	1.9	1.3	2.3

[1]Number below the poverty level as a percent of the total in the labor force for 27 weeks or more.

Note: Data for 1999, which were collected in the March 2000 supplement to the Current Population Survey, are not strictly comparable with data for 1998 and earlier years because of the introduction in January 2000 of revised population controls used in the survey.

SOURCE: " Table 3: Persons in the labor force for 27 weeks or more: Poverty status by educational attainment, race, and sex, 1999," in *A Profile of the Working Poor, 1999,* U.S. Department of Labor, Bureau of Labor Statistics, Washington, DC, 2001

CHAPTER 5

THE WORKFORCE OF TOMORROW

Making informed career decisions requires reliable information about job opportunities in the future. Job opportunities result from the relationships between the population, labor force, and the demand for goods and services. Population ultimately limits the size of the labor force, which, in turn, drives how much can be produced. Demand for various goods and services determines employment in the industries providing them. Occupational employment opportunities then result from skills needed within specific industries. Opportunities for registered nurses and other health-related specialists, for example, have surged in response to the rapid growth in demand for health services as the population has aged.

Based on population and economic growth, the U.S. Bureau of Labor Statistics (BLS) predicts where future job growth is expected, by industry and occupation, and what the demographic makeup of the workforce is likely to be. The latest predictions released are for the decade 2000 to 2010. These 10-year projections are widely used for studying long-range economic and employment trends, planning education and training programs, and developing career information.

LABOR FORCE

The civilian labor force comprises individuals age 16 and older who are either working or looking for work. They represent the supply of workers available to fill all the jobs that will be created. The population and labor force will continue to grow over the 2000 to 2010 period, at roughly the same rate as the previous 10-year period. The labor force is projected to increase by 17 million (12 percent) between 2000 and 2010, reaching 158 million workers in 2010. (See Figure 5.1 and Table 5.1.) The labor force is projected to grow slightly faster than the population, because a larger proportion of the population will be working or looking for work. This includes a larger number of women and minority workers.

A special report, "Working in the 21st Century," published by the BLS in 2002 disagreed somewhat with these figures. It projected a slowdown in the pace of growth of the labor force between 2000 to 2015, then a substantial downturn in labor force as the baby boomers—those born between 1946 and 1964—retire.

Older Workers

The labor force is getting older as the baby boomers age. According to the BLS, workers between the ages of 55 to 64 will be the fastest-growing portion of the

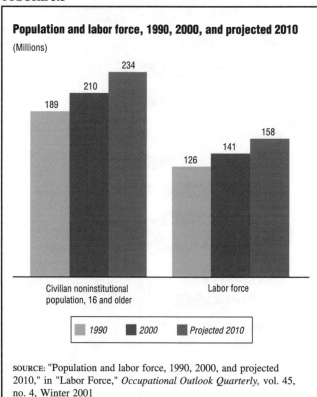

FIGURE 5.1

Population and labor force, 1990, 2000, and projected 2010

(Millions)

SOURCE: "Population and labor force, 1990, 2000, and projected 2010," in "Labor Force," *Occupational Outlook Quarterly,* vol. 45, no. 4, Winter 2001

TABLE 5.1

Civilian labor force by sex, age, race, and Hispanic origin, 1990, 2000, 2010

[Numbers in thousands]

Group	Level			Change		Percent change		Percent distribution		
	1990	2000	2010	1990-2000	2000-10	1990-2000	2000-10	1990	2000	2010
Total, 16 years and older	125,840	140,863	157,721	15,023	16,858	11.9	12.0	100.0	100.0	100.0
16 to 24	22,492	22,715	26,081	223	3,366	1.0	14.8	17.9	16.1	16
25 to 54	88,322	99,974	104,994	11,652	5,020	13.2	5.0	70.2	71.0	66
55 and older	15,026	18,175	26,646	3,149	8,471	21.0	46.6	11.9	12.9	16
Men, total	69,011	75,247	82,221	6,236	6,974	9.0	9.3	54.8	53.4	52
Women, total	56,829	65,616	75,500	8,787	9,884	15.5	15.1	45.2	46.6	47
White, total	107,447	117,574	128,043	10,127	10,470	9.4	8.9	85.4	83.5	81
Black, total	13,740	16,603	20,041	2,863	3,439	20.8	20.7	10.9	11.8	12
Asian and other, total[1]	4,653	6,687	9,636	2,034	2,950	43.7	44.1	3.7	4.7	6
Hispanic origin, total	10,720	15,368	20,947	4,648	5,579	43.4	36.3	8.5	10.9	13
Other than Hispanic origin, total	115,120	125,495	136,774	10,375	11,279	9.0	9.0	91.5	89.1	86
White non-Hispanic	97,818	102,963	109,118	5,144	6,155	5.3	6.0	77.7	73.1	69

[1]The "Asian and other" group includes (1) Asians and Pacific Islanders and (2) American Indians. The historical data are derived by subtracting "black" and "white" from the total; projections not by subtraction.

SOURCE: "Table 5. Civilian labor force by sex, age, race, and Hispanic origin, 1990, 2000, 2010," in *News: Bureau of Labor Statistics,* U.S. Department of Labor, Bureau of Labor Statistics, Office of Occupational Statistics and Employment Projections, Washington, DC, June 6, 2002 [Online] http://www.bls.gov/news.release/ecopro.t05.htm [accessed June 20, 2002]

FIGURE 5.2

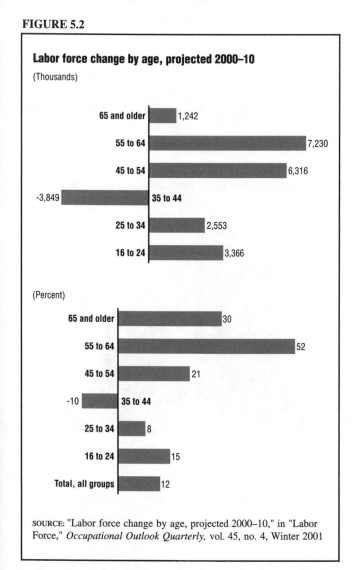

Labor force change by age, projected 2000–10

SOURCE: "Labor force change by age, projected 2000–10," in "Labor Force," *Occupational Outlook Quarterly,* vol. 45, no. 4, Winter 2001

workforce between 1996 and 2006. The median age of U.S. workers will increase to 41 years in 2006, up from 38 years in 1996. This, coupled with a population growth rate that is expected to lag behind the job growth rate, is predicted to create a situation in which employers will need to rely on older workers to fill or keep jobs.

Baby boomers seem willing to stay in their jobs. A 1998 poll presented at an annual American Association of Retired Persons (AARP) conference showed that 80 percent of baby boomers intend to keep working at least part-time after retirement age. Reasons for continuing to work ranged from job enjoyment, to the desire to start a business, to the need for income.

The labor force participation rate changes with age. Participation is low for young persons because of school and child care, rises during the prime working ages of 25 to 54, and then declines after age 55 as workers retire. In 2000, for example, the labor force participation rate for those age 16 to 24 was 16.1 percent, and for those age 25 to 54, it was 71 percent. (See Table 5.1.) For persons age 55 and older, the participation rate was 12.9 percent.

The number of workers in the two age groups with large numbers of baby boomers are projected to increase—the numbers of people age 45 to 54 in the labor force will grow by 21 percent and those age 55 to 64 will increase by 52 percent by 2010. (See Figure 5.2.)

Gender

From 2000 to 2010 women will continue to make up a growing proportion of the labor force, rising from 47 to 48 percent. (See Figure 5.3.) The labor force participation

FIGURE 5.3

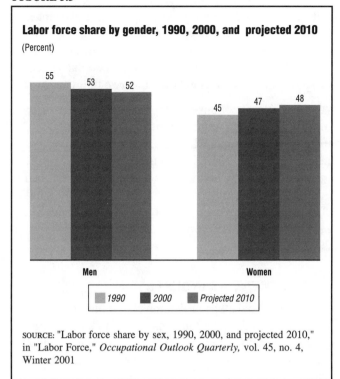

Labor force share by gender, 1990, 2000, and projected 2010

(Percent)

SOURCE: "Labor force share by sex, 1990, 2000, and projected 2010," in "Labor Force," *Occupational Outlook Quarterly,* vol. 45, no. 4, Winter 2001

FIGURE 5.4

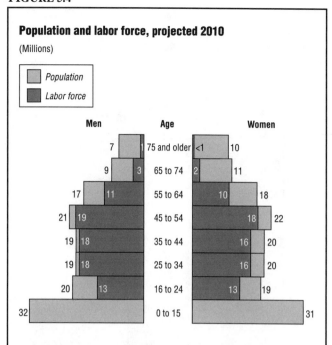

Population and labor force, projected 2010

(Millions)

SOURCE: "Population and labor force, projected 2010," in "Labor Force," *Occupational Outlook Quarterly,* vol. 45, no. 4, Winter 2001

rate for women rose from 57 percent in 1988 to 60 percent in 1998 and is projected to increase even more by 2010. However, men's labor force participation rates have declined steadily, from 76 percent in 1988 to 75 percent in 1998. Men will continue to have higher rates of participation in the labor force than women, but women's rates will be higher in all age categories than in previous decades. (See Figure 5.4.)

Race and Ethnicity

Due to the effects of immigration, the labor force growth of Hispanics, Asians, and others will be much faster than that of blacks and non-Hispanic whites. Asians are projected to be the fastest-growing group during the 2000 to 2010 period, increasing more than three times as fast as the overall labor force, followed closely by Hispanics. (See Table 5.1.) As a result, by 2010 more Hispanics will be in the labor force than blacks. Despite a slower rate of growth than Hispanics and Asians, non-Hispanic whites will still be the largest group of workers between 2000 and 2010. (See Figure 5.5.)

ECONOMIC GROWTH

The economy's need for workers stems from the demand for goods and services, which is measured by the gross domestic product (GDP). The GDP is projected to grow at a rate of 2.1 percent per year during the 1996 to 2006 period and to reach approximately $9.5 trillion by 2008. By comparison, the GDP grew at an average annual

FIGURE 5.5

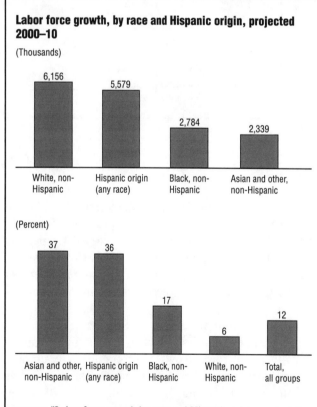

Labor force growth, by race and Hispanic origin, projected 2000–10

(Thousands)

(Percent)

SOURCE: "Labor force growth by race and Hispanic origin, projected 2000–10," in "Labor Force," *Occupational Outlook Quarterly,* vol. 45, no. 4, Winter 2001

FIGURE 5.6

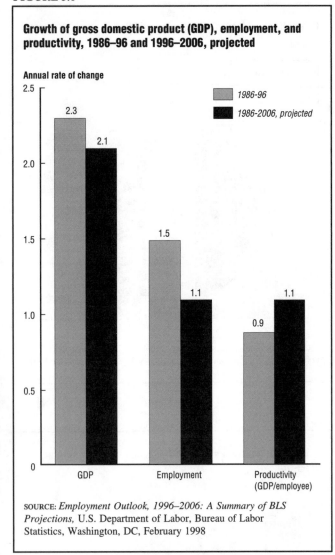

Growth of gross domestic product (GDP), employment, and productivity, 1986–96 and 1996–2006, projected

Annual rate of change

Legend:
- 1986-96
- 1986-2006, projected

GDP: 2.3 / 2.1
Employment: 1.5 / 1.1
Productivity (GDP/employee): 0.9 / 1.1

SOURCE: *Employment Outlook, 1996–2006: A Summary of BLS Projections,* U.S. Department of Labor, Bureau of Labor Statistics, Washington, DC, February 1998

rate of 2.3 percent during the 1986 to 1996 period. (See Figure 5.6.)

The slowdown in GDP growth reflects slower labor force growth, from an average annual rate of 1.5 percent over the 1986 to 1996 period to a projected 1.1 percent between 1996 and 2006. Along with this slowdown, the projection calls for rising productivity (more output per worker) in order to meet the ever-growing demand for goods and services. (See Figure 5.6.) Faster, more powerful machines and new equipment will enable workers to produce more efficiently, increasing output faster than the company's workforce grows. High-productivity companies are more likely to prosper in a globally competitive environment, increasing their output even further and either hiring additional workers or expecting more production from existing workers.

Domestic and foreign consumers, including individuals, businesses, and governments, purchase thousands of American products. Shifts in consumer tastes and govern-

ment priorities can affect the growth of and demand for different kinds of goods and services. Technical changes in products also affect demand. For example, the use of more plastics instead of steel in automobiles increases demand for plastics and decreases demand for steel. Such changes can have a significant effect on industry employment.

Traditionally, households have spent most of their income on housing, transportation, and medical care. This trend should continue. However, the BLS projects, for the period 2000 to 2010, that consumers will spend an increasing share of their income on durable goods, such as computers and furniture, and a comparatively smaller share on nondurable goods, such as food and fuel. These projections were made prior to the economic downturn of 2001 and 2002.

EMPLOYMENT BY INDUSTRY

The BLS develops projections of employment for 262 industries or industry groups that make up the economy as a whole. Because of expected shifts in spending, employment growth rates will vary significantly among industries. As a consequence, the structure of industry employment will change over the 1998 to 2008 period.

Changes in demand for an industry's products constitute the most important cause of differences in employment growth rates among industries. Technological change is another factor affecting industry employment. For example, automated equipment in manufacturing plants enables fewer workers to produce more goods, and its use is a major reason for declining employment in manufacturing. This decline in generally better-paying blue-collar jobs in manufacturing is a major reason that the earnings of the less educated have fallen behind from 1980 to 2000.

Changes in business practices also have an impact on employment. When businesses use contractors or temporary help services, they reduce their total employment. At the same time, employment rises for contractors and the temporary help supply services industry. This often means a loss of better-paying jobs and a gain in lower-paying jobs.

For analytical purposes, industries fall into the goods-producing sector and the services-producing sector. The divisions within the goods-producing sector are agriculture production, forestry, and fishing; mining; construction; and manufacturing. In the services-producing sector, the divisions are transportation, communications, and utilities; wholesale trade; retail trade; finance, insurance, and real estate; services; and government. Within each division, industries are combined into groups. For example, within the retail trade division, food stores is an industry group that comprises the industry's grocery stores, meat and fish markets, and retail bakeries.

FIGURE 5.7

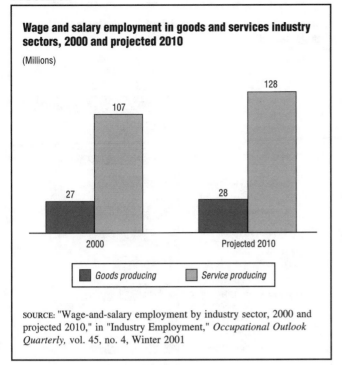

Wage and salary employment in goods and services industry sectors, 2000 and projected 2010

(Millions)

SOURCE: "Wage-and-salary employment by industry sector, 2000 and projected 2010," in "Industry Employment," *Occupational Outlook Quarterly*, vol. 45, no. 4, Winter 2001

Growth

Job growth can be measured both by percentage and numerical change. The fastest-growing occupations do not necessarily provide the largest number of jobs. A larger occupation with slower growth may produce more openings than a smaller occupation with faster growth.

Services-producing industries are projected to account for most of the growth of wage and salary employment over the 2000 to 2010 period, just as they did between 1988 and 1998. Almost all wage and salary employment growth will be in the service-producing sector, which is projected to increase nearly 20 percent by 2010. Wage and salary employment in the services-producing sector rose 3.9 million, from 96.6 million to 100.5 million between 1996 and 1998. Over the 2000 to 2010 period, it is projected to increase another 21 million. (See Figure 5.7.) Goods-producing employment is forecasted to grow slightly over the same period.

Figure 5.8 and Figure 5.9 show industries with the largest projected wage and salary employment growth and decline in the number of workers. Personnel supply services and computer and data processing services are expected to have the largest wage and salary employment growth by 2010. Private household work, federal government jobs, and apparel manufacturing will have the greatest decline in wage and salary employment by 2010, followed by the railroad transportation industry. Figure 5.10 shows the industries with the fastest-growing wage and salary employment by percent of change. Again, the computer and data processing service industry is project-

FIGURE 5.8

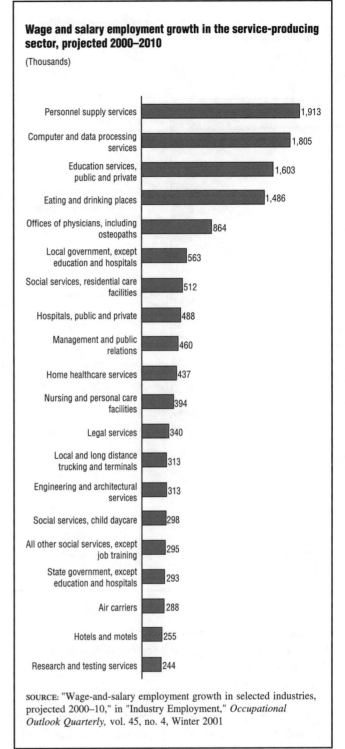

Wage and salary employment growth in the service-producing sector, projected 2000–2010

(Thousands)

SOURCE: "Wage-and-salary employment growth in selected industries, projected 2000–10," in "Industry Employment," *Occupational Outlook Quarterly*, vol. 45, no. 4, Winter 2001

ed to have an 86 percent increase in wage and salary employment growth by 2010.

Services-Producing Industries

Job growth in the services division is projected to be greater than all the other divisions within the services-producing sector combined. (The services division includes business services, health services, social services,

FIGURE 5.9

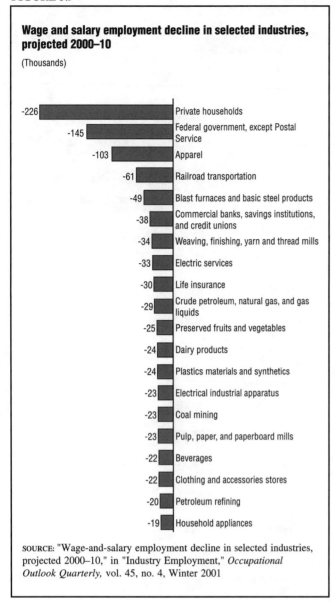

Wage and salary employment decline in selected industries, projected 2000–10

(Thousands)

Value	Industry
-226	Private households
-145	Federal government, except Postal Service
-103	Apparel
-61	Railroad transportation
-49	Blast furnaces and basic steel products
-38	Commercial banks, savings institutions, and credit unions
-34	Weaving, finishing, yarn and thread mills
-33	Electric services
-30	Life insurance
-29	Crude petroleum, natural gas, and gas liquids
-25	Preserved fruits and vegetables
-24	Dairy products
-24	Plastics materials and synthetics
-23	Electrical industrial apparatus
-23	Coal mining
-23	Pulp, paper, and paperboard mills
-22	Beverages
-22	Clothing and accessories stores
-20	Petroleum refining
-19	Household appliances

SOURCE: "Wage-and-salary employment decline in selected industries, projected 2000–10," in "Industry Employment," *Occupational Outlook Quarterly*, vol. 45, no. 4, Winter 2001

FIGURE 5.10

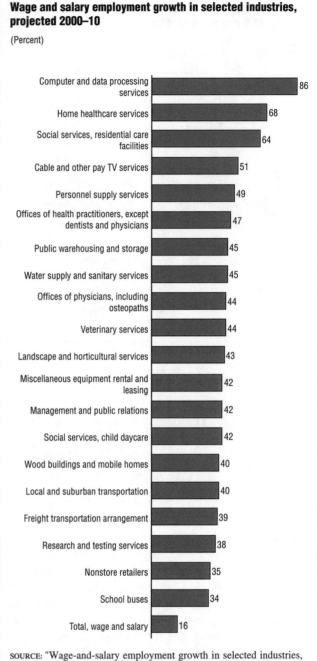

Wage and salary employment growth in selected industries, projected 2000–10

(Percent)

Industry	Value
Computer and data processing services	86
Home healthcare services	68
Social services, residential care facilities	64
Cable and other pay TV services	51
Personnel supply services	49
Offices of health practitioners, except dentists and physicians	47
Public warehousing and storage	45
Water supply and sanitary services	45
Offices of physicians, including osteopaths	44
Veterinary services	44
Landscape and horticultural services	43
Miscellaneous equipment rental and leasing	42
Management and public relations	42
Social services, child daycare	42
Wood buildings and mobile homes	40
Local and suburban transportation	40
Freight transportation arrangement	39
Research and testing services	38
Nonstore retailers	35
School buses	34
Total, wage and salary	16

SOURCE: "Wage-and-salary employment growth in selected industries, projected 2000–10," in "Industry Employment," *Occupational Outlook Quarterly*, vol. 45, no. 4, Winter 2001

engineering, management, and educational services.) Wage and salary jobs in the services division over the 2000 to 2010 period are forecasted to grow by 13.7 million. (See Figure 5.11.)

By 2010 more than 75 percent of employment gains are expected to take place in the services and retail trade divisions. Figure 5.12 shows the projected change in wage and salary employment within the services division for 2000 to 2010. Business services, the fastest-growing industry group, led by computer and data processing services and personnel supply services, is the fastest-growing industry in the economy. Business services is expected to gain 5 million in employment through 2010.

The health services industry follows business services in growth. Health services are projected to grow by 2.8 million jobs by 2010. Factors contributing to growth in the health services industry include the aging population, which will require more services, and the greater use of innovative medical technology. Patients will increasingly be shifted out of hospitals and into outpatient facilities, nursing homes, and home health care in an attempt to contain costs. This will likely lead to a declining hospital service staff, such as licensed practical nurses, since patients will be expected to take care of themselves or hire their own attendants.

Within the services division, engineering, management, and other services as well as social services are

FIGURE 5.11

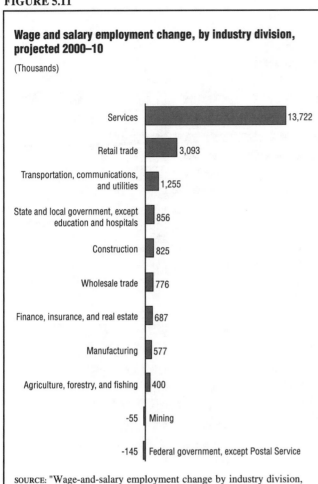

Wage and salary employment change, by industry division, projected 2000–10

(Thousands)

Industry	Value
Services	13,722
Retail trade	3,093
Transportation, communications, and utilities	1,255
State and local government, except education and hospitals	856
Construction	825
Wholesale trade	776
Finance, insurance, and real estate	687
Manufacturing	577
Agriculture, forestry, and fishing	400
Mining	-55
Federal government, except Postal Service	-145

SOURCE: "Wage-and-salary employment change by industry division, projected 2000–10," in "Industry Employment," *Occupational Outlook Quarterly,* vol. 45, no. 4, Winter 2001

FIGURE 5.12

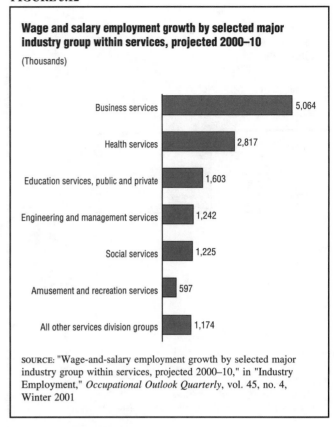

Wage and salary employment growth by selected major industry group within services, projected 2000–10

(Thousands)

Industry	Value
Business services	5,064
Health services	2,817
Education services, public and private	1,603
Engineering and management services	1,242
Social services	1,225
Amusement and recreation services	597
All other services division groups	1,174

SOURCE: "Wage-and-salary employment growth by selected major industry group within services, projected 2000–10," in "Industry Employment," *Occupational Outlook Quarterly*, vol. 45, no. 4, Winter 2001

projected to add jobs by 2010, though not at the rates of computer and data processing and business services. (See Figure 5.12.) Education is projected to grow by 1.6 million jobs by 2010. Engineering, management, and other services are expected to increase by 1.2 million jobs. Social services is due to increase by 1.2 million jobs as well. The projected increase in the older population is also a driving force in the growth of employment in this industry.

Jobs in the retail trade are forecasted to increase by 3.1 million. (See Figure 5.11.) The transportation group is due to have 1.3 million jobs in 2010, a decrease in growth rate over previous years. Employment in finance, insurance, and real estate should add 687,000 jobs between 2000 and 2010, also reflecting slower growth. Rising productivity, stemming from expanded use of automated and computerized services that replaced tellers and other bank workers, and continuing mergers and acquisitions will also contribute to the projected decline in employment.

Government employment is expected to increase by only 856,000 jobs, a slower rate of growth than previously experienced. (See Figure 5.11.) All of this employment growth will take place in state and local government, as the growth in school-age population will cause an increase in teachers. Federal government employment between 2000 and 2010 is due to decline by 145,000, as downsizing continues.

Goods-Producing Industries

Employment in the goods-producing sector is projected to vary over the 1998 to 2008 period. Construction is expected to grow in employment opportunities by 9 percent between 1998 and 2008. (See Figure 5.13.) Agriculture, forestry, and fishing are due to grow by 4 percent, and manufacturing and mining are due to decrease by 1 percent and 19 percent, respectively.

EMPLOYMENT BY OCCUPATION

The economy's occupational and industrial structures form a close relationship. Workers in various occupations provide the skills needed in different industries. Nurses, physicians, orderlies, and medical record technicians are needed in hospitals; cooks, waiters and waitresses, and food preparation workers are needed in restaurants. Consequently, the demand for the occupations concentrated in an industry often rises or falls with the fortunes of that industry. At the same time, it is important to remember that members of the same industry may not share the

FIGURE 5.13

Percentage change in wage and salary employment in goods-producing industries, 1988–98 and projected 1998–2008

SOURCE: "Chart 6. Percent change in wage and salary employment, goods-producing industry divisions, 1990–2000 and projected 2000–10," in *Occupational Outlook Handbook, 2000-01 Edition,* U.S. Department of Labor, Bureau of Labor Statistics, Washington, DC, 2000

FIGURE 5.14

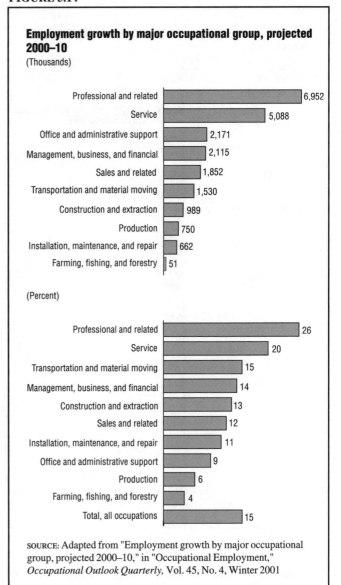

Employment growth by major occupational group, projected 2000–10
(Thousands)

SOURCE: Adapted from "Employment growth by major occupational group, projected 2000–10," in "Occupational Employment," *Occupational Outlook Quarterly,* Vol. 45, No. 4, Winter 2001

same concerns. For example, in the health industry, the goals of the hospital administrator, the doctor, and the licensed practical nurse may differ dramatically.

Changes in technology usually affect how industries use workers. For example, technological advances will continue to reduce the need for typists, directory assistance telephone operators, and bookkeeping, accounting, and auditing clerks. Changes in business practices and operations also can affect occupational staffing. For example, many companies are eliminating middle managers, thereby intending to put more authority in the hands of nonmanagerial frontline workers.

The U.S. Bureau of Labor analyzes these factors to project employment for more than 500 detailed occupations. These occupations can be grouped in different ways to provide a better understanding of broad occupational employment trends. Two of the grouping methods used are by type of work performed and by education and training usually required.

Types

Employment in professional and related occupations is projected to grow the fastest of the major occupational groups and to add the most jobs between 2000 and 2010. This occupational group is expected to add 6,952,000 jobs, representing a rate increase of 26 percent. (See Fig-

ure 5.14.) Professional and related occupations (actuaries, radiological technologists, teachers, lawyers, photographers, drafters, computer software engineers, and others) will account for almost one-third (31 percent) of all new jobs over the 2000 to 2010 period. This proportion reflects both the group's size and its projected growth among the major occupational groups.

The group with the second fastest projected growth rate (20 percent) is service occupations (police, firefighters, cooks, nursing aides, flight attendants, child-care workers, barbers, embalmers, and others). This group is expected to account for the second largest numerical increase in jobs (5,088,000). The next fastest-growing group (with a 15 percent rate of increase) is transportation and material-moving occupations (airline pilots, truck drivers, bus drivers, sailors, hand packers and packagers, pumping station operators, parking lot attendants, and others). (See Figure 5.14.)

Professional and related occupations and service occupations, which are on opposite ends of the educational attainment and earnings spectrum, are expected to provide more than one-half (54 percent) of the 2000 to 2010 projected total job growth. (See Figure 5.14.)

Employment in all other areas is expected to increase, but at a slower rate than total employment (the total average rate of growth is 15 percent). Employment in farming, fishing, and forestry occupations will show very little increase (4 percent) over the 2000 to 2010 period. (See Figure 5.14.)

These different projected growth rates among the major occupational groups will result in changes to the structure of total employment between 2000 and 2010. Service occupations and professional and related occupations are projected to increase their shares of total employment over the 2000 to 2010 period.

Demand for Information Technology Workers

Industry reports and numerous newspaper and magazine articles claimed that severe shortages of information technology (IT) workers could cripple the growth of the economy. In response, the U.S. Department of Commerce studied the alleged problem and issued its conclusions in *America's New Deficit: The Shortage of Information Technology Workers* (Washington, DC, 1997).

In its report, the Department of Commerce presented BLS projections that between 1994 and 2005 the United States would require slightly more than 1 million additional IT workers, such as computer programmers, systems analysts, and computer scientists and engineers. These workers would fill 820,000 newly created jobs and replace another 227,000 workers who are leaving these fields as a result of retirement, change of profession, or other reasons. The report noted that the number of systems analysts would grow 92 percent. (See Table 5.2.) The number of computer engineers and scientists would increase by 90 percent, while the number of computer programmer positions would rise by only 12 percent.

Since the report was released, the Department of Commerce has issued an update with revised BLS projections showing even stronger growth. The number of IT workers will grow from 1.5 million in 1996 to 2.6 million in 2006, a 42 percent increase. Another 244,000 workers will be needed to replace existing IT professionals.

The Department of Commerce found that 24,553 students earned bachelor's degrees in computer and information sciences in 1994, a decline of more than 40 percent from 1986. As of 1999, data indicated that the decline had come to a halt. There was modest but steady growth in the number of computer and information science bachelor's degrees awarded between 1993 and 1996, rising to 26,837

TABLE 5.2

Number of workers in computer related fields, 1994 and projected 2005

Occupation	Numbers of workers in thousands		Percentage change
	1994	2005 (projected)	
IT occupations	1,365	2,184	60
Systems analysts	483	928	92
Computer scientists and engineers	345	655	90
Computer programmers	537	601	12
All other occupations	125,649	142,524	13
Total, all occupations	127,014	144,708	14

SOURCE: "Table 1: BLS Projected Job Growth for Systems Analysts, Computer Engineers and Scientists, and Computer Programmers," in *Information Technology: Assessment of the Department of Commerce's Report on Workforce Demand and Supply*, GAO/HEHS-98-106, U.S. General Accounting Office, Washington, DC, 1998

in 1996. Despite this, the department concluded that there would be an inadequate supply of IT workers.

The report cites four observations upon which their conclusions were based: rising salaries for IT workers, reports of unfilled vacancies for IT workers, the recruiting of foreign workers, and the outsourcing of work to foreign companies. The estimated supply of IT workers (based on students graduating with bachelor's degrees in computer and information sciences) is less than its estimated demand.

For example, the Department of Commerce cited a 1997 *Business Week* article, "Forget the Huddled Masses: Send Nerds," to illustrate that companies are searching for IT workers in foreign labor markets. It also reported that India had more than 200,000 programmers and, in conjunction with predominantly U.S. partners, has developed into one of the world's largest exporters of software. In 1996 and 1997 outsourced software development accounted for 41 percent of India's software exports.

The House Committee on Commerce asked the General Accounting Office (GAO) to assess the Department of Commerce's analysis. The GAO study (*Information Technology Workers,* Washington, DC, 1998) concluded that the Department of Commerce failed to provide clear, complete, and compelling evidence for a shortage or a potential shortage of IT workers. First, although some data show rising salaries for IT workers, other data indicate that those increases in earnings have been commensurate with the rising earnings of all professional specialty occupations.

Second, the survey by the Information Technology Association of America (ITAA), a trade association that the Department of Commerce used to estimate unfilled IT jobs, had an inadequate response rate to form a basis for a nationwide estimate of unfilled jobs. Third, although the report cited instances of companies drawing upon talent pools outside the United States to meet their demands for

TABLE 5.3

Fastest growing occupations, projected 2000–10

[Numbers in thousands of jobs]

	Employment		Change	
Occupation	2000	2010	Number	Percent
Computer software engineers, applications	380	760	380	100
Computer support specialists	506	996	490	97
Computer software engineers, systems software	317	601	284	90
Network and computer systems administrators	229	416	187	82
Network systems and data communications analysts	119	211	92	77
Desktop publishers	38	63	25	67
Database administrators	106	176	70	66
Personal and home care aides	414	672	258	62
Computer systems analysts	431	689	258	60
Medical assistants	329	516	187	57
Social and human service assistants	271	418	147	54
Physician assistants	58	89	31	53
Medical records and health information technicians	136	202	66	49
Computer and information systems managers	313	463	150	48
Home health aides	615	907	291	47
Physical therapist aides	36	53	17	46
Occupational therapist aides	9	12	4	45
Physical therapist assistants	44	64	20	45
Audiologists	13	19	6	45
Fitness trainers and aerobics instructors	158	222	64	40
Computer and information scientists, research	28	39	11	40
Veterinary assistants and laboratory animal caretakers	55	77	22	40
Occupational therapist assistants	17	23	7	40
Veterinary technologists and technicians	49	69	19	39
Speech-language pathologists	88	122	34	39
Mental health and substance abuse social workers	83	116	33	39
Dental assistants	247	339	92	37
Dental hygienists	147	201	54	37
Special education teachers, preschool, kindergarten, and elementary school	234	320	86	37
Pharmacy technicians	190	259	69	36

SOURCE: Adapted from Daniel E. Hecker, "Table 3. Fastest growing occupations 2000–2010," in "Occupational employment projections to 2010," *Monthly Labor Review,* vol. 124, no. 11, November 2001

workers, not enough information was provided to determine the magnitude of this phenomenon. Finally, while the report discussed various sources of potential supplies of IT workers, it used only the number of students earning bachelor's degrees in computer and information sciences. Workers who receive certifications and degrees in other fields could be qualified, as could large numbers of workers who have been or will be retrained for these occupations.

The Department of Commerce responded that its report was not a definitive analysis of the labor market for IT workers and that the GAO analysis contained several inaccuracies. The Department of Commerce wrote that its report did not conclude that there would definitely be a shortage of workers, but that the demand for them was increasing, and industry practices showed clear indications of a tight labor market for IT workers. The GAO stood by its conclusions. The debate is important since many information technology industries have been lobbying Congress to let in a greater number of high-skilled foreign workers. Critics say that American workers can be trained to take these jobs.

The debate continues. In a projection of the fastest-growing occupations, put together by the BLS in its *Monthly Labor Review,* November 2001, eight of the top ten occupations were computer-related jobs. (See Table 5.3.)

EDUCATION

Although jobs are available at all levels of education and training, most jobs do not require postsecondary education or training. The economy will produce 22 million new jobs between 2000 and 2010, a 15.2 percent increase in employment. Over three-quarters (80 percent) of the growth will be in occupations requiring less education than a bachelor's degree. However, these positions generally offer the lowest pay and benefits. (See Table 5.4 and Figure 5.15.)

The education category with the highest-expected growth (32 percent) consists of jobs that require at least an associate degree. (See Figure 5.16.) Occupations requiring a bachelor's degree or higher are expected to increase faster than average. All categories that do not require some college are projected to grow equally or more slowly than average.

The largest education and training category is short-term on-the-job training in which workers can learn job skills in a few weeks or less. By 2010, 60.9 million workers will be in occupations that usually require short-term on-the-job training. (See Table 5.4.) Moderate-term on-the-job training in which workers can generally learn their skills after 1 to 12 months on the job will account for 30.8 million workers.

Occupations in which workers require more than a year of on-the-job experience and formal training will employ 13.4 million workers. (See Table 5.4.) An additional 11.6 million workers will be employed in occupations that require experience in another occupation. Almost 117 million workers, representing 69.5 percent of total employment, will be in jobs that generally require on-the-job training or experience.

Bachelor's Degree or Higher

Occupations requiring a bachelor's degree or more accounted for 30 million jobs in 2000. (See Table 5.4.) More than 17 million workers were in jobs that routinely require bachelor's degrees. By 2010 more than one-fifth (22.5 percent) of those employed will be in occupations requiring a bachelor's degree or higher.

A large amount of employment growth is expected in occupations usually requiring a bachelor's degree or work experience plus a bachelor's degree or higher from 2000 to 2010. General and operations managers and computer software engineers, applications are projected to grow by 363,000 and 380,000 employees, respectively. (See Figure 5.17.)

TABLE 5.4

Employment and total job openings by education or training category, projected 2000–10

[Numbers in thousands of jobs]

Most significant source of education or training	Employment				Change, 2000-2010			Total job openings due to growth and net replacements, 2000–2010*	
	Number		Percent distribution		Number	Percent distribution	Percent	Number	Percent distribution
	2000	2010	2000	2010					
Total, all occupations	145,594	167,754	100.0	100.0	22,160	100.0	15.2	57,932	100.0
Bachelor's or higher degree	30,072	36,556	20.7	21.8	6,484	29.3	21.6	12,130	20.9
First professional degree	2,034	2,404	1.4	1.4	370	1.7	18.2	691	1.2
Doctoral degree	1,492	1,845	1.0	1.1	353	1.6	23.7	760	1.3
Master's degree	1,426	1,759	1.0	1.0	333	1.5	23.4	634	1.1
Bachelor's or higher degree, plus work experience	7,319	8,741	5.0	5.2	1,422	6.4	19.4	2,741	4.7
Bachelor's degree	17,801	21,807	12.2	13.0	4,006	18.1	22.5	7,304	12.6
Associate degree or postsecondary vocational award	11,761	14,600	8.1	8.7	2,839	12.8	24.1	5,383	9.3
Associate degree	5,083	6,710	3.5	4.0	1,626	7.3	32.0	2,608	4.5
Postsecondary vocational award	6,678	7,891	4.6	4.7	1,213	5.5	18.2	2,775	4.8
Work-related training	103,760	116,597	71.3	69.5	12,837	57.9	12.4	40,419	69.8
Work experience in a related occupation	10,456	11,559	7.2	6.9	1,102	5.0	10.5	3,180	5.5
Long-term on-the-job training	12,435	13,373	8.5	8.0	938	4.2	7.5	3,737	6.5
Moderate-term on-the-job training	27,671	30,794	19.0	18.4	3,123	14.1	11.3	8,767	15.1
Short-term on-the-job training	53,198	60,871	36.5	36.3	7,673	34.6	14.4	24,735	42.7

* Total job openings represent the sum of employment increases and net replacements. If employment change is negative, job openings due to growth are zero and total job openings equal net replacements.
Note: Detail may not equal total or 100 percent due to rounding.

SOURCE: "Table 4. Employment and total job openings by education or training category, 2000–10," in *Economic and Employment Projections*, U.S. Department of Labor, Bureau of Labor Statistics, Washington, DC, 2002 [Online] http://www.bls.gov/news.release/ecopro.t04.htm [accessed June 20, 2002]

FIGURE 5.15

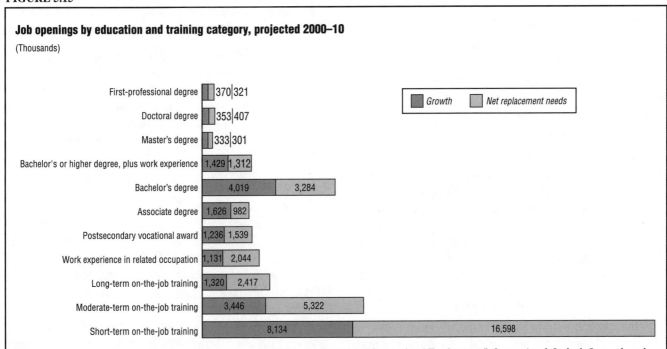

Job openings by education and training category, projected 2000–10

(Thousands)

- First-professional degree 370 | 321
- Doctoral degree 353 | 407
- Master's degree 333 | 301
- Bachelor's or higher degree, plus work experience 1,429 | 1,312
- Bachelor's degree 4,019 | 3,284
- Associate degree 1,626 | 982
- Postsecondary vocational award 1,236 | 1,539
- Work experience in related occupation 1,131 | 2,044
- Long-term on-the-job training 1,320 | 2,417
- Moderate-term on-the-job training 3,446 | 5,322
- Short-term on-the-job training 8,134 | 16,598

Legend: Growth | Net replacement needs

SOURCE: "Job openings by education and training category, projected 2000–10," in "Occupational Employment," *Occupational Outlook Quarterly*, vol. 45, no. 4, Winter 2001

FIGURE 5.16

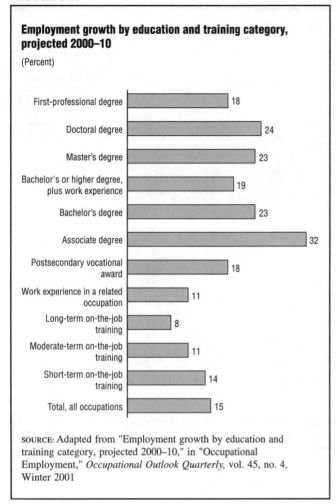

Employment growth by education and training category, projected 2000–10

(Percent)

Category	Percent
First-professional degree	18
Doctoral degree	24
Master's degree	23
Bachelor's or higher degree, plus work experience	19
Bachelor's degree	23
Associate degree	32
Postsecondary vocational award	18
Work experience in a related occupation	11
Long-term on-the-job training	8
Moderate-term on-the-job training	11
Short-term on-the-job training	14
Total, all occupations	15

SOURCE: Adapted from "Employment growth by education and training category, projected 2000–10," in "Occupational Employment," *Occupational Outlook Quarterly*, vol. 45, no. 4, Winter 2001

Postsecondary Vocational Training

Twenty occupations that usually require postsecondary vocational training will have employment growth between 2000 and 2010. The fastest-growing occupations in this group include registered nurses and computer support specialists. (See Figure 5.18.)

Twenty selected occupations that usually require short- or moderate-term on-the-job training are projected to increase employment growth between 2000 and 2010. Of the 20 occupations, the fastest-growing ones are expected to be food preparation and service workers (673,000 jobs), customer service representatives (631,000 jobs), and retail sales workers (510,000 jobs). (See Figure 5.19.)

WHICH WILL BE THE BEST JOBS?

Many criteria are used for determining job quality. Occupational characteristics generally accepted as a measure of future job quality include whether the number of jobs in that field will increase, how much the position pays, and whether a high percentage of those in that field are unemployed. In addition, individuals have personal desires and values that bring other factors into play in determining job quality, such as opportunities for self-employment for those who want to be their own boss or the opportunity to travel.

Remember, job growth can be measured both by percentage and numerical change. The fastest-growing occupations do not necessarily provide the greatest number of jobs. A larger occupation with slower growth may produce more openings than a smaller occupation with faster growth. See Table 5.5 for both the fastest-growing occupations and occupations having the largest numerical increase in employment from 2000 to 2010, by level of education and training.

Fastest Projected Growth

Figure 5.20 shows the 20 occupations with the fastest projected employment growth over the 2000 to 2010 period. (See also Table 5.3 for 2000 to 2010 information on fastest-growing occupations.) Most of the high-growth occupations have high earnings and low unemployment rates. Ten of these occupations have a large proportion of employment in the health services sector and seven are in computer-related services.

The health services sector will add more than 3 million jobs by 2010. Personal and home care aides and home health aides will be in great demand to provide care for an increasing number of elderly people and for persons who are recovering from surgery and other serious health conditions. This category is increasing, as hospitals and insurance companies require shorter stays for recovery in order to reduce costs.

Computer engineers and systems analysts jobs are expected to grow rapidly in order to satisfy expanding needs of scientific research and applications of computer technology. The three fastest-growing occupations are in computer-related fields. This industry will more than double its employment over the 2000 to 2010 period.

Largest Job Growth

According to the BLS, the 20 occupations with the largest projected employment growth rate account for more than one-third (39 percent) of the projected change in total employment over the 2000 to 2010 period. Three of these occupations have growth rates that are below average. The fastest-growing occupations in this list include computer engineers, computer support specialists, and computer systems analysts. Twelve of the 20 occupations require short-term training on the job; four occupations require a bachelor's degree or higher education. Figure 5.21 shows the occupations projected to gain the largest number of jobs between 2000 and 2010. (See also Table 5.6 for 2000 to 2010 information on fastest-growing occupations.)

FIGURE 5.17

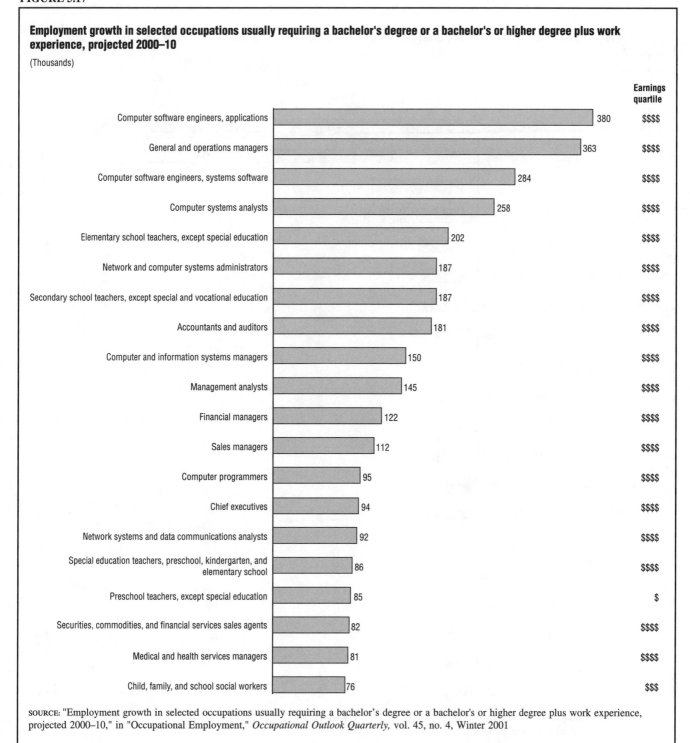

Employment growth in selected occupations usually requiring a bachelor's degree or a bachelor's or higher degree plus work experience, projected 2000–10

(Thousands)

Occupation		Earnings quartile
Computer software engineers, applications	380	$$$$
General and operations managers	363	$$$$
Computer software engineers, systems software	284	$$$$
Computer systems analysts	258	$$$$
Elementary school teachers, except special education	202	$$$$
Network and computer systems administrators	187	$$$$
Secondary school teachers, except special and vocational education	187	$$$$
Accountants and auditors	181	$$$$
Computer and information systems managers	150	$$$$
Management analysts	145	$$$$
Financial managers	122	$$$$
Sales managers	112	$$$$
Computer programmers	95	$$$$
Chief executives	94	$$$$
Network systems and data communications analysts	92	$$$$
Special education teachers, preschool, kindergarten, and elementary school	86	$$$$
Preschool teachers, except special education	85	$
Securities, commodities, and financial services sales agents	82	$$$$
Medical and health services managers	81	$$$$
Child, family, and school social workers	76	$$$

SOURCE: "Employment growth in selected occupations usually requiring a bachelor's degree or a bachelor's or higher degree plus work experience, projected 2000–10," in "Occupational Employment," *Occupational Outlook Quarterly,* vol. 45, no. 4, Winter 2001

Highest Earnings

Projections for 1996 to 2006 show the 20 occupations with the highest earnings all requiring at least a bachelor's degree. (See Figure 5.22.) Engineering and health occupations dominated the list. Some of these occupations were very small and slow growing and will provide few opportunities for workers in the future. A few are projected to decline, generating openings only from replacement needs. All have low (L) to very low (VL) unemployment rates.

LARGEST DECLINE IN EMPLOYMENT

An occupation's employment can decline because it is concentrated in a declining industry or because of changes to occupational staffing patterns. Office automation and other technological advances, declining industry employment, and changing legislation have adversely affected the occupations with the largest projected employment declines. Manufacturing and agriculture-related jobs, such as sewing machine operators and

FIGURE 5.18

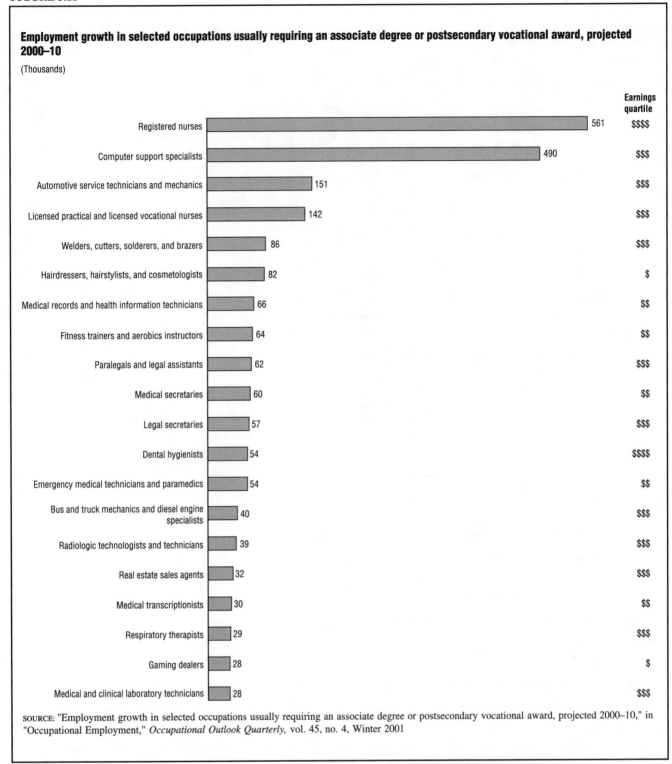

Employment growth in selected occupations usually requiring an associate degree or postsecondary vocational award, projected 2000–10

(Thousands)

Occupation	Growth	Earnings quartile
Registered nurses	561	$$$$
Computer support specialists	490	$$$
Automotive service technicians and mechanics	151	$$$
Licensed practical and licensed vocational nurses	142	$$$
Welders, cutters, solderers, and brazers	86	$$$
Hairdressers, hairstylists, and cosmetologists	82	$
Medical records and health information technicians	66	$$
Fitness trainers and aerobics instructors	64	$$
Paralegals and legal assistants	62	$$$
Medical secretaries	60	$$
Legal secretaries	57	$$$
Dental hygienists	54	$$$$
Emergency medical technicians and paramedics	54	$$
Bus and truck mechanics and diesel engine specialists	40	$$$
Radiologic technologists and technicians	39	$$$
Real estate sales agents	32	$$$
Medical transcriptionists	30	$$
Respiratory therapists	29	$$$
Gaming dealers	28	$
Medical and clinical laboratory technicians	28	$$$

SOURCE: "Employment growth in selected occupations usually requiring an associate degree or postsecondary vocational award, projected 2000–10," in "Occupational Employment," *Occupational Outlook Quarterly,* vol. 45, no. 4, Winter 2001

farmers, are examples of occupations that will lose employment due to declining employment in some goods-producing industries. The use of typists will decline dramatically because of productivity improvements in office automation and the increased use of word processing equipment by professional and managerial employees. (See Figure 5.23 and Table 5.7 for 2000 to 2010 data.)

Between 2000 and 2010 some occupations are projected to decline by 50 percent or more—the numbers of railroad brake, signal, and switch operators will decline by 61 percent. (See Table 5.7.) The number of telephone operators is expected to decline by 35 percent. The conversion to desktop publishing technology in the printing and publishing industry will affect several other occupations.

FIGURE 5.19

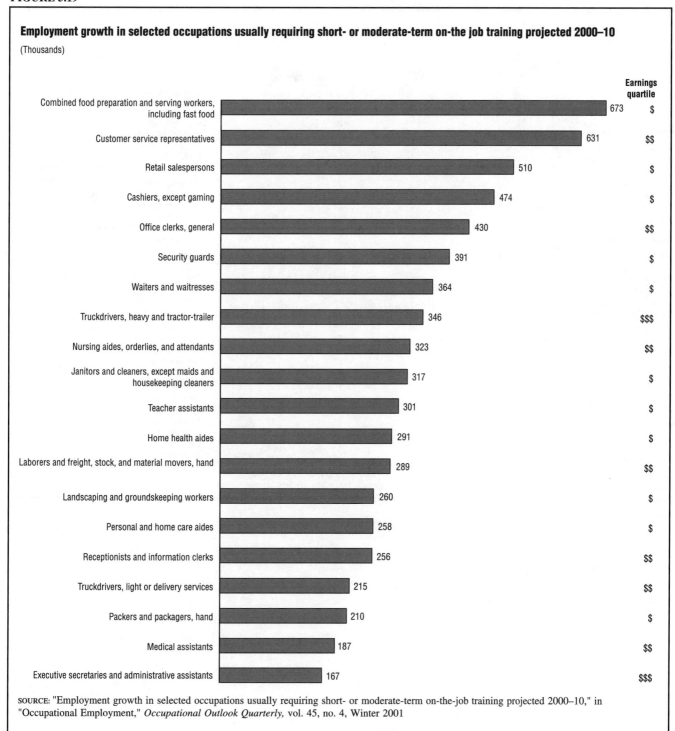

Employment growth in selected occupations usually requiring short- or moderate-term on-the-job training projected 2000–10

(Thousands)

Occupation	Value	Earnings quartile
Combined food preparation and serving workers, including fast food	673	$
Customer service representatives	631	$$
Retail salespersons	510	$
Cashiers, except gaming	474	$
Office clerks, general	430	$$
Security guards	391	$
Waiters and waitresses	364	$
Truckdrivers, heavy and tractor-trailer	346	$$$
Nursing aides, orderlies, and attendants	323	$$
Janitors and cleaners, except maids and housekeeping cleaners	317	$
Teacher assistants	301	$
Home health aides	291	$
Laborers and freight, stock, and material movers, hand	289	$$
Landscaping and groundskeeping workers	260	$
Personal and home care aides	258	$
Receptionists and information clerks	256	$$
Truckdrivers, light or delivery services	215	$$
Packers and packagers, hand	210	$
Medical assistants	187	$$
Executive secretaries and administrative assistants	167	$$$

SOURCE: "Employment growth in selected occupations usually requiring short- or moderate-term on-the-job training projected 2000–10," in "Occupational Employment," *Occupational Outlook Quarterly,* vol. 45, no. 4, Winter 2001

BEST OPPORTUNITIES FOR SELF-EMPLOYMENT

Many types of jobs provide opportunities for self-employment. Between 1996 and 2006, the largest concentration was projected to be made up of occupations requiring creativity, artistic ability, or design skills. It is expected that artists, designers, writers, photographers, and architects will account for one-fourth of the projected new jobs for self-employed or unpaid family workers. In 2000 farmers accounted for large numbers of self-employed, although those numbers are projected to decline. (See Figure 5.23, Table 5.7, and Figure 5.24.)

TABLE 5.5

Percent change in employment in fastest growing occupations, projected 2000–10

Occupation	Employment change, 2000-2010		Most significant source of education or training
	Number	Percent	
Computer software engineers, applications	380	100	Bachelor's degree
Computer support specialists	490	97	Associate degree
Computer software engineers, systems software	284	90	Bachelor's degree
Network and computer systems administrators	187	82	Bachelor's degree
Network systems and data communications analysts	92	77	Bachelor's degree
Desktop publishers	25	67	Postsecondary vocational award
Database administrators	70	66	Bachelor's degree
Personal and home care aides	258	62	Short-term on-the-job training
Computer systems analysts	258	60	Bachelor's degree
Medical assistants	187	57	Moderate-term on-the-job training
Social and human service assistants	147	54	Moderate-term on-the-job training
Physician assistants	31	53	Bachelor's degree
Medical records and health information technicians	66	49	Associate degree
Computer and information systems managers	150	48	Bachelor's or higher degree, plus work experience
Home health aides	291	47	Short-term on-the-job training
Physical therapist aides	17	46	Short-term on-the-job training
Occupational therapist aides	4	45	Short-term on-the-job training
Physical therapist assistants	20	45	Associate degree
Audiologists	6	45	Master's degree
Fitness trainers and aerobics instructors	64	40	Postsecondary vocational award
Computer and information scientists, research	11	40	Doctoral degree
Veterinary assistants and laboratory animal caretakers	22	40	Short-term on-the-job training
Occupational therapist assistants	7	40	Associate degree
Veterinary technologists and technicians	19	39	Associate degree
Speech-language pathologists	34	39	Master's degree
Mental health and substance abuse social workers	33	39	Master's degree
Dental assistants	92	37	Moderate-term on-the-job training
Dental hygienists	54	37	Associate degree
Special education teachers, preschool, kindergarten, and elementary school	86	37	Bachelor's degree
Pharmacy technicians	69	36	Moderate-term on-the-job training

SOURCE: "Table 1. Fastest growing occupations covered in the 2002–03 occupational outlook handbook, 2000–2010," U.S. Department of Labor, Bureau of Labor Statistics, Washington, DC, 2002 [Online] http://www.bls.gov/news.release/ooh.t01.htm [accessed June 20, 2002]

FIGURE 5.20

Percentage employment growth in selected occupations, projected 2000–10

(Percent)

Occupation	Percent	Earnings quartile
Computer software engineers, applications	100	$$$$
Computer support specialists	97	$$$
Computer software engineers, systems software	90	$$$$
Network and computer systems administrators	82	$$$$
Network systems and data communications analysts	77	$$$$
Desktop publishers	67	$$$
Database administrators	66	$$$$
Personal and home care aides	62	$
Computer systems analysts	60	$$$$
Medical assistants	57	$$
Social and human service assistants	54	$$
Physician assistants	53	$$$$
Medical records and health information technicians	49	$$
Computer and information systems managers	48	$$$$
Home health aides	47	$
Physical therapist aides	46	$$
Occupational therapist aides	45	$$
Physical therapist assistants	45	$$$
Audiologists	45	$$$$
Fitness trainers and aerobics instructors	40	$$
Total, all occupations	15	

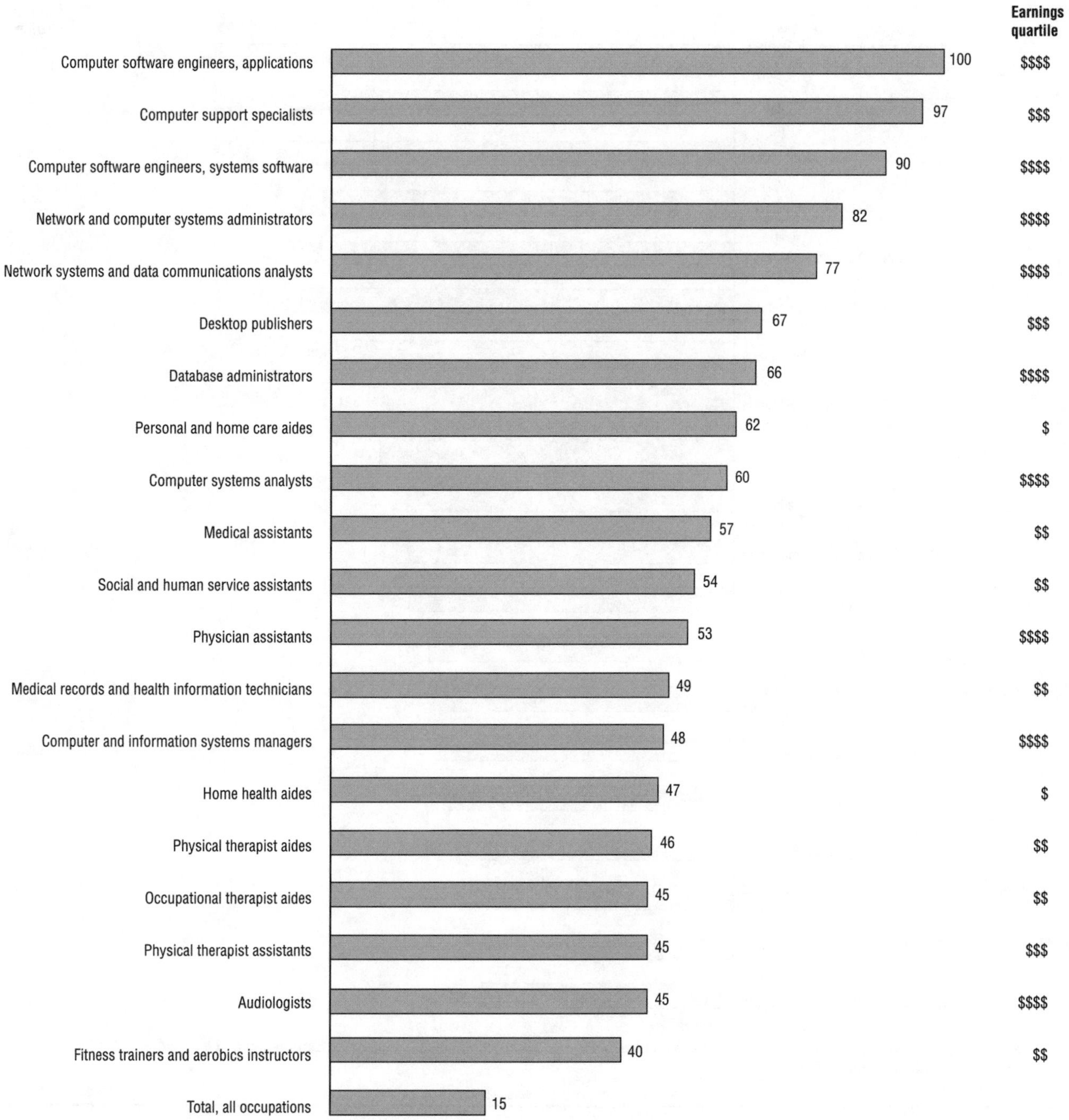

SOURCE: "Employment growth in selected occupations, projected 2000–10 (Percent)," in "Occupational Employment," *Occupational Outlook Quarterly*, vol. 45, no. 4, Winter 2001

FIGURE 5.21

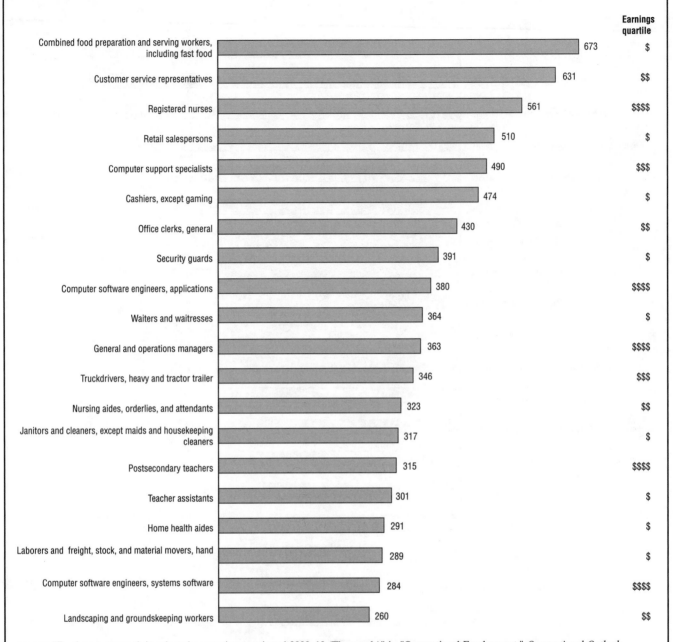

Employment growth in selected occupations, projected 2000–10

(Thousands)

Occupation	Growth	Earnings quartile
Combined food preparation and serving workers, including fast food	673	$
Customer service representatives	631	$$
Registered nurses	561	$$$$
Retail salespersons	510	$
Computer support specialists	490	$$$
Cashiers, except gaming	474	$
Office clerks, general	430	$$
Security guards	391	$
Computer software engineers, applications	380	$$$$
Waiters and waitresses	364	$
General and operations managers	363	$$$$
Truckdrivers, heavy and tractor trailer	346	$$$
Nursing aides, orderlies, and attendants	323	$$
Janitors and cleaners, except maids and housekeeping cleaners	317	$
Postsecondary teachers	315	$$$$
Teacher assistants	301	$
Home health aides	291	$
Laborers and freight, stock, and material movers, hand	289	$
Computer software engineers, systems software	284	$$$$
Landscaping and groundskeeping workers	260	$$

SOURCE: "Employment growth in selected occupations, projected 2000–10 (Thousands)" in "Occupational Employment," *Occupational Outlook Quarterly,* vol. 45, no. 4, Winter 2001

TABLE 5.6

Occupations with the largest job growth, 2000–10

[Numbers in thousands of jobs]

Occupation	Employment		Change	
	2000	2010	Number	Percent
Combined food preparation and serving workers, including fast food	2,206	2,879	673	30
Customer service representatives	1,946	2,577	631	32
Registered nurses	2,194	2,755	561	26
Retail salespersons	4,109	4,619	510	12
Computer support specialists	506	996	490	97
Cashiers, except gaming	3,325	3,799	474	14
Office clerks, general	2,705	3,135	430	16
Security guards	1,106	1,497	391	35
Computer software engineers, applications	380	760	380	100
Waiters and waitresses	1,983	2,347	364	18
General and operations managers	2,398	2,761	363	15
Truck drivers, heavy and tractor-trailer	1,749	2,095	346	20
Nursing aides, orderlies, and attendants	1,373	1,697	323	24
Janitors and cleaners, except maids and housekeeping cleaners	2,348	2,665	317	13
Postsecondary teachers	1,344	1,659	315	23
Teacher assistants	1,262	1,562	301	24
Home health aides	615	907	291	47
Laborers and freight, stock, and material movers, hand	2,084	2,373	289	14
Computer software engineers, systems software	317	601	284	90
Landscaping and groundskeeping workers	894	1,154	260	29
Personal and home care aides	414	672	258	62
Computer systems analysts	431	689	258	60
Receptionists and information clerks	1,078	1,334	256	24
Truck drivers, light or delivery services	1,117	1,331	215	19
Packers and packagers, hand	1,091	1,300	210	19
Elementary school teachers, except special education	1,532	1,734	202	13
Medical assistants	329	516	187	57
Network and computer systems administrators	229	416	187	82
Secondary school teachers, except special and vocational education	1,004	1,190	187	19
Accountants and auditors	976	1,157	181	19

SOURCE: Adapted from Daniel E. Hecker, "Table 4. Occupations with the largest job growth, 2000–2010," in "Occupational employment projections to 2010," *Monthly Labor Review,* vol. 124, no. 11, November 2001

FIGURE 5.22

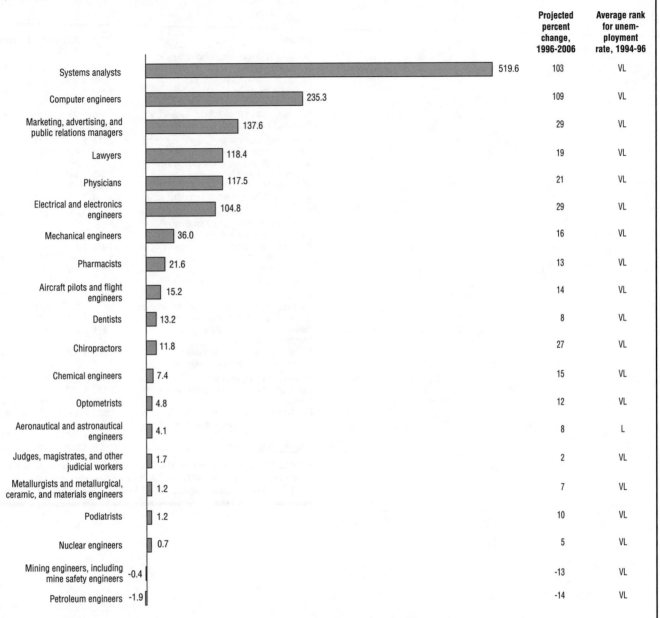

Employment growth of occupations with highest earnings, projected 1996–2006

(Thousands)

Occupation	Growth	Projected percent change, 1996-2006	Average rank for unemployment rate, 1994-96
Systems analysts	519.6	103	VL
Computer engineers	235.3	109	VL
Marketing, advertising, and public relations managers	137.6	29	VL
Lawyers	118.4	19	VL
Physicians	117.5	21	VL
Electrical and electronics engineers	104.8	29	VL
Mechanical engineers	36.0	16	VL
Pharmacists	21.6	13	VL
Aircraft pilots and flight engineers	15.2	14	VL
Dentists	13.2	8	VL
Chiropractors	11.8	27	VL
Chemical engineers	7.4	15	VL
Optometrists	4.8	12	VL
Aeronautical and astronautical engineers	4.1	8	L
Judges, magistrates, and other judicial workers	1.7	2	VL
Metallurgists and metallurgical, ceramic, and materials engineers	1.2	7	VL
Podiatrists	1.2	10	VL
Nuclear engineers	0.7	5	VL
Mining engineers, including mine safety engineers	-0.4	-13	VL
Petroleum engineers	-1.9	-14	VL

VL: Very low; L: Low

SOURCE: "Projected employment growth of occupations with highest earnings, 1996–2006," in *Occupational Outlook Quarterly,* vol. 41, no. 4, Winter 1997

FIGURE 5.23

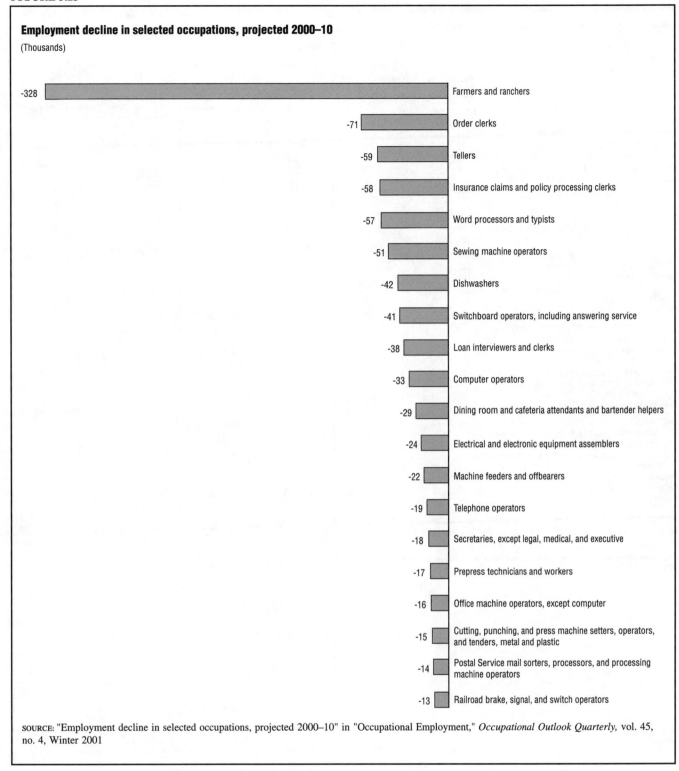

Employment decline in selected occupations, projected 2000–10

(Thousands)

Occupation	Value
Farmers and ranchers	-328
Order clerks	-71
Tellers	-59
Insurance claims and policy processing clerks	-58
Word processors and typists	-57
Sewing machine operators	-51
Dishwashers	-42
Switchboard operators, including answering service	-41
Loan interviewers and clerks	-38
Computer operators	-33
Dining room and cafeteria attendants and bartender helpers	-29
Electrical and electronic equipment assemblers	-24
Machine feeders and offbearers	-22
Telephone operators	-19
Secretaries, except legal, medical, and executive	-18
Prepress technicians and workers	-17
Office machine operators, except computer	-16
Cutting, punching, and press machine setters, operators, and tenders, metal and plastic	-15
Postal Service mail sorters, processors, and processing machine operators	-14
Railroad brake, signal, and switch operators	-13

SOURCE: "Employment decline in selected occupations, projected 2000–10" in "Occupational Employment," *Occupational Outlook Quarterly,* vol. 45, no. 4, Winter 2001

TABLE 5.7

Occupations with the largest job decline, 2000–10

[Numbers in thousands of jobs]

Occupation	Employment		Change	
	2000	2010	Number	Percent
Farmers and ranchers	1,294	965	-328	-25
Order clerks	348	277	-71	-20
Tellers	499	440	-59	-12
Insurance claims and policy processing clerks	289	231	-58	-20
Word processors and typists	297	240	-57	-19
Sewing machine operators	399	348	-51	-13
Dishwashers	525	483	-42	-8
Switchboard operators, including answering service	259	218	-41	-16
Loan interviewers and clerks	139	101	-38	-28
Computer operators	194	161	-33	-17
Dining room and cafeteria attendants and bartender helpers	431	402	-29	-7
Electrical and electronic equipment assemblers	379	355	-24	-6
Machine feeders and offbearers	182	159	-22	-12
Telephone operators	54	35	-19	-35
Secretaries, except legal, medical, and executive	1,864	1,846	-18	-1
Prepress technicians and workers	107	90	-17	-16
Office machine operators, except computer	84	68	-16	-19
Cutting, punching, and press machine setters, operators, and tenders, metal and plastic	372	357	-15	-4
Postal service mail sorters, processors, and processing machine operators	289	275	-14	-5
Railroad brake, signal, and switch operators	22	9	-13	-61
Wholesale and retail buyers, except farm products	148	135	-13	-9
Meter readers, utilities	49	36	-13	-26
Butchers and meat cutters	141	128	-13	-9
Parts salespersons	260	248	-12	-4
Inspectors, testers, sorters, samplers, and weighers	602	591	-11	-2
Eligibility interviewers, government programs	117	106	-11	-9
Door-to-door sales workers, news and street vendors, and related workers	166	156	-10	-6
Procurement clerks	76	67	-9	-12
Railroad conductors and yardmasters	45	36	-8	-19
Barbers	73	64	-8	-12

SOURCE: Adapted from Daniel E. Hecker, "Table 5. Occupations with the largest job decline, 2000–10," in "Occupational employment projections to 2010," *Monthly Labor Review,* vol. 124, no. 11, November 2001

FIGURE 5.24

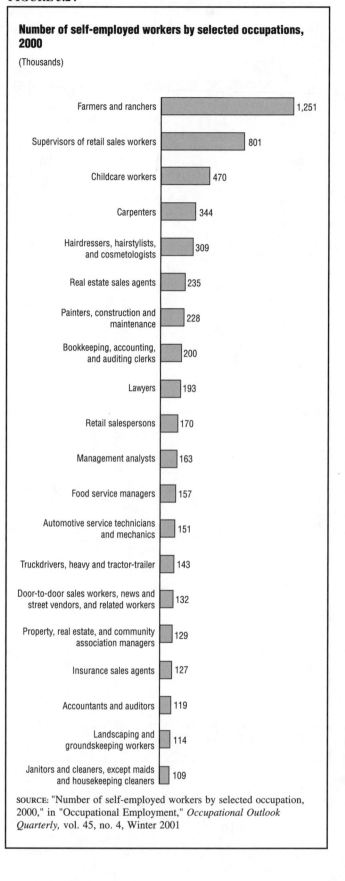

Number of self-employed workers by selected occupations, 2000

(Thousands)

SOURCE: "Number of self-employed workers by selected occupation, 2000," in "Occupational Employment," *Occupational Outlook Quarterly,* vol. 45, no. 4, Winter 2001

CHAPTER 6
EARNINGS AND BENEFITS

EARNINGS

The federal government measures both the mean (average) of the nation's workers and the median earnings (one-half earn more than this figure, and one-half earn less than this figure) of the nation's workers. Income is the total amount brought in by an individual or family, including earnings and money received from interest, pensions, and more.

In 1998 the population aged 15 and older had mean (average) earnings of $33,688. Whites earned slightly more ($34,610) than the mean, while blacks ($26,423) and those of Hispanic origin ($23,118) earned less. (See Table 6.1.) Males earned an average salary of $41,927, compared to $24,472 for females. The median earnings were $31,039 for males and $20,309 for females. (See Table 6.2.)

Full-Time, Year-Round Workers

Of the 79.2 million men 15 years old and over who reported working in 2000 (with or without earnings), 74 percent worked full-time, year-round. Of the 70.8 million

women 15 years old and over who reported working in 2000, 59 percent worked full-time, year-round. (See Table 6.2.)

In 1998 women working full-time, year-round earned a median of $27,355, compared to $37,339 for men. Women's median earnings increased 0.5 percent in 1999 ($27,208), while men's decreased by 1 percent ($37,701), measured in year 2000 dollars. (See Table 6.3.) Figure 6.1 shows that since the mid-1970s through 1996, with the exception of a couple of years, men's median earnings have generally been declining or staying level, while women's earnings have been increasing since the 1960s. These contrasting changes in earnings brought the female earnings closer than ever to male earnings; in 2000 the median earnings for women were about 73 percent of the median for men.

The reduction in the gap between female and male earnings have been due more to declines in the earnings of men than to increases in the earnings of women. (See

TABLE 6.1

Source of income of people 15 years old and over by age, race, and Hispanic origin, 2000

	All races		White		Black		Hispanic origin		White non-Hispanic	
	Number with Income	Mean income (Dollars)	Number with Income	Mean income (Dollars)	Number with Income	Mean income (Dollars)	Number with Income	Mean income (Dollars)	Number with Income	Mean income (Dollars)
Both sexes total – 15 years and over										
Total	196,957	31,169	165,115	32,106	22,648	24,104	19,336	21,552	146,694	33,457
Earnings	149,816	33,688	125,050	34,610	17,467	26,423	16,077	23,118	109,731	36,249
Wages and salary	141,025	33,419	117,215	34,409	16,993	25,960	15,526	22,750	102,423	36,102
Nonfarm self-employment	12,462	24,175	10,990	24,595	798	16,314	784	19,450	10,245	24,978
Farm self-employment	2,619	12,494	2,363	10,325	171	43,182	112	28,789	2,261	10,646

Note: Numbers in thousands.

SOURCE: Adapted from "PINC-09. Source Of Income In 2000-Number With Income And Mean Income Of Specified Type In 2000 Of People 15 Years Old And Over By Age, Race and Hispanic Origin," in *Current Population Survey,* U.S. Department of Labor, Bureau of Labor Statistics, Washington, DC, November 2001

TABLE 6.2

Work experience of people 15 years old and over by total money earnings, age, race, and sex, 2000

	Total	Total worked	Worked at full time jobs			
			Total	50 weeks or more	27 to 49 weeks	26 weeks or less
Male						
15 Years and Over						
All Races						
Total	104,273	79,180	68,985	58,765	6,106	4,114
Without Earnings	25,175	82	49	31	2	15
With Earnings	79,098	79,098	68,937	58,734	6,104	4,099
$1 to $2,499 or Loss	4,403	4,403	1,377	525	97	756
$2,500 to $4,999	2,707	2,707	1,157	190	121	846
$5,000 to $7,499	2,990	2,990	1,494	475	359	660
$7,500 to $9,999	2,085	2,085	1,290	479	403	408
$10,000 to $12,499	3,666	3,666	2,748	1,816	568	364
$12,500 to $14,999	2,320	2,320	2,029	1,436	407	186
$15,000 to $17,499	3,703	3,703	3,301	2,535	564	202
$17,500 to $19,999	2,651	2,651	2,456	2,074	326	56
$20,000 to $22,499	4,473	4,473	4,132	3,591	407	134
$22,500 to $24,999	2,441	2,441	2,360	2,100	211	50
$25,000 to $27,499	4,131	4,131	3,955	3,518	357	80
$27,500 to $29,999	1,926	1,926	1,895	1,629	234	32
$30,000 to $32,499	4,937	4,937	4,812	4,404	356	51
$32,500 to $34,999	1,509	1,509	1,468	1,369	91	9
$35,000 to $37,499	3,825	3,825	3,724	3,449	225	51
$37,500 to $39,999	1,609	1,609	1,562	1,443	114	5
$40,000 to $42,499	3,641	3,641	3,577	3,325	178	73
$42,500 to $44,999	1,066	1,066	1,038	957	67	14
$45,000 to $47,499	2,433	2,433	2,419	2,253	160	6
$47,500 to $49,999	1,190	1,190	1,173	1,108	62	4
$50,000 to $52,499	3,091	3,091	3,032	2,883	123	27
$52,500 to $54,999	662	662	652	617	30	5
$55,000 to $57,499	1,714	1,714	1,703	1,622	78	2
$57,500 to $59,999	606	606	582	563	14	4
$60,000 to $62,499	2,430	2,430	2,394	2,273	106	15
$62,500 to $64,999	451	451	445	425	15	4
$65,000 to $67,499	1,152	1,152	1,138	1,119	16	3
$67,500 to $69,999	397	397	394	386	7	0
$70,000 to $72,499	1,395	1,395	1,365	1,282	75	8
$72,500 to $74,999	224	224	221	212	10	0
$75,000 to $77,499	1,312	1,312	1,289	1,255	31	2
$77,500 to $79,999	286	286	279	266	11	2
$80,000 to $82,499	1,052	1,052	1,030	985	41	4
$82,500 to $84,999	154	154	149	149	0	0
$85,000 to $87,499	568	568	549	524	24	1
$87,500 to $89,999	72	72	72	65	5	2
$90,000 to $92,499	614	614	609	579	30	1
$92,500 to $94,999	91	91	89	87	2	0
$95,000 to $97,499	256	256	254	244	10	0
$97,500 to $99,999	144	144	140	134	5	1
$100,000 and over	4,723	4,723	4,586	4,387	163	35
Median earnings (dollars)	31,039	31,039	34,992	37,339	21,273	6,698
Standard error (dollars)	112	112	247	138	376	190
Mean earnings (dollars)	41,927	41,927	46,320	50,521	29,075	11,814
Standard error (dollars)	350	350	389	441	726	711
Gini ratio	.474	.474	.432	.403	.429	.563
Standard error	.0049	.0049	.0053	.0057	.0175	.0268
B-Cell	2454	2454	2454	2454	2454	2454

Figure 6.1.) Between 1993 and 1996 men's earnings declined by 2.6 percent. There was a rise in 1997 to 1999, followed by another decline. For women, the change between 1990 to 2000 has been a fairly steady rise.

Production or Nonsupervisory Earnings

In 2001 production or nonsupervisory workers on private nonfarm payrolls worked an average of 34.2 hours a week and earned a mean salary of $14.32 per hour. (See Table 6.4.) Hourly salaries varied by industry. People employed in the services industry worked an average of 32.7 hours and earned more than the total average—$14.67. On the other hand, those in retail trade worked fewer hours (28.9) and earned an average hourly wage of $9.77. Mining and construction workers earned more than the total average earnings, bringing in $17.56 and $18.34 per hour, respectively. Workers in both categories also worked longer hours per week.

TABLE 6.2

Work experience of people 15 years old and over by total money earnings, age, race, and sex, 2000 [CONTINUED]

	Total	Total worked	Worked at full time jobs			
			Total	50 weeks or more	27 to 49 weeks	26 weeks or less
Female						
15 Years and Over						
All Races						
Total	111,735	70,827	51,687	41,600	5,980	4,106
Without Earnings	41,017	109	37	29	3	5
With Earnings	70,718	70,718	51,650	41,571	5,977	4,102
$1 to $2,499 or Loss	6,292	6,292	1,539	376	92	1,071
$2,500 to $4,999	4,124	4,124	1,255	266	160	829
$5,000 to $7,499	4,495	4,495	1,710	610	413	686
$7,500 to $9,999	3,520	3,520	1,688	835	490	363
$10,000 to $12,499	5,442	5,442	3,339	2,253	757	329
$12,500 to $14,999	3,121	3,121	2,308	1,802	394	112
$15,000 to $17,499	4,734	4,734	3,838	3,102	559	177
$17,500 to $19,999	3,038	3,038	2,632	2,273	305	53
$20,000 to $22,499	4,806	4,806	4,229	3,647	457	124
$22,500 to $24,999	2,621	2,621	2,392	2,140	210	43
$25,000 to $27,499	4,568	4,568	4,155	3,699	393	63
$27,500 to $29,999	2,062	2,062	1,943	1,796	119	29
$30,000 to $32,499	3,968	3,968	3,635	3,305	285	45
$32,500 to $34,999	1,452	1,452	1,349	1,249	94	6
$35,000 to $37,499	2,757	2,757	2,597	2,365	203	29
$37,500 to $39,999	1,208	1,208	1,131	1,040	81	11
$40,000 to $42,499	2,536	2,536	2,417	2,197	183	37
$42,500 to $44,999	613	613	585	538	45	2
$45,000 to $47,499	1,314	1,314	1,249	1,179	64	7
$47,500 to $49,999	734	734	700	629	66	5
$50,000 to $52,499	1,569	1,569	1,499	1,319	159	22
$52,500 to $54,999	415	415	410	352	50	8
$55,000 to $57,499	710	710	686	612	69	6
$57,500 to $59,999	324	324	317	285	30	2
$60,000 to $62,499	811	811	756	691	53	12
$62,500 to $64,999	235	235	224	206	11	6
$65,000 to $67,499	486	486	472	435	37	0
$67,500 to $69,999	169	169	162	149	13	0
$70,000 to $72,499	502	502	473	429	42	2
$72,500 to $74,999	125	125	125	109	10	6
$75,000 to $77,499	318	318	308	269	36	4
$77,500 to $79,999	81	81	81	76	5	0
$80,000 to $82,499	213	213	202	197	2	3
$82,500 to $84,999	75	75	75	68	7	0
$85,000 to $87,499	137	137	137	132	5	0
$87,500 to $89,999	30	30	25	21	4	0
$90,000 to $92,499	106	106	96	90	3	3
$92,500 to $94,999	30	30	28	26	2	0
$95,000 to $97,499	68	68	65	65	0	0
$97,500 to $99,999	24	24	24	18	6	0
$100,000 and over	886	886	795	725	63	6
Median earnings (dollars)	20,309	20,309	25,539	27,352	18,509	5,550
Standard error (dollars)	108	108	107	108	496	183
Mean earnings (dollars)	24,472	24,472	29,736	32,621	23,941	8,939
Standard error (dollars)	164	164	206	240	418	294
Gini ratio	.444	.444	.370	.330	.393	.539
Standard error	.0045	.0045	.0053	.0060	.0155	.0220
B-Cell	2454	2454	2454	2454	2454	2454

Note: Numbers in thousands.

SOURCE: Adapted from "PINC-05. Work experience in 2000—People 15 Years Old and Over by Total Money Earnings in 2000, Age, Race, Hispanic Origin, and Sex," in *Current Population Survey,* U.S. Department of Labor, Bureau of Labor Statistics, Washington, DC, November 2001

Occupations

In 2001 full-time wage and salary workers earned a median of $597 per week. Those working in managerial and professional specialties and in precision production, craft, and repair earned more. However, within each occu-pational grouping, many categories earned significantly more or less than the median wage. Among managerial occupations, managers in marketing, advertising, and public relations had the highest weekly wages ($1,095), while managers of food-serving and lodging establishments

TABLE 6.3

Comparison of summary measures of income by selected characteristics, 1993, 1999, and 2000

(Households and people as of March of the following year.)

Characteristic	2000 Median income — Number (1,000)	2000 Median income — Value (dollars)	2000 Median income — 90-percent confidence interval (±) (dollars)	Median income in 1999 (in 2000 dollars) — Value (dollars)	Median income in 1999 (in 2000 dollars) — 90-percent confidence interval (±) (dollars)	Median income in 1993 (in 2000 dollars) — Value (dollars)	Median income in 1993 (in 2000 dollars) — 90-percent confidence interval (±) (dollars)	Percent change in real income 1999 to 2000 — Percent change	Percent change in real income 1999 to 2000 — 90-percent confidence interval (±)	Percent change in real income 1993 to 2000 — Percent change	Percent change in real income 1993 to 2000 — 90-percent confidence interval (±)
Households											
All households	106,417	42,148	324	42,187	325	36,746	282	−0.1	0.9	[1]14.7	1.2
Type of household											
Family households	72,375	51,751	390	51,618	464	44,090	402	0.3	1.0	[1]17.4	1.4
Married-couple families	55,598	59,346	620	58,736	519	50,729	505	1.0	1.1	[1]17.0	1.7
Female householder, no husband present	12,525	28,116	650	27,043	614	21,813	551	[1]4.0	2.7	[1]28.9	4.4
Male householder, no wife present	4,252	42,129	1,346	43,243	1,355	35,109	1,383	−2.6	3.5	[1]20.0	6.1
Nonfamily households	34,042	25,438	380	25,391	459	22,207	431	0.2	1.9	[1]14.5	2.8
Female householder	18,824	20,929	424	20,586	469	17,506	441	1.7	2.5	[1]19.6	3.9
Male householder	15,218	31,267	525	31,786	587	29,086	642	−1.6	2.0	[1]7.5	3.0
Race and Hispanic origin of householder											
All races[2]	106,417	42,148	324	42,187	325	36,746	282	−0.1	0.9	[1]14.7	1.2
White	88,545	44,226	452	43,932	406	38,768	371	0.7	1.1	[1]14.1	1.6
Non-Hispanic	79,376	45,904	434	45,856	474	40,195	387	0.1	1.1	[1]14.2	1.5
Black	13,352	30,439	757	28,848	882	22,974	747	[1]5.5	3.4	[1]32.5	5.4
Asian and Pacific Islander	3,527	55,521	2,443	52,925	3,191	45,105	3,649	4.9	6.4	[1]23.1	11.3
Hispanic origin[3]	9,663	33,447	1,114	31,767	772	26,919	890	[1]5.3	3.0	[1]24.3	5.8
Age of householder											
15 to 24 years	6,392	27,689	827	26,017	712	22,740	784	[1]6.4	3.5	[1]21.8	5.6
25 to 34 years	18,554	44,473	1,022	43,591	684	36,793	567	2.0	2.3	[1]20.9	3.3
35 to 44 years	23,904	53,240	906	52,582	675	48,063	588	1.3	1.8	[1]10.8	2.3
45 to 54 years	21,797	58,218	1,277	58,829	905	54,350	979	−1.0	2.2	[1]7.1	3.0
55 to 64 years	13,943	44,992	1,002	46,095	1,098	39,373	1,002	−2.4	2.6	[1]14.3	3.9
65 years and over	21,828	23,048	423	23,578	388	20,879	416	[1]−2.2	1.9	[1]10.4	3.0
Nativity of the householder											
Native	94,059	42,586	410	42,773	347	37,332	298	−0.4	1.0	[1]14.1	1.4
Foreign born	12,359	38,929	1,206	37,259	981	31,017	938	[1]4.5	3.4	[1]25.5	5.4
Naturalized citizen	5,740	44,456	1,969	45,423	2,499	37,357	1,556	−2.1	5.6	[1]19.0	7.2
Not a citizen	6,618	35,413	1,313	32,247	1,066	27,592	1,117	[1]9.8	4.4	[1]28.3	7.0
Region											
Northeast	20,212	45,106	926	43,394	723	39,694	716	[1]3.9	2.2	[1]13.6	3.1
Midwest	24,497	44,646	814	44,113	860	36,933	563	1.2	2.2	[1]20.9	2.9
South	38,525	38,410	614	38,700	566	33,453	524	−0.7	1.7	[1]14.8	2.6
West	23,183	44,744	834	44,155	809	39,685	758	1.3	2.1	[1]12.7	3.0
Residence											
Inside metropolitan areas	85,737	44,984	449	44,222	471	39,074	406	[1]1.7	1.2	[1]15.1	1.7
Inside central cities	32,030	36,987	503	36,768	522	31,221	443	0.6	1.6	[1]18.5	2.3
Outside central cities	53,706	50,262	472	49,311	646	44,945	522	[1]1.9	1.3	[1]11.8	1.7
Outside metropolitan areas	20,681	32,837	795	34,130	962	29,769	604	[1]−3.8	2.9	[1]10.3	3.5
Earnings of full-time, year-round workers											
Male	58,731	37,339	225	37,701	231	35,765	226	[1]−1.0	0.7	[1]4.4	0.9
Female	41,567	27,355	176	27,208	192	25,579	184	0.5	0.8	[1]6.9	1.0
Per capita income											
All races[2]	276,540	22,199	230	21,893	217	18,319	166	[1]1.4	1.2	[1]21.2	1.7
White	226,401	23,415	271	23,127	255	19,497	194	1.2	1.4	[1]20.1	1.8
Non-Hispanic	194,161	25,278	313	24,919	299	20,941	214	1.4	1.5	[1]20.7	1.9
Black	35,919	15,197	444	14,881	396	11,534	322	2.1	3.4	[1]31.8	5.3
Asian and Pacific Islander	11,384	22,352	1,221	21,844	1,221	18,456	1,247	2.3	6.7	[1]21.1	10.5
Hispanic origin[3]	33,863	12,306	377	12,011	416	10,317	354	2.5	3.5	[1]19.3	5.5

[1]Statistically significant change at the 90-percent confidence level.
[2]Data for American Indians and Alaska Natives are not shown separately in this table.
[3]Hispanics may be of any race.

SOURCE: Carmen DeNavas-Walt, Robert W. Cleveland, and Marc I. Roemer, "Table A. Comparison of Summary Measures of Income by Selected Characteristics: 1993, 1999, and 2000," in "Money Income in the United States: 2000," *Current Population Reports,* U.S. Census Bureau, Washington, DC, September 2001

FIGURE 6.1

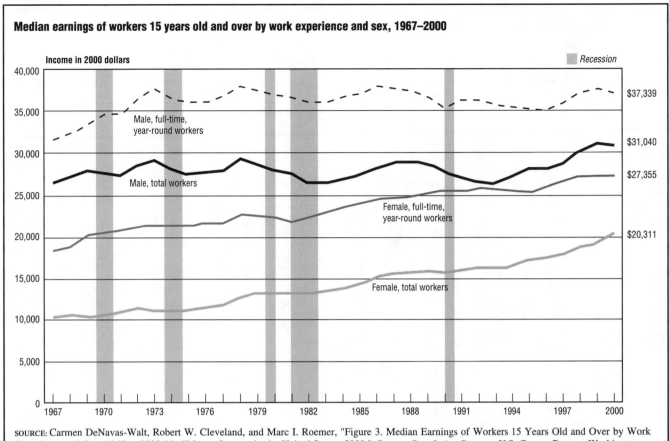

Median earnings of workers 15 years old and over by work experience and sex, 1967–2000

SOURCE: Carmen DeNavas-Walt, Robert W. Cleveland, and Marc I. Roemer, "Figure 3. Median Earnings of Workers 15 Years Old and Over by Work Experience and Sex: 1967 to 2000," in "Money Income in the United States: 2000," *Current Population Reports,* U.S. Census Bureau, Washington, DC, September 2001

earned the least ($598). In regard to professional specialty occupations, pharmacists ($1,366), chemical engineers ($1,350), physicians ($1,258), and aerospace engineers ($1,246) headed the list of salaries. However, recreation workers ($471), prekindergarten and kindergarten teachers ($480), dietitians ($520), and social workers ($644) made the lowest median weekly earnings. (See Table 6.5.)

While those in sales occupations ($574) generally earned less than the median earnings of all workers, sales representatives of commodities, except retail ($839), earned far more than others. Sales workers in retail and personal services ($363) had the lowest salaries among those in sales occupations. Administrative support personnel earned a median salary of $486. Supervisors earned $621, while secretaries received $475. (See Table 6.5.)

In the technical, sales, and administrative support field, airline pilots and navigators ($1,150) and computer programmers ($952) earned far more than the median salaries. Service occupations were among the lowest paid workers. Within this category, child-care workers ($246) and private household workers ($255) earned the lowest salaries. Protective services police and detectives ($949) had the highest. (See Table 6.5.)

In the precision production, craft, and repair grouping, supervisors of mechanics and repairers ($783) and telephone line installers and repairers ($953) earned the highest salaries, while several categories in precision jobs were among the lowest. (See Table 6.5.) In the operators, fabricators, and laborers category, textile sewing machine operators ($316) and pressing machine operators ($288) were among the lowest paid. Separating, filtering, and clarifying machine operators earned $793, the highest in this category. Among transportation and material-moving occupations, stock handlers and baggers ($324) and garage and service station-related jobs ($326) were among the lowest paid, while those in railroad transportation earned $947. See the *Occupational Outlook Handbook* (Bureau of Labor Statistics [BLS]) for detailed descriptions of each job.

Starting Salaries for New College Graduates

L. Patrick Scheetz, in *Recruiting Trends: 1997–98* (27th Edition, Career Services and Placement, Michigan State University, East Lansing, Michigan, December 5, 1997), found that the expanding economy offered recent graduates greater opportunities in the workplace. The engineering fields offered the highest starting salaries for

TABLE 6.4

Average hours and earnings of production or nonsupervisory workers* on private nonfarm payrolls by major industry, 1981–2001

	Total private[1]			Mining			Construction		
Year and month	Weekly hours	Hourly earnings	Weekly earnings	Weekly hours	Hourly earnings	Weekly earnings	Weekly hours	Hourly earnings	Weekly earnings
	Annual averages								
1981	35.2	7.25	255.20	43.7	10.04	438.75	36.9	10.82	399.26
1982	34.8	7.68	267.26	42.7	10.77	459.88	36.7	11.63	426.82
1983	35.0	8.02	280.70	42.5	11.28	479.40	37.1	11.94	442.97
1984	35.2	8.32	292.86	43.3	11.63	503.58	37.8	12.13	458.51
1985	34.9	8.57	299.09	43.4	11.98	519.93	37.7	12.32	464.46
1986	34.8	8.76	304.85	42.2	12.46	525.81	37.4	12.48	466.75
1987	34.8	8.98	312.50	42.4	12.54	531.70	37.8	12.71	480.44
1988	34.7	9.28	322.02	42.3	12.80	541.44	37.9	13.08	495.73
1989	34.6	9.66	334.24	43.0	13.26	570.18	37.9	13.54	513.17
1990	34.5	10.01	345.35	44.1	13.68	603.29	38.2	13.77	526.01
1991	34.3	10.32	353.98	44.4	14.19	630.04	38.1	14.00	533.40
1992	34.4	10.57	363.61	43.9	14.54	638.31	38.0	14.15	537.70
1993	34.5	10.83	373.64	44.3	14.60	646.78	38.5	14.38	553.63
1994	34.7	11.12	385.86	44.8	14.88	666.62	38.9	14.73	573.00
1995	34.5	11.43	394.34	44.7	15.30	683.91	38.9	15.09	587.00
1996	34.4	11.82	406.61	45.3	15.62	707.59	39.0	15.47	603.33
1997	34.6	12.28	424.89	45.4	16.15	733.21	39.0	16.04	625.56
1998	34.6	12.78	442.19	43.9	16.91	742.35	38.9	16.61	646.13
1999	34.5	13.24	456.78	43.2	17.05	736.56	39.1	17.19	672.13
2000	34.5	13.76	474.72	43.1	17.22	742.18	39.3	17.88	702.68
2001	34.2	14.32	489.74	43.5	17.56	763.86	39.3	18.34	720.76
	Monthly data, not seasonally adjusted								
2001:									
May	34.1	$14.21	$484.56	44.1	$17.42	$768.22	40.2	$18.18	$730.84
June	34.4	14.20	488.48	43.8	17.53	767.81	40.1	18.22	730.62
July	34.7	14.26	494.82	43.7	17.61	769.56	40.4	18.33	740.53
August	34.5	14.26	491.97	43.6	17.47	761.69	40.2	18.44	741.29
September	34.4	14.50	498.80	44.0	17.61	774.84	39.9	18.51	738.55
October	34.0	14.49	492.66	43.6	17.72	772.59	39.7	18.57	737.23
November	34.0	14.54	494.36	43.4	17.61	764.27	39.1	18.54	724.91
December	34.4	14.62	502.93	43.9	17.58	771.76	38.5	18.69	719.57
2002:									
January	33.6	14.65	492.24	42.2	17.89	754.96	38.5	18.56	714.56
February	33.9	14.67	497.31	42.9	17.76	761.90	38.5	18.62	716.87
March	33.9	14.67	497.31	42.7	17.73	757.07	38.4	18.66	716.54
April(p)	34.0	14.69	499.46	42.3	17.68	747.86	38.8	18.68	724.78
May(p)	34.1	14.67	500.25	42.9	17.68	758.47	39.0	18.65	727.35

	Manufacturing				Transportation and public utilities			Wholesale trade		
Year and month	Weekly hours	Hourly earnings	Hourly earnings, excluding overtime	Weekly earnings	Weekly hours	Hourly earnings	Weekly earnings	Weekly hours	Hourly earnings	Weekly earnings
	Annual averages									
1981	39.8	7.99	7.72	318.00	39.4	9.70	382.18	38.5	7.55	290
1982	38.9	8.49	8.25	330.26	39.0	10.32	402.48	38.3	8.08	309
1983	40.1	8.83	8.52	354.08	39.0	10.79	420.81	38.5	8.54	328
1984	40.7	9.19	8.82	374.03	39.4	11.12	438.13	38.5	8.88	341
1985	40.5	9.54	9.16	386.37	39.5	11.40	450.30	38.4	9.15	351
1986	40.7	9.73	9.34	396.01	39.2	11.70	458.64	38.3	9.34	357
1987	41.0	9.91	9.48	406.31	39.2	12.03	471.58	38.1	9.59	365
1988	41.1	10.19	9.73	418.81	38.2	12.24	467.57	38.1	9.98	380
1989	41.0	10.48	10.02	429.68	38.3	12.57	481.43	38.0	10.39	394
1990	40.8	10.83	10.37	441.86	38.4	12.92	496.13	38.1	10.79	411
1991	40.7	11.18	10.71	455.03	38.1	13.20	502.92	38.1	11.15	424
1992	41.0	11.46	10.95	469.86	38.3	13.43	514.37	38.2	11.39	435
1993	41.4	11.74	11.18	486.04	39.3	13.55	532.52	38.2	11.74	448
1994	42.0	12.07	11.43	506.94	39.7	13.78	547.07	38.4	12.06	463
1995	41.6	12.37	11.74	514.59	39.4	14.13	556.72	38.3	12.43	476
1996	41.6	12.77	12.12	531.23	39.6	14.45	572.22	38.3	12.87	492
1997	42.0	13.17	12.45	553.14	39.7	14.92	592.32	38.4	13.45	516
1998	41.7	13.49	12.79	562.53	39.5	15.31	604.75	38.3	14.07	538
1999	41.7	13.90	13.17	579.63	38.7	15.69	607.20	38.3	14.59	558
2000	41.6	14.37	13.62	597.79	38.4	16.21	622.46	38.5	15.22	585
2001	40.7	14.83	14.15	603.58	38.2	16.79	641.38	38.2	15.86	605

TABLE 6.4

Average hours and earnings of production or nonsupervisory workers* on private nonfarm payrolls by major industry, 1981–2001 [CONTINUED]

Year and month	Manufacturing				Transportation and public utilities				Wholesale trade		
	Weekly hours	Hourly earnings	Hourly earnings, excluding overtime	Weekly earnings	Weekly hours	Weekly hours	Hourly earnings	Weekly earnings	Weekly hours	Hourly earnings	Weekly earnings
				Monthly data, not seasonally adjusted							
2001:											
May	40.7	$14.75	$14.08	$600.33	38.1	$16.65	$634.37	38.2	$15.71	$600
June	40.8	14.79	14.10	603.43	38.4	16.69	640.90	38.2	15.81	603
July	40.4	14.84	14.16	599.54	38.7	16.81	650.55	38.5	15.92	612
August	40.9	14.89	14.15	609.00	38.4	16.78	644.35	38.3	15.80	605
September	41.1	15.01	14.26	616.91	38.2	16.91	645.96	38.6	16.08	620
October	40.6	14.97	14.27	607.78	38.0	16.98	645.24	38.0	15.95	606
November	40.7	15.07	14.37	613.35	37.9	17.05	646.20	38.3	15.96	611
December	41.2	15.17	14.45	625.00	38.6	17.11	660.45	38.7	16.21	627
2002:											
January	40.4	15.15	14.48	612.06	37.7	17.18	647.69	37.8	16.11	608
February	40.3	15.16	14.50	610.95	37.9	17.18	651.12	38.0	16.21	615
March	40.9	15.16	14.45	620.04	38.0	17.24	655.12	38.1	16.13	614
April(p)	40.8	15.20	14.50	620.16	38.0	17.31	657.78	38.2	16.09	614
May(p)	40.9	15.23	14.50	622.91	38.3	17.24	660.29	38.3	16.09	616

Year and month	Retail trade			Finance, insurance, and real estate			Services		
	Weekly hours	Hourly earnings	Weekly earnings	Weekly hours	Hourly earnings	Weekly earnings	Weekly hours	Hourly earnings	Weekly earnings
				Annual averages					
1981	30.1	5.25	158.03	36.3	6.31	229.05	32.6	6.41	208.97
1982	29.9	5.48	163.85	36.2	6.78	245.44	32.6	6.92	225.59
1983	29.8	5.74	171.05	36.2	7.29	263.90	32.7	7.31	239.04
1984	29.8	5.85	174.33	36.5	7.63	278.50	32.6	7.59	247.43
1985	29.4	5.94	174.64	36.4	7.94	289.02	32.5	7.90	256.75
1986	29.2	6.03	176.08	36.4	8.36	304.30	32.5	8.18	265.85
1987	29.2	6.12	178.70	36.3	8.73	316.90	32.5	8.49	275.93
1988	29.1	6.31	183.62	35.9	9.06	325.25	32.6	8.88	289.49
1989	28.9	6.53	188.72	35.8	9.53	341.17	32.6	9.38	305.79
1990	28.8	6.75	194.40	35.8	9.97	356.93	32.5	9.83	319.48
1991	28.6	6.94	198.48	35.7	10.39	370.92	32.4	10.23	331.45
1992	28.8	7.12	205.06	35.8	10.82	387.36	32.5	10.54	342.55
1993	28.8	7.29	209.95	35.8	11.35	406.33	32.5	10.78	350.35
1994	28.9	7.49	216.46	35.8	11.83	423.51	32.5	11.04	358.80
1995	28.8	7.69	221.47	35.9	12.32	442.29	32.4	11.39	369.04
1996	28.8	7.99	230.11	35.9	12.80	459.52	32.4	11.79	382.00
1997	28.9	8.33	240.74	36.1	13.34	481.57	32.6	12.28	400.33
1998	29.0	8.74	253.46	36.4	14.07	512.15	32.6	12.84	418.58
1999	29.0	9.09	263.61	36.2	14.62	529.24	32.6	13.37	435.86
2000	28.9	9.46	273.39	36.4	15.14	551.10	32.7	13.93	455.51
2001	28.9	9.77	282.35	36.1	15.80	570.38	32.7	14.67	479.71
				Monthly data, not seasonally adjusted					
2001:									
May	28.7	$9.67	$277.53	35.6	$15.72	$559.63	32.5	$14.52	$471.90
June	29.2	9.70	283.24	36.2	15.68	567.62	32.8	14.45	473.96
July	29.7	9.70	288.09	36.6	15.82	579.01	33.1	14.52	480.61
August	29.4	9.71	285.47	36.0	15.77	567.72	32.9	14.52	477.71
September	28.9	9.86	284.95	36.7	15.96	585.73	32.8	14.85	487.08
October	28.6	9.87	282.28	35.8	15.91	569.58	32.5	14.87	483.28
November	28.5	9.91	282.44	35.9	15.97	573.32	32.5	14.99	487.18
December	29.3	9.89	289.78	36.7	16.14	592.34	32.9	15.15	498.44
2002:									
January	28.1	9.96	279.88	35.8	16.07	575.31	32.2	15.14	487.51
February	28.6	9.95	284.57	36.1	16.13	582.29	32.5	15.17	493.03
March	28.7	9.98	286.43	35.9	16.17	580.50	32.5	15.16	492.70
April(p)	28.8	10.01	288.29	35.8	16.23	581.03	32.4	15.15	490.86
May(p)	29.1	9.97	290.13	35.8	16.20	579.96	32.4	15.13	490.21

*Data relate to production workers in mining and manufacturing; construction workers in construction; and nonsupervisory workers in transportation and public utilities; wholesale and retail trade; finance, insurance, and real estate; and services.
p = preliminary.

SOURCE: Adapted from "B-2. Average hours and earnings of production or nonsupervisory workers[1] on private nonfarm payrolls by major industry, 1964 to date," *Current Population Survey* U.S. Department of Labor, Bureau of Labor Statistics, Washington, DC [Online] ftp://ftp.bls.gov/pub/suppl/empsit.ceseeb2.txt [accessed July 9, 2002]

TABLE 6.5

Median weekly earnings of full-time wage and salary workers by detailed occupation and sex, 2001

(Numbers in thousands)

Occupation	2001 Both sexes Number of workers	Both sexes Median weekly earnings	Men Number of workers	Men Median weekly earnings	Women Number of workers	Women Median weekly earnings
Total, 16 years and over	99,599	$597	55,928	$672	43,671	$511
Managerial and professional specialty	32,221	859	16,265	1,038	15,956	732
Executive, administrative, and managerial	15,795	867	8,349	1,060	7,446	706
Administrators and officials, public administration	686	889	337	1,051	349	747
Administrators, protective services	62	891	44	(*)	18	(*)
Financial managers	682	1,016	330	1,262	352	816
Personnel and labor relations managers	209	924	68	1,113	141	861
Purchasing managers	135	919	76	1,125	59	749
Managers, marketing, advertising, and public relations	727	1,095	451	1,219	276	853
Administrators, education and related fields	717	945	272	1,189	445	819
Managers, medicine and health	665	789	157	1,146	508	725
Managers, food serving and lodging establishments	971	598	520	707	451	486
Managers, properties and real estate	348	702	162	880	187	620
Management-related occupations	4,197	758	1,724	942	2,473	670
Accountants and auditors	1,374	773	581	954	793	687
Underwriters	98	780	26	(*)	73	732
Other financial officers	729	861	357	1,065	371	712
Management analysts	270	1,084	152	1,214	117	969
Personnel, training, and labor relations specialists	590	710	175	876	414	670
Buyers, wholesale and retail trade, except farm products	162	649	79	797	84	586
Construction inspectors	54	670	50	698	4	(*)
Inspectors and compliance officers, except construction	215	858	121	923	94	749
Professional specialty	16,426	854	7,916	1,021	8,510	749
Engineers, architects, and surveyors	2,148	1,131	1,920	1,142	228	989
Architects	152	981	116	1,039	36	(*)
Engineers	1,979	1,142	1,787	1,149	191	1,022
Aerospace engineers	84	1,246	75	1,249	9	(*)
Chemical engineers	75	1,350	65	1,401	9	(*)
Civil engineers	270	1,041	244	1,059	26	(*)
Electrical and electronic engineers	695	1,174	634	1,171	61	1,200
Industrial engineers	255	1,053	211	1,104	44	(*)
Mechanical engineers	309	1,131	295	1,134	14	(*)
Mathematical and computer scientists	1,878	1,074	1,329	1,159	549	898
Computer systems analysts and scientists	1,603	1,100	1,173	1,161	430	918
Operations and systems researchers and analysts	223	931	126	1,074	97	819
Natural scientists	513	901	332	996	181	758
Chemists, except biochemists	151	954	97	1,087	54	800
Biological and life scientists	109	743	61	826	49	(*)
Medical scientists	88	811	45	(*)	43	(*)
Health diagnosing occupations	581	1,172	388	1,372	193	883
Physicians	494	1,258	333	1,410	161	958
Health assessment and treating occupations	2,233	831	370	983	1,863	811
Registered nurses	1,604	829	145	933	1,459	820
Pharmacists	157	1,366	92	1,421	66	1,261
Dietitians	72	520	9	(*)	63	545
Therapists	346	788	100	810	246	782
Respiratory therapists	68	765	27	(*)	42	(*)
Physical therapists	106	859	41	(*)	65	806
Speech therapists	68	834	4	(*)	63	836
Physicians' assistants	54	839	24	(*)	30	(*)
Teachers, college and university	663	1,009	420	1,126	244	844
Teachers, except college and university	4,421	730	1,189	780	3,232	707
Teachers, prekindergarten and kindergarten	495	480	8	(*)	487	476
Teachers, elementary school	1,959	740	362	770	1,596	731
Teachers, secondary school	1,155	774	504	826	651	759
Teachers, special education	314	761	53	742	261	764
Counselors, educational and vocational	225	766	67	854	157	734
Librarians, archivists, and curators	181	724	33	(*)	148	713
Librarians	159	726	27	(*)	132	713
Social scientists and urban planners	298	870	135	1,056	163	750
Economists	107	945	49	(*)	58	733
Psychologists	151	818	64	914	87	757
Social, recreation, and religious workers	1,218	643	569	689	649	614
Social workers	711	644	211	677	500	630

TABLE 6.5

Median weekly earnings of full-time wage and salary workers by detailed occupation and sex, 2001 [CONTINUED]

(Numbers in thousands)

	2001					
	Both sexes		**Men**		**Women**	
Occupation	**Number of workers**	**Median weekly earnings**	**Number of workers**	**Median weekly earnings**	**Number of workers**	**Median weekly earnings**
Recreation workers	81	471	22	(*)	59	451
Clergy	303	699	269	723	34	(*)
Lawyers and judges	611	1,380	405	1,535	206	1,062
Lawyers	572	1,398	377	1,547	195	1,073
Writers, artists, entertainers, and athletes	1,455	750	758	843	697	683
Technical writers	70	941	29	(*)	41	(*)
Designers	511	742	258	884	253	639
Actors and directors	85	774	47	(*)	39	(*)
Painters, sculptors, craft artists, and artist printmakers	102	647	67	662	35	(*)
Photographers	54	667	35	(*)	19	(*)
Editors and reporters	230	762	112	866	118	705
Public relations specialists	151	819	58	917	93	789
Athletes	55	761	44	(*)	11	(*)
Technical, sales, and administrative support	28,145	521	10,733	667	17,411	473
Technicians and related support	3,753	673	1,870	783	1,883	580
Health technologists and technicians	1,389	562	290	698	1,099	534
Clinical laboratory technologists and technicians	289	609	68	717	220	575
Radiologic technicians	140	707	49	(*)	91	694
Licensed practical nurses	287	567	16	(*)	271	562
Engineering and related technologists and technicians	924	713	736	743	187	608
Electrical and electronic technicians	437	727	352	751	84	628
Drafting occupations	198	703	164	737	35	(*)
Surveying and mapping technicians	62	666	56	680	6	(*)
Science technicians	237	625	139	689	98	558
Biological technicians	93	535	40	(*)	53	491
Chemical technicians	62	761	47	(*)	15	(*)
Technicians, except health, engineering, and science	1,203	827	704	949	499	705
Airplane pilots and navigators	101	1,150	98	1,145	3	(*)
Computer programmers	602	952	438	975	164	867
Legal assistants	344	645	55	665	289	637
Sales occupations	10,173	574	5,599	692	4,574	429
Supervisors and proprietors	3,380	618	1,957	712	1,423	502
Sales representatives, finance and business services	1,983	753	1,113	897	870	627
Insurance sales	397	670	186	850	211	583
Real estate sales	382	747	184	838	198	695
Securities and financial services sales	434	980	293	1,156	140	716
Advertising and related sales	157	707	73	782	84	663
Sales occupations, other business services	614	707	377	775	236	544
Sales representatives, commodities, except retail	1,301	839	1,012	876	289	694
Sales workers, retail and personal services	3,474	363	1,504	460	1,971	313
Sales workers, motor vehicles and boats	294	656	267	675	27	(*)
Sales workers, apparel	139	336	32	(*)	107	329
Sales workers, furniture and home furnishings	125	496	78	545	48	(*)
Sales workers, radio, television, hi-fi, and appliances	189	506	134	509	55	465
Sales workers, hardware and building supplies	227	480	172	490	55	430
Sales workers, parts	136	458	120	471	16	(*)
Sales workers, other commodities	732	382	287	428	445	351
Sales counter clerks	93	329	33	(*)	60	310
Cashiers	1,383	299	309	327	1,075	292
Street and door-to-door sales workers	94	497	37	(*)	57	492
Administrative support, including clerical	14,219	486	3,264	576	10,954	469
Supervisors	696	621	245	703	451	587
General office	403	592	110	763	293	552
Financial records processing	97	722	14	(*)	83	703
Distribution, scheduling, and adjusting clerks	186	636	117	639	69	629
Computer equipment operators	285	559	135	644	149	498
Computer operators	280	565	132	647	148	499
Secretaries, stenographers, and typists	2,333	479	48	(*)	2,285	478
Secretaries	1,846	475	25	(*)	1,821	475
Stenographers	99	517	5	(*)	94	511
Typists	388	487	18	(*)	370	485
Information clerks	1,384	421	164	511	1,220	414
Interviewers	106	444	15	(*)	91	448

TABLE 6.5

Median weekly earnings of full-time wage and salary workers by detailed occupation and sex, 2001 [CONTINUED]

(Numbers in thousands)

	2001					
	Both sexes		**Men**		**Women**	
Occupation	**Number of workers**	**Median weekly earnings**	**Number of workers**	**Median weekly earnings**	**Number of workers**	**Median weekly earnings**
Hotel clerks	89	348	22	(*)	66	347
Transportation ticket and reservation agents	209	525	69	681	141	475
Receptionists	712	401	15	(*)	697	401
Records processing, except financial	752	473	152	484	601	469
Order clerks	272	517	67	506	205	522
Personnel clerks, except payroll and timekeeping	52	540	9	(*)	43	(*)
Library clerks	68	400	10	(*)	58	398
File clerks	181	402	37	(*)	144	398
Records clerks	172	478	26	(*)	146	479
Financial records processing	1,529	483	143	519	1,386	479
Bookkeepers, accounting, and auditing clerks	1,058	477	83	506	975	474
Payroll and timekeeping clerks	150	549	11	(*)	139	553
Billing clerks	172	480	29	(*)	143	474
Billing, posting, and calculating machine operators	109	483	9	(*)	100	478
Communications equipment operators	126	418	20	(*)	107	397
Telephone operators	118	424	16	(*)	102	400
Mail and message distributing	800	660	492	700	307	593
Postal clerks, except mail carriers	280	697	146	738	133	654
Mail carriers, postal service	317	721	225	753	91	641
Mail clerks, except postal service	115	471	53	497	62	436
Messengers	89	503	68	545	21	(*)
Material recording, scheduling, and distributing clerks	1,723	489	963	513	760	457
Dispatchers	207	563	111	634	96	483
Production coordinators	223	675	93	775	130	580
Traffic, shipping, and receiving clerks	589	450	420	468	169	413
Stock and inventory clerks	366	467	203	493	164	431
Meter readers	51	529	45	(*)	6	(*)
Expediters	234	440	73	550	161	416
Adjusters and investigators	1,723	508	435	581	1,288	497
Insurance adjusters, examiners, and investigators	449	575	122	662	328	546
Investigators and adjusters, except insurance	998	497	247	545	752	487
Eligibility clerks, social welfare	78	497	6	(*)	72	485
Bill and account collectors	197	481	61	504	136	468
Miscellaneous administrative support occupations	2,822	449	446	520	2,376	437
General office clerks	624	465	87	481	536	462
Bank tellers	303	376	33	(*)	270	372
Data-entry keyers	546	446	84	483	462	441
Statistical clerks	88	428	7	(*)	82	419
Teachers' aides	415	361	31	(*)	384	356
Service occupations	11,143	377	5,331	438	5,812	335
Private household	354	255	15	(*)	340	255
Child care workers	135	246	2	(*)	132	245
Cleaners and servants	207	254	10	(*)	197	254
Protective services	2,166	629	1,783	658	383	509
Supervisors	200	894	175	920	24	(*)
Police and detectives	111	949	100	970	11	(*)
Guards	53	595	40	(*)	13	(*)
Firefighting and fire prevention	256	792	245	796	10	(*)
Firefighting	242	795	235	793	6	(*)
Police and detectives	1,038	691	856	717	182	594
Police and detectives, public service	545	782	471	796	73	725
Sheriffs, bailiffs, and other law enforcement officers	163	647	125	651	37	(*)
Correctional institution officers	330	573	259	603	71	502
Guards	673	424	507	447	167	391
Guards and police, except public service	629	440	488	451	142	413
Service occupations, except private household and protective	8,622	349	3,532	374	5,089	332
Food preparation and service occupations	3,285	322	1,648	343	1,638	309
Supervisors	292	394	135	445	157	350
Bartenders	178	369	89	408	89	338
Waiters and waitresses	558	331	162	363	396	317
Cooks, except short order	1,382	326	836	347	546	305
Food counter, fountain, and related occupations	114	266	39	(*)	75	261
Kitchen workers, food preparation	138	315	42	(*)	95	308
Waiters' and waitresses' assistants	278	315	138	319	140	310

TABLE 6.5

Median weekly earnings of full-time wage and salary workers by detailed occupation and sex, 2001 [CONTINUED]

(Numbers in thousands)

Occupation	2001					
	Both sexes		Men		Women	
	Number of workers	Median weekly earnings	Number of workers	Median weekly earnings	Number of workers	Median weekly earnings
Miscellaneous food preparation occupations	346	291	207	288	139	296
Health service occupations	1,867	367	227	408	1,640	363
Dental assistants	130	435	3	(*)	127	433
Health aides, except nursing	266	375	62	438	204	364
Nursing aides, orderlies, and attendants	1,472	360	162	397	1,309	356
Cleaning and building service occupations	2,228	361	1,335	399	893	315
Supervisors	159	444	113	500	46	(*)
Maids and housemen	471	316	96	385	375	308
Janitors and cleaners	1,536	365	1,070	389	466	318
Pest control	53	475	51	483	3	(*)
Personal service occupations	1,242	370	323	404	919	355
Supervisors	69	521	31	(*)	38	(*)
Hairdressers and cosmetologists	326	381	35	(*)	291	374
Attendants, amusement and recreation facilities	146	371	90	388	56	343
Public transportation attendants	85	552	17	(*)	68	561
Welfare service aides	74	394	12	(*)	62	395
Early childhood teachers' assistants	239	306	10	(*)	229	306
Precision production, craft, and repair	12,030	629	11,018	648	1,012	479
Mechanics and repairers	4,153	665	3,951	670	201	594
Supervisors	251	783	228	794	23	(*)
Mechanics and repairers, except supervisors	3,901	656	3,723	661	179	586
Vehicle and mobile equipment mechanics and repairers	1,495	614	1,475	615	20	(*)
Automobile mechanics	641	541	633	545	8	(*)
Bus, truck, and stationary engine mechanics	309	686	306	685	3	(*)
Aircraft engine mechanics	127	791	121	803	7	(*)
Automobile body and related repairers	175	577	174	575	1	(*)
Heavy equipment mechanics	143	688	142	690	1	(*)
Industrial machinery repairers	420	650	403	659	18	(*)
Electrical and electronic equipment repairers	884	748	789	760	95	651
Electronic repairers, communications and industrial equipment	181	695	172	692	9	(*)
Data processing equipment repairers	275	708	231	743	44	(*)
Telephone line installers and repairers	54	953	52	976	1	(*)
Telephone installers and repairers	278	803	243	803	35	(*)
Heating, air conditioning, and refrigeration mechanics	265	714	261	713	4	(*)
Miscellaneous mechanics and repairers	817	627	776	637	40	(*)
Millwrights	63	813	61	827	2	(*)
Construction trades	4,501	611	4,407	613	94	437
Supervisors	559	749	546	749	13	(*)
Construction trades, except supervisors	3,942	593	3,861	595	81	424
Brickmasons and stonemasons	183	545	179	551	4	(*)
Tile setters, hard and soft	57	530	57	530	-	-
Carpet installers	71	497	71	497	-	-
Carpenters	1,036	573	1,020	576	16	(*)
Drywall installers	136	517	131	522	5	(*)
Electricians	752	714	739	716	14	(*)
Electrical power installers and repairers	146	758	140	767	6	(*)
Painters, construction and maintenance	359	460	347	460	13	(*)
Plumbers, pipefitters, steamfitters, and apprentices	466	672	458	674	8	(*)
Concrete and terrazzo finishers	104	545	104	547	-	-
Insulation workers	55	542	52	547	3	(*)
Roofers	131	491	130	491	2	(*)
Structural metalworkers	71	701	69	699	2	(*)
Extractive occupations	125	784	123	789	2	(*)
Precision production occupations	3,252	618	2,537	680	714	451
Supervisors	1,028	707	833	732	195	571
Precision metalworking occupations	811	687	761	697	50	510
Tool and die makers	109	811	106	817	3	(*)
Machinists	476	671	453	680	23	(*)
Sheet-metal workers	110	674	104	673	5	(*)
Precision woodworking occupations	83	510	74	537	10	(*)
Cabinet makers and bench carpenters	56	550	53	558	3	(*)
Precision textile, apparel, and furnishings machine workers	99	422	42	(*)	57	390
Precision workers, assorted materials	459	474	220	517	239	418

TABLE 6.5

Median weekly earnings of full-time wage and salary workers by detailed occupation and sex, 2001 [CONTINUED]

(Numbers in thousands)

	2001					
	Both sexes		Men		Women	
Occupation	Number of workers	Median weekly earnings	Number of workers	Median weekly earnings	Number of workers	Median weekly earnings
Optical goods workers	61	530	31	(*)	29	(*)
Electrical and electronic equipment assemblers	299	448	114	506	184	411
Precision food production occupations	355	424	240	472	115	375
Butchers and meat cutters	200	445	168	471	33	(*)
Bakers	117	406	62	461	54	363
Precision inspectors, testers, and related workers	157	716	118	760	39	(*)
Inspectors, testers, and graders	150	726	114	763	36	(*)
Plant and system operators	259	783	248	789	10	(*)
Water and sewage treatment plant operators	67	748	67	746	1	(*)
Stationary engineers	102	779	97	788	5	(*)
Operators, fabricators, and laborers	14,568	467	11,310	501	3,258	368
Machine operators, assemblers, and inspectors	6,073	457	3,954	512	2,119	369
Machine operators and tenders, except precision	3,797	449	2,496	509	1,301	360
Metalworking and plastic working machine operators	305	531	246	554	59	458
Punching and stamping press machine operators	91	464	64	525	27	(*)
Grinding, abrading, buffing, and polishing machine operators	86	512	75	516	11	(*)
Metal and plastic processing machine operators	122	485	97	521	25	(*)
Molding and casting machine operators	73	475	52	511	21	(*)
Woodworking machine operators	84	415	71	431	14	(*)
Sawing machine operators	51	399	42	(*)	9	(*)
Printing machine operators	312	562	246	618	66	418
Printing press operators	250	565	212	607	38	(*)
Textile, apparel, and furnishings machine operators	615	330	193	373	422	319
Textile sewing machine operators	317	316	86	345	231	311
Pressing machine operators	55	288	18	(*)	37	(*)
Laundering and dry cleaning machine operators	133	324	46	(*)	87	306
Machine operators, assorted materials	2,338	463	1,627	508	712	372
Packaging and filling machine operators	286	380	107	446	179	346
Mixing and blending machine operators	103	550	91	559	12	(*)
Separating, filtering, and clarifying machine operators	53	793	47	(*)	6	(*)
Painting and paint spraying machine operators	152	498	139	508	13	(*)
Furnace, kiln, and oven operators, except food	57	607	52	630	5	(*)
Slicing and cutting machine operators	130	454	98	490	32	(*)
Photographic process machine operators	54	353	22	(*)	32	(*)
Fabricators, assemblers, and hand working occupations	1,623	464	1,134	505	489	376
Welders and cutters	500	539	485	546	15	(*)
Assemblers	1,015	433	584	481	431	381
Production inspectors, testers, samplers, and weighers	652	484	323	592	329	400
Production inspectors, checkers, and examiners	469	495	223	616	246	410
Production testers	69	603	48	(*)	21	(*)
Graders and sorters, except agricultural	108	334	50	388	58	313
Transportation and material moving occupations	4,505	573	4,149	587	356	439
Motor vehicle operators	3,303	575	3,004	591	299	422
Supervisors	72	609	57	683	15	(*)
Truck drivers	2,530	593	2,421	600	108	456
Drivers—sales workers	144	630	137	647	7	(*)
Bus drivers	346	457	203	487	143	415
Taxicab drivers and chauffeurs	162	487	143	509	19	(*)
Transportation occupations, except motor vehicles	151	911	144	919	6	(*)
Rail transportation	102	947	98	950	5	(*)
Locomotive operating occupations	57	947	56	950	1	(*)
Material moving equipment operators	1,052	536	1,001	540	51	486
Operating engineers	231	675	226	675	5	(*)
Crane and tower operators	64	726	63	718	1	(*)
Excavating and loading machine operators	72	665	71	661	-	-
Grader, dozer, and scraper operators	55	568	54	571	1	(*)
Industrial truck and tractor equipment operators	538	474	504	476	34	(*)
Handlers, equipment cleaners, helpers, and laborers	3,990	389	3,207	401	783	342
Helpers, construction and extractive occupations	89	394	86	391	3	(*)
Helpers, construction trades	83	389	79	386	3	(*)
Construction laborers	878	424	849	427	29	(*)
Freight, stock, and material handlers	1,277	384	972	398	305	341
Stock handlers and baggers	595	324	388	330	207	317
Machine feeders and offbearers	72	399	47	(*)	25	(*)

TABLE 6.5

Median weekly earnings of full-time wage and salary workers by detailed occupation and sex, 2001 [CONTINUED]

(Numbers in thousands)

Occupation	Both sexes		Men		Women	
	Number of workers	Median weekly earnings	Number of workers	Median weekly earnings	Number of workers	Median weekly earnings
Garage and service station related occupations	127	326	118	328	9	(*)
Vehicle washers and equipment cleaners	211	339	183	346	28	(*)
Hand packers and packagers	291	326	108	344	182	321
Laborers, except construction	1,037	400	824	410	212	365
Farming, forestry, and fishing	1,493	354	1,271	366	222	308
Farm operators and managers	77	510	59	560	18	(*)
Farm managers	65	525	48	(*)	18	(*)
Other agricultural and related occupations	1,354	342	1,155	353	199	303
Farm occupations, except managerial	540	319	463	328	77	283
Farm workers	491	313	421	319	70	284
Related agricultural occupations	814	360	692	370	122	315
Supervisors, related agricultural occupations	82	561	73	625	9	(*)
Groundskeepers and gardeners, except farm	609	356	574	358	36	(*)
Animal caretakers, except farm	80	341	25	(*)	55	323

*Data not shown where base is less than 50,000.

SOURCE: "39. Median weekly earnings of full-time wage and salary workers by detailed occupation and sex" in *Employment and Earnings*, vol. 48, no. 1, January 2001

college graduates. Those majoring in education and tele-communications had the lowest starting salaries. According to the National Association of Colleges and Employers (NACE), starting salaries for liberal arts majors were higher in 1996 than in 1995. For example, the salaries of journalism graduates went up 14.9 percent to an average of $22,897. Political science majors had a 9.2 percent rise in their salaries, starting with an average of $26,924.

By 2002 opportunities for new college graduates in the labor market had reduced somewhat. The summer 2002 edition of the NACE quarterly publication *Salary Survey* reported decreases in starting salaries in many sectors, due to reduced demand by employers and increased competition among new graduates. In the business disciplines, the most severe decline hit logistics/materials management graduates, with a 9.1 percent drop in the average offer from the previous year to $39,407. Management information systems graduates experienced a 6.3 percent decrease to $42,705. Business administration starting salaries fell 5.3 percent to $36,429. Technology graduates also felt the pinch. Computer engineers, while still among the highest paid engineering graduates, had a 4.3 percent decrease in average starting salary to $51,587. Electrical engineers faced a 3.4 percent decrease to $50,123. Declines in salary offers were also seen in most of the liberal arts disciplines. With an ongoing need for health care workers, graduate nurses saw an increase of 4.8 percent in starting salaries over the previous year to $38,459.

EMPLOYEE BENEFITS

Private Companies

In 2000 most workers had paid holidays (77 percent) and paid vacations (80 percent). (See Table 6.6.) The pro-portion has gone down somewhat from 1984, when 99 percent had paid holidays and paid vacations.

Only 54 percent of employees were participants in life insurance plans in 2000, and just over a quarter of employees (26 percent) had long-term disability insurance plans. (See Table 6.7.) About half (52 percent) of workers had employer-provided medical care plans in 2000, down dramatically from 97 percent in 1984. Of those with medical coverage in 2000, employers fully paid the premiums for only 32 percent of those with individual coverage plans and 19 percent of those with family coverage. (See Table 6.8.) The average monthly contribution rose from about $12.00 in the mid-1980s to $54.40 for individual coverage in 2000.

State and Local Governments

About three-fourths (73 percent) of employees of state and local governments had paid holidays in 1998. (See Table 6.9.) More than one-third (38 percent) of government workers obtained paid personal leave, and 96 percent received paid sick leave. Also as a benefit, 95 percent of state and local government employees were offered unpaid family leave. Most (89 percent) participated in employer-provided life insurance plans and 86 percent had medical care plans with 51 percent of the participants paying a monthly contribution of $31.94 to the health plan. Most government employees (98 percent) were provided with retirement income benefits.

TYPES OF EMPLOYEES. In 2000 blue-collar and service employees were less likely than other types of employees to participate in employee benefit programs. For example,

TABLE 6.6

Percent of workers with access to selected benefits, by worker and private employer characteristics, 2000

| Characteristics | Paid vacations | Paid holidays | Employer assistance for child care | | | | Adoption assistance | Long-term care insurance | Flexible work place |
			Total [1]	Employer provided funds	On-site child care	Off-site child care			
Total	80	77	4	2	2	1	5	7	5
Worker characteristics:[2]									
Professional, technical, and related employees[3]	88	85	11	4	6	3	12	14	12
Clerical and sales employees[3]	80	80	5	3	1	2	5	74	
Blue-collar and service employees[3]	77	73	2	1	1	([4])	2	4	1
Full time	91	87	5	2	2	1	6	8	5
Part time	39	39	3	1	1	1	2	2	2
Union	93	89	8	6	2	([4])	5	15	3
Nonunion	79	76	4	2	2	1	5	6	5
Establishment characteristics:									
Goods-producing	89	89	2	1	([4])	([4])	6	5	4
Service-producing	78	74	5	2	3	1	4	8	5
1-99 workers	73	70	1	([4])	([4])	1	1	5	2
100 workers or more	89	86	9	4	4	2	9	10	7

| Characteristics | Non-wage cash payments | | | Subsidized commuting | Education assistance | | Travel accident insurance | Health promotion benefits | |
	Nonpro-duction bonuses	Supple-mental unem-ployment benefits	Severance pay		Work related	Non-work related		Wellness programs	Fitness centers
Total	48	1	20	3	38	9	15	18	9
Worker characteristics:[2]									
Professional, technical, and related employees[3]	52	1	35	6	62	19	30	35	19
Clerical and sales employees[3]	48	1	24	3	37	8	15	17	10
Blue-collar and service employees[3]	46	1	12	2	28	6	9	11	4
Full time	51	1	23	3	44	11	17	21	10
Part time	36	([4])	10	1	15	3	9	7	5
Union	38	8	31	2	57	18	23	38	11
Nonunion	49	([4])	19	3	36	8	14	16	9
Establishment characteristics:									
Goods-producing	51	4	21	1	45	14	19	19	10
Service-producing	47	([4])	20	4	36	8	14	17	9
1-99 workers	49	([4])	11	2	26	3	5	6	4
100 workers or more	46	2	32	5	52	17	28	31	16

Note: Data are from the National Compensatation Survey 2000, which covers all 50 States and the District of Columbia. Collection was conducted between February and December 2000. The average reference period was July 2000. Because of rounding, sums of individual items may not equal totals. Where applicable, dash indicates no employees in this category or data do not meet publication criteria.

[1] The total may be less than the sum of individual items because some employees were receiving more than one type of employer assistance for child care.
[2] Employees are classified as working either a full-time or part-time schedule based on the definition used by each establishment. Union workers are those whose wages are determined through collective bargaining.
[3] A classification system including about 480 individual occupations is used to cover all workers in the civilian economy.
[4] Less than 0.5 percent.

SOURCE: "Table 2. Percent of workers with access to selected benefits, by worker and establishment characteristics, private industry, National Compensation Survey, 2000," in *Employee Benefits in Private Industry, 2000,* U.S. Department of Labor, Bureau of Labor Statistics, Washington, DC, July 16, 2002 [Online] http://www.bls.gov/ncs/ebs/sp/ebnr0007.pdf [accessed August 1, 2002]

50 percent of clerical and sales employees, and 64 percent of professional, technical, and related employees had medical care benefits, as compared to 47 percent of blue-collar and service employees. (See Table 6.7.) In regard to paid holidays, nearly three-fourths (73 percent) of the blue-collar and service workers received this benefit, whereas 80 percent of clerical and sales employees and 85 percent of

professional, technical, and related employees were awarded paid holidays. (See Table 6.6.)

Blue-collar and service employees of state and local governments in most cases fared better than other state and local government employees. More of the blue-collar and service workers (92 percent) received paid holidays and

TABLE 6.7

Percent of workers participating in selected benefits, by worker and private employer characteristics, 2000

Characteristics	Retirement benefits			Health care benefits		
	All	Defined benefit	Defined contri-bution	Medical care	Dental care	Vision care
Total	48	19	36	52	29	17
Worker characteristics:[1]						
Professional, technical, and related employees[2]	66	27	53	64	42	24
Clerical and sales employees[2]	50	18	40	50	30	17
Blue-collar and service employees[2]	39	17	27	47	24	15
Full time	55	22	42	61	35	21
Part time	18	6	12	13	6	4
Union	83	69	38	75	53	41
Nonunion	44	14	36	49	27	15
Establishment characteristics:						
Goods-producing	57	–	44	–	33	20
Service-producing	45	18	33	48	28	17
1-99 workers	33	8	27	43	19	10
100 workers or more	65	33	46	61	41	26

Characteristics	Survivor benefits			Disability benefits	
	Life insurance	Accidental death and dismem-berment	Survivor income benefits	Short-term disability	Long-term disability
Total	54	41	2	34	26
Worker characteristics:[1]					
Professional, technical, and related employees[2]	76	58	3	50	51
Clerical and sales employees[2]	52	39	2	32	27
Blue-collar and service employees[2]	47	36	2	28	14
Full time	65	50	2	39	31
Part time	11	8	1	12	4
Union	82	66	6	69	28
Nonunion	51	39	2	30	25
Establishment characteristics:					
Goods-producing	69	58	3	45	31
Service-producing	50	36	2	30	24
1-99 workers	37	24	2	22	13
100 workers or more	75	62	3	47	40

Note: Data are from the National Compensation Survey, 2000, which covers all 50 States and the District of Columbia. Collection was conducted between February and December 2000. The average reference period was July 2000. Because of rounding, sums of individual items may not equal totals. Where applicable, dash indicates no employees in this category or data do not meet publication criteria.
[1] Employees are classified as working either a full-time or part-time schedule based on the definition used by each establishment. Union workers are those whose wages are determined through collective bargaining.
[2] A classification system including about 480 individual occupations is used to cover all workers in the civilian economy.

SOURCE: "Table 1. Percent of workers participating in selected benefits, by worker and establishment characteristics, private industry, National Compensation Survey, 2000," in *Employee Benefits in Private Industry, 2000*, U.S Department of Labor, Bureau of Labor Statistics, Washington, DC, July 16, 2002 [Online] www.bls.gov/ncs/ebs/sp/ebnr0007.pdf [accessed August 1, 2002]

vacations than the white-collar employees, except teachers (86 and 83 percent, respectively). (See Table 6.9.) Less than one-third of the teachers (31 percent) were awarded paid holidays, and only 10 percent got paid vacations. (Teachers are typically paid to work a specific number of days per year.) Health care benefits appear to be a basic benefit for all government workers since about the same proportion of blue-collar and service employees, teachers, and white-collar employees participated in health care benefits.

FIRMS PROVIDING BENEFITS

For more than 50 years, the U.S. Chamber of Commerce has surveyed a cross section of businesses in regard to the benefits offered. The average benefit payment expended by the approximately 600 firms who replied to the survey in 1998 amounted to 37.2 percent of their total payroll, down from 41.3 percent in 1996. In 1965 benefits were 21.5 percent of the payroll.

TABLE 6.8

Percent of participants required to contribute to private-employer-provided medical care benefits and average employee contribution, 2000

	Single Coverage			Family Coverage		
	Employee contributions not required	Employee contributions required	Average[1] flat monthly contribution in dollars	Employee contributions not required	Employee contributions required	Average[1] flat monthly contribution in dollars
Total	32	68	$54.40	19	81	$179.75
Worker characteristics:[2]						
Professional, technical, and related employees[3]	25	75	54.32	15	85	183.51
Clerical and sales employees[3]	28	72	54.14	16	84	187.07
Blue-collar and service employees[3]	38	62	54.63	23	77	172.69
Union	–	–	–	–	–	–
Nonunion	27	73	55.63	13	87	185.79
Full time	31	69	53.93	19	81	180.16
Part time	–	–	–	–	–	–
Establishment characteristics:						
Goods-producing	36	64	57.59	25	75	189.76
Service-producing	30	70	53.34	17	83	176.41
1-99 workers	34	66	60.12	19	81	182.32
100 workers or more	30	70	49.56	20	80	177.47

Note: Data are from the National Compensation Survey, 2000, which covers all 50 States and the District of Columbia. Collection was conducted between February and December 2000. The average reference period was July 2000. Because of rounding, sums of individual items may not equal totals. Where applicable, dash indicates no employees in this category or data do not meet publication criteria.

[1] The average is presented for all covered workers and excludes workers without the plan provision. Averages are for plans stating a flat monthly cost.

[2] Employees are classified as working either a full-time or part-time schedule based on the definition used by each establishment. Union workers are those whose wages are determined through collective bargaining.

[3] A classification system including about 480 individual occupations is used to cover all workers in the civilian economy.

SOURCE: "Table 3. Medical care benefits: Percent of participants required to contribute and average employee contribution, private industry, National Compensation Survey, 2000," in *Employee Benefits in Private Industry, 2000*, U.S. Department of Labor, Bureau of Labor Statistics, Washington, DC, July 16, 2002 [Online] http://www.bls.gov/ncs/ebs/sp/ebnr0007.pdf [accessed August 1, 2002]

Benefits as Percentage of Total Payroll

Table 6.10 breaks down the types of benefits for all employees as a percent of payroll for 1994, 1995, and 1996. Almost 9 percent were legally required payments, such as Social Security, unemployment insurance, and workers' compensation. Medical benefits (about 10 percent) and payment for vacations, holidays, and sick leave (about 10 percent) accounted for one-fifth of the percentage of payroll. Legally required benefits as a percentage of payrolls for hourly workers were slightly more than for salaried workers, while retirement benefit percentages were significantly higher for salaried workers. (See Table 6.11.)

Distribution of Benefit Spending

Figure 6.2 shows how the benefit dollars were spent in 1996. More than one-fifth of all benefit dollars went to legally required benefits; another 23.2 percent were for medical benefits. Companies paid almost one-fourth of benefit dollars for paid leave and holidays. Life insurance took only 1 percent of the benefit dollars.

According to a U.S. Chamber of Commerce survey, average annual benefits per employee amounted to $14,086 in 1996. (See Figure 6.3.) The 802 firms responding to the survey paid an average annual wage of $29,371; this, along with payroll taxes and more, made the total gross payroll $34,109. Benefits were 41.3 percent of the total gross payroll. The entire pay package for an employee was $43,457, of which 32.4 percent were employee benefits. (See Figure 6.4.)

Based upon its 1996 questionnaire, the survey estimated that benefits amounted to a total of $1.5 trillion. In 1975 benefits were $244.4 billion, 30 percent of the gross payroll. Some of the increase came from rising health insurance costs, as well as paid vacations and holidays, but almost half came from the growth of mandated benefits, such as Social Security.

Employee Benefits Policy at the Beginning of the Twenty-first Century

Initiatives that were pursued by the U.S. government during 2000 promise to have an impact on the realm of employee benefits. Debate concerned a policy that will

TABLE 6.9

Participation in selected employee benefit programs by full-time employees of state and local governments, 1998

Benefit	All employees	White-collar employees, except teachers	Teachers	Blue-collar and service employees
Paid time off:				
Holidays	73	86	31	92
Vacations	67	83	10	92
Personal leave	38	31	55	31
Funeral leave	65	62	61	71
Jury duty leave	95	95	96	95
Military leave	76	81	60	82
Family leave	4	3	4	5
Unpaid family leave	95	95	94	96
Disability benefits[1]:				
Paid sick leave	96	94	97	97
Short-term disability	20	20	15	24
Long-term disability insurance	34	36	38	28
Survivor benefits:				
Life insurance	89	90	88	88
Accidental death and dismemberment	58	57	63	56
Survivor income benefits	1	1	1	1
Health care benefits:				
Medical care	86	86	86	86
Dental care	60	59	62	60
Vision care	43	41	40	48
Outpatient prescription drug coverage	84	85	82	84

TABLE 6.10

Types of benefits for all employees as a percent of payroll, 1994–96

	Benefits as a percent of payroll All employees		
	Year		
Types of Benefits	1994	1995	1996
Legally required payments	8.9	8.9	8.8
Retirement and savings	7.2	7.5	6.3
Life insurance and death benefits	0.4	0.4	0.4
Medical and medically related benefits	10.4	10.5	9.6
Paid rest periods, lunch periods, etc.	2.2	2.2	3.7
Payment for vacations, holidays, sick leave, etc.	9.7	10.2	10.2
Miscellaneous benefits	1.9	2.2	2.3
Total	**40.7**	**42.0**	**41.3**

SOURCE: "Benefits as a Percent of Payroll, All Employees," in *Employee Benefits,* U.S. Chamber of Commerce, Washington, DC, 1997

TABLE 6.9

Participation in selected employee benefit programs by full-time employees of state and local governments, 1998 [CONTINUED]

Benefit	All employees	White-collar employees, except teachers	Teachers	Blue-collar and service employees
Retirement income benefits:				
All retirement[2]	98	98	98	98
Defined benefit	90	89	92	91
Defined contribution[3]	14	15	11	14
Savings and thrift	5	5	1	6
Money purchase pension	10	11	9	10
Simplified employee pension	(4)	(4)	-	(4)
Cash or deferred arrangements:				
With employer contributions	13	14	10	13
Salary reduction	6	6	5	7
Savings and thrift	4	5	1	6
Money purchase pension	1	(4)	3	1
Other[5]	7	9	5	7
No employer contributions	22	22	25	19

Notes: Only current employees are counted as participants. Participants in insurance and retirement benefits have met minimum length-of-service requirements and paid any required employee share of the benefit cost. Participants in all other benefits include all employees in occupations offered the benefit.

Employee benefit programs in this survey almost always include those sponsored by employers, who pay some share of the cost. Except for unpaid family leave, postretirement medical care and life insurance, dependent life insurance, supplemental life insurance, and some salary reduction plans, benefits for which the employees pay the full cost are excluded from the survey.

Because of rounding, sums of individual items may not equal totals. Where applicable, dash indicates no employees in this category.

[1] The definitions for paid sick leave and short-term disability (previously sickness and accident insurance) were changed for the 1995 survey. Paid sick leave now only includes plans that either specify a maximum number of days per year or unlimited days. Short-term disability now includes all insured, self-insured, and state-mandated plans available on a per disability basis as well as the unfunded per disability plans previously reported as sick leave. Sickness and accident insurance, reported in years prior to the 1995 survey, only included insured, self-insured, and state-mandated plans providing per disability benefits at less than full pay.
[2] Includes defined benefit pension plans and defined contribution retirement plans. The total is less than the sum of the individual items because many employees participated in both types of plans.
[3] The total is less than the sum of the individual items because some employees participated in more than one type of plan.
[4] Less than 0.5 percent.
[5] Includes required contributions made to money purchase pension plans on a pretax basis.

SOURCE: "Table 1. Summary: Participation in selected employee benefit programs, full-time employees, State and local governments, 1998," in *Employeee Benefits in State and Local Governments, 1998,* Bulletin 2531, U.S. Department of Labor, Bureau of Labor Statistics, Washington, DC, December 2000 [Online] www.bls.gov/ncs/ebs/sp/ebbl0018.pdf [accessed August 1, 2002]

---

finance voluntary family leave for employees with funds from unemployment insurance. The new policy, crafted by the Federal Department of Labor, will allow states to use unemployment insurance trust funds to pay for employees taking leave for instances like the birth or the adoption of a child. According to the Employment Policy Foundation (EPF), a research group in Washington, D.C., half of employees receive full pay during these leaves and an additional one of five employees receive partial pay on such leaves. The EPF argues that the policy would cause state unemployment insurance trust funds to decrease below solvency levels by 2003. Additionally, the group projects that payroll taxes will need to be increased by 145 percent to implement the policy. According to the EPF, the cost of running the unemployment insurance system will increase by two times.

Congressional debate concerning legislation (the Norwood-Dingell Bill, H.R. 2723) that had the capacity to

TABLE 6.11

Comparison of benefits for salaried workers with hourly paid employees, 1996

	Benefits as a % of payroll		
	Salaried	Hourly	Difference
Total	42.9	41.2	+1.7
Legally required	8.3	8.9	-0.6
Retirement	10.6	6.0	+4.6
Life insurance	0.6	0.3	+0.3
Medically related	8.6	9.7	-1.1
Paid rest periods*		4.0	
Payment for time not worked	12.4	10.0	+2.4
Miscellaneous	2.5	2.3	+0.2

*Since salaried workers are not paid strictly on time, payments for rest periods are not used for salaried workers

SOURCE: "Comparison of Benefits for Salaried Workers with Hourly Paid Employees," in *Employee Benefits,* U.S. Chamber of Commerce, Washington, DC, 1997

FIGURE 6.2

How the benefit dollars were spent, 1996

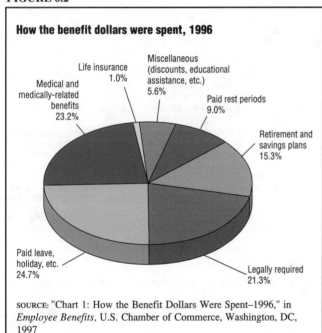

SOURCE: "Chart 1: How the Benefit Dollars Were Spent–1996," in *Employee Benefits,* U.S. Chamber of Commerce, Washington, DC, 1997

FIGURE 6.3

Average annual employee benefits and earnings, 1996

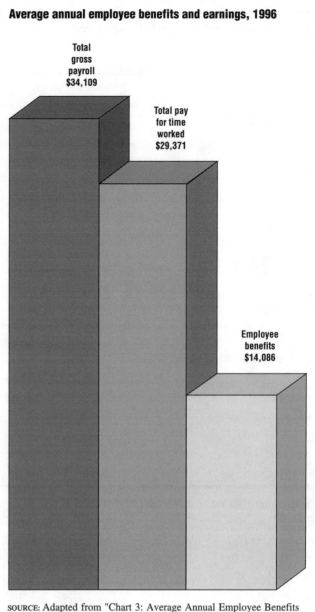

SOURCE: Adapted from "Chart 3: Average Annual Employee Benefits and Earnings, 1996," in *Employee Benefits,* U.S. Chamber of Commerce, Washington, DC, 1997

greatly impact employer-sponsored health insurance continued through mid-2000. The bill will make it possible for employees to sue health plans, insurers, and employers for personal injury or death under state tort law. It was felt such legislation would increase employers' costs by an estimated $16.7 billion per year. Employers who were surveyed noted that these rising costs would result in reduced benefits coverage and lower wage increases. The bill, with amendments, was passed by the House and was joined to Senate bill 1052 to become the Bipartisan Patient Protection Act in 2001. Further amendments protected employers from being sued and required a series of exhaustive reviews before a patient can sue a health care provider.

EMPLOYER-SPONSORED HEALTH INSURANCE

Health insurance became a major issue during the late 1990s. As a result, many employees do not change jobs because they fear losing their health coverage. Welfare recipients often stay on welfare to avoid losing Medicaid coverage. If they take a job, it may not offer health insurance.

Health care has been debated at all levels of government. As of 1995, 45 states had passed legislation regulating the small-employer health insurance market, and 44 states included premium-rate restrictions as part of reforms. Almost all reforms included portability of health insurance (in which employees who had coverage at their previous place of employment are immediately eligible at their next jobs) and preexisting condition limitations (in which an insurer could not deny coverage because of a preexisting physical ailment). Since the passage of the 1996 Health Care Portability and Accountability Act (PL 104-191), such reforms apply to all states.

While Congress was debating the 1993 Health Security Act (which failed to pass), the President's Task Force on Health Care Reform identified a number of unanswered questions on employer-sponsored health insurance. The *National Employer Health Insurance Survey (NEHIS)* was developed to gather data for policymakers and researchers to use in developing and evaluating alternative health care policies.

Employer-sponsored health insurance is a major source of private health care coverage in the United States. At the end of 1993, 40 percent of private sector establishments, employing 80.3 percent of all private workers, offered health insurance to their employees. (See Table 6.12.) About 56 percent participated in the employer-sponsored health plans. (The *NEHIS* found that 99 percent of public employees had health insurance available at their jobs.) By 2000 two-thirds of all American employees obtained employer-sponsored health insurance.

Firm size was one of the most important determinants of whether a business offered health insurance. One-third (33.2 percent) of firms with less than ten employees offered health insurance, compared to 95.7 percent of establishments with 100 or more employees. (See Table 6.12 and Table 6.13.) The percent of establishments offering health insurance at the end of 1993 varied widely by state, ranging from 40 percent in Montana to 86 percent in Hawaii. Most of the variation across states occurred among firms with fewer than 50 employees.

Types of Establishments

Table 6.13 and Figure 6.5 show that the provision of health insurance also varies by type of industry. Over 60 percent of private establishments in mining; transportation, communication, and utilities; wholesale trade; and finance, insurance, and real estate offered health benefits to workers. Employers in agriculture, forestry, fishing, and in construction were least likely to offer health benefits to employees.

The seasonality of agricultural workers and the contractual nature (involving site-specific jobs) of construction workers may discourage these employers from offering health benefits. Agricultural and construction establishments were also more likely to be small businesses. Finally, these trades often employ less-educated workers and recent immigrants who are less likely to expect or ask for health coverage. Only 51.3 percent of service establishments and 43.6 percent of retail trade establish-

FIGURE 6.4

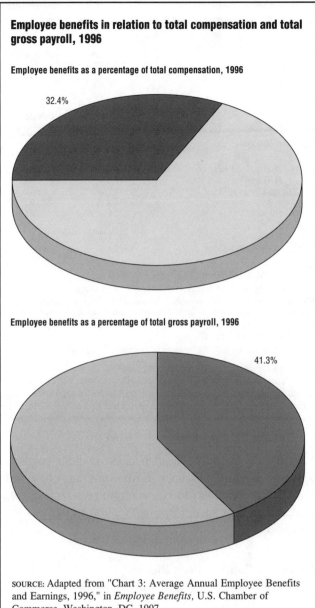

Employee benefits in relation to total compensation and total gross payroll, 1996

Employee benefits as a percentage of total compensation, 1996

32.4%

Employee benefits as a percentage of total gross payroll, 1996

41.3%

SOURCE: Adapted from "Chart 3: Average Annual Employee Benefits and Earnings, 1996," in *Employee Benefits,* U.S. Chamber of Commerce, Washington, DC, 1997

ments offered health insurance. (See Table 6.13.) Retail and service industries likely offered less health insurance because they tend to be smaller businesses, often employing many part-time workers, low-wage workers, and recent immigrants.

Workforce Characteristics

The likelihood of a firm offering health benefits depends not only on employer characteristics, such as size, industry, age, and corporate structure of the firm, but also on employee demand for health benefits. Employer-sponsored health insurance is attractive because it is the least expensive way to obtain health insurance. Employees with lower incomes, however, may not even be able to afford to pay the employee share of the premium. Thus

TABLE 6.12

Private establishments offering health insurance and private employees enrolled in employers' health plans, by firm size, 1993

	Private establishments[1]			Private employees			
Firm size[2]	Number of establishments	Percent distribution	Percent offering health insurance	Number of employees	Percent distribution	Percent working in establishments that offer health insurance	Percent enrolled in employer's health plan
Total, United States	**11,210,800**	**100.0**	**40.0**	**103,257,100**	**100.0**	**80.3**	**56.1**
1 employee (SENE's[3])	4,934,000	44.0	25.2	4,934,000	4.8	25.2	25.2
SENE's 18–64 years	4,456,600	39.8	27.9	4,456,600	4.3	27.9	27.9
SENE's 65 years and over	477,400	4.3	[4]	477,400	0.5	[4]	[4]
2 or more employees	6,276,800	56.0	51.6	98,323,100	95.2	83.1	57.6
2–9	3,914,400	34.9	33.2	15,725,700	15.2	39.2	25.8
10–24	870,800	7.8	67.1	10,726,800	10.4	68.8	44.3
25–99	596,400	5.3	83.0	16,250,000	15.7	84.2	53.8
100–999	406,800	3.6	94.6	20,910,700	20.3	95.9	65.0
1,000 or more	488,400	4.4	96.7	34,710,000	33.6	99.3	73.4

[1] Establishments are defined as single business locations.

[2] Number of employees nationwide as reported by respondent.

[3] Self-employed with no employee (SENE) businesses. For these businesses, those who directly purchase health insurance for themselves or those who obtain health insurance through union, association, or business arrangements were considered as "offering health insurance."

[4] Since virtually all SENE's 65 years old or older are covered by Medicare, other supplementary health plans (for example, Medigap) that were privately purchased were not counted as "offering health insurance."

Note: Estimates in this table are based on a December 31, 1993, reference period. Figures may not add to totals because of rounding.

SOURCE: Karen Allen and Christina Park, "Table 2. Number and percent distribution of private establishments and percent offering health insurance, and number and percent distribution of employees and percent of employees in establishments offering health insurance and percent enrolled in employer's health plan by firm size: United States, 1993," in *Health Insurance Coverage for the Self-Employed with No Employees,* U.S. Department of Health and Human Services, Centers for Disease Control and Prevention, National Center for Health Statistics, Hyattsville, MD, 1999

they may choose not to enroll in, or even ask for, employer-sponsored health insurance. Firms with many low-wage employees and fewer full-time employees tended not to have health insurance. Firms with union employees were most likely to have insurance.

Employee Contributions Rising

By the late twentieth century, employees were paying more for their medical insurance than ever before. The proportion of those required to pay more rose between 1991 and 2000. In 1991, 51 percent of the employees who purchased medical care coverage through their employers were required to contribute for single coverage and more than two-thirds (69 percent) paid for family coverage. By 2000, two of three (68 percent) full-time employees with medical insurance contributed to the cost of single coverage, with the employer picking up the balance. (See Table 6.8.) More than four-fifths (81 percent) of employees contributed to the cost of family coverage.

Blue-collar and service workers were less likely to contribute towards either single or family coverage than their white-collar counterparts. In 2000, 62 percent of blue-collar and service workers helped pay for single coverage, and 77 percent contributed to family coverage. (See Table 6.8.) Among white-collar workers, 75 percent contributed towards single coverage, and 85 percent did so for family coverage. In 2000 average monthly employee

contributions were $54.40 for single coverage and over $179.75 for family coverage.

PARTICIPATION IN SAVINGS AND THRIFT PLANS

The 1998 Survey of Consumer Finances, prepared by the Federal Reserve Board, showed that from 1995 to 1998, the mean or average net worth of Americans rose for all income groups except the lowest. The greatest gain was for families with incomes of $100,000 or more, a group likely to have had large gains in the stock market. Continuing the trend from earlier years, ownership of tax-deferred retirement accounts, such as Individual Retirement Accounts (IRAs), Keogh accounts, and 401(k) plans rose from 45.2 percent of families in 1995 to 48.8 percent in 1998. In addition to tax-deferred accounts, many working families also have defined-benefit plans, which typically provide an annuity income at retirement. The amount is based on the employees' salaries and years of service.

In 2000, according to the BLS report *Employee Benefits in Private Industry,* 48 percent of employees in private industry had retirement benefits of at least one type, either a defined-benefit plan (19 percent) or a defined-contribution plan (36 percent). (See Table 6.7.) Approximately 7 percent had both types of coverage.

In regard to savings and thrift plans, such as the 401(k), employee contributions are made with pretax

TABLE 6.13

Percent of private establishments offering health insurance by firm size, according to selected characteristics, 1993

Establishment characteristics	All firm sizes	Less than 10 employees	10-24 employees	25-99 employees	100 or more employees	Less than 50 employees	50 or more employees
				Firm size[1]			
			Percent of establishments offering health insurance[2]				
United States	51.6	33.2	67.1	83.0	95.7	42.2	94.3
Industry group							
Agriculture, forestry, and fishing	30.2	21.8	60.9	85.5	93.6	29.1	84.7
Mining	67.3	40.4	87.8	98.0	99.2	53.2	98.7
Construction	40.4	31.7	62.9	80.0	94.5	37.6	91.5
Manufacturing	60.8	36.8	75.5	89.3	99.2	49.8	97.4
Transportation, communication, and utilities	65.8	41.0	75.4	86.4	97.6	52.3	95.6
Wholesale trade	64.9	43.3	79.9	94.5	99.2	55.6	98.8
Retail trade	43.6	22.5	48.1	69.3	95.5	29.9	93.2
Finance, insurance, and real estate	64.8	38.9	85.1	96.2	97.6	49.9	97.4
Services	51.3	36.9	70.4	82.0	91.5	45.4	90.5
Ownership							
For profit	52.3	34.3	68.0	83.2	97.1	43.1	95.4
Incorporated	66.0	45.2	73.0	85.7	97.5	55.6	96.3
Unincorporated	28.4	23.6	47.2	64.1	90.8	26.2	84.5
Nonprofit	66.1	48.6	70.5	86.5	89.2	58.0	89.9
Other	65.3	37.8	76.6	94.1	89.3	52.1	91.2
Age of firm							
Less than 5 years	34.8	26.8	48.2	68.2	91.1	31.3	88.5
5-9 years	41.2	29.7	59.0	75.8	92.5	36.4	89.0
10-24 years	50.0	35.7	70.0	83.3	94.4	44.4	93.2
25 years or more	71.8	45.7	78.8	90.8	97.0	58.1	96.3
Location of establishments in firm							
1 location only	40.9	33.1	66.8	80.5	92.2	39.7	89.9
2 or more locations, all in same State	73.5	35.4	66.8	85.7	94.4	62.2	92.4
2 or more locations, multiple States	93.0	54.9	78.7	87.7	96.8	74.5	96.4
Metropolitan area indicator							
Metropolitan area	53.7	34.9	69.0	83.4	96.0	44.2	94.6
Nonmetropolitan area	43.7	27.7	59.0	81.5	94.3	35.3	92.8
Percent of employees that are full-time							
Less than 25 percent	26.6	10.7	20.0	52.5	84.7	15.6	79.9
25-49 percent	41.0	23.0	46.4	64.4	92.0	29.6	89.3
50-74 percent	43.5	27.9	63.0	78.0	95.4	34.7	94.0
75 percent or more	59.4	40.0	77.7	90.2	97.7	50.6	96.7
Presence of union employees							
No union employees	51.9	34.7	67.9	83.4	95.2	43.6	93.8
Has union employees	84.0	62.1	85.7	97.0	98.5	74.7	98.2
Percent of low-wage employees[3]							
50 percent or more of employees are low-wage	25.2	15.4	26.9	49.4	83.9	18.5	79.7
50 percent or more of employees are not low-wage	58.3	40.9	74.0	88.2	96.5	50.8	95.5

[1] Number of employees nationwide as reported by respondent.

[2] An establishment is defined as a business at a single physical location.

[3] Low-wage employees earned less than $5 per hour or less than $10,000 per year.

SOURCE: "Table 1. Percent of private establishments offering health insurance by firm size, according to selected characteristics: United States, 1993," in *Employer-Sponsored Health Insurance,* Centers for Disease Control and Prevention, National Center for Health Statistics, Hyattsville, MD, 1997

dollars. This means the employee's taxable income is reduced by the amount of the contribution. However, taxes are deferred, not eliminated. When the employee starts withdrawing funds from the plan, taxes must be paid on the pretax contributions, any employer-matching funds, and any earnings on these contributions.

All savings and thrift plans require a basic employee contribution, which may be matched by the employer. However, not all employers make matching contributions. Many plans allow an additional contribution by the employee in excess of the maximum amount matched by the employer. This is called a voluntary employee contribution.

Who Participates?

The BLS *Employee Benefits in Private Industry, 2000* examined the relationship between selected savings and thrift plan provisions and employee participation in such plans. Overall, 69 percent of employees participated in available programs. (See Table 6.7.) Professional, technical and related (66 percent), and clerical and sales employees (50 percent) were more likely than blue-collar and service employees (39 percent) to participate in such plans.

Laws related to employee retirement plans are likely to change, following the 2001 accounting scandal and subsequent bankruptcy of Enron Corporation, which left

FIGURE 6.5

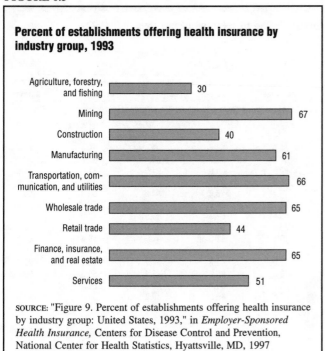

Percent of establishments offering health insurance by industry group, 1993

Industry	Percent
Agriculture, forestry, and fishing	30
Mining	67
Construction	40
Manufacturing	61
Transportation, communication, and utilities	66
Wholesale trade	65
Retail trade	44
Finance, insurance, and real estate	65
Services	51

SOURCE: "Figure 9. Percent of establishments offering health insurance by industry group: United States, 1993," in *Employer-Sponsored Health Insurance,* Centers for Disease Control and Prevention, National Center for Health Statistics, Hyattsville, MD, 1997

employee 401(k) accounts ravaged. Many Enron employees, with management's encouragement, were heavily invested in their own company. A large number of former Enron employees lost their jobs and their retirement savings. Congress began to discuss restricting the percentage of an employee's 401(k) that can be invested in the employee's own company.

CHAPTER 7
GETTING A JOB

A journey of a thousand miles begins with a single step.

— A Chinese proverb

Being out of work, changing careers, or trying to get one's first job can be a very scary experience. It takes some people a great deal of time and effort to find a job they will enjoy. Others may walk right into an ideal employment situation. In any case, the journey to a career begins with the single step of doing something to get a job.

Many job counselors liken the job-hunting process to a race. They say to "get on the mark" by researching the job market. Next, "get ready" with the information and training needed to work in a particular field. Then "get set" by finding out about possible employers. Finally "go" for the job, by putting together a good resume. A job seeker should also be prepared to meet prospective employers with courteous manners, a good appearance, and sound interview skills.

SOURCES OF CAREER INFORMATION

Personal Contacts

Families and friends can be extremely helpful in providing career information. While they may not always have the information needed, they may know other knowledgeable people and be able to put the job seeker in touch with them. These contacts can lead to an "information interview," talking to someone who provides information about a company or career. This person should have the experience to describe how he or she trained for the job, received promotions, and likes or dislikes the job. Not only can the person advise what to do, he or she can advise what not to do.

Libraries and Career Centers

Libraries have a lot of information about careers and job training. Begin with the card catalog or computer listings under "vocations" or "careers" and then look under

specific fields of work. For instance, for those who like working with animals, there are veterinarians and veterinarian assistants, zoologists, animal trainers, breeders, groomers, and many other occupations that involve working with animals. Trade publications and magazines describe and discuss many kinds of work in various fields.

In addition the Bureau of Labor Statistics of the U.S. Department of Labor publishes the *Occupational Outlook Handbook,* which describes about 250 occupations in detail. School career centers often offer individual counseling and testing, guest speakers, field trips, and career days. Information in career guidance materials should be current. It is wise to find a number of sources since one resource might glamorize the occupation, overstate the earnings, or exaggerate the demand for workers in the field.

Counselors

Counselors are professionals trained to help their clients discover their strengths and weaknesses, evaluate their goals and values, and determine what they want in a career. Counselors can be found in:

• High school guidance offices,

• Placement offices in private vocational/technical schools,

• College career planning and placement offices,

• Vocational rehabilitation agencies,

• Counseling service offices offered by community organizations,

• Private counseling agencies, and

• State employment service offices.

The Internet

The Internet provides much of the same job information that is available through libraries, career centers, and guidance offices. However, no single network or resource

TABLE 7.1

Where to learn about job openings

- Personal contacts
- School career planning and placement offices
- Classified ads
  - National and local newspapers
  - Professional journals
  - Trade magazines
- Internet networks and resources
- State employment service offices
- Federal Government
- Professional associations
- Labor unions
- Private employment agencies and career consultants
- Community agencies

SOURCE: "Where to learn about job openings," in *Occupational Outlook Handbook, 2002-03 Edition,* U.S. Department of Labor, Bureau of Labor Statistics, Washington, DC, 2002

will contain all the desired information. As in a library search, one must look through various lists by field or discipline or by using particular keywords.

Organizations

Professional societies, trade associations, labor unions, business firms, and educational institutions offer a variety of free or inexpensive career material. *The Guide to American Directories, The Directory of Directories* and *The Encyclopedia of Associations,* found at local libraries, are useful resources. Trade organizations are particularly important if one already has a job and is seeking another or fears being "downsized" by one's present employer.

Education and Training Information

Every job requires some kind of training, even one that uses simple, everyday skills. Most people get some kind of training in life during the process of growing up. Most jobs, however, require more training.

Free training may be available through vocational courses in public schools, local branches of state employment offices, or apprenticeship programs. Some occupations require a few months of training, while others may take many years of education and be very costly. Physicians, for instance, may spend as many as 15 years and many tens of thousands of dollars to learn a specialty in medicine.

Colleges, schools, and training institutes readily reply to requests for information about their programs. Professional and trade associations have lists of schools that offer career preparation in their fields. Information on financial aid for study or training is available from a variety of sources—high school guidance counselors, college financial aid officers, banks and credit unions, the Internet, and state and federal governments. Directories and guides to sources of student financial aid can be found in guidance offices and public libraries.

JOB SEARCH METHODS

Table 7.1 provides sources of job listings.

Personal Contacts—Networking

A good place to start collecting information is from family, friends, and acquaintances. One should not be afraid to ask friends or relatives if they know of an available job. Many people get jobs through personal contacts. Although it may be difficult to ask, often a friend or relative will be glad to put one in touch with someone else who can help. Such networking can lead to meeting a person who is hiring for his or her firm or who knows of specific job openings.

Classified Ads

The "Help Wanted" advertisements in newspapers list hundreds of jobs. However, these listings do not contain all of the job openings in the area, and they usually do not give all of the pertinent information about the available positions. Many offer little or no description of the jobs, working conditions, or pay. Some advertisements do not identify the employer. They may simply give a post office box for sending a resume. This makes follow-up inquiries very difficult. Furthermore, some advertisements are for employment agencies rather than actual employment opportunities. Some helpful hints on using classified advertisements include:

- Do not rely solely on the classified ads to find a job; follow other leads as well.

- Answer ads promptly since openings may be filled quickly, even before the ad stops appearing in the paper.

- Read the ads every day, particularly the Sunday edition, which usually includes the most listings.

- Know that "no experience necessary" ads often signal low wages, poor working conditions, or commission work.

- Keep a record of all ads responded to, including the specific skills, educational background, and personal qualifications required for the positions.

Internet Networks and Resources

A variety of information is available on the Internet, including job listings and job search resources and techniques. Internet resources are available 7 days a week, 24 hours a day. No single network or resource will contain all of the information on employment or career opportunities, so be prepared to search a bit. Job listings may be posted by field or discipline, so begin the search by using keywords.

A good place to start the job search is at *America's Job Bank* (http://www.ajb.dni.us/). *America's Job Bank,* run by the U.S. Department of Labor's Employment and Training Administration, provides information on preparing resumes and using the Internet for job searches. It also discusses trends in the U.S. job market and, as of July 2002, lists about 1 million job openings. Job seekers also can post their resumes on the site for potential employers. As of 2002 there are also a number of private Web sites such as the *Monster Network* (http://www.monster.com) or *HotJobs* (http://www.hotjobs.com) that can assist in the job search.

Public Employment Services

States operate employment services, sometimes called the Job Service, in coordination with the U.S. Employment Service of the U.S. Department of Labor. As of July 2002 the Federal Trade Commission's Web site reported that there were about 1,700 local, full-time, full-service offices to help job seekers find positions and employers find qualified workers at no cost to themselves. Telephone listings under "Job Service" or "Employment" in the state government telephone listings will show the nearest offices.

Private Employment Agencies

These agencies can be helpful, but they are in business to make money. Most agencies operate on a commission basis, with the fee dependent upon a percentage of the salary paid to a successful applicant. The newly hired employee or the hiring company will have to pay a sizable fee. Job seekers should find out the exact cost and who is responsible for paying the fees before using the service.

College Career Planning and Placement Offices

College placement offices facilitate job placement for their students and alumni. They set up appointments and provide facilities for interviews with recruiters. Placement offices usually list part-time, temporary, and summer jobs offered on campus. They also list jobs in regional business, nonprofit, and government organizations. Students can receive career counseling, testing, and job search advice and can also use career resource libraries maintained by placement offices. Access to these resources is usually included in tuition fees.

Community Agencies

Many nonprofit organizations, including churches, synagogues, and vocational rehabilitation agencies, offer counseling, career development, and job placement services. These are often targeted to a particular group, such as women, youth, minorities, ex-offenders, or older workers.

Employers

It is possible to apply directly to employers without a referral. Potential employers can be found in the Yellow Pages, directories of local chambers of commerce, other publications that provide information about employers, and the Internet.

TABLE 7.2

What usually goes into a resume

- Name, address, e-mail address, and telephone number.
- Employment objective. State the type of work or specific job you are seeking.
- Education, including school name and address, dates of attendance, curriculum, and highest grade completed or degree awarded. Consider including any courses or areas of focus that might be relevant to the position.
- Experience, paid and volunteer. For each job, include the job title, name and location of employer, and dates of employment. Briefly describe your job duties.
- Special skills, computer skills, proficiency in foreign languages, achievements, and membership in organizations.
- References, only when requested.
- Keep it short; only one page for less experienced applicants.
- Avoid long paragraphs; use bullets to highlight key skills and accomplishments.
- Have a friend review your resume for any spelling or grammatical errors.
- Print it on high quality paper.

SOURCE: "What Usually Goes into a Resume," in *Occupational Outlook Handbook, 2002-03 Edition*, U.S. Department of Labor, Bureau of Labor Statistics, Washington, DC, 2002

APPLYING FOR A JOB

Resumes and Application Forms

Sending a resume (summary of a job applicant's previous employment, education, and skills) and filling out an application form are two ways to provide employers with written evidence of one's qualifications. Some employers prefer that prospective employees present a resume, while others require a completed application.

There are many ways to organize a resume. A variety of books on the topic are available in local libraries and bookstores. The Internet is also a good source for finding resume-writing techniques. See Table 7.2 for the basic information that is included in a resume. The company to which the job seeker is applying usually supplies an application form, which should be filled out completely and correctly.

Cover Letters

A cover letter is sent with a resume or application form as a way to introduce the job seeker to prospective employers. It should capture the employer's attention, follow a business-letter format, and include the following information:

- The name and address of the specific person to whom the letter is addressed,

- The reason for the applicant's interest in the company and type of job the applicant is seeking,

- A brief list of qualifications for the position, including education, job experience, and unpaid experience,

- Any special skills,

- References (if requested),

- A request for an interview, and

- Home and work phone number.

TABLE 7.3

Job interview tips

Preparation:
- Learn about the organization.
- Have a specific job or jobs in mind.
- Review your qualifications for the job.
- Prepare answers to broad questions about yourself.
- Review your resume.
- Practice an interview with a friend or relative.
- Arrive before the scheduled time of your interview.

Personal Appearance:
- Be well groomed.
- Dress appropriately.
- Do not chew gum or smoke.

The Interview:
- Relax and answer each question concisely.
- Respond promptly.
- Use good manners. Learn the name of your interviewer and shake hands as you meet.
- Use proper English—avoid slang.
- Be cooperative and enthusiastic.
- Ask questions about the position and the organization.
- Thank the interviewer when you leave and, as a follow up, in writing.

Test (if employer gives one):
- Listen closely to instructions.
- Read each question carefully.
- Write legibly and clearly.
- Budget your time wisely and don't dwell on one question.

Information to Bring to an Interview:
- Social Security card.
- Government-issed identification (driver's license).
- Resume. Although not all employers require applicants to bring a resume, you should be able to furnish the interviewer information about your education, training, and previous employment.
- References. Employers typically require three references. Get permission before using anyone as a reference. Make sure they will give you a good reference. Try to avoid using relatives.

SOURCE: "Job Interview Tips," in *Occupational Outlook Handbook, 2002-03 Edition,* U.S. Department of Labor, Bureau of Labor Statistics, Washington, DC, 2002

Interviewing

An interview showcases qualifications to an employer. Table 7.3 provides some helpful hints about interviewing. Preparation, personal appearance, and information presented at an interview are all very important, but being prepared is perhaps the most important. Adequate preparation shows that the candidate is knowledgeable and confident and helps the interviewee feel more at ease with answering questions and taking any tests required.

For every interview, a job candidate should be well groomed and appear polished and confident. It is always better to be overdressed than underdressed. Job candidates should never smoke, chew gum, or accept an alcoholic beverage at an interview.

Whether the position is offered or not, it is important that the job seeker follow through with a brief note of thanks to the interviewer. The note can also be another opportunity for the job candidate to "sell" his or her strong qualities. This is a courtesy that leaves a positive impression on a potential employer. If another job becomes available, the interviewer may remember the gracious gesture and approach the candidate about the position.

Testing

Many employers require prospective employees to take skills, drug, alcohol, and/or psychological tests in order to be considered for positions at their companies. Such tests are regulated by state and federal laws, including the Americans with Disabilities Act.

EVALUATING A JOB OFFER

When a job is offered, the job seeker needs to evaluate the offer carefully. There are many issues to be considered. Will the organization be a good place to work? Will the job be interesting? Are the people easy to work with? How are opportunities for advancement? Is the salary fair? Does the employer offer good benefits? Rarely will anyone ever find the perfect job, especially the first time out. A person should be open to a number of possibilities, even those not exactly matching his or her skills.

CHAPTER 8
WORKERS' RIGHTS

Over the past 100 years, federal, state, and local governments have created a body of laws, rules, and regulations to protect the rights of workers. These laws cover many aspects of work. As it is impossible to review all of these elements and the many situations to which they apply, the following covers some of the major work-related laws. Most of this material is based on an article by Larry Drake and Rachel Moskowitz, "Your Rights in the Workplace," *Occupational Outlook Quarterly,* volume 41, number 2, summer, 1997.

WAGES AND HOURS

Passed in 1938, the Fair Labor Standards Act (FLSA-52 Stat 1060) is the most important wage and hour law. It applies to all businesses involved in interstate commerce and established rules covering minimum hourly wages, overtime pay, and the work of children. Many states also have statutes that set higher standards than the FLSA. Employers must abide by the more stringent rules.

The minimum wage was increased to $5.15 an hour on September 1, 1997. With a few minor exceptions, the FLSA requires that workers earning an hourly wage be paid overtime pay at least one and one-half times the regular pay rate for all hours worked in the workweek after the first 40 hours.

The FLSA also contains provisions that regulate the wages at which young people may work and the hours they may work. Employers may pay youth under 20 years of age a minimum wage—$4.25 an hour during their first 90 consecutive calendar days of employment with an employer. Individuals under the age of 16 may work only under certain conditions. Youths 14 and 15 years old may work outside of school hours in various nonmanufacturing, nonmining, nonhazardous jobs. They may work up to 3 hours on a school day or 8 hours on a nonschool day for a total of 18 hours in a school week and 40 hours in a nonschool

week. In addition, work must be performed between the hours of 7 A.M. and 7 P.M., except from June 1 through Labor Day, when evening hours are extended to 9 P.M.

Although the federal minimum wage remains at $5.15 an hour, an initiative called the Living Wage Campaign proposed a national minimum wage rate of $8.00 per hour, or enough to support a family of four at the local poverty level. An attempt in Congress in 2001 to increase the minimum wage to $6.65 did not pass. Even though federal policymakers were debating whether to raise the federal minimum wage $1.00 over two to three years, some state, county, and city governments increased the range to $6.25 to $10.75 in the late 1990s and early 2000s. The Bureau of Labor Statistics reports that as of January 1, 2002, Alaska, California, Connecticut, Delaware, the District of Columbia, Hawaii, Maine, Massachusetts, Oregon, Rhode Island, Vermont, and Washington all had higher minimum wage rates than the federal standard.

FAMILY AND MEDICAL LEAVE

The Family and Medical Leave Act, enacted in 1993, gives employees the right to take up to 12 weeks unpaid leave, for certain circumstances, without losing their jobs. This leave can be for childbirth (either parent), for adoption of a child (either parent), in order to care for an immediate family member with a serious health condition, or if the employee has a serious medical condition.

UNEMPLOYMENT

The Social Security Act of 1935 (49 Stat 620) created a federal unemployment compensation system. Shortly afterward, the federal government empowered states to create their own unemployment systems, which every state subsequently implemented. Along with meeting minimum federal standards each state must determine who is eligible for benefits, how much unemployed workers will receive, and how long the benefits will last.

Unemployment insurance benefits are paid entirely by taxes imposed on employers, except in three states (Alaska, New Jersey, and Pennsylvania), where the employees also contribute to the benefits.

During the late 1990s changes in the economy, workforce, and workplace prompted the U.S. Department of Labor to reassess the unemployment insurance system to better ensure that it meets the needs of the changing U.S. employment arena. The department invited peer comment on unemployment insurance issues. Generally, participants agreed that the program accomplished its goals and provided incentives for the unemployed to return to work. Furthermore, it would continue to fulfill these goals with consistent funding.

However, policy during 2000 was proposed by the Clinton administration that would provide paid employee family leave using unemployment insurance funds. Opponents claimed that such policy could draw any state unemployment insurance programs below solvency and could raise payroll taxes an average of 145 percent. Clinton's proposal went to the House of Representatives as part of HB 5619, but it did not pass.

Benefits

Unemployment insurance pays benefits to qualified workers who are unemployed and looking for work. Most states pay a maximum of 26 weeks of benefits. People may be disqualified from receiving benefits for various reasons, such as voluntarily leaving work without good cause or being fired for misconduct. Another reason is the refusal of suitable work without good cause. "Good cause" must be connected with the job, rather than with the individual's personal life. Also, with few exceptions, workers are not eligible for benefits if their unemployment is caused by a labor dispute.

ON-THE-JOB SAFETY

In 1970 Congress passed the Occupational Safety and Health Act (PL 91-596). This law set up a comprehensive national policy to guarantee workers a safe and healthy workplace. The Labor Department's Occupational Safety and Health Administration (OSHA) enforces this statute.

Under the law, employers must furnish employment "free from recognized hazards" that are "likely to cause death or serious physical harm." OSHA has established hundreds of detailed occupational safety and health standards that regulate specific workplace hazards so employers will know what is required of them. Things covered include personal protective equipment, machine protections, structural protections, fire protection, and protection against hazardous materials, such as flammable gases.

While OSHA has established many required standards, it also issues nonbinding regulations. For example,

in April 1998 OSHA recommended that retail outlets, such as convenience stores with a history of crime, use bulletproof glass or employ at least two clerks at night. It also suggested that such stores keep a minimum amount of cash on hand, use drop safes (the cashier can put money in but cannot take the money out) and security cameras, be well lit, and train workers how to behave during an armed robbery.

OSHA also gives workers the right to information about the kinds of hazards to which they are exposed in the workplace. Workers may be entitled to recover damages if they are harmed by unsafe and unhealthy workplace conditions. In certain rare circumstances, workers can walk off the job rather than expose themselves to an imminently dangerous situation.

At the beginning of the twenty-first century OSHA proposed an ergonomics standard. According to OSHA, 33 percent of all work-related injuries and illnesses are a result of work-related musculoskeletal disorders (MSDs). In 1997 compensation for such injuries comprised $1 out of every $3 spent on workers' compensation. Costs of MSDs were expected to rise from $20 billion to $54 billion per year. Ergonomic programs incorporate seating and office furniture that minimize the occurrence of MSDs such as repetitive stress disorder. The Employment Policy Foundation (EPF) criticized the OSHA proposed standard, claiming that it would cost business up to $100 billion annually and override any benefits. EPF claimed that companies had already made good progress in implementing ergonomic changes, and that the federal proposal was an unwise expenditure of taxpayer dollars.

For young people, workplace safety is covered by FLSA, in addition to the OSHA regulations covering all workers. FLSA prohibits employing minors under age 18 to work at 17 hazardous nonfarm jobs. These prohibited jobs include driving a motor vehicle, being an outside helper on a motor vehicle, operating various power-driven machines, and performing roofing operations. Limited exemptions are provided for apprentices and student-learners under specified conditions.

COMPENSATION FOR WORK-RELATED INJURIES AND ILLNESSES

If a person is injured on the job or becomes ill because of the work environment, he or she will likely come in contact with the workers' compensation program (workers' comp). Workers' comp is an insurance program that pays compensation to injured workers for their lost wage-earning capability. It also pays workers' medical and rehabilitation expenses and provides benefits for dependents of workers who are killed on the job.

This program is financed primarily by insurance premiums paid by employers. Both workers and employers benefit from this program. Workers receive compensation in the event they are injured and unable to work. Employers benefit because the program makes the costs of workers' compensation a predictable business expense that can be included in production costs. Each state administers its own workers' comp programs.

For workers' comp to apply, there needs to be an "injury by accident." Generally, the accident must occur when the person is working. The injured worker and the workers' comp insurance company, or state insurance fund, tries to reach a settlement. If they cannot, there is an appeal process. Many states have a payment schedule that specifies definite amounts for particular injuries. In most cases, workers' comp will pay a worker a weekly amount equal to a percentage of his or her average weekly pay, up to a maximum set by law.

DISCRIMINATION AND HARASSMENT

Employers are not allowed to discriminate on the basis of sex, race, religion, national origin, or disability. Furthermore, they must ensure that workers are not subjected to sexual harassment.

Discrimination

There are many national laws protecting employees from discrimination in the workplace with respect to hiring, compensation, terms, conditions, and privileges of employment. These laws cover employees of all types of businesses, from very large to very small. They also apply to employment agencies and labor organizations.

The Equal Pay Act of 1963 (PL 88-38) establishes that employers cannot pay lower wages to an employee based on gender. Equal pay must be paid to workers for equal work if the jobs they perform require "equal skill, effort, and responsibility and are performed under similar working conditions."

The Civil Rights Act of 1964 (PL 88-352) makes it unlawful for an employer to discriminate against individuals on the basis of race, color, religion, national origin, or sex. This law was amended (PL 95-555) in 1978, making it unlawful for an employer to discriminate on the basis of pregnancy, childbirth, or a related medical condition. This law not only applies to hiring but also to promotion and termination. In 1997 the Supreme Court ruled in *Robinson v. Shell Oil Company* (No. 95-1376) that the Civil Rights Act of 1964 protected workers from retaliation for filing complaints about discrimination on the job. This ruling included forbidding retaliation in the form of a bad job recommendation after the worker is no longer employed.

The Age Discrimination in Employment Act of 1967 (PL 90-202) makes it unlawful for an employer to discriminate against individuals aged 40 or older with respect to hiring, compensation, and employment on the basis of age.

The Americans with Disabilities Act (ADA) of 1990 (PL 101-336) makes it unlawful for an employer to discriminate in hiring, compensating, or employing individuals with disabilities. This law applies to companies that have 15 or more employees. The law requires reasonable accommodation for disabled applicants and employees. For example, if an employee cannot fit his or her wheelchair through the entrance to the workplace, the employer may be required to alter that entrance or provide a different work area. The ADA affected 43 million Americans at the beginning of the twenty-first century.

In November 1999, Congress passed the Ticket to Work and Work Incentives Improvement Act (TWWIIA) to give Americans with disabilities both the incentive and the means to seek employment. In part, this provides assurance to disabled workers that they will not lose their medical insurance if their income or savings exceed certain levels.

State and local laws extend the coverage of the federal statutes in different ways. Some state laws extend federal protections to employers who are covered by those statutes because of their small size, for example. Other states protect against discrimination based on factors not covered by federal law, such as sexual preference.

Sexual Harassment

Workers have the right to be free from sexual harassment—unwelcome sexual advances or conduct—from supervisors and coworkers, as well as from customers and clients. There are two main forms of sexual harassment. One is demanding sexual favors in return for job benefits over which the individual has some control, such as promotions. This is known as quid pro quo sexual harassment. Another type is "hostile work environment" sexual harassment. When individuals use obscene language, post lewd pictures, make unwelcome sexual advances, or talk about sex in an offensive manner, they are creating a hostile work environment.

Sexual harassment is a violation of the 1964 Civil Rights Act, as amended in 1972 (PL 92-261). Under the Civil Rights Act of 1991 (PL 102-166), victims of sexual harassment are entitled to damages for pain and suffering, as well as to lost pay. The Equal Employment Opportunity Commission defines sexual harassment as unwelcome sexual advances, requests for sexual favors, and other verbal or physical conduct of a sexual nature.

THE RIGHT TO JOIN A UNION

The National Labor Relations Act of 1935 (49 Stat 449) guarantees nonsupervisory employees the right to organize a union, choose their own representatives, and bargain collectively with their employer for higher pay, better benefits, improved working conditions, and more relaxed work rules. Workers have the right to join a union if one exists or to help organize one if one does not exist. The law prohibits employers from punishing employees who exercise their right to join a union and participate in union activities. Workers in a company who want to form a union must ask a federal or state agency, such as the National Labor Relations Board, to hold an election to determine if a majority of workers want to be represented by a union.

Workers may be required to join a union after they are hired; such workplaces are called union shops. Twenty-one states have enacted right-to-work laws that prohibit the union shop. This means that to get or hold a job, workers do not have to join a union if one exists. Closed shops, in which only union members in good standing could be hired to begin with, are illegal.

By law, all workers in a bargaining unit are entitled to the benefits gained through union collective bargaining, whether they are union members or not. Nonunion workers employed by a unionized company get the same benefits as union members, even if they do not join the union.

While unions historically represent the working class, they also have a growing presence in professional specialties. As an example, medical doctors began organizing unions during 2000. Their initiative to organize was driven partly by policy that made it possible for patients to sue for malpractice under state laws. As of July 2002, an unresolved issue remains—whether doctors in organized labor unions should have the right to strike.

EMPLOYER TESTING

Employers may administer various tests to potential or current employees in order to determine their fitness to perform the duties of a position. Recently, many companies have introduced testing for the use of drugs and are administering polygraph (lie detector) exams and psychological tests.

Drug and Alcohol Testing

Growing concern over the impact of drug and alcohol abuse in the workplace has led to an increase in the number of employers who test for drug and alcohol abuse. These tests are performed on employees and, increasingly, on job applicants. Workers in some jobs, such as airline pilots, are required by law to submit to drug and alcohol testing, but an increasing number of employers are requiring employees to submit to testing as a condition of employment.

Some programs use mandatory and random testing. Others test only on the basis of reasonable suspicion. Workers in jobs that are particularly related to safety or security concerns are more likely to be tested. Certain workers, such as those who operate airplanes, buses, and large trucks, are required to take a drug and alcohol test upon employment. They also must submit to testing if they have been involved in an accident.

Tyler D. Hartwell, Paul D. Steele, and Nathaniel F. Rodman, in "Workplace Alcohol-Testing Programs: Prevalence and Trends" (*Monthly Labor Review,* Bureau of Labor Statistics, June 1998), surveyed the nation's companies with 50 or more employees in 1993 and 1995 to determine how many tested for alcohol and/or drug abuse. They found that more than twice as many worksites test job applicants for drugs (45.9 percent) than for alcohol (21.7 percent). (See Table 8.1.) When it comes to employees, the figures are closer, with 33.7 percent testing for drugs and 28.4 percent testing for alcohol.

The larger the company, the more likely employees were tested. (See Table 8.2.) Also, alcohol and drug testing varies greatly, depending on the industry. Those working in communications, mining and construction, manufacturing, and wholesale and retail were more likely to be tested than those in finance and services. Those working in the Northeast were less likely to be tested than those living in other regions.

While 48 percent of the companies had drug testing according to the 1993 study, only 24 percent examined all their employees. Fourteen percent tested only job applicants, 4 percent inspected only employees that the Department of Transportation requires be analyzed, 1 percent assessed only safety or security employees, and 6 percent tested various combinations of types of employees.

What happens to job applicants or employees who refuse to take drug tests? That depends on where they work and the state law, if there is one. In many cases refusal to take the test is grounds for not getting a job or being fired.

If a job applicant takes the test and tests positive, he or she may not get the job. If a worker tests positive on a random drug test, treatment and counseling sponsored by the company may be given or employment may be terminated.

These tests have led to controversy throughout the country because many people think the tests invade personal privacy. By 1998, 17 states had some type of regulation to control drug testing in the private sector. Some states ban or restrict random drug testing, while others require that a second, confirmatory drug test be given if the first one is positive. Some states require that the results of these tests be kept confidential, while others limit the type of discipline employers can mete out to employees who fail drug tests.

Polygraph Exams

At one time it was popular among many employers to use polygraph tests on their employees. Many workers resented these tests, and their aversion eventually led a number of

TABLE 8.1

National estimates of alcohol and drug testing among applicants, employees, and combinations of both groups in private nonagricultural worksites, 1995

[In percent]

		Worksite conducts drug testing on applicants		
		Yes	No	Total (alcohol testing)
Worksite conducts alcohol testing on applicants	Yes	20.6 (1.4)	1.1 (.3)	21.7 (1.4)
	No	25.2 (1.4)	53.0 (1.7)	78.3 (1.4)
	Total (drug testing)	45.9 (1.7)	54.1 (1.7)	100.0

More than twice as many worksites test applicants for drugs (45.9 percent) than for alcohol (21.7 percent).

		Worksite conducts drug testing on current employees		
		Yes	No	Total (alcohol testing)
Worksite conducts alcohol testing on current employees	Yes	22.7 (1.4)	5.7 (.8)	28.4 (1.5)
	No	11.0 (1.1)	60.6 (1.7)	71.6 (1.5)
	Total (drug testing)	33.7 (1.6)	66.3 (1.6)	100.0

Slightly more worksites test current employees for drugs (33.7 percent) than for alcohol (28.4 percent).

		Worksite conducts drug testing*		
		Yes	No	Total (alcohol testing)
Worksite conducts alcohol testing	Yes	33.5 (1.6)	2.6 (1.6)	36.0 (1.6)
	No	20.2 (1.4)	43.7 (1.7)	63.9 (1.6)
	Total (drug testing)	53.7 (1.7)	46.3 (1.7)	100.0

*Worksites that test applicants only, current employees only, and both applicants and current employees.
Note: Data in parentheses represent the standard error. When a worksite tests for drugs, it usually also tests for alcohol. Only 2.6 percent of worksites test for alcohol and not drugs. Conversely, many worksites test for drugs and not alcohol (20.2 percent).

SOURCE: Tyler D. Hartwell, Paul D. Steele, and Nathanial F. Rodman, "Exhibit 1. National estimates of alcohol and drug testing among applicants, employees, and combinations of both groups in private nonagricultural worksites, 1995," in "Workplace alcohol-testing programs: prevalence and trends," *Monthly Labor Review*, vol. 121, no. 6, June 1998

TABLE 8.2

National estimates of alcohol testing among private nonagricultural worksites by size, industry, and census region, 1995

[In percent]

	Worksites that test—				Government regulation requires testing, 1995[2]
Characteristic	Applicants 1995	Current employees 1993	Current employees 1995	Applicants and/or employees[1] 1995	
All worksites	21.7 (1.4)	20.3 (1.0)	[3]28.4 (1.5)	36.0 (1.6)	31.7 (2.5)
Worksite size					
50–99 employees	19.2 (2.4)	15.8 (1.6)	[3]25.0 (2.6)	31.4 (2.8)	33.7 (5.1)
100–249 employees	19.7 (2.3)	19.3 (1.6)	[3]26.8 (2.5)	33.6 (2.7)	26.2 (3.9)
250–999 employees	26.5 (3.0)	28.4 (2.0)	34.1 (3.2)	42.9 (3.3)	33.8 (4.9)
1,000 employees or more	33.3 (5.0)	37.5 (3.5)	40.0 (5.2)	55.2 (5.6)	38.3 (6.1)
Industry					
Manufacturing	33.7 (2.8)	25.1 (1.9)	[3]38.1 (2.8)	49.5 (2.9)	24.3 (3.5)
Wholesale/retail	19.4 (3.5)	18.0 (2.5)	26.3 (3.9)	33.1 (4.1)	37.3 (7.4)
Communications, utilities, and transportation	30.3 (4.1)	32.3 (3.0)	[3]47.4 (4.6)	52.7 (4.7)	67.7 (6.5)
Finance, insurance, and real estate	5.8 (1.4)	6.8 (1.3)	7.3 (2.3)	11.0 (2.5	11.6 (6.0)
Mining and construction	29.3 (4.1)	26.6 (3.4)	[3]39.0 (4.6)	45.5 (4.8)	46.3 (6.4)
Services	13.3 (2.3)	16.1 (1.7)	20.2 (2.7)	26.5 (3.1)	21.4 (5.3)
Region					
Northeast	19.2 (3.1)	11.7 (1.6)	[3]20.1 (2.9)	27.2 (3.4)	39.2 (7.1)
Midwest	24.5 (2.7)	21.0 (2.0)	27.3 (2.8)	36.0 (3.1)	26.3 (4.0)
South	19.2 (2.3)	23.2 (1.7)	[3]37.9 (2.9)	41.9 (3.0)	32.7 (4.1)
West	24.7 (3.4)	23.2 (2.5)	22.3 (3.1)	34.7 (3.8)	31.3 (5.9)

[1] Worksites that test applicants only, current employees only, and both applicants and current employees. Columns 1 through 4 are not exclusive categories.
[2] Percent of worksites that test for alcohol in which Government regulation requires testing.
[3] Difference between 1993 and 1995 is significant at the .05 level.
Data in parentheses represent the standard error.

SOURCE: Tyler D. Hartwell, Paul D. Steele, and Nathanial F. Rodman, "Table 1. National estimates of alcohol-testing among private nonagricultural worksites by size, industry, and census region, 1995," in "Workplace alcohol-testing programs: prevalence and trends," *Monthly Labor Review*, vol. 121, no. 6, June 1998

states to pass laws limiting their use. In 1988 Congress passed the Employee Polygraph Protection Act (PL 100-347), which prohibits most private employers from using lie detector tests either for preemployment screening or during the course of employment. In most circumstances employers are prohibited from requiring or requesting any employee or job applicant to take a lie detector test. Employers are also prevented from discharging, disciplining, or discriminating against an employee or prospective employee for refusing to take a test or for exercising other rights under this act.

Still, many employers may administer these tests. Federal, state, and local governments are exempt from the Employee Polygraph Protection Act, and the law does not apply to tests given by the federal government to certain private individuals engaged in national security-related activities. Furthermore, the act permits polygraph tests to be administered in the private sector to certain prospective employees of security service firms and pharmaceutical manufacturers, distributors, and dispensers.

The act also permits polygraph testing of certain employees who are reasonably suspected of involvement in a workplace incident, such as theft or embezzlement, that resulted in economic loss to the employer. Some restrictions may apply in these cases, and state or local law or collective bargaining agreements may be more restrictive.

Where polygraph tests are permitted, they are subject to numerous strict standards concerning the conduct and length of the test. Persons who take polygraph tests have a number of specific rights, including the right to a written notice before testing, the right to refuse or discontinue a test, and the right not to have test results disclosed to unauthorized persons.

In cases where employers cannot legally administer polygraph testing, they may instead be able to administer what is known as honesty testing. This form of testing is typically a written true or false test that offers choices of alternatives of behavior in given circumstances. There are no wrong answers, but evaluators feel they can determine patterns of behavior and, therefore, predict who is at high risk for dishonest behavior. Honesty testing has opponents, including some labor unions and others that are concerned about where to draw the line regarding privacy. On the other hand, such methods sustain interest from employers, who wish to make the best hiring decisions and minimize, in some cases, company theft. Employers may also request information such as applicants' credit reports or criminal records.

Psychological Testing

Concerned about the high costs and legal problems that can result from hiring the wrong person for the job, some employers are administering psychological tests to prospective employees and to employees who are under consideration for promotions. For instance, employers may administer personality tests to determine a prospective employee's suitability for a particular job, especially when the job is a sensitive position in the public trust, such as police officer or firefighter. This is usually done after there has been a conditional offer of employment. The candidate in those cases will usually be sent to a psychologist or psychiatrist to be tested.

In 2001 the American Management Association (AMA), a global not-for-profit, membership-based association in New York, found that 29.2 percent of the 1,627 responses from AMA member and client companies surveyed said they gave psychological exams to job applicants. These tests included cognitive ability, career directions, personality measurements, and physical simulation of job tasks. This survey does not accurately portray the testing policies in the U.S. economy since the companies surveyed employ only one-fourth of the U.S. workforce; the rest consist of smaller firms.

According to Rochelle Kaplan, legal counsel for the National Association of Colleges and Employers and a specialist in employment and labor law, any requested psychological test results should relate directly to the job. Additionally, access to such test results should be limited to those making the hiring decision.

CHAPTER 9
BUSINESS OPPORTUNITIES

Starting or acquiring a business has long been considered an American dream. For many, this dream has become a reality. The Dun & Bradstreet Corporation (D & B) compiles data on entrepreneurial activity in the United States. Every year, people start thousands of businesses. Other firms fail, discontinue, are sold, or continue operating. As of 2002, according to D & B, nearly 1 million changes are made daily to its database of more than 75 million global businesses.

The number of small businesses in the United States reported by D & B can differ dramatically from the U.S. Census Bureau figures. In 1992 D & B listed 11 million businesses, while the U.S. Census Bureau, according to its *1992 Economic Census,* counted 17 million. D & B counts small businesses that become part of its database through an application for credit at a bank or other lending facility. D & B also includes businesses whose owners respond to mailers asking them to voluntarily become part of the D & B database. Companies that did not apply for credit, wanted confidentiality, or ignored the mailer would not be included in the D & B database and therefore would not be counted.

The U.S. Census Bureau counts Schedule C businesses (individual proprietorship or self-employed persons) and Subchapter S corporations (usually small corporations in which the profits pass through to the owners without being taxed first). It does not count the large number of small businesses incorporated as standard corporations.

As a result, both surveys undercount the number of small businesses in the United States. Recognizing this, both surveys are used as indicators. While neither survey may be completely accurate, a base of 11 or 17 million is a sufficient amount upon which to base observations.

In addition, every five years, in years ending in "2" and "7," the U.S. Census Bureau surveys business enterprises. Any business that filed an Internal Revenue Service

(IRS) form 1040, Schedule C, form 1065 (partnership), or form 1120S (Subchapter S corporation) was counted. The latest U.S. Census Bureau survey with available data is the *1997 Economic Census.* In some instances, this five-year census report does not analyze the data for the same criteria used previously. Therefore, some earlier data, specifically from the 1992 census, is used in this chapter.

BUSINESS STARTS

In 1998, according to D & B, business starts decreased by 7 percent to total 155,141 (down from 166,740 startups in 1997). The 1998 startups employed 906,105 people. D & B speculated that startups declined due to the strong U.S. economy; startups are assumed to increase when people face unemployment and consider other methods of earning a living.

The largest percentages of business startups in 1998 were in the service and retail sectors; together they comprised 53 percent of 1998 startups and 54 percent of 1998 jobs created by startups. However, these represented declines from 1997 figures, and figures in almost every industry sector declined. For 1998 business startups increased over 1997 in agriculture, forestry, and fishing, as well as finance, insurance, and real estate. On a regional basis, 1998 business startups increased employment only in the southeast part of the United States. The U.S. Census Bureau's *Statistical Abstract of the United States: 2001* indicated 151,016 business startups in 1999, a further decline in the rate over the previous year. By mid-2000, 2,394 businesses in the United States were started weekly, down from 3,009 weekly startups at the same time in 1999. (See Table 9.1.) Figure 9.1 illustrates the overall decline of business startups from 1994 through 1997.

Most businesses that start up are very small. In 1997, 54 percent of the new businesses employed just two people or less. Only 10 percent of the firms employed more than 11 people. (See Figure 9.2 and Table 9.2.)

TABLE 9.1

Weekly business starts, 2000 vs. 1999

Week number	2000 week ending	1999 week ending	2000 weekly starts	1999 weekly starts	2000 13-week moving average	2000 52-week moving average	2000 year-to-date starts	1999 year-to-date starts	Change 2000 vs 1999
21	5/26/00	5/28/99	2,394	3,009	2,495	2,718	50,912	58,372	-12.8%
20	5/19/00	5/21/99	2,311	2,920	2,478	2,729	48,518	55,363	-12.4%
19	5/12/00	5/14/99	2,223	2,811	2,469	2,741	46,207	52,443	-11.9%
18	5/5/00	5/7/99	2,230	2,713	2,498	2,752	43,984	49,632	-11.4%
17	4/28/00	4/30/99	2,436	3,089	2,506	2,762	41,754	46,916	-11.0%
16	4/21/00	4/23/99	2,254	3,397	2,495	2,774	39,318	43,830	-10.3%
15	4/14/00	4/16/99	2,632	3,096	2,502	2,796	37,064	40,433	-8.3%
14	4/7/00	4/9/99	2,765	2,939	2,519	2,805	34,432	37,337	-7.8%
13	3/31/00	4/2/99	2,546	3,409	2,436	2,808	31,667	34,398	-7.9%
12	3/24/00	3/26/99	2,686	2,534	2,463	2,825	29,121	30,989	-6.0%
11	3/17/00	3/19/99	2,323	2,765	2,458	2,822	26,435	28,455	-7.1%
10	3/10/00	3/12/99	2,635	2,588	2,557	2,831	24,112	25,690	-6.1%
9	3/3/00	3/5/99	3,006	2,644	2,621	2,830	21,477	23,102	-7.0%
8	2/25/00	2/26/99	2,169	2,729	2,633	2,823	18,471	20,458	-9.7%
7	2/18/00	2/19/99	2,189	2,201	2,640	2,834	16,302	17,729	-8.0%
6	2/11/00	2/12/99	2,609	2,245	2,757	2,834	14,113	15,528	-9.1%
5	2/4/00	2/5/99	2,333	2,784	2,813	2,827	11,504	13,283	-13.4%
4	1/28/00	1/29/99	2,294	2,816	2,885	2,835	9,171	10,499	-12.6%
3	1/21/00	1/22/99	2,344*	2,451*	3,010	2,845	6,877	7,683	-10.5%
2	1/14/00	1/15/99	2,843	2,420	3,089	2,848	4,533	5,232	-13.4%
1	1/7/00	1/8/99	1,690*	2,812	3,131	2,839	1,690	2,812	-39.9%

* Four-day week

Note: The 13-week moving average represents the average level of starts for a period of approximately one quarter ending with the current week. This average presents a better measure of the trend in new business activity by eliminating the volatility often associated with monthly or weekly comparisons of data. The 52-week moving average column indicates change in business starts over the course of a year and hence is a useful indicator of the relative level of activity. Comparisons of year-to-date figures in the first few weeks of the year are not conclusive.

SOURCE: Economics Analysis Department, The Dun and Bradstreet Corp., Murray Hill, NJ, May 31, 2000

FIGURE 9.1

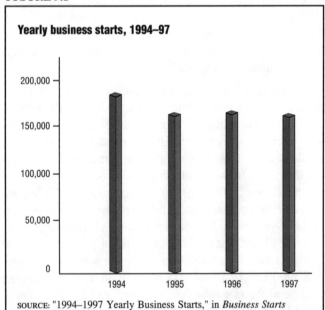

Yearly business starts, 1994–97

SOURCE: "1994–1997 Yearly Business Starts," in *Business Starts Record,* Neil DiBernardo, ed., The Dun and Bradstreet Corp., Murray Hill, NJ, 1998

FIGURE 9.2

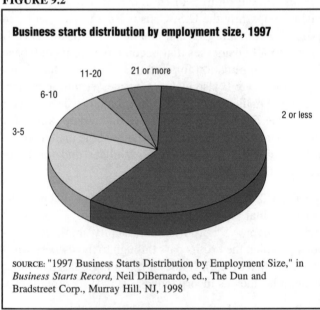

Business starts distribution by employment size, 1997

SOURCE: "1997 Business Starts Distribution by Employment Size," in *Business Starts Record,* Neil DiBernardo, ed., The Dun and Bradstreet Corp., Murray Hill, NJ, 1998

The U.S. Census Bureau, in a January 2002 report, stated more than 16 million businesses were non-employer businesses, with no paid employees, in 1999; this figure was up 2.8 percent from 1998. This represents just a portion of the small business startups over that period, since many small businesses have some employees. Nearly 60 percent of non-employer sales were from four sectors of the economy: real estate and rental and leasing ($125 billion); construction ($103 billion); professional, scientific and technical services ($85 billion); and retail trade ($73 billion).

BUSINESS FAILURES

In 1997 D & B found that 83,384 businesses failed. (See Table 9.3.) The failure rate of 88 per 10,000 businesses listed with D & B was well below a high of 120 in 1986. Previous- ly, the high was 154 per 10,000 failures in 1932, a Great Depression year. In 1997 each failed firm owed an average liability (debt) of $448,970. (See Figure 9.3.) The *1992 Economic Census* reported that 71.7 percent of discontinued businesses attributed their failure to inadequate cash flow or low sales. Another 8.2 percent thought they were unsuccessful because of lack of access to business loans or credit.

NUMBER OF BUSINESSES

The U.S. Census Bureau identified 20.8 million firms in 1997 with sales and receipts of $18.6 trillion. Of these businesses, 14.6 percent, over 3 million businesses, were owned by minorities, generating more than $591 billion in revenues. (See Table 9.4.) Between 1992 and 1997, minority businesses increased in number four times as fast as the number of total businesses in the United States. Although Hispanics owned the largest number of minority-owned businesses, Asian-owned firms brought in the largest share of revenues. Women owned 5.4 million businesses in 1997, with sales and receipts of $819 billion.

TABLE 9.2

Business starts distribution by employment size, 1996–97

	1996		1997	
	Firms	Percent	Firms	Percent
Employees				
2 or less	98,671	57.9%	89,927	53.9%
3 to 5	38,129	22.4%	40,304	24.2%
6 to l0	18,135	10.6%	19,393	11.6%
11 to 20	8,727	5.1%	9,402	5.6%
21 or more	6,813	4.0%	7,714	4.6%
Total	**170,475**	**100.0%**	**166,740**	**100.0%**

SOURCE: "Business Starts Distribution by Employment Size," in *Business Starts Record,* Neil DiBernardo, ed., The Dun and Bradstreet Corp., Murray Hill, NJ, 1998

TABLE 9.3

Business failures, 1927–97

	Number of failures	Total failure liabilities	Failure rate per 10,000 listed concerns	Average liability per failure		Number of failures	Total failure liabilities	Failure rate per 10,000 listed concerns	Average liability per failure
1927	23,146	$ 520,105,000	106	$22,471	1962	15,782	$ 1,213,601,000	61	$ 76,898
1928	23,842	489,559,000	109	20,534	1963	14,374	1,352,593,000	56	94,100
1929	22,909	483,252,000	104	21,094	1964	13,501	1,329,223,000	53	98,454
1930	26,355	668,282,000	122	25,357	1965	13,514	1,321,666,000	53	97,800
1931	28,285	736,310,000	133	26,032	1966	13,061	1,385,659,000	52	106,091
1932	31,822	928,313,000	154	29,172	1967	12,364	1,265,227,000	49	102,332
1933	19,859	457,520,000	100	23,038	1968	9,636	940,996,000	39	97,654
1934	12,091	333,959,000	61	27,621	1969	9,154	1,142,113,000	37	124,767
1935	12,244	310,580,000	62	25,366	1970	10,748	1,887,754,000	44	175,638
1936	9,607	203,173,000	48	21,148	1971	10,326	1,916,929,000	42	185,641
1937	9,490	$ 183,253,000	46	$19,310	1972	9,566	$ 2,000,244,000	38	$ 209,099
1938	12,836	246,505,000	61	19,204	1973	9,345	2,298,606,000	36	245,972
1939	14,768	182,520,000	70	12,359	1974	9,915	3,053,137,000	38	307,931
1940	13,619	166,684,000	63	12,239	1975	11,432	4,380,170,000	43	383,150
1941	11,848	136,104,000	55	11,488	1976	9,628	3,011,271,000	35	312,762
1942	9,405	100,763,000	45	10,713	1977	7,919	3,095,317,000	28	390,872
1943	3,221	45,339,000	16	14,076	1978	6,619	2,656,006,000	24	401,270
1944	1,222	31,660,000	7	25,908	1979	7,564	2,667,362,000	28	352,639
1945	809	30,225,000	4	37,361	1980	11,742	4,635,080,000	42	394,744
1946	1,129	67,349,000	5	59,654	1981	16,794	6,955,180,000	61	414,147
1947	3,474	$ 204,612,000	14	$58,898	1982	24,908	$15,610,792,000	88	$ 626,738
1948	5,250	234,620,000	20	44,690	1983	31,334	16,072,860,000	110	512,953
1949	9,246	308,109,000	34	33,323	1984	52,078	29,268,646,871	107	562,016
1950	9,162	248,283,000	34	27,099	1985	57,253	36,937,369,478	115	645,160
1951	8,058	259,547,000	31	32,210	1986	61,616	44,723,991,601	120	725,850
1952	7,611	283,314,000	29	37,224	1987	61,111	34,723,831,429	102	568,209
1953	8,862	394,153,000	33	44,477	1988	57,097	39,573,030,341	98	693,084
1954	11,086	462,628,000	42	41,731	1989	50,361	42,328,790,375	65	840,507
1955	10,969	449,380,000	42	40,968	1990	60,747	56,130,073,898	74	923,996
1956	12,686	562,697,000	48	44,356	1991	88,140	96,825,314,741	107	1,098,539
1957	13,739	615,293,000	52	44,784	1992	97,069	94,317,500,288	110	971,653
1958	14,964	728,258,000	56	48,667	1993	86,133	47,755,514,259	109	554,438
1959	14,053	692,808,000	52	49,300	1994	71,558	28,977,866,378	86	404,956
1960	15,445	938,630,000	57	60,772	1995	71,128	37,283,550,627	82	524,175
1961	17,075	1,090,123,000	64	63,843	1996	71,931	29,568,731,719	80	411,071
					1997p	83,384	37,436,934,664	88	448,970

p = preliminary

SOURCE: "Failure Trends Since 1927," in *Business Failure Record,* Neil DiBernardo, ed., The Dun and Bradstreet Corp., Murray Hill, NJ, 1998

FIGURE 9.3

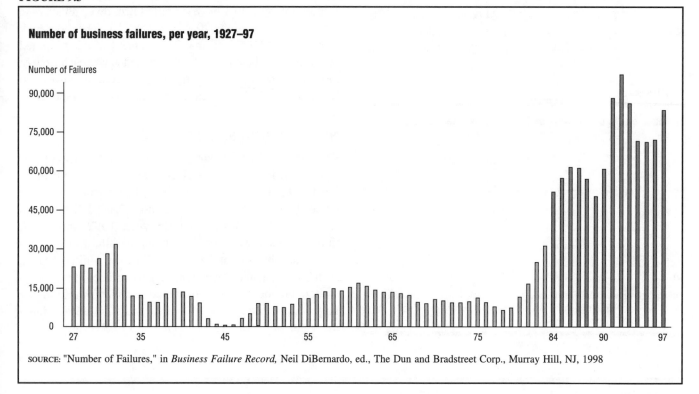

Number of business failures, per year, 1927–97

Number of Failures

SOURCE: "Number of Failures," in *Business Failure Record,* Neil DiBernardo, ed., The Dun and Bradstreet Corp., Murray Hill, NJ, 1998

TABLE 9.4

Business ownership by minority group, 1997

	All firms[1]		Percent of minority-owned firms	
Minority group	Firms (number)	Sales and receipts (million dollars)	Firms	Sales and receipts
All minority firms	**3,039,033**	**591,259**	**X**	**X**
Black	823,499	71,215	27.1	12.0
Hispanic	1,199,896	186,275	39.5	31.5
American Indian and Alaska Native	197,300	34,344	6.5	5.8
Asian and Pacific Islander	912,960	306,933	30.0	51.9

[1]All firms data include both firms with paid employees and firms with no paid employees.
Note: Detail in this table does not add to total because of duplication of some firms. Hispanics may be of any race and, therefore, may be included in more than one minority group.

SOURCE: "Table A. Comparison of Business Ownership by Minority Group: 1997," in *1997 Economic Census: Survey of Minority-Owned Business Enterprises: Summary,* U.S. Census Bureau, Washington, DC, July 2001

Most of the firms were concentrated in the service industries. Forty-three percent of all U.S. firms, 47 percent of the minority-owned firms, and 56 percent of the firms owned by women were classified as services. Retail trade had the next largest share—14 percent of all U.S. firms, 15 percent of the minority-owned firms, and 17 percent of the women-owned firms.

HOW OWNERS ACQUIRED THEIR BUSINESSES

The U.S. Census Bureau published a special report, *Characteristics of Business Owners, 1992 Economic Census,* in which they studied the process of starting a business. Most owners (68.9 percent) founded their own businesses. (See Table 9.5.) Others (10.5 percent) had the businesses transferred to them, generally as a gift, while another 10.1 percent bought the businesses. About 3 percent inherited their firms.

REASONS FOR BECOMING A BUSINESS OWNER

One-fifth (21.3 percent) of owners reported that they became an owner to have a primary source of income, while one-fourth (25.6 percent) wanted to have a secondary source of income. (See Table 9.5.) Another one-fifth (21.5 percent) wanted to be their own boss. Less than 3 percent wanted to bring a new idea to the marketplace. Approximately 8 percent wanted to have more freedom to meet family responsibilities.

CAPITAL REQUIREMENTS

Most 1992 business owners (57 percent) started their enterprises with less than $5,000. In fact, one-fourth (25 percent) required no capital. (See Table 9.5.) Forty-four percent of the owners did not borrow their starting capital but used money or assets of their own or from their families. Only 19 percent used capital based on a personal loan, which could have included borrowing against the home mortgage, using credit cards, or borrowing from a family member.

TABLE 9.5

TABLE 9.6

Startup issues of business owners, 1992

[Detail may not add to total due to rounding]

Item	All businesses
How the owner acquired the business	
Founded	68.9
Received transfer of ownership/gift	10.5
Purchased	10.1
Inherited	2.7
Other means	2.2
Not reported	5.6
Reason for becoming an owner in the business	
To have a primary source of income	21.3
To have a secondary source of income	25.6
To have work which conforms to owner's health limitations	1.6
To have work not available elsewhere in the job market	1.5
To have more freedom to meet family responsibilities	7.6
To bring a new idea to the marketplace	2.6
To advance in my profession	6.2
To be my own boss	21.5
Other reason	6.7
Not reported	5.5
Total capital needed by owner to start/acquire the business	
None	25.0
Less than $5,000	32.0
$5,000 to $9,999	9.6
$10,000 to $24,999	11.4
$25,000 to $49,999	5.7
$50,000 to $99,999	4.6
$100,000 to $249,999	3.0
$250,000 to $999,999	1.4
$1,000,000 or more	.5
Not reported	6.8

SOURCE: Adapted from Durwin Knutson, "Table 1. Summary Characteristics of Business Owners and Their Businesses: 1992," in *Characteristics of Business Owners Survey,* U.S. Census Bureau, Washington, DC, September 1997

Profits and income of business owners, 1992

[Detail may not add to total due to rounding.]

Item	All businesses
Business's net profit (or loss) before taxes as reported on its tax return	
Net Profit	
$100,000 or more	2.2
$25,000 to $99,999	8.0
$10,000 to $24,999	8.3
Less than $10,000	38.5
Net Loss	
Less than $10,000	15.6
$10,000 to $24,999	2.6
$25,000 to $99,999	1.5
$100,000 or more	.7
Not reported	22.5
During 1992, the percent of owner's total personal income produced as a result of the business	
None	12.9
Less than 10 percent	22.9
10 to 24 percent	8.4
25 to 49 percent	6.7
50 to 74 percent	5.5
75 to 99 percent	11.1
100 percent	24.1
Not reported	8.5

SOURCE: Adapted from Durwin Knutson, "Table 1. Summary Characteristics of Business Owners and Their Businesses: 1992," in *Characteristics of Business Owners Survey,* U.S. Census Bureau, Washington, DC, 1992

PROFITABILITY

In 1992 about 35 percent of business owners reported that 75 percent or more of their personal income was produced as a result of their business, while nearly 36 percent reported that none or less than 10 percent of their income came from the business. (See Table 9.6.)

Almost 39 percent of businesses reported a net profit of less than $10,000 from their businesses, while 18.5 percent claimed a profit of $10,000 or more. On the other hand, about 20 percent of the businesses reported experiencing a net loss in 1992. (See Table 9.6.)

HOME-BASED BUSINESSES

In 1992 approximately half (50 percent) of all businesses were home-based. Not surprisingly, the percentage of firms operated from a home tended to be higher for smaller firms. Fifty-seven percent of businesses with receipts less than $25,000 were home-based, compared to 26 percent of firms with receipts of $25,000 to $199,999, 16 percent of firms with receipts of $200,000 to $999,000, and only 5 percent of firms with receipts of $1,000,000 or more.

Of the home-based businesses, male-owned firms were most likely to use the residence to do clerical work only or for phone calls or e-mail. In contrast, home-based women-owned firms were more likely to use their residences to produce goods or services on the premises. (See Table 9.7.)

OWNER'S WORK EXPERIENCE

Sixty-six percent of the business owners stated that the business they owned in 1992 was the first one they had owned. Approximately 69 percent of the business owners reported that they were the original founders of the business. About 21 percent purchased their share of the business or received a transfer of ownership in the business. For a firm with $50,000 or more in receipts in 1992, the larger the receipts, the less likely the business was to be owned by the original founder. Prior to beginning or acquiring the business, half of the owners (49.9 percent) had close relatives who owned a business or who had been self-employed.

Two-thirds (65.5 percent) had never owned another business. (See Table 9.8.) About one-fifth (21.3 percent) reported having worked for relatives. Fifty-two percent of business owners had 10 or more years of work experience prior to starting or acquiring their businesses. More than one-third (33.9 percent) had no managerial experience

TABLE 9.7

Location of business, 1992

[Detail may not add to total due to rounding.]

Item	All businesses	Hispanic-owned businesses	Black-owned businesses	Other minority-owned businesses	Women-owned businesses	Nonminority male-owned businesses	Standard error of estimate for column-				
	A	B	C	D	E	F	A	B	C	D	E
Operated primarily from or in a home when first established											
Yes	52.1	46.2	48.7	34.3	55.2	51.7	.6	1.4	1.2	1.0	.8
No	40.0	43.4	36.7	56.9	35.4	41.7	.6	.8	1.0	1.1	.4
Don't know	1.7	2.0	2.1	3.3	1.7	1.8	.3	.3	.2	.2	.3
Not reported	6.2	8.4	12.5	5.5	7.7	5.0	.3	.9	.4	.2	.7
Operated primarily from or in a home during 1992											
Yes	49.6	44.2	47.2	33.8	53.2	46.8	.6	1.6	1.1	1.0	.7
No	43.2	45.7	37.7	59.9	38.2	45.2	.4	1.0	.9	1.1	.4
Not reported	7.2	10.1	15.1	6.3	8.6	6.0	.4	I.0	.4	.5	.8
Home-based businesses' primary use of the home											
To produce goods/services on the premises	20.2	17.4	18.5	15.8	26.4	17.3	.6	1.2	.8	1.1	.8
To do clerical work (goods/services produced off the premises)	23.7	18.9	21.2	13.9	22.6	24.9	.7	1.0	.7	.7	.8
To telecommute (outside employment doing office work at home)	8.2	8.1	8.1	7.0	6.8	9.0	.4	.2	.4	.7	.5
Not reported	13.1	17.8	21.8	13.1	14.3	11.9	.5	1.3	.8	.5	.8
Not applicable	34.9	38.1	30.3	50.3	30.0	36.8	.4	.6	.9	.9	.5

SOURCE: Adapted from Durwin Knutson, "Table 1. Summary Characteristics of Business Owners and Their Businesses: 1992," in *Characteristics of Business Owners Survey,* U.S. Census Bureau, Washington, DC, 1992

when they started their businesses. One-fifth (19.6 percent) had 10 or more years of managerial experience.

Fifty-one percent of the business owners managed or worked in their business the entire year (48 weeks or more). About 35 percent of business owners averaged more than 40 hours per week in their business, while 36 percent worked less than 20 hours per week. The percentage of business owners working less than 20 hours per week was highest in the finance, insurance, and real estate sector (55 percent). (See Table 9.9.)

OWNER CHARACTERISTICS

In 1992 half of the business owners (50 percent) in each group were between the ages of 35 and 54 years of age, and over half of these individuals were in the 35- to 44-year age-bracket. (See Table 9.10.) Seven of ten (71.9 percent) of the owners were married when they began or acquired their businesses. Most (84.1 percent) were born in the United States, 8.7 percent were born outside the United States, and 7.2 percent did not report their status. Asians and Pacific Islanders dominated the foreign-born percentages. (See Figure 9.4.)

Fewer than 10 percent (9.4) of business owners had less than a high school education; 22.6 percent had completed high school or had a GED equivalency. (See Table

9.11.) About one-fifth (20.2 percent) had attained a bachelor's degree. Another 14.7 percent had attained an advanced degree. One of six business owners (17.3 percent) who had attended school beyond high school studied business; another 11.7 percent had a liberal arts/general studies education.

Minority Business Owners

A survey by D & B, conducted in early 1999, showed that minorities were becoming less optimistic about the performances of their small businesses. Minority business owners showed lowered expectations for customer growth, revenue growth, profit growth, and economic outlook, among others. The biggest challenge to minorities in running their businesses was keeping good employees. Future challenges that concerned minorities included government regulations and cash flow. Previously, minority attitudes about their businesses had tended to be more optimistic than the rest of the small business population in the United States.

IMPACT OF THE INTERNET

A D & B 2000 survey indicated that between 1998 and 1999, the proportion of small business owners with Internet access jumped 57 percent. By 1999, 71 percent of small businesses had online access. (See Table 9.12.)

TABLE 9.8

Work experience of business owners, 1992

Detail may not add to total due to rounding.

Item	All businesses	Hispanic-owned businesses	Black-owned businesses	Other minority-owned businesses	Women-owned businesses	Nonminority male-owned businesses	Standard error of estimate for column-					
	A	B	C	D	E	F	A	B	C	D	E	F
Years of work experience prior to starting/acquiring the business												
None (did not work)	7.6	12.8	9.7	13.7	9.0	6.3	.4	.5	.6	.9	.7	.5
Less than 2 years	6.3	7.8	6.4	8.5	6.9	5.7	.4	.6	.3	.8	.8	.5
2 to 5 years	14.2	16.5	12.7	18.9	13.8	14.1	.5	.7	.5	1.1	.5	.8
6 to 9 years	14.1	13.0	13.2	14.7	13.4	14.5	.5	.6	.4	.8	.6	.9
10 to 19 years	26.4	25.4	26.2	23.6	27.6	26.0	.6	.9	.6	.6	.8	1.0
20 years or more	25.9	17.7	22.3	14.8	23.3	28.3	.9	.5	.3	.6	1.2	1.6
Not reported	5.5	6.7	9.4	5.8	6.0	5.0	.3	.5	.4	.5	.5	.5
Previous years of work experience in a managerial capacity												
None	33.9	35.1	40.6	28.1	36.0	32.7	.7	.8	.7	.9	.8	1.1
Less than 2 years	8.0	7.9	7.4	9.1	7.9	7.9	.5	.4	.6	.6	.6	.6
2 to 5 years	13.8	12.6	12.1	16.0	13.2	14.2	.4	.6	.5	1.0	.6	.7
6 to 9 years	9.0	7.9	6.7	9.4	9.0	9.0	.3	.5	.4	.8	.6	.5
10 to 19 years	11.4	9.3	8.3	10.3	10.2	12.3	.6	.6	.5	.5	.5	.9
20 years or more	8.2	4.5	3.6	4.6	5.8	10.0	.5	.5	.2	.5	.3	.8
Not sure	2.4	2.9	2.4	3.1	2.5	2.3	.2	.5	.1	.5	.4	.2
Not reported	5.7	7.0	9.1	5.7	6.5	5.1	.3	.5	.6	.5	.4	.5
Not applicable	7.6	12.8	9.7	13.7	9.0	6.3	.4	.5	.6	.9	.6	.5
Previous years of work experience as the owner of another business												
None	65.5	65.5	69.9	56.9	67.8	64.6	.7	1.3	1.0	.8	.5	1.2
Less than 2 years	3.0	2.6	2.7	4.4	3.3	2.7	.2	.2	.3	.4	.5	.3
2 to 5 years	5.6	4.8	4.3	7.4	4.9	5.9	.3	.4	.3	.8	.4	.4
6 to 9 years	3.3	2.4	1.5	3.9	2.4	3.9	.2	.2	.2	.4	.2	.4
10 to 19 years	4.8	2.9	1.6	4.7	3.2	5.9	.4	.3	.2	.5	.3	.5
20 years or more	3.9	1.6	.8	2.1	2.3	5.1	.5	.2	.2	.2	.1	.7
Not sure	.8	1.0	.8	1.6	.8	.9	.1	.2	.2	.2	.1	.2
Not reported	5.4	6.3	8.7	5.4	6.3	4.8	.3	.6	.5	.4	.3	.5
Not applicable	7.6	12.8	9.7	13.7	9.0	6.3	.4	.5	.8	.9	.6	.5

SOURCE: Adapted from Durwin Knutson, "Table 1. Summary Characteristics of Business Owners and Their Businesses: 1992," in *Characteristics of Business Owners Survey,* U.S. Census Bureau, Washington, DC, 1992

Regardless, half of these businesses claimed that the Internet had no significant impact on their business. The data showed that the use of the Internet for marketing and research had actually declined. According to D & B, this seemed to indicate that small businesses were proceeding cautiously into the realm of e-commerce. Only 26 percent of businesses used the Internet to sell or market products. The top use of online access was e-mail (71 percent).

Small businesses were increasingly maintaining an online presence through Web site development. Small business Web sites increased 10 percent between 1999 and 2000 for businesses overall. (See Table 9.13.) Sixty-five percent of businesses with 26 to 100 employees indicated that they had a Web page or site in 2000. Businesses with 6 to 25 employees showed the slowest growth in Web site development between 1999 and 2000 (2 percent).

TABLE 9.9

Weeks and hours owner spends managing or working, by industry division, 1992

[All data are shown as percents, except firms.]

Type of firm and industry division	Firms (number)	Number of weeks spent managing or working in the business							Average number of hours per week spent managing or working in the business			
		None	Less than 12	12 to 23	24 to 35	36 to 47	48 or more	Not reported	None	Less than 10	10 to 19	20 to 29
	A	B	C	D	E	F	G	H	I	J	K	L
1 All businesses	17,253,143	8.4	12.4	6.2	6.4	7.1	51.3	8.3	8.4	17.1	10.5	8.9
2 Agricultural services, forestry, fishing, and mining	53,253	14.2	9.9	7.7	9.1	6.9	41.4	10.9	13.5	13.8	10.2	9.4
3 Construction	1,829,620	8.6	8.6	5.4	7.1	8.1	56.8	5.5	8.5	9.4	6.3	8.9
4 Manufacturing	517,714	10.6	11.2	5.6	6.6	4.7	55.7	5.6	10.8	12.6	10.1	7.9
5 Transportation, communications, and utilities	698,903	5.6	7.3	6.9	6.7	9.4	54.3	9.8	5.5	13.1	8.1	6.3
6 Wholesale trade	538,339	6.3	8.7	5.0	3.7	4.4	64.7	7.1	6.4	11.9	8.3	5.5
7 Retail trade	2,470,045	5.3	9.1	6.6	6.6	6.7	57.1	8.6	5.8	14.2	11.2	9.2
8 Finance, insurance, and real estate	1,941,029	20.7	19.7	3.2	3.3	4.5	41.4	7.2	20.7	29.1	5.2	5.3
9 Services	7,784,016	4.6	12.6	7.1	7.4	8.1	52.1	8.2	4:6	16.9	13.9	10.7
10 Industries not classified	882,224	7.4	12.7	8.9	6.0	7.7	39.9	17.3	7.4	17.5	8.6	8.6

SOURCE: Adapted from Durwin Knutson, "Table 18a. Weeks and Hours Owner Spent Managing or Working by Industry Division: 1992," in *Characteristics of Business Owners Survey,* U.S. Census Bureau, Washington, DC, 1992

TABLE 9.10

Age, citizenship, and marital status of business owners, 1992

[Detail may not add to total due to rounding.]

Item	All businesses
Age as of December 31, 1992	
Under 25	2.3
25 to 34	14.2
35 to 44	27.1
45 to 54	22.9
55 to 64	17.5
65 Or over	10.4
Not reported	5.7
Born in the United States	
Yes	84.1
No	8.7
Not reported	7.2
Marital status when the business was started/acquired	
Never married	12.2
Married	71.9
Divorced/separated	8.3
Widowed	1.8
Not reported	5.8

SOURCE: Adapted from Durwin Knutson, "Table 1. Summary Characteristics of Business Owners and Their Businesses: 1992," in *Characteristics of Business Owners Survey,* U.S. Census Bureau, Washington, DC, 1992

FIGURE 9.4

Foreign born business owners, 1992

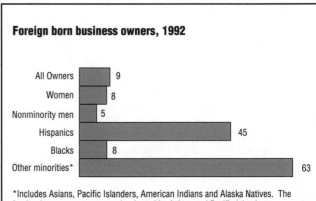

*Includes Asians, Pacific Islanders, American Indians and Alaska Natives. The foreign-born percentages are dominated by Asians and Pacific Islanders.

SOURCE: *Census and You,* U.S. Census Bureau, Washington, DC, 1992

TABLE 9.11

Educational attainment of business owners, 1992

[Detail may not add to total due to rounding.]

| Item | All businesses | Hispanic-owned businesses | Black-owned businesses | Other minority-owned businesses | Women-owned businesses | Nonminority male-owned businesses | Standard error of estimate for column | | | | | |
							A	B	C	D	E	F
	A	B	C	D	E	F						
Highest level of education completed or degree received when business was started/acquired												
Less than 9th grade	3.7	14.8	6.0	5.3	3.2	3.3	.2	.7	.3	.4	.4	.2
Some high school, but no diploma	5.7	10.6	10.4	6.4	4.9	5.7	.2	.6	.4	.6	.5	.4
High school graduate or GED equivalency	22.6	18.2	21.3	14.8	22.4	23.2	.6	.7	.5	.6	.7	.8
Technical, trade, or vocational school	7.0	7.9	8.6	4.7	7.6	6.7	.2	.7	.5	.5	.4	.4
Some college, but no degree	16.1	16.6	16.6	12.9	17.7	15.4	.6	.9	.4	.8	.8	.8
Associate Degree	4.0	4.1	4.9	4.4	4.7	3.5	.4	.4	.4	.3	.6	.5
Bachelor's Degree	20.2	11.9	11.9	23.7	20.6	20.6	.6	.7	.6	1.5	.9	1.0
Master's Degree	5.8	3.9	6.7	8.9	7.0	5.0	.3	.2	.6	.7	.5	.5
Professional School or Doctorate	8.9	5.4	6.0	12.1	5.2	10.8	.2	.4	.4	.9	.5	.4
Not reported	6.1	6.6	7.7	6.5	6.7	5.6	.3	.4	.5	.8	.3	.5
If attended college or other school beyond high school, area of concentration												
Architecture/Engineering	5.0	4.9	2.6	9.6	3.3	5.7	.2	.4	.3	.5	.3	.3
Biological/Medical Science	6.9	5.6	5.8	11.8	6.9	6.7	.3	.5	.2	.9	.4	.5
Business	17.3	14.2	14.2	17.6	16.0	18.3	.4	.6	.5	.9	.5	.8
Computer Science	1.0	1.5	1.5	2.8	1.1	.8	.1	.2	.1	.4	.2	.2
Construction Trade/Industrial Arts	1.9	1.6	1.9	1.2	1.3	2.3	.2	.2	.1	.3	.3	.2
Law and Legal Studies	3.5	2.2	2.4	2.2	2.0	4.4	.2	.2	.2	.3	.2	.4
Liberal Arts/General Studies	11.7	7.6	10.1	7.7	14.9	10.5	.5	.5	.5	.8	.5	.8
Mathematics	.8	.5	.9	1.3	.8	.8	.1	.1	.1	.2	.1	.2
Military Technologies	.5	.2	.3	.3	.1	.7	.1	.1	.1	.1	.1	.2
Other college	5.9	3.8	5.5	5.3	8.2	4.9	.3	.4	.3	.4	.6	.5
Other vocational	5.5	5.0	7.5	5.1	6.2	5.1	.3	.5	.5	.5	.4	.6
Not reported	8.0	9.1	9.8	8.5	8.6	7.6	.3	.5	.4	.8	.5	.6
Not applicable	32.0	43.6	37.6	26.5	30.5	32.2	.6	1.0	.4	.6	.9	.9

SOURCE: Durwin Knutson, *Characteristics of Business Owners Survey,* U.S. Census Bureau, Washington, DC, 1992

TABLE 9.12

Internet use by small businesses, 1998–99

Used Internet for . . .	in 1999	in 1998
E-Mail	71%	76%
Business Research	58%	71%
Personal Research	50%	64%
Purchase Goods/Services (business use)	43%	38%
Purchase Goods/Services (personal use)	31%	35%
Sell/Market Products	26%	29%

SOURCE: Economics Analysis Department, The Dun and Bradstreet Corp., Murray Hill, NJ, May 25, 2000

TABLE 9.13

Small business presence on the web, 1999–2000

Has web page/site	All small businesses	1-5 empl.	6-25 empl.	26-100 empl.	Home-based	Women-owned	Minority-owned
2000	38%	28%	47%	65%	24%	41%	40%
1999	28%	22%	45%	43%	16%	22%	30%

SOURCE: Economics Analysis Department, The Dun and Bradstreet Corp., Murray Hill, NJ, May 25, 2000

IMPORTANT NAMES AND ADDRESSES

AFL-CIO
American Federation of Labor-Congress of
Industrial Organizations
815 16th St., NW
Washington, DC 20006
(202) 637-5000
FAX: (202) 637-5058
E-mail: feedback@aflcio.org
URL: http://www.aflcio.org

Center on Budget and Policy Priorities
820 First St., NE, Suite 510
Washington, DC 20002
(202) 408-1080
FAX: (202) 408-1056
E-mail: bazie@cbpp.org
URL: http://www.cbpp.org

**Committee on Education and
the Workforce**
2181 Rayburn House Office Bldg.
Washington, DC 20515
(202) 225-4527
URL: http://www.house.gov/ed_workforce/

**Committee on Health, Education, Labor,
and Pensions**
428 Dirksen Senate Office Bldg.
Washington, DC 20510-6300
(202) 224-5375
URL: http://www.senate.gov/~labor

Dun & Bradstreet
One Diamond Hill Rd.
Murray Hill, NJ 07974-1218
(908) 665-5000
FAX: (908) 665-5803
URL: http://www.dnb.com

Employment Policy Foundation
1015 15th St., NW, Suite 1200
Washington, DC 20005
(202) 789-8685
FAX: (202) 789-8684
E-mail: info@epf.org
URL: http://www.epf.org

Employment Standards Administration
U.S. Department of Labor
200 Constitution Ave., NW
Washington, DC 20210
(202) 693-0023
URL: http://www.dol.gov/esa/welcome.htm

Employment and Training Administration
U.S. Department of Labor
200 Constitution Ave., NW
Washington, DC 20210
(202) 693-3900
FAX: (202) 693-3839
(877) US-2JOBS
URL: http://www.doleta.gov

**Equal Employment
Opportunity Commission**
1801 L St., NW
Washington, DC 20507
(202) 663-4900
URL: http://www.eeoc.gov

National Alliance of Business
1201 New York Ave., NW, Suite 700
Washington, DC 20005
(202) 289-2888
(800) 787-2848
URL: http://www.nab.com

National Association of Manufacturers
1331 Pennsylvania Ave., NW
Washington, DC 20004-1790
(202) 637-3000
FAX: (202) 637-3182
E-mail: manufacturing@nam.org
URL: http://www.nam.org

**National Association of Temporary
and Staffing Services (American
Staffing Association)**
277 South Washington St., Suite 200
Alexandria, VA 22314
(703) 253-2020
FAX: (703) 253-2053

E-mail: asa@staffingtoday.net
URL: http://www.natss.org

National Center for Health Statistics
U.S. Department of Health and
Human Services
6525 Belcrest Rd.
Hyattsville, MD 20782-2003
(301) 458-4636
URL: http://www.cdc.gov/nchs

National Labor Relations Board
1099 14th St.
Washington, DC 20570-0001
(202) 273-1991
FAX: (202) 273-1789
URL: http://www.nlrb.gov

National Safety Council
1121 Spring Lake Dr.
Itasca, IL 60143-3201
(630) 285-1121
FAX: (630) 285-1315
customerservice@nsc.org
URL: http://www.nsc.org

**Occupational Safety and Health
Administration (OSHA)**
U.S. Department of Labor
200 Constitution Ave., NW
Washington, DC 20210
(202) 693-1999
(800) 321-OSHA (6742)
URL: http://www.osha-slc.gov

Society for Human Resource Management
1800 Duke St.
Alexandria, VA 22314
(703) 548-3440
FAX: (703) 535-6490
(800) 283-SHRM
E-mail: shrm@shrm.org
URL: http://www.shrm.org

U.S. Bureau of the Census
4700 Silver Hills Rd.

Suitland, MD 20746
(301) 457-3030
FAX: (301) 457-3670
E-mail: comments@census.gov
URL: http://www.census.gov

U.S. Bureau of Labor Statistics
U.S. Department of Labor
2 Massachusetts Ave., NE
Washington, DC 20212-0001
(202) 691-5200
FAX: (202) 691-6325
E-mail: blsdata_staff@bls.gov
URL: http://www.bls.gov

U.S. Chamber of Commerce
1615 H St., NW
Washington, DC 20062-2000
(202) 659-6000
URL: http://www.uschamber.org

U.S. Department of Commerce
1401 Constitution Ave., NW
Washington, DC 20230
(202) 482-4883
FAX: (202) 482-5168
URL: http://www.doc.gov

U.S. Department of Education
400 Maryland Ave., SW

Washington, DC 20202-0498
FAX: (202) 401-0689
(800) USA-LEARN
E-mail: customerservice@inet.ed.gov
/index.jsp
URL: http://www.ed.gov

U.S. Department of Labor
200 Constitution Ave., NW
Washington, DC 20210
(202) 693-4676
(866) 4-USA-DOL
URL: http://www.dol.gov

RESOURCES

The Bureau of Labor Statistics (BLS), a branch of the U.S. Department of Labor, is an important source of information on employment and unemployment in the United States. *Employment and Earnings,* a monthly BLS publication, gives complete statistics on employment in the United States. The BLS also releases special reports, such as *A Profile of the Working Poor, 1999* (2001) and *Working in the 21st Century* (2002).

In addition, the BLS publishes the *Monthly Labor Review,* which contains articles on issues relating to jobs and how workers are affected by changes in the labor market. The *Monthly Labor Review* also provides historical data and supplies information on employee benefits, including medical and life insurance, disability insurance, and retirement.

The monthly *BLS News* examines employment situations. The BLS also prints *Issues in Labor Statistics,* which may include items such as "How Long Is the Workweek?" (1997), "Workers Are on the Job More Hours over the Course of the Year" (1997), and "Are Workers More Secure?" (1998). The BLS periodically surveys employee benefits. *Employee Benefits in Private Industry: 2000* (2000) and *Employee Benefits in State and Local Governments: 1998* (2000) are two of the surveys on benefits. The Employment Policy Foundation also provides information about employee benefits, including topics on paid family leave, unemployment insurance, and employer-sponsored medical coverage.

The BLS annual *Occupational Outlook Handbook* is one of the most complete sources on jobs available. The handbook outlines future job projections. It also provides detailed descriptions of most jobs and directs the reader to further information. The BLS *Occupational Outlook Quarterly* contains valuable articles on employment and the labor market.

The quarterly *Family Economics and Nutrition Review,* prepared by the Agricultural Service of the U.S.

Department of Agriculture, contains articles on family living as well as jobs and workers. *The Survey of Consumer Finances, 1998,* by the Federal Reserve Board discusses income and participation in savings and thrift plans.

The U.S. Census Bureau, a branch of the U.S. Department of Commerce, is a major source of information about the American people. Some of its studies concern employment and employee earnings. Helpful publications from the U.S. Census Bureau include *Money Income in the United States, 1998* (1999), *Characteristics of Business Owners, 1992 Economic Census* (1997), and *Statistical Abstract of the United States: 2001* (2002).

The U.S. Department of Education also publishes research on educational levels and their relationship to career opportunities. Its publications include *Digest of Education Statistics: 1999* (2000), *Condition of Education, 1999* (1999), and *Projections of Education Statistics to 2009* (1999).

The General Accounting Office reported its findings on information technology workers to the House Committee on Commerce in its *Information Technology: Assessment of the Department of Commerce's Report on Workforce Demand and Supply* (1998). The National Center for Health Statistics (Hyattsville, Maryland) writes about health insurance in its *National Employer Health Insurance Survey* (1997).

The Society for Human Resource Management's (Alexandria, Virginia) *1996 Issues Management Survey* is based on a poll of its membership. The series includes the *1996 Workplace Violence Survey* (1996) and the *1996 Job Security and Layoffs Survey* (1996).

Dun and Bradstreet, a company of The Dun and Bradstreet Corporation, (Murray Hill, New Jersey) compiles the annual *Business Starts Records* (1998 and 1999–2000) and *Business Failure Records* (1997). Dun and Bradstreet also supplies data on business Internet usage and minority business owners' attitudes toward their businesses.

The Center on Budget and Policy Priorities, a private research group, gives information on employment and earnings of former welfare recipients. The National Association of Colleges and Employers discusses salaries in its quarterly publication *Salary Survey*. The American Management Association as well as the National Association of Colleges and Employers provides data on psychological testing of employees. The Career Services and Placement Office of Michigan State University has published *Recruiting Trends: 1997–1998* (December 1997).

The U.S. Chamber of Commerce (Washington, D.C.) provides information on employee benefits. The National Association of Temporary and Staffing Services has printed a survey on temporary work in *Contemporary Times* magazine (spring 1998). Online sources from the Department of Labor, the Federal Trade Commission, the Access Board of the Americans with Disabilities Act, and Occupational Safety and Health Administration (OSHA) supply information on current topics such as reassessing the Americans with Disabilities Act (ADA) and proposing an ergonomics standard.

Information Plus sincerely thanks all of the organizations listed above for the valuable information they provide.

INDEX